Translation and Multilingual Natural Language Processing

Editors: Oliver Czulo (Universität Leipzig), Silvia Hansen-Schirra (Johannes Gutenberg-Universität Mainz), Reinhard Rapp (Hochschule Magdeburg-Stendal), Mario Bisiada (Universitat Pompeu Fabra)

In this series (see the complete series history at https://langsci-press.org/catalog/series/tmnlp):

11. Fantinuoli, Claudio (ed.). Interpreting and technology.

12. Nitzke, Jean. Problem solving activities in post-editing and translation from scratch: A multi-method study.

13. Vandevoorde, Lore. Semantic differences in translation.

14. Bisiada, Mario (ed.). Empirical studies in translation and discourse.

15. Tra&Co Group (ed.). Translation, interpreting, cognition: The way out of the box.

16. Nitzke, Jean & Silvia Hansen-Schirra. A short guide to post-editing.

17. Hoberg, Felix. Informationsintegration in mehrsprachigen Textchats: Der Skype Translator im Sprachenpaar Katalanisch-Deutsch.

18. Kenny, Dorothy (ed.). Machine translation for everyone: Empowering users in the age of artificial intelligence.

19. Kajzer-Wietrzny, Marta, Adriano Ferraresi, Ilmari Ivaska & Silvia Bernardini. Mediated discourse at the European Parliament: Empirical investigations.

20. Marzouk, Shaimaa. Sprachkontrolle im Spiegel der Maschinellen Übersetzung: Untersuchung zur Wechselwirkung ausgewählter Regeln der Kontrollierten Sprache mit verschiedenen Ansätzen der Maschinellen Übersetzung.

21. Frittella, Francesca Maria. Usability research for interpreter-centred technology: The case study of SmarTerp.

22. Prandi, Bianca. Computer-assisted simultaneous interpreting: A cognitive-experimental study on terminology.

ISSN: 2364-8899

Computer-assisted simultaneous interpreting

A cognitive-experimental study on terminology

Bianca Prandi

language science press

Bianca Prandi. 2023. *Computer-assisted simultaneous interpreting: A cognitive-experimental study on terminology* (Translation and Multilingual Natural Language Processing 22). Berlin: Language Science Press.

This title can be downloaded at:
http://langsci-press.org/catalog/book/348
ISBN: 978-3-96110-397-3 (Digital)
       978-3-98554-055-6 (Hardcover)

ISSN: 2364-8899
DOI: 10.5281/zenodo.7143056
Source code available from www.github.com/langsci/348
Errata: paperhive.org/documents/remote?type=langsci&id=348

Cover and concept of design: Ulrike Harbort
Proofreading: Amir Ghorbanpour, Andreas Hölzl, Christopher Straughn, Elen Le Foll, Jean Nitzke, Jeroen van de Weijer, Marten Stelling, Neneng Sri, Robin Lemke
Fonts: Libertinus, Arimo, DejaVu Sans Mono
Typesetting software: XƎLATEX

Language Science Press
xHain
Grünberger Str. 16
10243 Berlin, Germany
http://langsci-press.org

Storage and cataloguing done by FU Berlin

Contents

Contents

Contents

Acknowledgements

For her invaluable advice, patience and feedback, I would like to express my deepest gratitude to my supervisor, Univ-Prof. Dr. Silvia Hansen-Schirra.

This endeavour would not have been possible without the students who participated in the experiments, my speaker, and the helping hand of the Tra&Co research team.

I would like to extend my sincere thanks to my mentor, Dr. Claudio Fantinuoli, for inspiring and supporting me throughout my research journey.

Finally, my heartfelt thanks goes to my parents Anna and Claudio, my sister Francesca, my partner Marek and all my friends, in particular Francesca and Elisa, for their unwavering support over the years.

Abbreviations

AI	Artificial Intelligence
AIIC	International Association of Conference Interpreters
ANOVA	Analysis of Variance
AOI	Area of Interest
API	Application Programming Interface
APR	Average Pause Ration
ASR	Automatic Speech Recognition
ATE	Automatic Term Extraction
BLEU	Bilingual Evaluation Understudy
CACI	Canadian Association of Conference Interpreters
CAI	Computer-Assisted Interpreting
CAIT	Computer-Assisted Interpreter Training
CASI	Computer-Assisted Simultaneous Interpreting
CAT	Computer-Assisted Translation
CDIP	Corpus-Driven Interpreter Preparation
CIUTI	International Standing Conference of University Institutes of Translators and Interpreters
CE	Cognitive Effort
CL	Cognitive Load
CLM	Cognitive Load Model
CLT	Cognitive Load Theory
CM	Conflict Matrix
COVID-19	Coronavirus Disease 2019
CRF	Cognitive Resource Footprint
CTS	Cognitive Translation Studies
DOT	Dolmetschorientierte Terminologiearbeit
EABM	Ergonomics for the Artificial Boothmate
EB	Episodic Buffer
EEG	Electroencephalography
EKS	Eye-Key Span
EM	Effort Model
ERP	Event-Related Potential

EU	European Union
EVS	Ear-Voice Span
fMRI	Functional Magnetic Resonance Imaging
HIAT	Halbinterpretative Arbeitstranskriptionen (Semi-Interpretative Working Transcriptions)
HMI	Human-Machine Interaction
HTER	Human-targeted Translation Edit Rate
IATE	Interactive Terminology for Europe
ICL	Intrinsic Cognitive Load
ICPD	Inter-Cluster Pause Duration
ICT	Information and Communication Technologies
ILO	International Labor Organization
IS	Interpreting Studies
KIT	Karlsruhe Institute of Technology
LSP	Language for Special Purpose
LTM	Long-Term Memory
LTS	Long-Term Store
MEG	Magnetoencephalography
MI	Machine Interpreting
MQM	Multidimensional Quality Metrics
MS	Microsoft
MT	Machine Translation
MTPE	Machine Translation Post-Editing
NASA-TLX	NASA Task-Load Index
NIR	Near-Infrared Spectroscopy
NLP	Natural Language Processing
NMT	Neural Machine Translation
PET	Positron Emission Tomography
PL	Phonological Loop
PWR	Pause to Word Ratio
RSI	Remote Simultaneous Interpreting
RTF	Real-Time Factor
RWL	Reading while Listening
SD	Standard Deviation
SDI	Sprachen & Dolmetscher Institut
SI	Simultaneous Interpreting
SIMTXT	Simultaneous Interpreting with Text
SR	Speech Recognition
ST	Sight Translation

ST	Source Text
STM	Short-Term Memory
STS	Short-Term Storage
STT	Speech to Text
SYNLE	Syntactic Left Embeddedness
TAP	Think-Aloud Protocol
TAUS-DQF	TAUS Dynamic Quality Framework
TE	Terminology Extraction
TET	Terminology Extraction Tool
TICQ	Translation and Interpreting Competence Questionnaire
TIS	Total Interference Score
TIS	Translation and Interpreting Studies
TKC	Terminological Knowledge Constellation
TKE	Terminological Knowledge Entity
TM	Translation Memory
TMS	Terminology Management System
TPR	Translation Process Research
TT	Target Text
UI	User Interface
UN	United Nations
VR	Virtual Reality
VSSP	Visual-Spatial Sketch Pad
WER	Word Error Rate
WM	Working Memory
WPM	Words per Minute
WPT	Word Production Time

Introduction

When conference interpreters interpret a speech simultaneously, they are often faced with the need to quickly and precisely render specialised terminology in the target language. Hence, pre-assignment preparation is fundamental to acquire specialised terminology to aptly express domain-specific knowledge in the target language. In the preparation phase, interpreters usually compile glossaries containing specialised terms likely to be used by the speaker (e.g. Rütten 2007, Fantinuoli 2017a, Will 2007, Gile 2009). Despite learning the terminological equivalents ahead of the event, interpreters may not always be able to retrieve the target-language equivalent from memory during interpreting. To cope with this difficulty, among other tactics (Gile 2009: 14), they may choose to look up the required term in their glossaries. Traditionally, specialised glossaries have been compiled on paper, or prepared in digital format and printed out for the booth (e.g. Jiang 2013, 2015).

With the increasing permeation of the profession by technology over the past couple of decades, the booth is now increasingly paper-less (Rütten 2017). On a laptop or a tablet, interpreters can now conduct glossary queries in the digital medium.

As for the software employed to create digital glossaries for interpreting assignments, traditionally this has consisted in text processing programmes or database applications aimed at the general public. For lack of dedicated tools, some interpreters have resorted to computer-assisted translation (CAT) tools. The use of tools for corpus-based terminology work, terminology extraction, and of speech recognition, to name but a few examples, is therefore not the exclusive preserve of translators and terminologists but can also be found in interpreters' terminology work.

Despite the potential usefulness of these technologies for interpreters, scholarship remarked that the nature of interpreting imposes specific demands, both cognitive and related to interpreters' workflow (e.g. Rütten 2004, Will 2000, 2007). Thus, around the same time when CAT tools started to appear, applications geared towards the specific needs of interpreters were created and later increasingly refined which fall under the name of computer-assisted interpreting (CAI) tools.[1] Their aim is to support interpreters along several phases of their workflow, especially during preparation, but also for terminology retrieval during the interpreting task. The recent advances in automatic speech recognition (ASR) technology have motivated its integration into CAI tools, which may now offer live support for terminology and other units of information without physical interaction between the interpreter and the machine. The first prototypes of ASR-enhanced CAI tools are already emerging (e.g. Fantinuoli 2017a).

In light of these developments, several studies have been conducted on the topic of CAI tools over the past few years. They have mainly explored the tools' potential to improve terminological accuracy during simultaneous interpreting (e.g. Prandi 2015a,b), the extent to which ASR improves the rendition of number words and specialized terms in the target language (e.g. Defrancq & Fantinuoli 2021), or their potential for offering support to interpreters in the consecutive mode (e.g. Wang & Wang 2019). With a few exceptions (Biagini 2015, Frittella 2022), the focus of such studies has been rather narrow, using specific performance indicators such as the accuracy of interpreted terms and numerals to assess the tools' impact on the overall quality of the interpretation (e.g. Pisani & Fantinuoli 2021), without taking stock of the interpretation beyond these individual items. Many findings have emerged from small-scale experiments conducted on students in the framework of master's theses (e.g. Canali 2018, Van Cauwenberghe 2020). Despite the emphasis on the postulated difficulty of integrating CAI tools into the interpreting process and, on the other hand, the widespread enthusiasm for the potential of ASR to alleviate cognitive load during SI, the impact of such solutions on the cognitive subprocesses underlying SI has so far remained largely unexplored. This represents an evident lacuna compared to the large body of research conducted on cognition in the translator-machine interaction. Such interaction has been addressed by numerous empirical studies in the area of Translation Process Research (TPR) from multiple perspectives and with a variety of methods (Tardel 2021: xvii). Indeed, as "a research tradition within cognitive translation studies (CTS) [...] exploring factors that determine human translation behavior" (ibid.), TPR may constitute a valuable reference point and provide useful tools to the analysis of computer-assisted simultaneous interpreting (CASI), especially from a methodological standpoint. However, no empirically-validated methodology for the combined collection of product- and process-oriented data with a markedly cognitive focus has yet been developed to explore the phenomenon of technology-supported SI.

---

[1] For a terminological clarification of the term "CAI tool" and its use in the present work, see §2.2.1.

The present doctoral thesis seeks to address this limitation by developing and testing an empirical methodology for a cognitive exploration of CASI. In particular, the present work derives its methods from TPR to analyse the impact on cognitive load of different forms of digital terminological support for interpreters through a within-subject experimental study.

To the best of my knowledge, this is the first study to address computer-assisted SI from a cognitive perspective. As such, it presents an exploratory character which aims to provide first findings and, at the same time, to identify open questions and formulate hypotheses for further investigations of the phenomenon.

The following section establishes the paradigm for the present research work and provides a conceptual framework for the cognitive inquiry into the phenomenon of CASI. The rest of the present chapter illustrates how the present work is organised and briefly describes the content of each chapter.

Choice of paradigm for the present study

Especially in the simultaneous mode, interpreting has often been described as a complex cognitive activity, involving concurrent information processing and temporary storage tasks competing for attentional resources. This view of interpreting[2] as cognitive information processing represents one of the "supermemes" of interpreting, as observed by Pöchhacker (2004: 51)[3].

Yet, even though this "internal" perspective has been particularly prolific in the academic inquiry into the phenomenon, interpreting may also be viewed as a socially embedded human activity, situated in a real communicative context. The supermeme of communicative activity elucidates interpreting as a combination of listening and speaking aimed at facilitating communication beyond the linguistic barrier.

For the scope of the present study, I chose to conduct my inquiry into interpreting from an explicitly cognitive perspective. Selecting one perspective does not, however, mean discarding or denying the other, but rather focusing the spotlight on one aspect of this multi-faceted activity, and is necessary to establish the theoretical framework guiding investigation. The next step lies into the defini-

---

[2] Here intended in the broader sense of the term and referring not only to the conference setting.
[3] Pöchhacker derives the notion of memes and supermemes from Chesterman (2016): as in translation, these "socio-biological concepts" have arisen as metaphors to illustrate particular views of interpreting as an object of study. From this perspective, the interpreter is seen as a "human processor" performing several "cognitive skills [...] the combination of which would account for the complex task of interpreting" (Pöchhacker 2004: 53).

tion of my research paradigm[4]. The two supermemes of interpreting as cognitive information processing and as communicative activity are at the core of a number of paradigms that can be divided into social, psycholinguistic, and cognitive approaches following Setton's classification (Setton 2003).

The social approach reflects a tradition which looks at interpreting within a broader framework including social and behavioural factors. Prominent issues deriving from this view of interpreting are the interaction between the actors involved in the communicative event, the role of the interpreter and the long-standing issue of neutrality, the view of quality assessment as a question of pragmatics (and not only of identity between the source text and the interpreted message), but also the issue of interpreting strategies. To this category may be ascribe the "target-text oriented, translation-theoretical" (Pöchhacker 2004: 77) paradigm exemplified by Salevsky (1987), Schjoldager (1995), Pöchhacker (1994) and Kalina (1998), as well as the "dialogic discourse-based interaction" paradigm (Pöchhacker 2004: 79) of which Roy (1996, 2000) and Wadensjö (1993, 1998) are the most prominent representatives.

Psycholinguistic approaches are grounded in theories of communication and focus on features of discourse rather than on the cognitive processing of interpreting. This perspective is at the core of the interpretive paradigm pioneered by Seleskovitch (1976) and Lederer (1981) with their *théorie du sens*. The models by Chernov (1979, 1994), Déjean Le Féal (1980, 1981), Donovan (1990), Laplace (1994) and Setton (1999) himself may also be included in this category.

Finally, interpreting has been studied from a cognitive perspective and viewed as a matter of information processing. The scholars belonging to this tradition focus on the exploration of the cognitive underpinnings of interpreting. It is not by chance that they derive their methods of investigation from the cognitive sciences. This third approach has generated the cognitive processing paradigm (Pöchhacker 2004: 73) initiated by Gerver (1976) and further exemplified by Lambert (1988), Massaro (1978), Moser (1978) and Moser-Mercer (1997), Kurz (1996), Shlesinger (2000) and Gile (1988, 1997, 1999) and Seeber (2007, 2011, 2017). To this perspective one can also ascribe the "neurophysiological/neurolinguistic paradigm" (Pöchhacker 2004: 75) exemplified by Fabbro & Gran (1994), Kurz (1994, 1996), Darò (1994, 1997), Petsche et al. (1993), Rinne et al. (2000), and Tommola & Hyönä (1990).

The focus of the present doctoral thesis lies on the way the use of digital terminological support tools during simultaneous interpreting affects the cognitive

---

[4]See Pöchhacker (2004, 2016) for a detailed account of research paradigms in Interpreting Studies.

processes involved in simultaneous interpreting. Hence, I situate my inquiry in the cognitive processing paradigm, while adopting an interdisciplinary approach to the exploration of simultaneous interpreting with digital terminology support. Methodologically, the study draws heavily on research methods developed and validated in the framework of empirical Translation Process Research (TPR). As translation and interpreting are rather similar activities in terms of their underlying cognitive processes and cognitive control functions, the approaches developed in TPR for the exploration of the translation process are expected to provide a valuable methodological reference point.

Organisation

The present thesis is organised as follows. Chapter 1 introduces the topic of terminology in interpreting. Specifically, it addresses terminology work in conference interpreting highlighting its commonalities and differences with terminology work in translation. Additionally, it underlines the role of terminology as an important quality factor in translation and interpreting, which motivates the focus on terminological support in the present study. The last section closes Chapter 1 with a discussion of the requirements for CAI tools and of the potential and limitations of non-bespoke terminology tools for interpreters. Against this background, Chapter 2 frames the technology object of inquiry, i.e. CAI tools, within the larger framework of technology applied to interpreting. After an overview of the available technologies for interpreting (§2.1), CAI tools are discussed in detail (§2.2.2), and InterpretBank, the CAI tool chosen for the experiment, in particular (§2.2.3). The chapter offers a review of interpreters' practices in compiling terminological resources ahead of and during the interpreting assignment, specifically in terms of their level of computerisation and choice of tools. This section closes with a review of how CAI tools have been studied in interpreting research thus far (§2.4) and illustrates current attitudes towards CAI tools (§2.3.4), which motivates the present work. Hence, in Chapter 3 I proceed to discuss simultaneous interpreting as a complex cognitive activity, specifically as a question of attention allocation and resource sharing between co-occurring subtasks (§3.1), a key issue in the inquiry into technology-supported (simultaneous) interpreting. §3.4 illustrates cognitive load as a fundamental construct often encountered in academic discourse around CAI tools, but not yet explored experimentally. These two sections pave the way for the discussion of interpreting as an issue of multi-tasking within the area of Interpreting Studies (§3.5). Here, I illustrate in detail two models of SI which address this activity from the perspective of the concurrent performance and coordination of cognitive sub-tasks. On this basis, I motivate the choice of framework to operationalise hypotheses on SI with digital terminological support (§3.5.3). Chapter 4 describes the methods adopted in TPR and neighbouring disciplines (e.g. cognitive psychology) to measure cognitive load. Chapter 5 presents and discusses the research approach (§5.3) and the methodology deployed to test the hypotheses formulated for the present study (§5.2). §5.4 presents the methods and results of the pilot study conducted to test the research methodology and validate the stimuli to be used for data collection. §5.5 goes into the details of the experimental design adopted in the main study, describing the adaptations conducted in light of the results of the pilot test. In Chapter 6, the results of the experiment are presented and discussed against the background of the hypotheses formulated in §5.2 and of relevant publications in the area of TPR and CAI research. §6.2.4 discusses and validates the application of Seeber (2007, 2011, 2017) CLM of SI to illustrate task interference and cognitive load in SI with the support of traditional digital glossaries, CAI tools with manual look-up, and ASR-enhanced CAI tools. The limitations of the present study are addressed in §6.3. Chapter 7 presents the methodological, didactic and practical implications of the present study and concludes this work with final remarks on potential avenues for future CAI research.

1 Terminology work in interpreting

The present chapter discusses the role of terminology in simultaneous interpreting at specialised conferences, highlighting the commonalities with translation while at the same time foregrounding the specific requirements of terminology work in interpreting. Against this background, the ideal features of a bespoke tool for terminology work in the different phases of interpreting are discussed. To conclude, the chapter highlights the limitations of terminology tools available to translators, thus motivating the need for interpreter-specific tools, which are discussed in the following chapter.

1.1 Translating and interpreting for LSP

Translation and interpreting share a large set of common features, as both activities concern the interlingual and intercultural transmission of a message. The most apparent element of distinction is perhaps the channel through which the target text is produced: written, in the case of translation, and oral or visual, in the case of interpreting and signed language interpreting, respectively. This distinction is usually adopted for ease of explanation, for instance in communication with laypeople. However, translation and interpreting are in numerous respects quite similar. For instance, hybrid forms of translation and interpreting are possible: one such instance is sight translation (ST), which consists in the spoken translation of a written source text. With the advent of new possibilities offered by technology, additional hybrid forms of translation and interpretation are emerging, such as live subtitling (or interlingual respeaking), in which the interpreter produces a live translation of the speaker's words that is, however, rendered in written form. Second, TPR has elucidated that cognitive control functions are very similar in translation and interpreting. Both translation and interpreting involve the performance of parallel sub-tasks (e.g. Vardaro et al. 2019) and the first draft of a translation does not require significantly more time to be produced than a target text (TT) in interpreting.

Translation and interpreting also share another characteristic: a large amount of texts translated or interpreted are specialised texts. The profile of translators is thus increasingly becoming that of a specialised translator (Campo 2005); specialised conferences, technical meetings, seminars or workshops represent the most common type of assignment for professional conference interpreters, both for those working in the private market and those employed by public institutions (e.g. Rütten 2008: 22).

When translating or interpreting in specialised fields, translators and interpreters face a common challenge: they are called upon to enable expert communication across languages despite not being subject-matter experts themselves. This is particularly true for interpreters, who often work "in very different thematic scenarios, usually for a public of experts, and are given the task of transmitting highly specialised knowledge" (Rodríguez & Schnell 2009: 21). Despite the increasing expertise acquired by translators and interpreters during their careers, specialised translation and interpretation in technical settings remains a complex task for both groups of professionals. This complexity is related to the demands imposed on translators and interpreters by specialised language (see §1.1.1) and to the expectations of expert readers or listeners (see §1.1.2).

1.1.1 Features of LSP

As specialised communication is considered primarily informative (Olohan 2013: 427), the focus is on the content, which must be conveyed with the highest accuracy possible. A key characteristic of specialised communication is thus the use of languages for special purposes (LSP, Desblache 2001, Scarpa 2010), the in-house jargon (Kalina 2006) adopted by experts in a specific subject matter to convey specialised knowledge to other experts or laypeople. LSP thus "has a precise purpose and function, that is, to specifically communicate concrete information clearly to a target set of users so that it can be productively used" (Folaron 2019: 207). LSP can therefore be seen as the way specialised knowledge manifests itself and is constituted in discourse. As compared to ordinary language, LSP presents several specific features concerning its lexicon as well as its phraseology and syntax. LSPs may therefore be described as "contextual-functional varieties of the ordinary language (Garzone 2006), [...] characterized by specific morpho-syntactic forms and by some discursive and pragmatic features" (Pignataro 2012: 134).

Especially in scientific contexts, one such characteristic is the widespread use of English as a lingua franca (Ammon 2011). As remarked for instance by Hansen-Schirra et al. (2017), this might result in shining-through effects in translation, especially if the language is particularly susceptible to Anglicism (as is the case for German). Additionally, Braun et al. (2014) evidence how academic texts present a high number of Latinisms and Grecisms in addition to Anglicisms.

This type of influence combined with similar etymology, especially for certain language pairs, may favour the use of cognates, i.e. "those translation words that have similar orthographic-phonological forms" (Costa et al. 2000: 1285), in the translation of specialised discourse. On a cognitive level, cognates have been found to be easier to process. This is referred to as the cognate facilitation effect (Costa et al. 2000). The use of terms with etymological roots shared by different languages may therefore to some extent facilitate access to scientific discourse.

Another feature of LSP is a certain preference for nominalisation and especially for complex noun phrases or compounds (Olohan 2008: 247), especially in English and other Germanic languages. These linguistic devices are functional to the economy of expression which is essential to specialised language (Pignataro 2012: 135). With reference to Halliday & Martin (2003), Olohan (2013: 428) remarks in this respect that:

> This shift from verb to noun, they argue, is significant because the meaning construed by the nominalization is a new one – an abstract theoretical entity which forms part of a scientific theory. These and other features, like expanded nominal groups, privilege experts and exclude others from accessing scientific discourse.

In translation and interpreting, these linguistic features of LSP pose an additional layer of difficulty as elliptical, multi-word expressions must be re-coded in the target language. This may prove particularly problematic if the target-language equivalent is not readily available (see §1.2.3.1).

Finally, LSP is characterised by specific phraseology and syntax (Olohan 2013: 426), as well as specialised terminology, which translators and interpreters must use "as a means to achieve the interlinguistic transfer of specialized knowledge units" (Velásquez 2002: 447).

1.1.2 Terminology as a parameter of quality

In light of the status of terminology for effective specialised communication, it is not surprising that terminology is acknowledged as an important parameter of quality in translation and interpreting. It may be affirmed that "the adequacy of the terminology in a text as well as its suitability for the level of specialization determines to a great extent the quality of a translation" (Martínez & Faber 2009: 91).

While terminology is not the only benchmark against which the quality of a translation may be assessed, its relevance as an important element of quality emerges for instance through its inclusion in many evaluation frameworks, both for human and for machine translation (MT). For instance, Mertin (2006) developed a typology of translation errors which includes terminology as one of the categories of the evaluation matrix. The Multidimensional Quality Metrics framework (MQM, see Lommel, Uszkoreit, et al. 2014, Lommel, Burchardt, et al. 2014) for the assessment of translation quality includes terminology as one of the higher-level issue types. Terminology is one of the 20 "core" issue types included in MQM Core, a simplified version of MQM, and it is included as a key issue type in the TAUS DQF Error Typology (Görög 2014a,b), a subset of MQM. The SAE J2450 Translation Quality Metric for Language Translation of Service Information (SAE International 2001) also includes the issue type "wrong term", which can be mapped to the "terminology" issue type in MQM. Similarly, Hjerson (Popovic 2011: 59), a framework for automatic classification of errors in machine translation output, includes "incorrect lexical choice" as one of the error classes. These are but a few examples, but they highlight the role attributed to terminology for the assessment of translation quality.

By the same token, especially in the context of interpreting settings where LSP is used, e.g. specialised conferences and technical meetings or workshops, terminology emerges as an important element of quality, although it is but one parameter (García de Quesada 2011: 231). The weight attributed to terminology for the evaluation of interpreting quality may also be said to reflect the overall approach to interpreting and its evaluation. As discussed by Pöchhacker (2001, 2004), interpreting has been addressed essentially from two perspectives: on the one hand, it has been viewed as a primarily linguistic task of text reception and production; on the other, as a chiefly communicative, socially-embedded task. Terminology as a quality parameter tends to play an important role in evaluation frameworks belonging to the first approach, as here the focus is on the product. This approach reflects the expectation of equivalence between the interpreted and the source speech, and is reflected in the notions of accuracy and fidelity (Gile 1991a), resulting in what Déjean Le Féal (1990: 155) defined as "equivalent effect". This approach is exemplified by Barik's (1971) taxonomy of error and omission types in simultaneous interpreting, seen primarily as linguistic production. The second approach focuses on interpreting as interaction. Here, the evaluation of quality focuses on the communicative aim of interpreting as situated in a real communicative event. Rather than equivalence, what is important for scholars choosing this approach is the efficacy in achieving a pragmatic communication goal. In this sense, important contributions stem from research on community interpreting, which by its nature promotes the involvement of all players in the communication triad, i.e. the interpreter and the communication parties. An example of this approach to the evaluation of interpretation is Wadensjö (1998, 2005) evaluation framework.

In the context of specialised conferences, the adequate use of specialised terminology is particularly relevant in terms of the clients' and end-users' expectations, because precision, economy of expression, and accuracy are considered key aspects of specialised discourse. It is not surprising, then, that several surveys on quality in simultaneous interpreting have highlighted the use of correct terminology as one of the most important benchmarks of perceived quality (e.g. Gile 1990, Pöchhacker 1994), both in terms of the expectations on and of the evaluation of the interpreting service, and both among end-users and interpreters themselves. Many such user surveys have been conducted over the years, predominantly through questionnaires sometimes combined with other methods, such as interviews (Mack & Cattaruzza 1995, Vuorikoski 1993, 1998, see García Becerra 2016 for a discussion on administration methods).

For instance, a survey by Kurz (1989, 1993) regarding user expectations on interpreting quality found that correct terminology was the third out of eight factors in order of importance, after "sense consistency with the original message" and "logical cohesion of the utterance".

Meak (1990) conducted a small-scale survey on 10 Italian doctors. The results on the role of correct terminology are less conclusive in this case, but this is to be expected considering the limited sample. Nonetheless, even the most lenient respondents stressed that too frequent imprecise use of vocabulary may prove distracting.

Marrone's (1993) survey on a sample of 87 conference attendees combined expectations and evaluation and found that "inaccurate terminological usage" (p. 37) was considered as a shortcoming by most respondents, more serious than unpleasant delivery. Quality of style and correct terminology were ranked second in order of importance after information completeness and before intonation and delivery.

Kopczynski (1994) explored the expectations of 57 Polish speakers and receptors of interpreting and found that although conference attendees may in some cases show a certain degree of leniency towards the use of incorrect terminology, this may be perceived as one of the main irritants. Terminological precision was identified as the second most important parameter of quality, independent of the respondents' role and professions. By the same token, in a survey by Pöchhacker (1994) on quality evaluation, "mastery of technical language" was ranked second in order of importance after the quality of verbal expression.

Mack & Cattaruzza (1995) surveyed user expectations in Italy. In their research, correct terminology was identified as the most important quality factor. The findings of Weller & Yanez's (1998) user survey are also in line with Mack and Cattaruzza's.

An AIIC survey presented in Moser (1995, 1996) involved 94 users of interpreting who were interviewed based on a structured questionnaire. Terminological accuracy was deemed important especially by experienced attendees of technical meetings. It was even considered more important than completeness. For general meetings, the opposite was true.

In sum, end-users attending technical conferences tend to rank the use of correct terminology among the top quality factors for interpreting. Completeness of rendition, knowledge of the subject matter and precise terminology tend to be assigned higher values than delivery-related aspects such as native accent or pleasant voice.

Interpreters also recognise the role of terminology as a key quality parameter. The first survey on interpreters' expectations was conducted by Bühler (1986) on 41 AIIC members and 6 members of the association's Admissions Committee. Both linguistic and extra-linguistic criteria were included. Among linguistic criteria, "use of correct terminology" (p. 232) was ranked particularly high (83% highly important) by the members of the Admissions Committee, similarly to the ranking for "sense consistency with the original message", which received the highest relative and absolute ranking by all participants. As Bühler suggests, this might indicate that using accurate terminology can promote a faithful rendition of the message. Indeed, the use of adequate terminology may contribute to improve performance as it favours cohesion and the correct transmission of the message (García de Quesada 2011: 219).

A larger number of respondents were reached through online questionnaires in the 2000s. In a survey by Chiaro & Nocella (2004), involving 286 respondents, interpreters ranked correct terminology usage as one of the second-most important factors in addition to fluency of delivery and correct grammatical usage.

Zwischenberger & Pöchhacker (2010) collected survey data on interpreters' expectations and self-perceptions, which the authors see as "inherently linked with the issue of quality" (p. 11). They partly replicated Bühler's survey by adopting the same quality criteria, although their questionnaire also involved an evaluation of recorded interpretations. As for the role of correct terminology, the results were similar to Bühler's. Zwischenberger and Pöchhacker, however, also explored how the relative weight assigned to the individual criteria is affected by the type of interpreted event. They found that correct terminology was listed as a top priority by 38% of the respondents who cited seminars and workshops as a setting with specific quality requirements (ibid., p. 16).

In light of these survey results, it appears clear that both interpreting service providers and users acknowledge terminology as an important quality criterion. Therefore, interpreters may more easily meet the quality expectations of their audience by using adequate specialised terminology. This goal can be achieved through effective domain knowledge acquisition and proper terminological preparation. Against this background, the following section will discuss the role of terminology work, with a focus on interpreting as compared to translation.

1.2 Terminology work in translation and interpreting

The contribution of the terminological discipline to the field of specialised translation has been fundamental. For this reason, translation scholars and practitioners tend to consider terminology as an integral part of the professional translation practice, as testified by its inclusion in training programmes. However, terminology work in translation and interpreting presents specific features which are related to the nature of translation and interpreting and to the purpose served by specialised terminology in these professions. For these reasons, while the terminological discipline has laid the foundations for terminology work in translation and interpreting, the approach to terminology in these fields has evolved to adapt to their specific requirements, giving rise to dedicated models of translators' and interpreters' terminology work.

1.2.1 Terminology and translation

Wüster (1931, 1979) may be considered as the nestor of terminology, for which he and the "Viennese school" (Drewer & Pulitano 2019) claimed the status of independent discipline. His normative intent, formulated in his "General Theory of Terminology", pursued the goal of ensuring unequivocal communication in technical fields. He saw terminology "as a tool for disambiguating scientific and technical documentation and communication" (Cabré Castellví 1998: 17). Specialised communication requires brevity and clarity, which is only achieved through adequate linguistic tools, i.e. terms.

Terminology thus emerges as essential both for intralingual and interlingual specialised communication (Arntz & Picht 1982), be it in the form of translation or interpreting. In Wüster's model, which expands de Saussure's (1959) triangle, the term is described as an entity made up of a denomination, the "symbol" in Ogden & Richards's (1923) semiotic triangle, or de Saussure's (1959) "signifier", and a concept, the signified. Wüster includes the distinction between *langue* and *parole* in the model itself (Mikkelsen 1991: 163), a distinction which appears both in the signified (content) and in the signifier (expression).

While Wüster's model lays the ground for a structured terminological discipline, it presents several limitations which determined its later expansion by loyalists or its firm critique and rejection by competing schools of thought (Cabré Castellví 2003, Drewer & Pulitano 2019).[1]

One such limitation is the exclusion of the individual contexts in which terminology is inevitably embedded, and which determines a certain degree of variability (Will 2007). Therefore, translators and interpreters should not rely on parallel texts as reliable sources for the mining of terminology and the creation of ontologies, since in Wüster's theory terminologies are seen as universal, superordinate structures, unaffected by cultural differences. To overcome the limitations of Wüster's approach, Gerzymisch-Arbogast (1996) proposed a context-specific term model which allows for a comparison of term meaning across texts, as used by the individual authors. The establishment of knowledge systems of this type requires static textual environments, as in translation.

1.2.2 Terminology work in translation

At the beginning of the 1980s, terminology positioned itself as a necessity for translation (Mayer 2019: 84). Perhaps the most influential contribution to terminology theory and practice applied to translation can be identified in Arntz & Picht's (1982) "Einführung in die übersetzungsbezogene Terminologiearbeit". The authors offer a detailed discussion of Wüster's model and provide indications for terminology work in translation. Unlike for terminologists, translators' terminology work is always descriptive rather than prescriptive, thus aiming to pin down the knowledge system of a particular field and its expression through terminology (intended both as terms and as syntagma and collocations). While ideal terminology work proceeds onomasiologically, i.e. from the signified to the signifier, translators (and especially interpreters, as discussed in §1.2.3) often proceed semasiologically, i.e. from the expression to the meaning. As Mayer (2019: 103) observes, the onomasiological approach is only rarely used in terminology work by translators because of the considerable effort it entails.

As remarked for interpreters (§1.1), it is not required of translators to be expert in a specific specialised field. Rather, like ad-hoc terminologists and terminographers (Wright & Wright 1997), they must be able to quickly acquire the elements of expert knowledge necessary to fill their knowledge gaps and deliver a high-quality translation. Thus, terminology work is conducted as part of the transla-

---

[1]Although, as Drewer & Pulitano (2019) rightly observe, "the differences between these schools [are] too small to be able to talk about different schools at all" [my translation from the German original].

tion process (Martínez & Faber 2009: 104) and is strictly intertwined with the individual context and co-text in which specialised terms are embedded. This further denotes how a prescriptive, onomasiological approach to terminology and terminography is not reflective of the way translators work on specialised texts. In their terminology work, translators can make use of a variety of tools and resources that "can contribute to facilitating and accelerating the identification, description, consultation and reuse of terminology in a translation context" (Kageura & Marshman 2019: 74). These tools and resources comprise terminology databases, terminology extraction tools (TET) from monolingual and bilingual comparable and parallel corpora (especially previous translations), concordancers, tools for terminology research, text-alignment software, and terminology management systems (TMS). A translator's workbench typically integrates all or most of these technologies (Hansen-Schirra 2012: 211). While translating a text, translators can consult multilingual glossaries and terminology databases to look up target-language equivalents, find definitions, etc. (Blancafort et al. 2011: 4).

A translation project often starts with monolingual term extraction from the source text or other documents. The source text can be pre-processed to identify and extract candidate terms; previously translated and aligned texts can be used to create terminology databases as parallel corpora. Terminology extraction can be performed both by project managers and in-house terminologists and made available to translators, either for entire domains or for individual translation projects and documents. In principle, terminology can be extracted manually, for instance by reading and annotating the text. However, due to the increasing volumes of texts to be translated and the increasingly shorter time to production, manual terminology extraction is often excessively time-consuming. Here, automatic terminology extraction (ATE) can provide valuable support in combination with subsequent refinement to exclude pseudo-terminological units (Pavel & Nolet 2001: 88). Bilingual ATE can be performed on parallel corpora (Vintar 2001), often in the form of translation memories (TM), to create termbases containing terminological pairs. Especially for non-standardised and emerging domains, parallel corpora (Blancafort et al. 2010: 263) or authoritative databases or handbooks may not be available (Heid & Gojun 2012: 586). This lack can be addressed by the use of comparable corpora, i.e. of "texts of the same domain (and possibly genre) in different languages which need not be translations of each other" (Blancafort et al. 2011: 1). Incidentally, the results of terminology extraction are not only directly useful to translators but can be fed to further tools which translators can use to support their translation workflow, such as computer-assisted translation

(CAT) tools or MT systems (Heid & Gojun 2012: 588). Most CAT tools include TETs, such as MultiTerm Extract in SDL Trados, which require parallel texts.

Corpora can be further analysed through concordancers to explore how terms are used in context to derive the most relevant phraseologisms (Pavel & Nolet 2001: 89). Some freely available examples are Linguee[2] or Reverso Context[3] for the exploration of parallel corpora. Sketch Engine[4] (Kilgarriff et al. 2014) is also a popular concordancer which offers monolingual, bilingual, or multilingual corpora analysis.

Terminological resources can be used for the immediate translation task, but they can also be further stored in dedicated terminology management tools to be consulted and reused in future translation tasks. Although dedicated tools are available to this aim (e.g. termbases in TMSs), the use of spreadsheet software or other general-purpose solutions to store and exchange terminology is also rather widespread (e.g. SDL 2008, Blancafort et al. 2011).

1.2.3 Terminology work in interpreting

Even though interpreting shares many similarities with translation, it presents some distinctive features that affect the way terminology work is conducted to ensure effective interlingual oral communication.

1.2.3.1 Distinctive features of terminology work in interpreting

Translators work with a source text fixed in writing, which they can revisit as often as needed during the task. They can scan the text to clarify doubts by analysing the co-text, conduct terminological and content-related queries to fill their knowledge gaps during the task, and in theory pace the translation process as they require. The final product is therefore seldom the first draft produced, but rather the result of a process of increasing refinement. In interpreting, the source text is seldom available. Even when interpreters have access to the script of the speech before the assignment, they encounter the final speech as pronounced by the speaker only in the moment in which it is actually delivered, i.e. during the assignment. Interpreters are therefore often faced with the task of foreseeing which topics will be addressed in the speech and, consequently, which terminology may be used. Therefore, they must strive to fill their domain-knowledge

---

[2] https://www.linguee.com (Accessed: 10.09.2021)
[3] https://context.reverso.net/translation/ (Accessed: 10.09.2021)
[4] http://www.sketchengine.eu/ (Accessed: 06.09.2021)

and terminological gaps ahead of the task (Rütten 2008: 22). Additionally, interpreting is performed under severe time constraints and cannot be interrupted. It would be unthinkable for interpreters to stop their rendition of the speaker's message because they need to acquire additional knowledge to correctly understand and transfer the meaning. The possibilities of revision and monitoring are also more limited in interpreting, as the target text produced by interpreters cannot be further refined or modified (Will 2020: 38). Indeed, self-corrections or reformulations are often regarded as undesirable in interpreting. For interpreting assignments, the process of knowledge and terminological acquisition is thus mainly relegated to the pre-process phase and can only be integrated to some extent into interpreting either peri- or in-process (Kalina 2005: 778), i.e. during the assignment.

Terminology work in interpreting thus aims to avoid knowledge gaps (Rütten 2008: 25). Such knowledge gaps are, however, not only related to an interpreter's overall general knowledge or knowledge of the subject field, but are also situation-related. While conferences and their interpretations can be recorded and made available even after the event has ended, the communication taking place during the conference is mostly meant to serve an immediate purpose and aimed at a specific audience. The situatedness of speeches and presentations also determines the situatedness of their interpretations. What matters in an interpreter's preparation is its suitability for the assignment at hand; terms are considered adequate if they help communication. Thus, terminological preparation is also more pragmatic and situation-oriented than the terminology work of translators (Rütten 2012b), because the product is usually meant to remain available for a longer period of time, and especially of terminologists, whose work must remain valid also beyond the individual text (Rütten 2013: 49). The pragmatism and situatedness of interpreters' terminology work emerge in the type of information contained in interpreters' glossaries: the terms chosen may be even very simple and general if the interpreter deems them more suitable to ensure effective multilingual communication. As remarked by Rütten (2012a: 43), "translators and terminologists are far less free to generalize (and interpreters, in a way, are meant to generalize if the situation calls for it)".

Another difference between terminology work in translation and interpreting is due to the interpreting mode used in specialised conferences. In this setting, interpreters mostly work in the simultaneous mode, while consecutive interpreting is reserved to short presentations or other settings characterised by a higher degree of interaction between the speaker and the audience, e.g. technical workshops. Unlike in the consecutive mode, in the simultaneous mode the interpreter does not deliver the speech after the delegate, but rather almost at the same time as the speaker (for a discussion of interpreting modes, see e.g. Pöchhacker 2015).

The immediacy which characterises both modes of interpreting (Pöchhacker 2011: 10) is particularly apparent in simultaneous interpreting; the external pacing of the task profoundly affects the cognitive and strategic processes underlying interpretation. Due to the limited amount of time and cognitive resources available during SI (Rütten 2013: 49), being able to quickly retrieve target-language equivalents from long-term memory to properly render specialised discourse is paramount. This foregrounds the key role of terminology work pre-, peri- and in-process in interpretation for specialised conferences. Conducting preparatory work ahead of the interpreting process allows for the internalisation of domain knowledge and specialised terminology, which can later be more easily recalled by interpreters, thus facilitating both their understanding of the source speech and their rendition in the target language. Gile (2009) describes the role of language availability in his gravitational model. When units of linguistic knowledge are readily available because they have been activated, for example through preparation, or because they are often used, they can be easily accessed by the interpreter, as they gravitate to the core of available lexicon. When this does not happen, i.e. when the units of linguistic knowledge (terms) "drift outwards", a series of issues can occur both at the comprehension and the production level. Activating terminology before the event is therefore paramount to prevent such problems. More specifically, shifting cognition upstream from the simultaneous phase (Stoll 2010: 3) allows for easier anticipation and faster understanding of the speaker and, in turn, for faster processing and a more accurate rendition. Finally, favouring the use of specific terminology over the adoption of alternative strategies such as paraphrasing, abstracting, or using hypernyms also helps interpreters avoid cognitive overload by freeing up cognitive resources thanks to a faster rendition. However, not all and not only domain-relevant terms are included in interpreters' glossaries: only those terms are noted which the interpreter fears not being able to retrieve from long-term memory, even though they are trivial words (Rütten 2011: 42). This shows that terminology work in interpreting is also highly personal, corresponding to the individual interpreter's preferences, working and memory structures (Rütten 2012a: 48, Wagener 2012: 9, Rütten 2018: 147).

1.2.3.2 Modelling terminology work in interpreting

For the reasons outlined thus far, interpreting does not allow for a direct application of Gerzymisch-Arbogast's (1996) model. In interpreting, the context is in fieri and co-created by the communication parties, albeit to different extents according to the individual interpreting modes. Additionally, the time constraints inherent to interpreting, especially in the simultaneous mode, determine an even clearer preference for the semasiological approach, which saves time when compared to the ideal onomasiological approach (Mikkelsen 1991: 168). It should be noted that expeditious terminology work is essential not only in terms of consultation, but increasingly also during the preparation phase, which has become progressively shorter (Rütten 2008). Speeding up preparation also seems convenient in terms of the profitability of interpreting, as preparing for an assignment seems to require a considerable amount of time.[5]

At the same time, interpreters need to constitute knowledge systems by relying on "external textual structures" (Will 2007: 67) to be able to understand the texts they are interpreting. Will's (2007) model of terminology work in SI closed the gap left open by previous models by considering the particular nature of interpretation and the conditions under which texts are produced and translated during SI.

Will's model represents an expansion and integration of his own model of knowledge management during a simultaneous interpreting assignment (Will 2000). In this first model, Will separated the interpreting assignment into three phases of knowledge acquisition: the preparation phase (Stage I), the conference itself (Stage II) and the de-briefing phase post-assignment (Stage III). Or, in Kalina's (2005: 778) terms, into the pre-process, peri- and in-process, and post-process stages, respectively. As Will argues, new knowledge in the form of single terminological units can only be constituted during Stage I and III and during the non-interpreting phases of Stage II (i.e. right before and right after the interpreting session). Additionally, Will draws on Gerzymisch-Arbogast's model as well as on Mudersbach's (1999) and Floros's (2003) models. Mudersbach's model integrates terminological units into their relative knowledge systems necessary for text comprehension, while Floros describes how relevant knowledge is selected.

As Will (2007: 65) observes, "it would be impossible [for conference interpreters] to acquire the same amount of knowledge as their specialised public". They "have thus to be able to constitute and to use relevant information in a very effective and specific way". With some rare exceptions, conference interpreters working with LSP do not possess the same level of domain knowledge as the speakers and audiences they are called to interpret for. They are therefore presented with an arduous task: that of compiling terminological resources and acquiring sufficient information on the subject matter at hand to be able to precisely convey the speaker's message despite not being experts themselves. Quite

---

[5]One or more working days according to AIIC's (2002) workload study.

often, this is further complicated by the limited time available for preparation. How, then, can they solve this conundrum?

According to Will's model of terminology work in SI, when preparing for a specialised conference, the interpreter must first of all attribute an individual term ("Texterm") to a specific knowledge system, by comparing it with a reference definition ("Systerm"). This process leads to the creation of a "Terminological Knowledge Entity" (TKE), "the smallest complete knowledge unit for understanding and producing technical texts" (Will 2007: 69). To obtain a picture of the general knowledge structures in a speech, TKEs are grouped to form what Will defines as "Terminological Knowledge Constellations" (TKC). The most relevant knowledge systems for the assignment in question should be further investigated, while the less relevant ones can be treated in a more "economic" way, which allows for a more effective approach to terminology work. According to Will, conference interpreters' terminology work can thus be equated to a detective's investigative work: rather than following an onomasiological approach, which would involve a top-down approach, i.e. starting from acquiring the knowledge and then identifying the terminology used to express the concepts, conference interpreters tend to follow a semasiological approach. They explore the corpus of preparation material looking for the relevant terminology, the "explicit units" that refer to a knowledge system, using terms as evidence to identify the units of knowledge they convey. Semantic links between terms reflect logical connections between the individual knowledge items. This process allows interpreters to acquire the necessary terminological knowledge and at the same time to link such knowledge to conceptual reference systems.

This "detective work" presupposes the availability of the "evidence", of sufficient preparation material to ensure effective terminology extraction and knowledge constitution. In order to face these limitations, Fantinuoli (2006) proposes the adoption of a corpus-driven preparation methodology. After creating corpora of specialised texts with corpora creation tools, conference interpreters can explore the topic with a concordancer starting from an automatically-extracted terminology list. This also facilitates the identification of "phraseological knowledge" (Fantinuoli 2017a: 29), primarily in the form of collocations, which in addition to the individual terms also characterise specialised terminology and the client's jargon. Thus, following a Corpus-Driven Interpreter Preparation (CDIP), "interpreters preparing for a conference can obtain a list of relevant terms and texts within minutes, even when targeted preparatory materials have not been made available by the conference organisers (as is often the case in professional settings)" (Fantinuoli 2006: 188).

1.3 Terminology tools for conference interpreters

The need for supporting terminology tools capable of optimising and automating the interpreting workflow clearly emerges against the background of what
was discussed in §1.2.3. Will's model of the terminology workflow in interpreting highlights that dedicated tools should address several requirements specific
to interpretation: they should lighten interpreters' preparation load by promoting targeted preparation and easy access to glossaries; be as little obtrusive and
complex as possible, especially during the in-process phase, in order not to interfere with the concurrent cognitive processes involved in interpreting; easily
adapt to the individual preparation styles of conference interpreters; facilitate
the goal of moving cognition upstream of the interpreting phase (Stoll 2009).

1.3.1 Requirements for a support tool for conference interpreters

To define the ideal architecture and features of a bespoke tool for interpreters,
Rütten (2000, 2004, 2007) laid down a model of the ideal interpreter-specific tool
which mirrors the workflow defined by Will (2000, 2007).

Rütten envisaged a five-tier structure organised around a "central starting
page" (Rütten 2004: 173, see Figure 1.1) from which the different modules can
be accessed. Each module serves a specific purpose and represents one phase of
an interpreter's workflow. According to Rütten, interpreters would benefit from:

- a modality allowing for online and offline research of documents and information;

- a module for document management, connected to

- a function for terminology extraction, also from parallel texts when available, for the compiling of multilingual dictionaries;

- a terminology management module synchronised to the previous one
  which would allow for the identification of duplicates or similar entries;

- a "trainer" to systematise vocabulary memorisation.

In addition to these interdependent modules, the author argues in favour of
an "overall quick-search key that can be used blindly and independently of the
module or function" (Rütten 2004: 175) for querying the whole database and all
the modules. For students, a dedicated training function with exercises to fine-
tune the sub-skills involved in interpreting could also prove beneficial. Rütten's

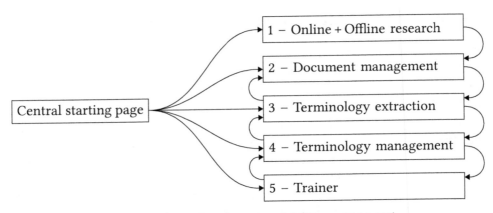

Figure 1.1: Rütten's software model (Rütten 2004: 173)

suggestions map the circularity of interpreters' terminology work, from preparation material to glossaries before and during interpreting, and back to glossaries after the assignment. The document management and terminology extraction modules facilitate the collection of textual material to constitute the necessary reference knowledge systems. The vocabulary trainer addresses another key necessity for interpreters: the acquisition and activation of relevant specialised vocabulary ahead of the interpreting task, as terminological resources, unlike for translators, can also be consulted to some extent during interpreting.

1.3.2 Usefulness and limitations of non-interpreter-specific tools

Against the background of Will's and Rütten's models, the question arises whether and to what degree the tools already available to translators may already satisfy the specific requirements of interpreters' terminology work.

As remarked by Rütten (2011: 43), CAT tools and other technologies such as TETs, TMSs, concordancers, etc., already cover several subphases of an interpreter's workflow. These tools have the potential to provide useful support to interpreters, although they have not been explicitly targeted to these professionals. Useful functions offered by translation memory tools and terminology management tools are for instance sorting and filtering functions or differentiated search functions (e.g. fuzzy search, see Rütten 2011: 43). It should be noted that complex searches or filtering are mainly feasible in the pre-, peri-, or post-process phase (Rütten 2013: 50, Wagener 2012: 8). Translation memories can represent useful tools especially for those interpreters also working as translators, who may reuse their terminological databases and save precious preparation time (Rütten 2013: 49). TMs can also be useful to show aligned parallel texts on screen. This function may be useful also during interpreting, for instance if texts are read out loud by speakers and the translation is already available. Translation memory systems which save all terminological entries in a single database can promote managing the data as a whole (Rütten 2012a: 44). Additionally, some TM tools and TMSs usually allow embedding a picture to illustrate a term, which can be useful to quickly grasp the term's meaning (ibid.) and support memorisation.

Tools for terminology extraction, either stand-alone or integrated into CAT tools, can save interpreters time by automatically identifying candidate terms and promote knowledge acquisition by allowing interpreters to focus on the meaning of the text. These tools can also represent useful emergency solutions when long documents are made available last-minute during the assignment (Rütten 2012a: 48).

Finally, tools for terminology search on the web or in online databases and dictionaries can prove useful to identify or check the validity of a target-language equivalent during glossary compilation. The application of TMs, TMSs, CAT tools, etc., to interpreting presents, however, some limitations, which emerge especially in relation to their in-process use. To start, while non-bespoke tools do address some operations and subprocesses, they do not cover the entire interpreting workflow satisfactorily (Rütten 2013: 49).

Non-interpreter-specific tools are often criticised by interpreters because they are perceived as too complex and not intuitive. TMSs, for instance, usually offer multiple data levels, which promote a systematisation of entries, but are often seen as too cumbersome or excessively complex (Rütten 2012a: 50, Stoll 2009: 141). The host of functions offered by non-bespoke tools does not necessarily have to be exploited completely. However, interpreters not familiar with these tools may perceive them as overwhelming and unnecessarily complex. Additionally, an interface offering too many functions or unoptimised entry structures may be difficult to process, especially for in-process terminology look-up when attention is already allocated to several subprocesses. None of the available tools offers "a mouse-free, blind and intuitive search function" (Rütten 2012a: 46).

The limitations of non-bespoke tools outlined above have led to the development of increasingly sophisticated tools dedicated to conference interpreters, known as CAI tools. The following chapter discusses them in detail, highlighting the postulated advantages they offer, as well as their unique features as compared to CAT tools and the other resources discussed thus far (see also §1.2.2). The chapter further explores whether and to what degree interpreters prefer CAI tools to other solutions for their terminology work and reviews the research conducted thus far on the topic of CAI.

2 Information technologies and interpreting

In view of the complexity and the necessity of terminology work in interpreting for LSP settings, interpreters have looked for ways to facilitate their terminology work through technology.

While interpreters can use tools that are also available to translators to prepare for their assignments and to access their terminological resources while interpreting, they can also adopt software developed specifically for interpreters. Known as CAI tools, these solutions aim to address interpreters' unique needs and overcome the limitations of traditional tools identified in §1.3.2.

With the aim to provide an in-depth discussion of CAI tools, the present chapter introduces the topic of technologies applied to interpreting and illustrates CAI tools within this larger framework. Special attention is dedicated to InterpretBank[1] (Fantinuoli 2012, 2017a), the CAI tool adopted in the present study. To determine whether and to what degree interpreters include CAI tools in their workflows, the terminographic practices of conference interpreters are presented. The potential and limitations of CAI tools in addressing interpreters' needs are discussed against the background of current CAI research, which motivates the contribution provided by the present work.

2.1 Overview and classification of technologies

Like translation and numerous other areas of human life and work, the interpreting profession has not remained indifferent to technological advances. Some developments in the field of technology have led to considerable progress in the interpreting practice, while other technologies have been perceived as a threat to its very existence since their inception. Something similar can be said of the translation profession, which has experienced radical changes that have optimised translators' workflows, but also threatened the status of human translation.

---

[1]https://interpretbank.com/ (Accessed: 24.07.2022)

Technologies can both mediate, generate and support interpretation (see Braun 2019). Supporting technologies include CAI tools. CAI tools can, however, also integrate technologies used to generate interpretation (e.g. ASR and MT), and may, in turn, be integrated into technologies mediating interpreting (see Will 2020: 65). To introduce the topic of CAI and define it in relation to other information and communication technologies (ICTs), the following sections provide an overview and a classification of interpreting technologies.[2]

2.1.1 Technologies mediating interpreting

The first category of technologies applied to interpreting comprises solutions that have led to the emergence of new interpreting modes, or that allow for the performance of interpreting in previously inaccessible settings. The most prominent example of the first is simultaneous interpreting technology. Up until the 1920s, interpreting was only performed in the consecutive mode, or in the form of whispered interpretation, i.e. synchronously but without any technological aid. The first (successful attempt) at using simultaneous interpreting at a conference was at the 1928 ILO conference, where real SI was used during entire meetings, involving up to seven different languages (Baigorri-Jalón 1999: 33). After this first experiment, SI reached its "coming of age" (ibid., p. 34) at the Nuremberg Trials almost 20 years later. The simultaneous mode faced initial resistance by consecutive interpreters, who feared a decay in the quality of interpretation and, as a result, of communication, and perceived headphones and SI equipment as foreign objects. Nonetheless, SI quickly imposed itself for its time-saving character and cost-effectiveness, and remains the most widespread interpreting mode in the conference setting to date.

If simultaneous interpreting can be perceived as the first revolution brought about by technology in the field of interpreting, distance interpreting can be viewed as the second. This innovation made it possible to perform both modes of interpreting in new settings and with multiple possible configurations in the speaker-listener-interpreter triad. Distance interpreting "covers a whole range of technologically different setups" (Ziegler & Gigliobianco 2018: 121), which vary according to the constellation in the communication, the interpreting mode (e.g. in terms of the range of audio frequencies required), but also according to whether only the audio signal or both audio and video data are to be captured and transmitted. Since its inception, distance interpreting has posed the conundrum

---

[2]This chapter focuses on applications to professional conference interpreting. Therefore, technologies which support training, known as Computer-Assisted Interpreter Training (CAIT) tools are not discussed here.

of "striking a balance between cost-effectiveness and quality of interpretation" (Baigorri-Jalón 1999: 36). Not only financial, but also organisational and logistical issues must be addressed, without sacrificing the quality of audio and video streams. Although some perceived and factual issues can be overcome through proper set-ups, a certain degree of resistance towards the "new technologies" remains among some conference interpreters. This extends to the other two categories of interpreting technologies, as discussed in the following sections. The successful implementation of distance interpreting in several settings has, however, shown that this technology is here to stay. Indeed, it could lay the foundations for the emergence of new conference interpreter profiles who fully embrace the home-office, location-independent alternative to traditional conference settings, as the COVID-19 pandemic has shown (Fantinuoli 2019). Additionally, distance interpreting will require adjustments not only in attitudes, but also in training, for instance through the development of "training modules designed specifically for this modality, addressing cognitive, communicative and technical aspects" (Ziegler & Gigliobianco 2018: 137). Furthermore, the integration of augmented reality technologies, such as VR glasses, could represent the next step in distance interpreting by helping address the perceived feeling of isolation through distance and the need for "self-control of the direction of sight" (ibid., p. 136).

In translation, a comparable level of innovation was introduced by the advent of personal computers, which allowed for the execution of this intellectual activity on a new medium. At the same time, this innovation brought about evident advantages in terms of productivity and quality, especially thanks to CAT technologies (see §2.1.3). Technology has also modified how translation is performed. For instance, moving translation to the cloud has led to the creation of collaborative translation platforms, which allow for an unprecedented level of interaction between translators cooperating despite geographical limitations. The resulting translation is thus the product of a joint intellectual effort. ASR has allowed translators to dictate their interpretation, rather than typing it, with evident gains in productivity and potentially also in quality (Carl, Lacruz, et al. 2016a). The use of machine translation has, to some extent, replaced translators' work, but it has also offered language service providers and individual translators ways to speed up human translators' work, e.g. through human post-editing of machine-translated texts. For this reason, machine-translation post-editing (MTPE) can be placed at the intersection of technology-generated and technology-mediated translation. The combination of ASR and MTPE has even made post-editing of ASR output in audio-visual translation possible, as explored in the CompASs (Computer-Assisted Subtitling) project, a joint EU-financed effort of the German

TV channel ZDF and of the Translation & Cognition Center (TRA&CO) of the University of Mainz (see Tardel et al. 2019, 2021).

2.1.2 Technologies generating interpreting

When considering technologies for the provision of intercultural communication services without the involvement of human interpreters, an inevitable parallel emerges between translation and interpreting. Over the years, although with different levels of perceived pressure, both translators and interpreters have increasingly been faced with what they consider a potential threat to their livelihood: machine translation, on the one hand, and machine interpreting (MI), or speech translation, on the other. Just like MT, MI also aims to generate interpreting without the contribution of human interpreters.

Despite its having long been discarded as a merely theoretical threat, the considerable advances brought about by neural networks and artificial intelligence (AI) have led to a resurfacing of machine interpreting.

Like MT, MI requires a combination of several technologies. The essential steps involve ASR or speech-to-text technology (STT) to turn the speaker's words into written text, a machine translation system to translate such text, and speech synthesis, or text-to-speech, to turn the translation into its oral form in the target language. The spoken output can, however, also be replaced by the creation of subtitles, without the use of speech synthesis.

At present, the two main models are cascading and end-to-end systems. In cascading systems, the above-mentioned steps are performed consecutively and the source speech must be segmented. End-to-end systems do not require the intermediate step of ASR. This last possibility has only recently started to be explored, but it is increasingly reaching the quality produced by cascading systems. End-to-end systems are exemplified by Google's Translatotron (Jia et al. 2019) and Translatotron 2 (Jia et al. 2022). The further development of the "neural paradigm" (Braun 2019: 296) could lead to rapid advances in the quality of MI output: "especially neural networks which can learn from previous tasks and shift attention according to the relevance of an element in the source speech may have the potential to make machine interpreting more human-like" (ibid.).

Most systems developed thus far work consecutively, i.e. the interpretation in written or oral form is made available after the speaker has produced an utterance. However, simultaneous machine interpreting has also been explored (e.g. Cho et al. 2013) and is attracting growing interest.

The first MI systems were of the consecutive type and relegated to limited domain applications. One example is the German Verbmobil project (Wahlster

2000), a consecutive speech translation system for the domain of appointment-making. It was one of the first projects combining ASR and speech synthesis. Another domain-specific system is VoiceTRAN Communicator, a cascading speech-to-speech system for the language pair Slovenian-English (Žganec-Gros et al. 2005).

These first systems had limited applications. However, in recent years, machine interpreting has become increasingly known to the general public, thanks to the implementation of general-purpose solutions capable of handling conversations on a variety of topics. A well-known example is Microsoft's Skype Translator[3], which offers "real-time machine translation in 10 languages in voice and video chats and 60 languages in text chats" (Hoberg 2021: 21). Microsoft Azure also offers a speech translation API.[4] Currently, there is growing interest for simultaneous machine interpreting systems capable of handling continuous speech. The Karlsruhe Institute of Technology (KIT) has developed a lecture translator to provide automatic simultaneous interpreting for foreign students who do not understand German. The output is made available in the form of written subtitles (see Dessloch et al. 2018 for a detailed description of the system). In addition to fostering accessibility in the university environment, the lecture translator further supports the students' learning as the recordings of the lectures and their translations are stored in a repository. Another key advantage of using the lecture translator is the greater affordability of the system compared to human interpreters, despite the lower quality (Dessloch et al. 2018: 89). User tests involving students suggest that the lecture translator is well received and considered useful, especially by foreign students.

A similar application of a system combining ASR with MT developed in the field of audiovisual translation is the CompAsS project (see also §2.1.1). The CompAsS tool aims at automating the subtitling process wherever possible, supporting the workflow of subtitlers. Initial studies suggest that the tool reduces the technical effort experienced by subtitlers (Tardel et al. 2019, 2021).

What could seem like a relatively easy feat considering the sizeable improvements made by machine translation is, however, complicated by the very nature of spoken discourse. Unlike written communication, speech presents a certain degree of spontaneity and ambiguity, which machines are still unable to deal with without human assistance. Nor are they capable of inference and context anticipation: as Fantinuoli (2019: 342) observes, "they still lack background and

---

[3]https://www.skype.com/it/features/skype-translator/ (Accessed: 11.09.2021)
[4]https://azure.microsoft.com/en-us/services/cognitive-services/speech-translation/ (Accessed: 15.09.2021)

context knowledge". There is, additionally, the issue of the suitability of input for MI processing: unlike MT, which allows for a quick test to verify whether a certain document can effectively be machine translated, MI does not allow for a re-do if things go south – if "a[n] MI system [...] fails to deliver a usable translation, the communication simply breaks down" (ibid.). The interplay of these factors, coupled with the immediacy of simultaneous interpreting, is one of the reasons why fully automated machine interpreting will probably require further effort and time. As Braun (2019: 295) points out, the application of MI systems "to situations in which highly accurate professional language mediation is required remains a nontrivial challenge". In order for MI to enter the third phase of human-machine interaction, i.e. that in which interpreters will go from machine-assisted to machine-assisting professionals, not only would the MI output need to be of a quality comparable to human interpreting, but it would also need to become more convenient in economic terms. Despite some scholars' assertions that a total replacement of human interpreters by machines will never be possible, "the real question is if AI will ever be able to tackle [the above-mentioned] issues at some point in the future" (Fantinuoli 2019: 345). There is no reason to affirm with absolute certitude that this will never be possible. At present, the question remains unanswered.

There is, however, no doubt that machine interpreting will impact the interpreting market in some way or another, at the very least in terms of the perception of conference interpreters' role and professionalism in the eyes of the public. Fantinuoli (2019) envisages a near future in which MI will start entering the low-end segment of the market, following its short-term entering of the recreational sector, where professional interpreting services were not used before. It is plausible to imagine that high-quality and highly professional human interpreting will be relegated to the higher end of the market, "at least until the advent of real human-like MI." (p. 345).

The use of machine interpreting in formal and high-level contexts should, however, not be excluded. There is growing interest for machine interpreting from business and institutional players,[5] and the quality of MI continues to improve. What remains to be determined is how the use of MI affects communication. Further insight into this aspect of MI-mediated communication may reasonably be expected to impact its adoption by end-users and its perception by interpreters. This has been a concern of interpreting scholars from the beginning, as consecutive systems applied to dialogic conversations have been explored from a

---

[5]For instance, Cisco Webex offers "real time translation" (Webex Help Center 2022). The European Parliament's innovation partnership also aims at the development of a "Live Speech to Text and Machine Translation Tool for 24 Languages" (European Parliament 2019)

discourse-oriented perspective (see e.g. Apfelbaum & Wadensjö 1997 for Verbmobil, Hoberg 2022 for Skype Translator). This type of evaluation is, however, still in its infancy for continuous systems in conference settings (see Fantinuoli & Prandi 2021). A valuable step in this direction is the QEMI-C corpus (Mauri 2021). QEMI-C is a manually-compiled and -annotated, trilingual parallel corpus comprising 40 authentic speeches. It can serve as a basis for the comparative quality evaluation of MI and human interpretation (ibid., p. 95) in conference settings, which research has yet to address to a large extent.

Understanding the effects of MI use on communication appears particularly urgent, especially considering the overall negative perception of this technology by interpreters. In translation, where MT has long entered the profession, translators' resistance towards this technology and a certain dislike of related translation tasks (e.g. MTPE) is well known, surfacing as negative attitudes for instance in surveys (e.g. Moorkens & O'Brien 2015) and in social media discourse (e.g. Läubli & Orrego-Carmona 2017), especially among experienced professionals. Nonetheless, MT can also be used as a support, for instance to speed up the translation process for certain types of texts. Similarly, MI, especially with written output, may also be integrated into CAI tools to alleviate part of interpreters' cognitive efforts (see §2.2 and e.g. Wang & Wang 2019 for consecutive interpreting). A deeper understanding of these technologies may help interpreters embrace them as valuable support tools.

2.1.3 Supporting technologies for interpreting

If technology-mediated and technology-generated interpreting may, for various reasons, encounter the adversity of practitioners, supporting technologies are the group of solutions which conference interpreters may be expected to embrace. This subset of technologies encompasses different types of applications, both hardware and software. The most remarkable examples are tablet interpreting, the sim-consec pen, supporting ICTs for terminology work also used by translators, and bespoke tools for interpreters (CAI).

2.1.3.1 Tablet interpreting

Tablets are a rather new addition to the interpreter's toolkit. The still rather scarce amount of research published on this subject has highlighted how tablets are applied in a variety of settings and can be used not only for consecutive interpreting (Rosado 2013, Behl 2013a,b, Goldsmith & Holley 2015, Goldsmith 2017,

Drechsel & Goldsmith 2016), which has been the main focus of the analyses conducted so far, but also for assignment preparation and during simultaneous interpreting (Paone 2016). As for tablet usage during consecutive interpreting, a pilot study conducted in 2015 by Goldsmith and Holley offers a comparative user evaluation of tools suitable for note-taking during consecutive interpreting, tablet features, and styluses. It highlights how tablet interpreters mostly seek reliability, durability and a good user experience when selecting tablets and tools. Research conducted thus far has identified several advantages provided by tablets over pen and paper for consecutive interpreting and over laptops in the interpreting booth. Tablets offer a "simplified user experience" (Drechsel & Goldsmith 2016: 11) and longer-lasting batteries, can easily fit in the small perimeter of a booth and are quieter than paper and most laptops. These aspects also favour their use for terminology look-up during interpreting. Drechsel & Goldsmith (2016: 17) even go so far as hypothesising that using such a "streamlined device may decrease cognitive load by allowing interpreters to focus on the necessary complements to the task at hand", although they recognise that research is needed to test such a hypothesis. As with all tools, it is reasonable to assume that training may improve users' command, and tablet interpreting performance as a consequence (Goldsmith 2017: 43). Goldsmith & Holley (2015) identify potential disadvantages: using tablets when moving can be cumbersome, tablets may generate mistrust in clients who are not familiar with this technology applied to interpreting, and they do come with additional stress, costs and a certain learning curve. As for the perceived professionalism, this largely depends on clients' knowledge of and attitudes towards this technology applied to interpreting.

2.1.3.2 Sim-consecutive and digital pen

The digital pen is another technology that can provide interesting advantages both for training and for practitioners. It belongs to the category of mobile computing platforms and consists of "a microphone, a built-in speaker, 3D recording headsets, and an infrared camera" (Orlando 2010: 77). Users can write as they would with any other pen, but must use special micro chipped paper onto which data is captured. Since the notes and the recording are synchronised, the interpreter can then play back the recording from the notes.

This technology opens up new possibilities for the profession, giving birth to a new hybrid mode of interpreting known as simultaneous consecutive interpreting, sim-consec, or consec-simul with notes. In this interpreting mode, the interpreter takes notes as usual using the digital pen, and can then deliver the speech simultaneously while playing back the recording from the pen's ear set and looking at her notes at the same time. The digital pen also allows for playback speed adjustment, which facilitates rendition and promotes precision. Overall, the advantages of the sim-consec pen have been identified by scholars as "better interpreting performance, which was seen in 'more fluid delivery, closer source-target correspondence' (Hamidi & Pöchhacker 2007: 14), greater accuracy, fewer 'disfluencies' (hesitation phenomena), greater interpreter confidence, and a more complete rendition" (Orlando 2014). Orlando (2010: 78) adds that "tablet PCs are more expensive and less portable than a pen and a notepad", which speaks in favour of a digital pen as an alternative to traditional pen and paper support for consecutive interpreting.

Digital pens also offer interesting advantages for the training of future interpreters. As Orlando (2010: 72) observes, trainers are often faced with the issue of "encouraging their students to develop their own personal [note-taking] systems freely", while at the same time being unable to "observe these systems in the process of being developed throughout the training". As a consequence, they are unable to intervene with effective feedback, or to address the issues underlying a poor rendition or an ineffective note-taking technique. The possibility of observing the notes while in the making and to link the audio and the video of the notes taken does not only support trainers, but could additionally prove beneficial in terms of students' self-awareness, self-evaluation and self-regulation, and encourage more objective, evidence-based assessment of the learners' notes.

2.1.3.3 Supporting ICTs for terminology work

Interpreters can make use of a host of technologies to support their terminology work before, during, and after the assignment. These supporting technologies include general-purpose tools, tools also used by translators, and bespoke tools for interpreters, i.e. CAI tools.

For instance, interpreters can use text-processing or database software (e.g. MS Word or Excel) to compile their glossaries. While not developed specifically for interpreters, these solutions are very flexible and can easily be adjusted to interpreters' individual needs. CAT tools and other resources and solutions commonly used in translation such as TETs and TMSs can also be applied to interpreters' terminology work. These tools can be used to process preparation documents and extract terminology to compile domain-specific glossaries. Online databases and electronic dictionaries can be used to look up terminology, while concordancers can be used to explore the use of terms in context. As pointed out in §1.3.2, however, these tools are not optimised for interpreters, and present a series of limitations.

CAI tools have been developed with the goal of addressing said limitations, targeting the specific needs of interpreters' terminology work. During the preparation phase, for instance, CAI tools can help "moving cognition upstream" (Stoll 2009) by helping interpreters extract terminology from ad-hoc corpora created through the automatic collection of texts on a particular subject, automatically annotating speech transcripts provided by clients, and looking up translation equivalents, definitions and other linguistic and extra-linguistic information from several sources simultaneously. They can help interpreters increase their productivity by speeding up glossary creation and terminology memorisation, facilitate information sharing through dedicated import and export tools, and provide seamless access to the terminology databases compiled during the preparation phase. Due to their relevance for the present work, CAI tools are discussed in detail in the following sections.

2.2 CAI tools

Among the technologies aimed to support the interpreting process, CAI tools have received an increasingly wider share of attention. Unlike technologies which mediate the provision of the interpreting service (see §2.1.1) and can be described as setting-oriented technologies, CAI tools fall into the category of process-oriented technologies (Fantinuoli 2018a). The rationale behind their creation is namely that of providing targeted support for each of the interdependent sub-processes involved in interpreting, thanks to a dedicated architecture and to features optimised for the interpreting workflow.

2.2.1 Definition

Due to the multitude of tools and resources which interpreters can use as support, there has been some inconsistency in the use of the term CAI (Will 2020: 46). As remarked by Will (2020), the term CAI tool can in principle be used broadly to indicate any kind of supporting technology applied to interpreting. Some authors (e.g. Fantinuoli 2018a, Prandi 2017, 2018) have discussed as CAI tools only those bespoke tools explicitly developed to address interpreters' needs. Other authors, on the other hand, use the term CAI tool in broader terms. For instance, Costa et al. (2014a) also include unit converters; Cavallo & Ortiz (2018) also mention "note-taking software, audio and video conference systems or learning platforms" (see also Will 2020: 47). Other authors have even used the term to indicate other categories of technologies applied to interpreting, including "terminology aids, such as laptops, notebooks, small handheld PDAs (Personal Digital Assistants) or similar instruments with Internet accessibility that may facilitate interpreters' work" (Tripepi Winteringham 2010: 90).

To provide some clarity in the use of the term, Will (2020: 47) proposes to define non-bespoke tools targeting the pre- and post-process phases as "secondary CAI tools". This term thus indicates "any computer-based applications to search, compile and record terminologically relevant structures for a subsequent interpretation" (Will 2020: 47). Secondary CAI tools are therefore mainly derived from computer linguistics and can also comprise corpus managers and corpus analysis tools, semantic networks (e.g. Babelnet, see Navigli & Ponzetto 2012, Navigli et al. 2021), terminology extraction tools, etc, i.e. the technologies discussed in §1.3.

In addition to secondary CAI tools, "primary CAI tools", i.e. tools explicitly targeted to interpreters, address the specific ergonomic and cognitive requirements of the in-process phase. Among primary CAI tools, Will (2020) identifies a subcategory defined as "integrated" CAI tools, i.e. those tools which represent a complete workstation for interpreters, integrating both primary and secondary CAI functions, similarly to what CAT tools represent for translators (although in principle, interpreters could also use CAT tools to cover many subphases of their workflow). For the purpose of the present study, I henceforth use the term CAI tools to indicate only those tools which Will (2020) defines as primary CAI tools.

2.2.2 Overview of CAI tools

Rütten's (2004) model of a CAI tool (see §1.2.3.2) envisages a software programme capable of providing support for each phase of the workflow and of optimising time-consuming operations. Not all tools currently available on the market, however, represent a complete technical implementation of the model. In their relatively short history, CAI tools have gone through an evolution from simple terminology management tools to all-around solutions for conference preparation, even going beyond what had been envisioned by the first scholarly speculations on the topic.

In providing an overview of the tools available, and of those no longer supported, I follow Fantinuoli's (2016: 44) classification of (primary) CAI tools according to their "architecture and functionality spectrum". This overview will serve as the basis to motivate the selection of the tool employed in the present study.

In addition to a zero generation of tools, comprising non-bespoke-tools applicable to interpreting (i.e. secondary CAI tools), CAI software can be subdivided into two generations (Fantinuoli 2016, 2018a). This categorisation should, however, not be interpreted in strictly chronological terms. Rather, it mirrors the degree of sophistication of the individual applications.

The first generation of tools consists of programs which offer little more than terminology management for interpreters (Hansen-Schirra 2012: 212). This category includes Terminus[6] (Wintringham 2009), Glossarmanager,[7] Glossary Assistant (Martin 2014), Interplex[8] (Sand 2003, 2010) and flashterm Interpreter [9] (Eisenrieth Dokumentations GmbH 2010). These tools can be used to organise terminological entries by topic, client, event and other criteria inside multilingual glossaries, the basic components of these tools' architecture. The only exception is flashterm Interpreter. This tool is not term-based, but rather concept-based: the terminological entries can be assigned to categories and tagged individually, and filtered to create ad-hoc glossaries. Some tools, such as Interplex, allow for the creation of multiple databases, while in most CAI tools (also of the second generation) all terminological entries are contained in a single database. Even though the basic functions offered by first-generation tools are similar (glossary creation and storage, basic import and export functions, a feature for glossary printing), some of the more recent tools provide additional functions that expand the range of elaboration by prospective users, such as the creation of ad-hoc term lists for quick terminology memorisation in flashterm Interpreter, or the inclusion of images in the terminological entries. These tools usually also provide a feature for quick terminology look-up, both within single glossaries and/or in the whole database.

To the second category of CAI tools can be ascribed applications that go beyond providing a structured way of organising terminological resources for interpreters. These solutions aim to offer a complete workstation for conference preparation and to support interpreters along the different phases of their workflow. Second-generation CAI tools typically provide the terminology management and glossary creation features present in first-generation solutions, but additionally offer further functions for workflow optimisation. Some examples are document integration and terminology extraction, quick search for translation equivalents and other linguistic and extra-linguistic information across multiple sources (such as online dictionaries and terminological databases), memorisation of relevant terminology and terminology look-up both during the preparation phase and on assignment thanks to the integration of search algorithms to

---

[6]http://www.wintringham.ch/cgi/ayawp.pl/t/terminus (Accessed: 01.11.2021)

[7]https://www.glossarmanager.de (Accessed: 01.11.2021)

[8]http://www.fourwillows.com/interplex.html# (Accessed: 01.11.2021)

[9]https://www.flashterm.eu/en/ (Accessed: 01.11.2021)

speed up the querying process and effectively deal with time constraints. Second-generation CAI tools thus represent, to a large extent, the actualisation of Rüt-ten's (2004) model. To this category one can ascribe Intragloss (discontinued), and Interpreter's Help[10] with its offline companion tool BoothMate.[11] Intragloss was only available for the Mac operating system, while Interpreter's Help is web-based and provides multi-platform offline applications. Intragloss allowed for quick terminology look-up across multiple online sources within the application itself, thus eliminating the need to switch between the tool and, for example, a search engine. Interpreter's Help is a community-oriented tool where glossaries can be accessed both through the online platform or offline from the compan-ion app BoothMate. In addition to the above-mentioned features common to all second-generation tools, Interpreter's Help also provides functions for managing assignments, sharing glossaries and assignment details online with colleagues, creating ad-hoc flashcards that allow users to memorise translation equivalents and other data, but also features that promote collaboration within the interpret-ing community: a public glossary database (Glossary Farm), a feature for upload-ing practice speeches, asking and providing feedback, and a community section with useful links and resources. BoothMate enables users to query their database thanks to a progressive search function that simply requires users to start typing the term they are looking for, and incrementally reduces the number of results presented.

While Fantinuoli distinguishes between two generations of CAI tools, the tech-nological advances provided by artificial intelligence hold great potential for fur-ther development of such tools towards fully-fledged virtual boothmates. This third generation of CAI tools, exemplified by InterpretBank (Fantinuoli 2012, 2017a), could represent the next step in human-machine interaction in the field of CAI. While first-generation tools mainly only provide a more rational and streamlined infrastructure for terminology work in interpreting with the bulk of the information processing still done by users, and second-generation tools take a step further by automatising and speeding up individual operations tradi-tionally carried out by the interpreter, third-generation, AI-enhanced CAI tools could provide a framework for optimising each step of the interpreting workflow through technology. When working with these tools, interpreters can focus on refining the work done by the tool, with the bulk of conference preparation hav-ing been pre-processed by the software. Even though this goal has not been fully achieved yet, and much will depend on the progress made by machine learning

---

[10]https://interpretershelp.com (Accessed: 01.11.2021)
[11]https://interpretershelp.com/boothmate (Accessed: 01.11.2021)

and AI, the CAI tool InterpretBank already presents some features that go beyond what is currently offered by second-generation tools and exemplifies third-
generation CAI tools. For its innovativeness, I chose InterpretBank as the tool
used in the study. In the following section, I therefore describe this CAI tool in
detail.

2.2.3 InterpretBank

InterpretBank combines a central Edit Modality – Rütten's (2007) central starting page (see §1.3.1) – with three modules each dedicated to a stage of conference
preparation: the Document Modality, the Memo Modality, and the Booth Modality.[12] From the Edit Modality, users can access the database, update old glossaries
and create new ones, merge glossaries and move terms to other glossaries, automatically search for translation equivalents and definitions both offline, in the
integrated resources, and online in pre-selected web pages. InterpretBank is currently the only tool that offers solutions for creating glossaries starting from
a single term thanks to the integration of corpus creation tools, and for automatically translating the whole glossary. The user's intervention is still required
to assess the results of automatic translation, but such a feature can help optimise interpreters' preparation under time pressure by enabling them to focus
on higher-level processing instead of devoting most of their time to manually
compiling glossaries ahead of the event. These functions might prove particularly useful when conference interpreters are faced with a scarcity of preparation
materials to be used as a basis for terminology extraction and key topic identification. While glossaries are organised within a single database, it is possible to
create subglossaries and group glossaries together with tags, which provides an
additional layer of structure and customisation.

When interpreters do receive preparation documents from their clients or have
found relevant resources on the internet, the Document Modality can assist them
in making the most of the available resources. InterpretBank is one of the few
tools that support users in extracting terminology from preparation documents,
allowing for an application of the corpus-driven interpreter preparation (CDIP,
see §1.2.3.2) put forward by Fantinuoli (2006). Like Interpreter's Help and Intragloss, InterpretBank makes it possible for users to select relevant terms while
reading through conference materials or other sources and add them to the glossary. When working with parallel texts, users can mark term pairs in parallel

---

[12]For a detailed and up-to-date description of InterpretBank's modules and functions, the reader
may refer to https://interpretbank.com/site/index.html#features and to the user guide at: https:
//www.interpretbank.com/site/docs/index.html (Accessed: 01.11.2021).

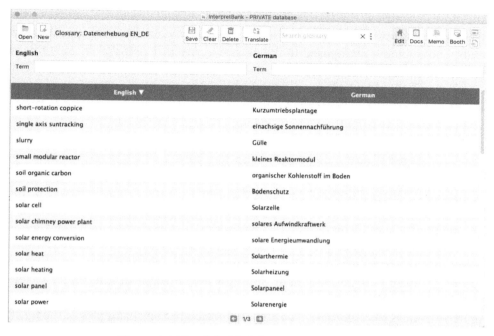

Figure 2.1: The Edit Modality in InterpretBank

in order to quickly add them to their glossary, a feature also available in the two second-generation CAI tools previously mentioned. A unique feature offered by InterpretBank is the automatic terminology extraction feature, which can be used to mine terminology either from the whole set or from subsets of available sources, or from single files. The SMART terminology extraction function learns from the user's behaviour to improve terminology extraction results in subsequent TE tasks. The tool helps effectively process speech transcripts by allowing for automatic document annotation, a function which can represent a useful emergency strategy when interpreters receive written speeches to be read aloud shortly before the conference starts. An additional feature which can prove useful for interpreters dealing with EU-related topics is the possibility of downloading the texts of EU legislation directly from EUR-Lex[13] into Interpret-Bank. Interpreters can mine these documents for terminology as with any other document added to the current glossary. The Edit and the Document Modality are therefore strictly intertwined: users can add entries to the glossary that they are currently working on from the Documents modality, and at a later time explore how terms are used in the context of their preparation documents from

---

[13]https://eur-lex.europa.eu/ (Accessed: 24.07.2022)

the glossary entries. The synergy between the two modalities also emerges from their presentation on the user's interface: the Documents modality appears as an additional window juxtaposed to the glossary currently being processed by the user.

After compiling terminological databases, interpreters can receive support in memorising event-related terminology in the Memory Modality, which creates virtual flashcards from the current glossary. Users can choose between manual and automatic presentation. The manual mode can prove particularly useful in the early stages of terminology memorisation, during which it can be useful for the user to mark the terms as "known" or "forgotten". Following the principle of spaced repetition, the tool presents the user with the forgotten terms at the end of the practice session, so that said terms can be practised once again. The automatic flashcard presentation can be used to test one's own reaction time to the term/stimulus, since presentation speed can be varied, but can also represent an easy way to quickly review the terminology right before the assignment begins or during breaks. A similar option is also present in Interpreter's Help, which provides the additional option of creating ad-hoc flashcard decks. InterpretBank offers two additional features: an option to view examples of the terms in the context of preparation documents, and the possibility of having the terms read aloud. This feature, which makes use of speech synthesis technology, is particularly suited to the needs of interpreters, who process oral stimuli (with the exception of sight and signed language translation). Additionally, it can prove particularly useful for highly non-phonemic languages such as English.

The phase of interpretation proper is covered by the Booth Modality, which completes the architecture of the tool. A similar function is also offered by Interpreter's Help companion app BoothMate. Like BoothMate, InterpretBank's Booth Modality can also be used offline. In this modality, interpreters can quickly search for terminology in their glossaries. Unlike in the Edit Modality, in which users can only work on one glossary at a time, in the Booth Modality it is possible to activate multiple glossaries which can all be queried simultaneously (the "active glossary"). Additionally, users can also choose to have InterpretBank perform the search inside the whole database or even exploit external resources as an emergency strategy.

The default search mode in the Booth Modality is the dynamic search, which progressively reduces the number of results with increasing input. It is, however, also possible to manually start the query. A host of additional options, such as the fuzzy search and the "case and access insensitive" search, facilitate the lookup process during interpreting.

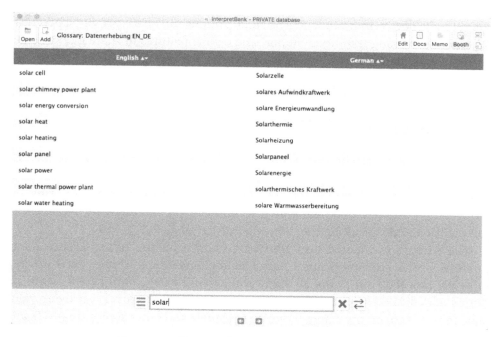

Figure 2.2: The Booth Modality in InterpretBank

Perhaps the most advanced feature offered by InterpretBank is the integration of ASR technology. While still marketed as an experimental feature in the freelance version, the integrated ASR option represents the next step in supporting interpreters through technology. The goal of ASR integration into the tool is that of presenting interpreters with elements typically deemed difficult to interpret, "problem triggers" (Gile 2009) such as numbers, specialised terminology, and named entities. This represents a step towards the creation of CAI tools serving as artificial boothmates and providing support without requiring extensive human-machine interaction. At the moment of writing, InterpretBank offers ASR support for specialised terminology and numbers. A similar feature is also offered for consecutive interpreting: users can create an "artificial notepad" allowing them to visualise the automatically-generated transcription of the source speech, looking up term equivalents with a click, automatically convert units, and share the ASR session with a colleague.

Like Interpreter's Help, InterpretBank also offers browser-based features that can be accessed through a private Cloud account. In the cloud, users can upload, edit, share and download glossaries, and access the memorisation and look-up features from the internet, an option particularly appreciated by interpreters who prefer to be device-independent. The cloud options can also represent a practical alternative to using traditional import and export features to share glossaries as text or Excel files.

2.3 Conference interpreters' use of supporting technologies

Given the role of terminology acquisition for the interpreting process, the distinctive features of terminology work in interpreting, and the availability of dedicated software for interpreters, scholars have taken interest in exploring interpreters' practices when compiling terminological databases for assignment preparation and consulting them during interpreting.

The surveys conducted over the years paint a picture of conference interpreters' level of computerisation, use of technological support pre-, peri-, in- and post-process (both in terms of hardware and software), and of their needs in terms of dedicated solutions for terminology work. These surveys provide valuable information on the extent to which CAI tools and other supporting ICTs are actually employed by interpreters in their professional workflows.

2.3.1 Conference interpreters' level of computerisation

When discussing the individual solutions chosen by interpreters as a support for their terminology work, their overall level of computerisation and their adoption of computer support in the various phases of interpretation is worth considering, as it may help put their practices into perspective.

The first inquiry into conference interpreters' preparation practices dates back to 1992. Moser-Mercer (1992) distributed a questionnaire among 260 interpreters, all AIIC active members with English among their working languages. Among the 130 respondents, the level of "computerisation" (Moser-Mercer 1992: 510), i.e. the percentage of respondents who own or have access to a computer, was already quite high (62.3%), and seemed to correlate positively with the years of professional experience and the number of interpreting days per year. Moser-Mercer speculated that this trend could be due to a higher level of specialisation among more experienced professionals, which would in turn promote computer use for terminology work. A survey conducted by Drechsel (2004) supports Moser-Mercer's (1992) findings, with only two respondents not using the PC in any of the phases of an interpreting assignment. It should be noted, however, that the sample was quite small and only representative of the German market (46 professional interpreters). A more nuanced picture of the use of computers as technological support for terminology emerges when considering the individual phases of the interpreting assignment.

2.3.2 Computer and software use for assignment preparation

Moser-Mercer's (1992) survey did not venture into a detailed analysis of the tools used for preparation. However, it provides valuable insight into which types of solutions interpreters used at a time when both CAT and CAI tools were starting to be developed. The survey reports that 51.3% of those who used a computer medium chose terminology databanks (40%), databases (35.5%) and spreadsheet software (31%) to compile and organise terminological information and documentation. The main sources for documentation ahead of the event were event documents and bilingual dictionaries, and a widespread use was made of terminology lists compiled personally or supplied by the clients. External databases were used only to a limited extent. These findings support the notion that terminology work in interpreting (as in translation) is performed ad-hoc and strictly interlinked with the individual assignment. The survey does, however, provide us with two interesting findings. At the time of her study, 67% of respondents showed an interest in terminology management software, while 72.7% expressed an interest in exchanging terminology in electronic form. This seems to speak in favour of a high degree of computerisation for preparation work. About a decade later, Valentini (2001, 2002) conducted a similar survey on a sample of 130 professional conference interpreters, both freelancers and staff, 40% of which with more than 20 years in the profession, working mostly (94.5%) in the simultaneous mode. In the preparation phase, a third of her sample used electronic terminology databases (37% used paper glossaries), and 11.3% conducted terminology extraction (TE) automatically. The most widespread programs for terminology work were Microsoft Word or similar (67.7%), followed by Excel or similar (11.4% of respondents). Users of these solutions generally showed a higher degree of satisfaction than users of dedicated terminology software.

A similar picture of the software used by conference interpreters emerges from the t-survey by Zielinski & Ramírez-Safar (2005): of the 81 interpreters involved, 63% performed terminology work; 66.1% used Word or Excel tables for terminology management, while 53.2% also used terminology management systems (TMS). In this survey, no mention of tools developed specifically for interpreters (see Chapter 3) is made, even though some of them were already available at the time (e.g. Interplex, LookUp/DolTerm, and TermDB). As for TE, the trend is similar to the study by Valentini (2001, 2002) (13.9% informants used terminology extraction tools).

Bilgen (2009) conducted a small-scale survey on a sample of experienced CACI members, the Canadian branch of AIIC. Bilgen's (2009) findings are along the lines of the surveys previously mentioned: 70% of respondents used word processors or spreadsheets for terminology management, while 85% recorded terms on paper (multiple answers were possible). On-screen work was preferred before and after conferences. Interestingly, 77% of the sample never used a TMS, and no mention was made of interpreter-specific software. This contrasts with Zielinski & Ramírez-Safar's (2005) findings, but in their sample most interpreters also worked as translators. Bilgen (2009) does not specify whether this is the case in her survey. Only one respondent reported using a TMS; another interpreter a database management programme. None of the surveyed interpreters mentioned interpreter-specific software.

In a survey conducted in 2010 on a sample of 222 conference interpreters (mostly AIIC members and/or working for the EU or the UN), Berber-Irabien (2010) found that ICTs were mainly used in the preparation phase, and only scarcely (15%) for post-assignment debriefing. Terminology databases (such as IATE) were used by 88% of her sample. Disappointingly, terminology management software, and in particular programs for interpreters such as Interplex or LookUp, were mentioned in the overview of tools for interpreters, but were not included in the questionnaire categories. Of all ICTs considered[14], search engines were those used with more frequency (in 38% of cases). While these findings overall support previously identified trends, no distinction was made between setting-oriented and process-oriented technologies, a limitation which hinders the direct comparison with previous studies.

In 2012, Wagener conducted a survey on 102 interpreters, mainly German. In line with previous survey work, she found that most interpreters in her sample used general-purpose tools such as MS Word and even paper, while MS Excel was less popular (less than 30% of the sample). Only 26% of her sample used interpreter-specific tools. Regrettably, it was not mandatory for her respondents to include the names of the tools used. An even smaller percentage (13%) used terminology software.

Jiang (2013) and Corpas Pastor & Fern (2016) conducted the two most recent surveys available on interpreters' terminology practices. Jiang's (2013) survey focused on conference interpreters' glossaries for SI. The response rate was very

---

[14]Berber-Irabien (2010) looked at search engines, online dictionaries and encyclopedias, terminology databases, electronic norms manuals, parallel texts, do-it-yourself corpora; technologies now considered obsolete – pocket electronic dictionaries, CD-ROM dictionaries, paper encyclopedias – and terminology databases, as well as setting-oriented technologies (Fantinuoli 2018a: 155) such as remote interpreting, videoconferencing and telephone interpreting.

high at 21%, and the large sample ($n = 476$) mostly consisted of AIIC members, two thirds of whom had more than 15 years of professional experience. Jiang (2013) analysed several aspects of glossary creation for SI, such as the items included in the glossary, the sources used and the frequency of glossary creation. A very interesting finding was that the preferred medium remained loose paper (57.6%), followed by Word glossaries (55.7%). Most interpreters seemed to combine digital glossaries with a printout, so it can be assumed that both were taken into the booth. A smaller percentage of the surveyed interpreters (15%) used "glossary software". An even smaller number of respondents use other tools such as Trados Multiterm and Interplex. An interpreter's glossary consists mainly of a table or a list with glossary items (93.7% of responses). Given the high response rate and large sample, Jiang's (2013) findings can be considered quite representative of the glossary creation practices of experienced, professional conference interpreters working in the simultaneous mode until some years ago.

Finally, Corpas Pastor & Fern (2016) aimed to explore interpreters' use of "technology tools" in the various interpreting modes and settings. For the purpose of this study, I will take into consideration the responses regarding simultaneous interpreting (a total of 92 out of 133). The respondents used mainly bilingual dictionaries, digital glossaries and thesauri, but also databases and term banks during preparation. Despite the rather small sample and the – in my opinion – somewhat arbitrary interpretation of data by the authors, their findings align with those of similar surveys.

The surveys presented above span over 25 years. The sample sizes vary, as does the specific focus of each survey, although they all relate to technology use during preparation. Even though these surveys are only comparable to some extent, they provide a picture of technology use for terminology work prior to the (simultaneous) interpreting task. On average, at least until 2016, conference interpreters tended to use computers for preparation, consult digital terminology databases and compile digital glossaries, mostly in the form of terminology lists and tables. General software prevailed, with a preference for Word or similar text processing programs, followed by Excel or other spreadsheet applications. The interest in software solutions for preparation identified by Moser-Mercer (1992) seems to have led to a widespread use of various technologies for assignment preparation. Despite these developments, which – there is reason to believe – will continue in the years to come, paper has not yet disappeared as an additional support medium for glossary work. On the contrary, paper seems to remain an integral component of interpreters' terminology work and is often combined with the afore-mentioned text-processing programs. To a limited extent, terminology management systems such as Trados Multiterm are also used, although it seems that especially interpreters who also work as translators use these kinds of tools. As emerges from the t-survey (Zielinski & Ramírez-Safar 2005), automatic terminology extraction with dedicated TET seems to be a rare practice among interpreters, who prefer manual TE. Considering the speed at which technology progresses, and the acceleration, also due to the COVID-19 pandemic, of what has been defined as "the technological turn" in interpreting (Fantinuoli 2019), these results are in all probability no longer representative of the situation in 2022. It can be reasonably assumed that the ratio of interpreter-specific technologies for assignment preparation compared to more "traditional" solutions has now shifted more towards the first. Regrettably, to the best of my knowledge, no survey on interpreters' use of technology pre-process has been conducted since 2016.

2.3.3 Computer and software use peri- and in-process

If the paper medium has not yet been entirely supplanted by the electronic one in the preparation of glossaries (Bilgen 2009, Jiang 2013), it is nonetheless undeniable that there has been a progressive penetration of technological support in the interpreting profession. As emerged from the surveys, however, at least until some years ago, the technological support inside the booth has remained limited. In Valentini's (2001) survey, dating back almost 20 years, only 27.6% of survey participants stated that they use a computer in the booth. The largest percentage of booth computer users in her sample worked for the European institutions. At EU institutions, "the greater availability of infrastructure [...] facilitates and encourages the penetration of information technology compared to other national and international institutions" (p. 162). A similar result emerged from Bilgen's (2009) and Berber-Irabien's (2010) surveys, which found that computer and software use was more popular before and after the assignment, while limited inside the booth. An encouraging piece of data that emerges from the survey conducted by Valentini (2001, 2002) is that 66.1% of respondents considered ICT support as potentially useful for SI. This is, however, a rather general claim and tells little about which ICTs are being referred to, nor which sub-processes they could support. Interestingly, 43.4% of the sample deemed terminology look-up with technological support "very useful". Bilgen's (2009) sample was also largely in favour of computer use in the booth, and half of the sample used one.

In Valentini's (2001, 2002) survey, no distinction was made between peri-process and in-process with reference to technology use in the booth. Drechsel (2004) did make this distinction. In the small sample he considered, 16 interpreters used a PC peri-process, 16 to help their boothmates and 13 to look up terminology themselves; 14 respondents used laptops to work on documents and 16 for follow-up work during the conference. As for the medium, 11 respondents out of 46 used paper glossaries in addition to digital glossaries.

The most recent inquiries in the terminology management practices of conference interpreters also show that, although with some limitations, the technological support has increasingly made its way into the interpreting booth. For instance, Berber-Irabien (2010) found that terminology databases are the preferred technology tool for accessing terminology during simultaneous interpreting. Corpas Pastor & Fern (2016) also came to a similar conclusion, identifying bilingual dictionaries and personal glossaries as the preferred digital tool used by interpreters to search for terminology during the task. Nonetheless, most conference interpreters seem not to rely on tools created specifically for interpreters. Corpas Pastor & Fern (2016) observe that "regarding technology tools during an interpreting task, most of our simultaneous interpreters do not count on help from technology resources. The only tools used in specific circumstances during an assignment are bilingual dictionaries, glossaries and, in some cases, web-based resources" (Corpas Pastor & Fern 2016: 26).

Wagener (2012) had also found a widespread use of online dictionaries, search engines and other search tools in the booth, pointing to terminology work also happening peri- and in-process and not only pre-process. On the other hand, she had found a very limited use of terminology management systems in the booth, similarly to what had been postulated by Stoll (2009) and Rütten (2011) (see Wagener 2012). However, the vast majority of her respondents bring a technological support into the booth, be it a laptop, a netbook, a smartphone or a tablet, almost always coupled with handwritten or printed documents (90% of surveyed interpreters).

To date, the only inquiry into conference interpreters' use of CAI tools for simultaneous interpreting is the survey conducted by the Sprachen und Dolmetscher Institut (SDI Munich) in 2007. The sample was made up of 135 AIIC members and conference interpreters members of other associations. Unfortunately, the survey was conducted in German, limiting the representativity of the sample. As for computer use, 68% of the sample brought a PC in the booth and 41% used it during interpreting, while 26% preferred booth-specific software. The participants who did not use CAI tools mainly used other tools, a good percentage also "during interpreting" (59%). It is unclear whether "during interpreting" ("während des Dolmetschens", SDI München 2007: 28) should be intended as during delivery itself, or whether this could also refer, for instance, to helping the boothmate with terminology look-up during their turn. A surprising finding, which would deserve further exploration, is that 41% used self-developed tools.

Because of the specificity of the sample, these findings cannot be generalised. Furthermore, the survey dates back to 2007 and is in all probability no longer representative. There is a need for an up-to-date inquiry into interpreters' level of computerisation and especially of their use of software in all phases of an interpreting assignment. Except for this survey, CAI tools are yet to be systematically integrated into such inquiries.

Despite the limitations of these surveys, they suggest a few trends in conference interpreters' use of terminology management software and other ICTs for terminology work, as well as in their level of computerisation. The average modern conference interpreter seems to make extensive use of ICTs in the pre-process phase, bringing a laptop into the booth, often together with some information on paper or a printed glossary, and conducts post-conference work on a laptop, mostly in the form of terminology update. The most popular technologies used to compile glossaries are general-purpose text-processing or database software, such as MS Word or Excel. Terminology extraction and terminology management tools are also used, especially by interpreters who also work as translators. However, the use of these tools is quite limited among interpreters, as is the use of CAI tools, although they seem to be more popular. This may suggest that there is still room for further optimisation and tailoring of these tools to interpreters' needs.

The widespread use of paper, despite the possibilities offered by modern technology for a paperless booth, may also point to a limitation of current CAI tools. It is possible, as Wagener (2012: 77) observes, that digital glossaries and paper are used for different purposes. The first support a kind of terminology work which aims at creating terminology resources that can be helpful also beyond the individual event. Having long-lasting terminological resources saves preparation time and makes terminology work more sustainable in the long run. Paper, on the other hand, may represent the ideal support for short-term terminological needs, i.e. to provide interpreters with the necessary *aide-memoires* for those terms which tend to be forgotten. CAI tools currently do not seem to address this specific need.

2.3.4 Attitudes towards CAI tools

Having considered the current state of CAI tool development, the specific interpreter needs and the potential of ASR for an even more efficient interpreter-tool interaction in-process, it is somewhat surprising that CAI tool usage is still relatively limited, as emerges from the surveys presented in §2.3.3. While providing a snapshot of interpreters' terminological practices at the moment of data collection, these surveys also bring to light some of the motivations behind the limited inclusion of CAI tools in interpreters' workflows. While some negative attitudes have subsided over time, when asked to comment on their tool choice or to provide their opinion on the adoption of computers and CAI tools, conference interpreters seem to share some common points of criticism.

Moser-Mercer (1992: 512) observed how the only tools that "met almost all requirements stipulated by interpreters" were Term-PC and SDL Multiterm. Both programs allowed for multilingual glossary creation, quick terminology retrieval, free definition of entry structures and options for glossary import, export and printing. Since then, several CAI tools were developed. Their use in the booth is, however, still considered problematic both by practitioners and researchers. In discussing the results of her survey on computer use in the interpreting booth, Valentini observed that terminology look-up while "on air" would only be possible for redundant terminology, i.e. when terms are repeated more than once within a speech. In her opinion, interpreters would prefer other strategies such as simplification through paraphrasing or the use of hypernyms to the more distracting search in their terminological resources, since clear and close rendition of the source message is a more prominent quality factor than terminological accuracy.

The distraction potential of CAI tools seems, indeed, to be a common point of criticism on CAI tools and, more generally, of terminology look-up during interpreting, as emerges from the SDI (2007) questionnaire and Bilgen's (2009) survey. In the first, the distracting effect ("ablenkende Wirkung", SDI München 2007: 29) of terminology software is mentioned by 6% of the 82 interpreters not using such solutions. The main reasons for the exclusion of such software from interpreters' toolkit are however the lack of necessity (57%), because more traditional solutions are preferred, the lack of knowledge about such tools (35%) and the fact that these tools were considered unconvincing or not yet sophisticated enough (22%). In view of the recent developments in CAI technology, this last point may not be as relevant as before. Other reasons mentioned are, in descending order of importance, lack of space in the booth, poor customisation and resistance to technology because of excessive complexity of use. Similarly, Bilgen's (2009) survey respondents observed that using the computer in the booth might be distracting for the interpreter and noisy, since the sound of typing could be picked up by the microphone, thus distracting the audience, too. This argument is, however, increasingly losing strength, as many modern laptops come with a silent keyboard, and some interpreters have already successfully replaced their laptops with tablets.

To explain the continued presence of paper as additional support in the booth, even considered the preferred medium used for interpreters' glossaries in her survey, Jiang (2013) advanced the hypothesis that interpreters' may jot down essential glossary items on loose paper sheets, which would make terminology access immediate. This is a necessity, since "accurate and just-in-time retrieval of glossary items is vital, especially at technical meetings" (Jiang 2013: 90). While this is true, Jiang seems not to take into consideration the quick search function in Word or Excel files and the progressive search function available in some CAI tools when stating that "physically turning a page is probably simpler and faster than having to access a given item or page in a sizeable computer file or database" (Jiang 2013: 91). Rather, the choice to include paper may be more of a strategic nature (see §2.3.3).

The potential disadvantages of CAI tools for terminology look-up have also been discussed in several publications on the application of technologies to conference interpreting. While CAI tools should theoretically "represent the most effective information interface when interpreting" (Tripepi Winteringham 2010: 90), the feasibility of their use is often questioned. These tools are described as potentially "time-consuming and distracting" (ibid.), or leading to a "loss of concentration" (Tripepi Winteringham 2010: 91). Berber-Irabien (2010) similarly observes that their use might interfere with listening and concentration. Given the complexity of the interpreting task, while using CAI tools "the interpreter [...] may not have the time or the cognitive ability to look up a word [...] or detect and choose the correct translation [...]" (Fantinuoli 2016: 49), because "typing an unknown word [...] requires an additional time-consuming effort which would affect the already existing efforts that interpreters support during their work" (Tripepi Winteringham 2010: 91). Additionally, "should the right word be found it may not be possible to incorporate it smoothly in speech" (Veisbergs 2007: 80).

The surveys and publications discussed suggest a certain interest in technologies for conference preparation and terminology work specifically developed to meet interpreters' requirements and the need for dedicated tools. While CAI tools' potential is overall acknowledged, their hypothesised and perceived limitations should not be ignored. The disadvantages that these analyses point to mainly concern the application of such tools on the simultaneous, in-process phase.

The negative attitudes and the indifference encountered among interpreters towards non-bespoke supporting technologies and CAI tools may be compared to translators' attitudes towards CAT tools and MT, a technology often integrated into CAT tools. While a considerable number of translators seem to have adopted CAT tools as a staple in their workflows, as suggested by recent surveys (e.g.

Moorkens & O'Brien 2016, Steurs et al. 2017), many translators express dissatisfaction towards their tools or frustration in their use. In translation, this feeling of frustration may be even more pronounced than in interpreting, as the use of specific tools is somehow imposed by the client, e.g. the translation agency. Translators' "cognitive friction" (Ehrensberger-Dow & O'Brien 2015) in using CAT tools manifests in the irritation and negative attitudes expressed in a number of surveys (e.g. O'Brien et al. 2017). Translators' dissatisfaction concerns complex user interfaces, a lack of intuitiveness and user-friendliness and suboptimal navigation within the tool which slows down the workflow. This contrasts with the identification of high working speed and intuitive user interfaces as essential features of translator tools (see O'Brien et al. 2017).

In interpreting, a certain amount of frustration may be avoided by simply choosing not to use tools perceived as useless or unsatisfactory, as the choice of supporting technologies is often left to the individual interpreter. This may, in part, be mirrored in the lower percentages of translation tools and CAI tools users among interpreters and the resulting digital divide with translators. However, if other players become involved in the development of CAI tools, e.g. RSI providers including CAI as support in their platforms, it is possible that interpreters may soon have to use tools they have not personally selected. As remarked by Hansen-Schirra (2012), most tools for translators and interpreters are yet to exploit computational linguistics and speech technologies to their fullest extent, which results in tools not entirely optimised for their end-users. As for translation tools, greater involvement of interpreters in the development of supporting tools may help to mitigate some of their limitations and perceived drawbacks. At the same time, research on the use of CAI tools can help define how they impact the product of interpretation and to what extent they may support or impair the cognitive processes underlying interpreting.

2.4 Research on CAI tools

The recent developments in the field of CAI have renewed and multiplied the interest of the interpreting community for this subject. This is demonstrated by the increasing number of publications on the topic. In addition to the foundational works by Rütten (2000, 2004, 2007), Stoll (2009) and Will (2000, 2007) providing a model of software programs for interpreters (see §1.2.3.2), the publications devoted to CAI tools address a number of topics and issues inherent to the tools, ranging from a simple presentation and comparison of the available solutions to the first empirical tests conducted on one or more tools.

Among the first publications which appeared on the topic, several contributions aim to provide prospective users with an overview of the CAI tools to choose from and a set of criteria for their selection. Several articles by Costa et al. (2014a,b, 2015) detail the tools available on the market and highlight the features addressing conference interpreters' needs. The authors offer "a tentative catalogue of current language technologies for interpreters, divided into terminology tools for interpreters, note-taking applications for consecutive interpreting, applications for voice recording and training tools" (Costa et al. 2015: 68). CAI and related terminology management tools, as well as other technologies relevant to interpreting, are discussed together. In Costa et al. (2015), the authors focus on CAI tools, analysing both three of the best-known CAI tools (Intragloss, InterpretBank and Interplex), and other lesser-known or non interpreter-specific terminology management software (i.e. SDL MultiTerm, AnyLexic, Lingo, Unilex and The Interpreter's Wizard). In their analysis, the authors evaluate the tools chosen for the comparison against a set of 15 features identified as priorities in relation to conference interpreters' needs. Of the 15 criteria, five are classified as fundamental and ten as secondary. The authors do not clarify the rationale behind this distinction, nor do they specify which features are deemed essential and which secondary. Additionally, they seem to base their evaluation on the rather unjustified goal of identifying the most complete solution. While this might be a useful piece of information, the tool so identified may not coincide with the one most suited to the needs of interpreters. In the authors' analysis, the programme which received the highest score is SDL MultiTerm. Overall, the evaluation appears rather arbitrary, as it excludes features which are particularly relevant to the interpreter's workflow such as quick terminology look-up or terminology extraction from preparation documents (Fantinuoli 2016).

Will (2015) proposes a similar evaluation of CAI tools and lays down a set of criteria for their assessment, with the goal of identifying deficits and proposing potential solutions to be implemented. Will's contribution has the merit of basing the definition of the evaluation criteria on a theoretical model of interpreters' terminological work, which he defines as "dolmetschorientierte Terminologiearbeit (DOT)" [interpreter-oriented terminology work] (Will 2015: 181), and is at the intersection of the terminology models by Wüster (1979) and Gerzymisch-Arbogast (1996), of Moser (1978) and Moser-Mercer's (1997) process model of simultaneous interpreting, and of Gile's (1995) effort model (see §3.5.1). The three principles thus identified as fundamental for the implementation of the model (adequacy and pattern building, simultaneity, and phase-specific usage) in CAI tools are used as a basis for the definition of three key criteria against which the tools should be evaluated: flexible visualisation, comprehensive database and help functions (1), ergonomics (2) and user-friendliness (3). Unlike Costa et al. (2014a,b, 2015), the author compares Interplex, Terminus, LookUp professional and InterpretBank 3, i.e. CAI tools as they are intended in the present work. The tool evaluation presents the limitation of being subjective, although based on clearly motivated criteria. The author does not involve additional raters. The involvement of a large sample of conference interpreters in the evaluation would have been welcome. Some of his suggestions (such as terminology extraction, automatic glossary population with definitions and translation equivalents) have, however, already been implemented into some tools, a sign of the rapid evolution of technology in this field.

In addition to these comparisons and evaluation attempts of several tools by scholars, a number of bachelor's and master's theses have been devoted to the subject. This suggests a growing interest for these tools among the newer generations of conference interpreters. In particular, De Merulis (2013) focused his analysis on the CAI tool InterpretBank, which he describes in detail. His was one of the first attempts at investigating the impact of CAI tool use on the quality of simultaneous interpreting in terms of terminological accuracy. Similarly, Gacek (2015) reviews several CAI tools and offers a detailed description of InterpretBank, defined as one of the most user-friendly tools available to interpreters. He reports the results of two experiments carried out with the tool, for which qualitative data was collected through questionnaires. Users were asked to rate the usability of InterpretBank during a simultaneous interpreting session (first experiment) and after two months of usage (second experiment) and to compare it with printed glossaries prepared in Word and Excel. Data analysis, although limited to a sample of 12 questionnaires, seems to indicate that InterpretBank provides an advantage in terms of efficiency, thanks to features such as the dynamic search function or the Memory Modality.

Drawing on trainee interpreters' interest into new technologies, interpreting research has looked at how CAI tools, in addition to more established technologies such as RSI, could be integrated into the interpreting curriculum. Prandi (2015a,b) carried out an exploratory study on the integration of CAI tools into the Master's degree in Interpreting at the University of Bologna/Forlì. The 12 study participants were divided into two groups: one group attended an introductory class on InterpretBank and then received practical training in the booth (three sessions), while the other attended three introductory classes on the topic and trained with the tool only once. Students worked in pairs and were free to establish how to interact with the software and with the boothmate while using the tool during SI. While the study was of qualitative nature and the sample relatively small, results seem to indicate that CAI tools may help achieve high terminological accuracy. InterpretBank was overall judged as user-friendly. Nonetheless, the study showed that hands-on training with the tool is also necessary: the group which enjoyed more booth time with InterpretBank before data collection showed a greater deal of independence in working with the tool during interpreting. The participants in this group had started to develop their own strategies for looking up terminology within the tool, for instance deciding beforehand whether terms should be searched by the active interpreter or by the boothmate. They also showed greater agility in coordinating CAI tool usage with more traditional methods for suggesting equivalents for specialised terms, such as writing down terms. While these results cannot be generalised, they seem to provide an argument for the introduction of these increasingly relevant technologies into the interpreting curriculum.

On the background of the increasing interest for CAI tools, it is interesting to consider their level of integration into the interpreting curriculum. In 2017, Prandi (2020) conducted a survey involving 25 higher education institution members of the CIUTI[15] network from 15 countries offering training programmes in conference interpreting. Survey results show that CAI tools are mostly seen as a secondary technology to be taught to prospective interpreters, whereas higher priority is given to remote interpreting technologies. With a few exceptions, the responses also pointed to a lack of knowledge on the topic among trainers, which emerged from the confusion around the term "computer-assisted interpreting", which is often interpreted to include other technologies applied to interpreting, such as RSI or computer-assisted interpreter training (CAIT). From the survey emerges, however, a certain openness towards conducting more research into the subject. The reasons why CAI has not yet been included in the curriculum are often of financial nature[16] or organisational, as this would require a restructuring of the training curriculum. Very often, the lack of knowledge on the subject among trainers makes it difficult to expand the curriculum to include this topic. There are, however, a few exceptions: notably the Universities of Bologna/Forlì, Mainz/Germersheim, Innsbruck and Heidelberg. These institutions either offer dedicated courses on CAI tools or organise workshops on the subject. The training usually involves a mix of theory and practice, and presents students with several tools. Suggestions for the inclusion of CAI tools and other interpreting technologies (RSI and MI) in interpreter training are offered by Fantinuoli & Prandi (2018), who proposed a training programme providing recommendations

---

[15]Conférence Internationale Permanente d'Instituts Universitaires de Traducteurs et Interprètes
[16]As mentioned by some respondents who may, however, be actually making reference to remote interpreting systems.

and best practices rooted in socio-constructivism. As the authors observe, "the introduction of CAI tools in interpreting courses should serve the purpose of exposing students to these solutions, and of providing them with the means to make an informed use of such tools. Thus, an introduction to CAI tools can be beneficial, even if trainees will not reach complete mastery of the tools." (Fantinuoli & Prandi 2018: 175). The authors thus put forward ideas on how to structure a training programme focused on CAI tool usage in the booth. The proposal involved a theoretical module to introduce students to the rationale behind CAI tool creation and integration into the interpreter's workflow, and a set of practical exercises of increasing complexity targeting the different sub-skills involved in SI with CAI. This approach aimed to foster the students' awareness of potential advantages and pitfalls in CAI usage, such as the risk of relying too much on the tool when faced with highly specialised terminology to be rendered into the target language (Prandi 2015b: 53).

Another strain of research, currently among the most prolific ones in the field of CAI research, focuses on exploring the impact of CAI tools usage on the quality of SI. The studies conducted so far are mostly pilot studies of exploratory nature, and do not attempt a holistic evaluation of the quality of the interpreting performance in broader terms, but rather narrow it down to terminological accuracy and omissions. The study by Prandi (2015a,b) included an evaluation of this type. She considered the percentage of terms included in the glossary that had been looked up and correctly identified. She found that the participants did not seem to have difficulties in using the tool to look for terms, as shown by the high percentage of terms looked up and found. The percentage of terms found and correctly interpreted as per glossary is not as high as the percentage of terms found, which could point to a difficulty in coordinating the look-up effort with the other subprocesses involved in SI. Drawing on Prandi's (2015a, 2015b) experimental design, Biagini (2015) was the first to empirically test the use of CAI tool glossaries in comparison with paper glossaries during SI. His study also involved a relatively small sample of advanced interpreting students. The participants were trained in using InterpretBank while interpreting terminology-dense texts. In the final experiment, they were asked to interpret two similar speeches while looking up terms in a printed paper glossary and using InterpretBank. The test-subjects' renditions were transcribed and rated on terminological accuracy and omissions. The difference between the paper glossary and the CAI tool proved statistically significant for the criteria "percentage of terms interpreted as per glossary" and "number of omissions". Based on these initial results, CAI tools seem to provide an advantage in terms of terminological accuracy and completeness of information (fewer cases of omissions were observed even after performing a search).

More recently, scholars have started investigating the potential of integrating ASR into CAI tools, a development which would signify a step closer to a third generation of AI-enhanced CAI tools. The goal of integrating an ASR system into a CAI tool is that of leveraging speech recognition to provide interpreters with live support during SI, with a view to reducing interpreters' active interaction with the machine. As Fantinuoli (2017b: 25) observes, "the main drawback [of traditional CAI tools] is that the database is queried manually, adding more cognitive effort to the interpreting process. This disadvantage could be addressed by automating the query through the use of Automatic Speech Recognition (ASR), as recent advances in Artificial Intelligence have considerably increased the quality of this technology." Fantinuoli first postulated the possibility of integrating ASR into a CAI tool in 2017, although this idea had already been put forward before (see Hansen-Schirra 2012). In his paper, he presents a model and a prototype of an ASR-CAI integration and discusses the requirements of both the CAI tool and the ASR system. In order for ASR integration to be possible, both systems need to fulfil a set of criteria.

First of all, the ASR system must be able to deal with the typical disfluencies of spoken language and cope with speaker variability, as well as with foreign accents and mispronunciations, especially in the context of English as *lingua franca*. Other issues inherent to spoken language are ambiguities, such as homophones, and poor articulation which can occur in the case of fast speech. Finally, speech is not segmented, but continuous, and pauses appear not at word boundaries, but are rather syntactical. The recognition of word boundaries is an issue that the ASR system must be able to deal with, or else the quality of the database querying mechanism necessary for producing the text may be compromised. Especially in consecutive interpreting, the ASR system must also be able to deal with background noise (Fantinuoli 2017b: 28). As Fantinuoli (2017b: 29) observes, an ASR system must also be able to "support large-vocabulary recognition" and "support vocabulary customisation" which is necessary to recognise specialised terminology. It must also have a low word error rate (WER), i.e. be highly accurate, and a low real-time factor (RTF), i.e. be fast. CAI tools must also present a certain profile: they must have high precision and recall, with priority given to precision if necessary, be able to deal with morphological variations, and have a sleek and user-friendly interface.

The prototype described recognises numerals and terms that have been added to the event database. The speech is first transcribed and pre-processed. The system then "queries the terminological database and identifies the entities from the text flow" (Fantinuoli 2017b: 30), which are extracted and visualised on the interpreter's screen. This initial prototype showed encouraging results: with a WER of 5.04% and a F1 score of 0.97[17], such a system could be used at least in standard settings. A recent study by Brüsewitz (2019) suggests that the commercial ASR solutions currently available already perform rather satisfactorily, at least for the recognition of numerals and specialised terminology, while for named entities there is still a certain margin for improvement. In the study, which tested solutions by Google, Watson (IBM), Sonix and Speechmatics on six parameters (numbers, proper names, terminology, homophones, nonsensical utterances, and speech rate), the Google API was the best-performing system.

Following up on the initial prototype proposition by Fantinuoli (2017b), the first investigations were conducted to further test the potential of an ASR-CAI system in experimental settings. So far, the focus has been on the issue of numerals, typically considered one of the most common problem triggers for interpreters (Gile 2009). Desmet et al. (2018) conducted a pilot study involving a small sample of advanced conference interpreting trainees. The objective was twofold: "to determine if limited technological support can improve the accuracy of interpreted numbers, and how this improvement breaks down over different number and error types" (p. 18). In the experiment, no commercially available CAI tool with integrated ASR was used. The authors created a prototype using PowerPoint presentations based on the speech transcripts which contained the numerals present in the speech, presented simultaneously to the occurrence of the oral stimulus. Thus, the results describe what an ideal system would be able to achieve, i.e., following the criteria outlined above, an ASR-CAI hybrid with perfect recognition and very low latency. The results support what has been outlined by Fantinuoli: in the case of numbers, a system with such characteristics is capable to improve accuracy (from 56.5 to 86.5%) with statistical significance, and to drastically reduce the occurrence of approximations (by 90% for the experiment), the second most frequent type of error after non-strategic omissions. Overall, intelligent CAI tools with integrated ASR seem to offer a promising upgrade to the toolkit currently available to interpreters. As the authors observe, however, there is still a lot to explore in this respect, and "further studies should be carried out on how interpreters deal with discrepancies between auditory input from a speaker and visual input from an automatic recognition system, increased delay or different modes of presentation" (Desmet et al. 2018: 26).

A follow-up experiment (Defrancq & Fantinuoli 2021) studied ASR support for numerals in a more naturalistic setting, using real-time transcription from the InterpretBank ASR tool. Data was collected through audio and video recordings and a follow-up questionnaire. Additionally, the study took a first look at the impact of a sudden loss of ASR support, which occurred in several cases during the

---

[17]The best possible value being 1, the worst 0.

experiment. The results confirm that the tool presents high precision (96%) and low enough latency to fit the interpreter's ear-voice-span (EVS). Overall, an increase in complete renditions (from 67.7% to 90.2%) and a drop in omissions (from 15.8% to 3.5%) due to ASR support was also observed. This aligns with previous findings, although the accuracy gain is less significant. This may be due, among other things, to the fact that numerical information was not presented in isolation like in the previous experiment, but rather highlighted within the context of the complete ASR transcription, requiring deeper processing by participants. Training would have probably led to even more significant improvements in the subjects' rendition. It should be noted that significant accuracy gains were observed intra-subject only for two participants out of six.

Interesting findings emerged from the questionnaire. The tool was judged positively in terms of ergonomics, although some participants would have preferred a more minimal presentation of the numerical information. A certain tendency to over-rely on the tool for support was also observed, which aligns with first observations by Prandi (2015a,b). Interestingly, the authors speculate that the provision of ASR support might have had a positive psychological effect: knowing numerals would be shown on the screen might reduce stress and/or boost confidence (Defrancq & Fantinuoli 2021: 93).

Van Cauwenberghe (2020) reached similar conclusions in his experiment on ASR support for terminology. However, like Defrancq & Fantinuoli (2021), he also contended that interacting with the tool may not be a trivial feat from a cognitive standpoint, and observed cases of imported errors from the ASR tool into the interpreters' renditions. In Defrancq & Fantinuoli (2021) and Van Cauwenberghe (2020), the system latency was deemed sufficiently short. On the topic of latency, Montecchio (2021) and Fantinuoli & Montecchio (2022) conducted a dedicated study precisely aimed at defining the maximum acceptable latency in ASR-enhanced CAI tools. Using an ASR mockup with increasing latencies varying from 1 to 5 seconds, Montecchio (2021) explored the impact of latency on the rendition accuracy for numerals and referents as well as the effect on the perceived delivery flow. She found that both accuracy and delivery flow declined with increasing latency, interpreting this loss in quality as evidence of increased cognitive load to cope with the longer ear-voice span (EVS).

A recent development in this area is the integration of AI-enhanced CAI tools into RSI platforms, as exemplified KUDO Interpreter Assist (Fantinuoli et al. 2022) and by SmarTerp (Rodríguez et al. 2021).

KUDO Interpreter Assist includes two features designed to support interpreters working remotely: an automatic glossary creation tool and a virtual boothmate for terms and numbers. This second feature presents a similar architecture to the ASR function offered by InterpretBank (see §2.2.3), comprising a cascade of ASR, identification of units of interest through a language model (LM), and automatic display of suggestions for terminology, numbers and named entities on the interpreter's screen. The terminological suggestions are based on the glossary curated by the interpreter[18], while numbers and proper names are extracted directly by the LM. The benchmark tests conducted on a general language and a specialised corpus show promising results in terms of precision, recall and F1 value, both for medium-sized and large glossaries (200 vs. 10,000 terms), with an average F1 value of around 98%. The tool performed better for named entities than for specialised terminology. Although the authors reported quite encouraging lowest F1 values of 84% and 81% respectively (Fantinuoli et al. 2022: 7), they also noted that individual terms and the glossary used can impact results considerably, as shown by a rather poor performance achieved for a speech about social issues (F1 = 76.19% for the medium and 68.90% for the large glossary). The average latency was of 1.6 seconds (minimum = 1.1s, maximum = 2.3s), i.e. low enough to fit into an interpreter's average EVS.

The CAI tool to be integrated into SmarTerp was tested on two components: its ASR system and its semantic interpretation module, which detects relevant entities of interest for the interpreter. For each interpreted session, the LM is adapted on the bases of the interpreter's event glossary, from which seed words are extracted to be added to the glossary and to select texts from the training corpora for the LM adaptation. The semantic interpretation module deploys three underlying resources: a multilingual general purpose, a domain-specific and a user-specific knowledge graph (Rodríguez et al. 2021: 105). The system evaluation showed rather positive results for the three languages analysed (English, Italian, Spanish), with F scores ranging from 0.82 (English) to 0.90 (Italian). The tests also showed a positive impact of the adaptation systems for all three languages and for all metrics (Rodríguez et al. 2021: 108).

In light of these initial results, the integration of CAI tools, particularly of those based on ASR, appears feasible. Nonetheless, a salient issue to be considered is the trade-off between the amount of information offered by a system of this kind and the additional cognitive load needed to operate a CAI tool during interpretation. This applies both to "traditional" in-booth CAI tools and CAI-ASR integration, and not only to numerals, but also to other problem triggers, such as specialised terminology. Stewart et al. (2018: 109) observe that "while

---

[18]In the glossary creation tool, the target-language equivalents for specialised terminology are first generated through MT and then validated by the interpreter.

displaying all terminology in a glossary achieves high recall of terms, it suffers from low precision. This could potentially have the unwanted effect of cognitively overwhelming the interpreter with too many term suggestions". For this reason, the authors explore the possibility of integrating an NLP tool capable of predicting the elements likely to be missed by interpreters, with a view to reducing errors and improving performance. Such a system would need to be trained on a corpus of data that have been processed to identify problem triggers using the combined criteria of "termhood" (is the term difficult to recall and non-ambiguous?), relevance (should the term necessarily be translated?) and interpreter coverage (has it been left untranslated or mistranslated?). In addition, such a system must also consider task-relevant criteria, such as fatigue at the end of the interpreting turn ("elapsed time"), speech rate ("word timing"), terms left untranslated because they are rare and thus more difficult to recall from memory ("word frequency"), or because they are long and thus likely to represent technical terminology ("word characteristics and syntactic features"). With a system of this kind, capable of processing the source speech and identifying potentially challenging terms based on these criteria, users could "theoretically adjust the precision-recall threshold" (Stewart et al. 2018: 115), even from speaker to speaker and for each assignment or presentation, in order to achieve a positive trade-off between useful term suggestions and additional cognitive effort required to deal with an extra source of information.

The findings of the empirical studies conducted thus far on the product of CASI appear encouraging. However, it should be noted that current investigations have been highly focused on individual units of information. Little is known as to how CAI tools' impact quality on a broader level, although first studies are starting to discuss the effects on the product more holistically and through qualitative analysis (Frittella 2022).

Regrettably, while research on the product of CASI is increasing, the hypotheses on CAI tools' impact on the cognitive subprocesses involved in CASI are yet to be tested empirically in controlled settings. Yet, gaining a more profound understanding of the CASI process and of interpreter-computer interaction during the in-process use of CAI tools appears to be essential in light of the postulated challenges in integrating CAI tools into the SI process. The insight gained through cognitive studies on CAI tools may prove helpful on different fronts. First, it may promote a better understanding of what discourages interpreters from using tools during SI. Second, it may help develop CAI tools truly targeting interpreters' needs and addressing the cognitive constraints inherent to SI. In turn, this may result in a wider acceptance of tools which have the potential to improve interpreters' workflow and the quality of interpretation.

The assumptions on the impact of CAI on mental processes in SI presented in §2.3.4 point to the idea of interference, of a limited amount of cognitive resources and time, and to the concepts of attention sharing and task coordination in view of the additional effort posed by terminology look-up. In order to formulate hypotheses on the impact of CAI tools on the cognitive processes involved in SI, which the present study aims to test, some attention should first be devoted to the exploration of such constructs both from a cognitive psychology perspective and within the context of simultaneous interpreting. This is the topic of the following chapter.

3 Simultaneous interpreting as a complex cognitive activity

As discussed in the previous chapter, the main points of criticism concerning the use of CAI tools for terminology look-up during interpreting, and in particular during SI, refer to the addition of yet another task to the concurrent mental processes involved in interpreting, i.e. that of interacting with a digital support tool to deal with specialised terminology perceived as an element of difficulty during interpreting (see §2.3.4). The hypotheses formulated on the cognitive implications of a CASI task, both when manual look-up is involved and when it is replaced by an ASR module are, however, mostly based on personal assumptions or unstructured observations and have not yet been grounded in empirical analysis aimed at investigating the effects of technological support on the interpreter's cognition. Such hypotheses refer to constructs that have been formulated and explored in the context of cognitive psychology, learning psychology and human factors research and which have been widely applied in TPR: the concept of interference between tasks, the assumption that humans have access to a limited amount of cognitive resources, the issue that attention must be allocated to and shared among different co-occurring tasks during a limited amount of time, and that this requires coordination and monitoring, and, finally, the construct of cognitive load (CL), often mentioned in reference to the presumed additional effort posed by CAI tool usage.

The present section will review and discuss these concepts, their application and empirical validation with the aim to provide a conceptual framework for the formulation of hypotheses on SI with digital terminological support and for the definition of the research questions guiding the present study.

I will start by discussing some basic assumptions about working memory (WM) and attention allocation (§3.1, §3.2), and discuss their relevance for the investigation of CL (§3.4) on the basis of related empirical research within the field of cognitive psychology and TPR. After defining and exploring these key concepts, I will consider how they have been integrated into cognitivist models of SI which view this process primarily as an issue of multitasking (§3.5), as this is the framework within which I conduct my analysis, define my research questions and formulate hypotheses on CL and task interference in SI with CAI tools (§3.6).

3.1 Working memory and information processing

The concept of WM was first introduced in the seminal work by Baddeley & Hitch (1974). Until the authors' investigations into the construct, little empirical evidence had been collected to support the idea of WM. The development of a construct of WM represents a step forward in the understanding of the role of memory in human information processing, specifically in how information is processed over a short period of time, for instance during reasoning, language comprehension, and learning, the three cases on which Baddeley and Hitch concentrated. The construct of short-term memory (STM, Atkinson & Shiffrin 1968) had been used to represent the temporary retention of a small part of information over a limited amount of time. As for processing in STM tasks, the role of the short-term store (STS) as WM, as proposed by Atkinson & Shiffrin (1968, 1971), had found little empirical evidence in non-memory related tasks. Baddeley and Hitch provided first evidence supporting the idea of a common WM system responsible for both short-term information retention and processing. Thus, they depart from Aktinson and Shiffrin's assumption that the STS is a single unit and that it is modality-independent. They describe WM as "a control system with limits on both its storage and processing capabilities" (Baddeley & Hitch 1974: 86): we can only store and process a limited amount of information over a brief period of time.

The role of WM is essential to interpreting as it is a highly complex cognitive activity which requires both retention of transient information and processing of said information during a short time-span. In addressing the issue of CAI tools integration into SI, it is often pointed out that interpreters may not always have the necessary resources (see §3.3) or sufficient time (see §3.4.3) to attend to the additional sub-processes required by glossary querying or by the interaction with an ASR system. As a consequence, an interpreter's WM may not be able to retain and process all stimuli that must be attended to. This hypothesis reflects one of the key assumptions about WM, i.e. its limited capacity. This fundamental tenet of WM plays an essential role in all models of WM, despite the ongoing debate on its nature (Seel 2012: 3474), which is, to some extent, still unresolved. One element of dispute lies in the architecture of WM: some scholars, as exemplified by the very successful modular model by Baddeley and Hitch, postulate a WM comprising a set of related components covering stimulus processing and attention allocation, while others, most notably Cowan (1988), view memory as a unitary store.

In Baddeley and Hitch's model, the WM system involves a phonological loop (PL), a visual-spatial sketch pad (VSSP) and a structure responsible for executive

functions, the Central Executive (CE). According to the authors, verbal information is "phonemically coded" (ibid.), and is rehearsed (either overtly or covertly)
in a limited-capacity phonemic buffer. Following Atkinson and Shiffrin's model,
Baddeley and Hitch postulate that rehearsal is necessary for information retention. They propose that WM is modality-dependent: while verbal information is
thought to be temporarily stored and encoded in the PL, visual-spatial information is encoded in the VSSP. Both substructures later received further specification. The PL was thus subdivided into a storage component, i.e. the phonological
store – where phonological traces are stored up to 2s (Baddeley 1990) due to the
word-length effect (Baddeley 1975) – and a rehearsal subsystem responsible for
refreshing memory traces in order to prevent their decay (the articulatory loop).
Similarly, the VSSP was divided by Logie (1995) into the visual cache (retention)
and the inner scribe (processing). Later on, Baddeley (2000) introduced the construct of an Episodic Buffer (EB) which stores and integrates information not only
from the PL and the VSSP, but also from long-term memory (LTM) to form a single percept. Baddeley and Hitch's model of WM posits important consequences
for our understanding of WM. According to the model, retention and processing
are managed by different memory structures. This in turn supports the idea of
multitasking, which is only possible if resources can be shared between retention and processing, and, conversely, if retention and processing correspond to
separate structures in WM.

The assumptions put forward by Baddeley and Hitch have received ample
empirical support. Of particular relevance to the task of SI are the PL, the CE
and the EB. The double function of the PL, i.e. perception and rehearsal, has
been evidenced by two related effects found in empirical testings of the model:
the phonological similarity effect (Baddeley et al. 2018) and the word-length effect (Baddeley 1975, Jacquemot et al. 2011). The first shows a reduced recall for
phonologically similar words, the second a decay in memory traces and thus an
impaired recall for visually presented words when articulatory rehearsal is suppressed. Neurological evidence also supports this distinction, as different brain
areas have been found to activate for storage and rehearsal tasks (Papagno et
al. 2017). Gieshoff (2012) found supporting evidence from interpreting as, in her
experiment, longer numbers were more difficult to recall. This aligns with the
word-length effect, as in interpreting phonological rehearsal is suppressed due
to the concurrent production of the interpretation. The concept of a CE responsible for focusing, dividing and switching attention and interacting with the LTM
store is supported by evidence from studies investigating executive functions
(e.g. Godefroy et al. 2010), although the notion that it is a unitary system may be
oversimplified (Stuss & Alexander 2007, Logie 2016). Finally, the introduction of

an EB was justified by findings that recall for longer sets of words was possible than what the PL would allow (Baddeley et al. 1987). More specifically, Baddeley (2012) postulates a capacity of four chunks of information. Further evidence of an integration and a facilitation effect between visual-spatially and verbal-vocally encoded information is provided by studies on bootstrapping data (Darling et al. 2017, Darling & Havelka 2010).

Concurring accounts of WM, exemplified by Cowan's (1988) unitary store model, propose an alternative to Atkinson and Shiffrin's multi-storage model, which, as discussed above, was highly influential in Baddeley and Hitch's development of their own model of WM. The development of Cowan's (2009) model was based on evidence that there might be interference between the auditory and the visual buffers, which does not support the notion of separate stores. In Cowan's model the existence of a single, long-term store (LTS) is postulated which contains units of information. STM is described as the activated portion of long term memory (LTM), while the items currently being processed are attended to in the so-called "focus of attention". Thus, WM, i.e. the processing of STM items, is located in the activated portion of LTM that is receiving attention at a certain moment in time. The main point of criticism for Cowan's model is its oversimplification inherent to the assumption that STM is only the activated portion of LTM. Additionally, studies on amnesic patients have identified impairment in STM, but not in LTM, or viceversa. This model of WM is valuable in that it poses the focus on the relationship between information processing and attention, an essential component in the interpreting process, as I will discuss in the following section (§3.2). Even if WM is structurally considered part of long term memory, its function is nonetheless distinct from LTM, as is the case in the multi-component model which further postulates a structural separation of the two stores.

Another key assumption about the human cognitive architecture is that control processes aimed at allocating attention to the stimuli to be processed must be governed by a dedicated cognitive structure. A CE responsible for voluntary processing and directing attention to relevant items is found both in modular and in unitary models of attention. In Baddeley and Hitch's model, for instance, the CE supervises the PL, the VSSP and the EB, i.e. the structures responsible for information retention and processing. Similarly, although based on largely different assumptions, Cowan also postulates the existence of a CE responsible for attention and voluntary processing, such as the activation and focusing of items. The CE also has the role to activate items stored in long term memory which are necessary for stimulus processing. The link between WM and a long term store emerges clearly in Cowan's model, which promotes a unitary view of human cognitive architecture, as discussed above.

The role of a CE is essential to free up cognitive capacity and avoid cognitive overload when capacity is exceeded. As postulated by Miller (1956), the (limited) capacity of our STM depends not on the amount of information, but on how it is compounded: chunks of information are more easily remembered than single elements of information. The CE is thought to intervene by re-coding information in order to free up capacity, re-combining single elements in larger chunks and thus reducing WM load. An example of chunking is present in instructional design theory (see Van Merrienboer & Sweller 2005) in the notion of schemata for information and knowledge organisation. The development of higher-order schemata allows learners to process information more easily, thus acting as a CE. This also relates to the translation process, in that the development of strategies to address a text to be translated or common sources of difficulty in speeches to be interpreted can alleviate WM by freeing up cognitive capacity for intentional processing. Studies on translation and interpreting competence have highlighted how one essential difference between novice and experts lies in the fact that the latter have developed more solid schemata (or strategies) which allow them to effectively process complex information and avoid cognitive overload, with important consequences for training (see for instance Riccardi 2005).

Both approaches to the definition of the architecture of WM present some shortcomings. As discussed above, the very influential multi-component model by Baddeley and Hitch has received repeated empirical support over the years from studies conducted in the field of cognitive psychology. In addition, it has been widely influential in TPR, where it has been adopted as a framework in a number of empirical studies (Darò & Fabbro 1994, Dragsted 2004, Mizuno 2005, Padilla et al. 2005, Kosma 2007, Hvelplund 2011, Köpke & Signorelli 2012, Timarová et al. 2015). In this framework, however, it is not clear how other types of sensory input may be processed in addition to auditory and visual information. This shortcoming emerges also on the basis of recent evidence which found that different areas of the brain are activated when different types of auditory and visual stimuli are processed. As discussed by Postle (2006), the consequence of such evidence for the "standard" model of WM is a potentially unlimited proliferation of subsystems, which would undermine the very role of the model:

> Followed to its logical extreme, the cognitive architecture of the standard model would eventually depict a WM system organized into hundreds (if not thousands or more) of domain-specific buffers, each responsible for the WM processing of a different kind of information.   (Postle 2006: 25)

On the other hand, an account of WM which views it as a unitary store also conflicts with such evidence. Additionally, it appears limited for its assumption that information is merely "activated" through focused attention, but does not offer a framework for the integration of new information in a long term store, presenting a unidirectional view of human memory architecture which brings information to the surface, but does not explain how information has entered the store in the first place. The value of Cowan's account of WM, taken to exemplify unitary models of WM, lies in its holistic view of information processing compared to the more rigid account by the more successful model by Baddeley and Hitch. A unifying view of WM may come from Postle (2006), who approaches WM from the perspective of cognitive neuroscience rather than cognitive psychology. He defines WM as a function that "arise[s] through the coordinated recruitment, via attention, of brain systems that have evolved to accomplish sensory-, representation-, and action-related functions" (Postle 2006: 23). It is this functional view which, in my opinion, best serves the discussion around WM for the translation and interpreting process. Thus, the separation of processing buffers for audio and visual stimuli is applied here functionally, rather than structurally. When referring to separate buffers for audio and visual stimuli, which will be pivotal in my discussion of task interference, I start from the assumption, backed by recent evidence, that there are indeed separate channels for the processing of this information. As I embed my methodological approach in the tradition of TPR, which has widely adopted and operationalised the model of WM by Baddeley and Hitch, I will be referring to two single channels dedicated to processing visual stimuli on the one hand and auditory on the other, while implicitly acknowledging that the cognitive structure underlying such systems may very well be more complex.

To sum up, though the approaches discussed present some differences in how they view the structure of WM, they share common assumptions in terms of its function. First of all, in both cases WM is considered to have both a retention capacity and a processing capacity. If the elements temporarily stored in WM are not attended to, not refreshed nor activated, their traces decay from memory. This, in turn, underlines the role of attention allocation, which must take place effectively in order to preserve such memory traces in WM. However, attentional capacity is considered to be limited. Thus, attention must necessarily be distributed, shared or switched to the different elements that require processing. The task of attention distribution, sharing and switching must be regulated by control functions, which in the models discussed is identified as a CE. How attention is allocated to the stimuli competing for attention is the object of theories of attention distribution and resource sharing, which will be the object of the following sections.

3.2 The role of attention in processing visual stimuli

Closely linked to WM is attention, which represents a key constituent in numerous models of human memory architecture, most notably in Baddeley and Hitch's and especially in Cowan's model, and in models of resource allocation among concurrent tasks, as I will discuss in §3.3. Attention is a multifaceted construct, which can be studied from different perspectives. Of particular interest for the present research object are the concepts of focused or selective attention and of divided attention. In particular, divided attention and its effects on information processing and performance has been in focus in Cognitive Load Theory (CLT), as will be discussed in §3.4.

Interpreting may be viewed as an activity requiring the allocation of attention to multiple streams of information (Seeber 2017). This is especially true today, as communication at multilingual events is rarely achieved through a single medium, but often foresees the combination of oral presentations and, for instance, slide presentations. This requires interpreters to process multiple types of inputs and several information flows in parallel derived from the external world (e.g. the speech, the presentation, support materials such as speech transcripts or glossaries), in addition to monitoring their own rendition. When a CAI tool or a conventional glossary is used as a support to deal with terminology, additional visual-verbal information enters the perceptual space of the interpreter. Some of these stimuli capture the interpreter's attention in a bottom-up way. However, it is required of the interpreter to actively divide their attention between the relevant streams of information and, for instance when the rendition of a specialised term requires additional effort, to actively focus their attention on a single input while at the same time keeping the other stimuli in the focus of attention. Thus, interpreting may be seen as an activity requiring both focused and divided attention, even more so when the processing of multimodal stimuli is involved – as is the case with a digital glossary or an ASR system – and involving both bottom-up and top-down attentional processes.

As a consequence, SI with digital terminological support may be seen as an activity imposing a high perceptual load as well as a high CL (see §3.4.1) on the interpreter's WM. The concept of perceptual load is pivotal in Lavie's (1995, 2000, 2005, 2010) perceptual load theory, which provides an explanation of how attention is selectively allocated to stimuli concurring for human attention. Her proposal outcomes the dichotomy of early selection models (Broadbent 1958, Treisman 1964) and late selection models (Deutsch & Deutsch 1963, Norman 1968). The first postulate, respectively, either an all-or-nothing filter which lets only salient items pass through and enter our focus of attention, or an attenuator which lets through only relevant enough elements. The latter, on the contrary, propose that selection occurs only at a later stage: everything is first perceived and processed, and then priority is assigned to the most relevant items.

In light of supporting empirical evidence for both models (e.g. Simons & Chabris 1999 for early selection or Stroop 1935 and Eriksen & Eriksen 1974 for late selection), Lavie put forward a model which overcomes the limitations of the preceding models and integrates their strengths. Her model thus represents a "resolution to the long-standing early and late selection debate on the extent to which irrelevant distractors can be ignored" and may be viewed as a "hybrid model of selection" (Lavie et al. 2004: 353). Lavie's theory is particularly relevant to the present research object as it has been tested within the framework of visual attention. According to Lavie, attention allocation is dependent on the perceptual load posed by the task. Low-load conditions allow for late selection (more stimuli can be processed and are only later selected), while high-load conditions require early selection of relevant information. The reduction in distractor processing under high perceptual load has been shown by several studies (for a review, see Lavie 2005). At the same time, in situations of high perceptual load, limited attentional capacity is left for processing. Therefore, we can hypothesise that during SI with terminological support, if the suggested terms are presented in a way that imposes high perceptual load (e.g. within the context of a glossary rather than in isolation), fewer resources will be left for the processing of other stimuli, such as the speaker's words or one's own rendition.

3.3 Attention sharing and task interference

Lavie's theory is helpful in understanding how visual stimuli to be processed are selected during high-load tasks such as SI. However, it is insufficient to formulate hypotheses on how multiple tasks interfere with each other. Additionally, in her model attention is viewed as a general resource, with no further specification. As a general theory of attention, her model is not sufficient to explain why certain concurrently performed tasks interfere with each other more than others, nor at which level this interference occurs, and which attentional resources are shared. The issue of task interference is highly relevant to a complex cognitive task such as interpreting, and even more so when the additional task of looking up terminology or processing a term presented automatically on a screen must be integrated with an already multi-layered task such as SI. Since in the present work SI is approached from the perspective of multitasking, I will now discuss attention allocation as a matter of resource sharing among concurrent tasks, focusing on two models which are reflected in models of the interpreting process seen as a matter of task coordination (see §3.5).

Similarly to Lavie, Kahneman (1973) postulates the presence of a single pool of attentional (or cognitive) resources that are shifted from one task to another. Kahneman's single resource theory can therefore be seen as a "general resource model of task interference" (Wickens 2002: 162), which explains a decrease in performance levels simply with the concurrent performance of the tasks at hand. According to Kahneman, variance in dual-task performance is due either to the level of difficulty of the individual tasks or to the preference given to one of the tasks (if a task is not favoured, its performance suffers, while the favoured task is carried out successfully). He distinguishes between the idea of load, i.e. the amount of resources demanded by a task, and that of effort, i.e. the amount of cognitive resources and energy the subject exerts in order to perform a task. When task demands are higher than the available capacities, performance suffers. Kahneman also addresses the role of arousal for the availability of cognitive resources: the higher the level of arousal, i.e. of conscious attention, the higher the amount of attentional capacities available. Kahneman's assumptions have, however, been challenged empirically (for a discussion in light of neuroscientific evidence, see Bruya & Tang 2018) and criticised for their vagueness. One major drawback of his theory is that it does not allow for a modulation of hypotheses on task interference based on the nature of the tasks. This stems from his equation of attention with effort, which does not allow for the integration of bottom-up processes of attention capturing. It does, however, focus the spotlight on one important quality of attention, which aligns with accounts of WM and is largely supported by empirical evidence: that attention is limited. Additionally, while limiting on the one hand, the model stresses the role of intentionality on the allocation of attention, which is essential in a complex activity such as interpreting.

In order to overcome the limitations of Kahneman's model, and to account for the fact that "differences in time-sharing efficiency" may be due to the quality of the resources concurrently recruited by multiple tasks (ibid.), as postulated by Kantowitz & Knight (1976) and Wickens (1976) himself, Wickens (1984, 2002) put forward an alternative model of resource sharing which posits that "time-sharing between two tasks [is] more efficient if the two [utilise] separate structures than if they [utilise] common structures" (ibid.).

At the core of Wickens's model are three underlying assumptions:

1. every non-automated task produces load;

2. two interacting tasks demand a higher amount of resources than the performance of any single task;

3. tasks recruiting the same type of resources exhibit a higher level of interference than tasks recruiting resources of discrete structures.

Unlike Kahneman, Wickens does not assume the existence of a single pool of resources, but rather of discrete attentional structures. As a consequence, what is shared among tasks are not the structures themselves, but rather their underlying resources. It follows that two or more tasks recruiting the same resources may be very difficult (or impossible) to perform simultaneously than tasks demanding separate resources. This would explain why we can simultaneously look at a painting and talk with a friend, while listening to the radio and to a friend at the same time will inevitably lead to a loss of information from one of the two sources. In the first case (simultaneous performance of a visual and an auditory task), resource sharing will be easier, and thus more efficient, than in the latter (two auditory tasks), which share the same underlying resources.

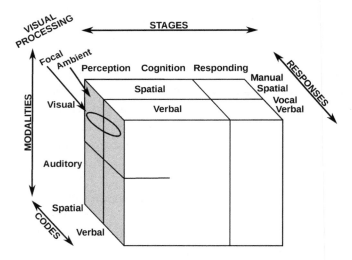

Figure 3.1: Wickens's multiple resource model (Wickens 2002: 163)

Wickens's model distinguishes between four dimensions, each further subdivided into two levels, as summarised in Table 3.1.

The fourth dimension (visual processing), with its respective levels, is a later addition (Wickens 2002) to the original model.

Table 3.1: Dimensions and respective levels in Wickens's multiple resource model

Dimensions	Levels		
processing stages	perception & cognition		response
perceptual modalities	visual		auditory
processing codes	spatial		verbal
visual processing	ambient		focal

According to the model (see Figure 3.1 for a graphic representation), processing occurs at two stages (perception and cognition are subsumed in a single stage, since one cannot occur without the other, and thus share the same pool of resources). Perception can be either visual or auditory. This points to the same distinction posited by Baddeley and Hitch and operationalised through the PL and the visuospatial sketchpad. The perceived information can be processed either as spatial or as verbal information. In addition to the four dimensions, Wickens also "concedes the existence of a residual pool of general resources which, albeit not reflected in his model, is available to and demanded by all tasks, modalities, codes, and stages as required" (Seeber 2007: 1382), and which may be, to some extent, equated to the CE.

This model of resource-sharing can be used to operationalise hypotheses on the level of task interference and thus to compute an "interference score", which can be adopted to predict the efficiency with which two tasks can be performed at the same time. Wickens develops a "conflict matrix" (CM) to show the level of resource recruitment by the single sub-tasks (expressed by "demand vectors") and the degree to which co-occurring sub-tasks are expected to interfere with each other (represented by the "conflict coefficients"), which is higher if the two tasks both demand the same level of a given dimension (Wickens 2002). Demand vectors can range from a value of 0 (no dependence on a certain resource) to 2 (extreme dependence on a resource) and are assigned for each dimension of a certain task. Conflict coefficients can be assigned a value between 0.2 and 1, where 1 represents two tasks that cannot be performed simultaneously, as they are both entirely dependent on the same resource, and 0.2 is the necessary interference cost of the simultaneous performance of two tasks. A conflict coefficient of 1 corresponds to a quantification of the central bottleneck assumed by several models of WM (Wickens 2002). The total interference score between tasks is thus calculated as the sum of demand vectors and conflict coefficients. A higher total interference score points to less efficient time-sharing between simultaneously performed tasks. Several findings support Wickens's model. For instance, experiments conducted by Treisman & Davies (2012) and McLeod (1977) support the notion that concurrent tasks in the same modality interfere with each other, while the research reviewed by Lu et al. (2013) provides support for reduced interference of tasks performed in different modalities.

One weakness of Wickens's model is the subdivision of tasks in a processing and response stage, which may represent too limiting an account of complex activities such as translation and interpreting, where these stages often overlap. It is, however, more in line with neurocognitive evidence suggesting that different areas of the brain are responsible for processing different types of stimuli, similarly to what has been discussed for Baddeley and Hitch's model (see §3.1), albeit with the same limitations. An additional benefit provided by the model is that it allows to operationalise and empirically test hypotheses on the interference of similar but different tasks, such as SI with different types of digital terminological support, as I will discuss further in §3.6. In turn, being able to test hypotheses at this level of granularity may prove particularly useful in practice in order to fine-tune the type of support provided to interpreters, where small differences may have a significant impact on the level of interference between tasks experienced and on the alleviation of WM demands. Therefore, Wickens's model will be especially relevant in the formulation of hypotheses for the present analysis (see §5.2) and in the present empirical investigation of CASI. Additionally, as I will discuss in §3.5, the model has already been operationalised in empirical interpreting research concerning itself with issues of attention allocation.

3.4 The construct of cognitive load

The notions of WM and attention allocation are particularly relevant to a complex cognitive activity such as SI. As such, they represent fundamental tenets for the construct of CL, ubiquitous in cognitive models of the interpreting process postulated within the framework of Interpreting Studies. In exploring the cognitive underpinnings of (simultaneous) interpreting, scholars have adopted a rather diverse terminology, not only referring to the notion of CL, but also to the concept of processing load or mental (work)load (see for instance Gieshoff 2018). Additionally, the notion of effort, which has been highly influential in Interpreting Studies (see §3.5.1), represents an important related construct.

The adoption of such diversified terminology reflects the interfacing of translation and interpreting studies with other disciplines, primarily cognitive psychology and human factors, in particular cognitive ergonomics. The former has been very influential in both areas of study, providing "the basic premise of the behavior– mind correlation" (Jakobsen 2017: 23). As the present study aims to approach the use of digital terminology support tools by interpreters from an explicitly cognitive perspective, investigating the "how" behind the "what" of the interpreting performance, the adoption of models and theories formulated within the field of cognitive psychology is expected to constitute a useful reference for the formulation of hypotheses about this research object. Additionally, although the present investigation does not directly aim to explore the ergonomics of the tools employed as terminological support[1], the interpreter's experience in interacting with the tools can reasonably be expected to influence cognition during SI, particularly in terms of the load experienced, similarly to how the interaction between translator/post-editors and CAT tools has been shown to play a crucial role for the disposition towards support technologies and for the load experienced by translators (see O'Brien 2012, O'Brien et al. 2017, Moorkens & O'Brien 2016).

In this section, I discuss the concept of CL from the perspective of cognitive psychology, focusing on the foundational model developed within the framework of CLT (Chandler & Sweller 1991), which has been widely adopted to model the translation and interpreting process and has received ample empirical support in TPR. I thus aim to provide first of all a terminological clarification of the concept, and to delineate a framework for the discussion of how the construct has been adopted by Interpreting Studies to discuss the cognitive implications of interpreting (§3.5). Particular attention will be devoted to the predictions of CLT for the load imposed on the interpreter by SI with digital terminological support and potential effects on attention and WM, which will serve as the theoretical basis for the discussion of results in §6.2.

3.4.1 Cognitive load in interpreter-computer interaction

The construct of CL was first delineated within the framework of Chandler & Sweller's (1991) CLT. In developing their theory, they were aiming to answer salient questions in instructional design, i.e. how to facilitate knowledge acquisition by effectively designing learning tasks that support students in their learning process. The authors distinguish between three types of CL: intrinsic, extraneous, and germane load.

---

[1]The interest in the cognitive ergonomics of CAI tools is picking up. A joint project currently underway at the University of Ghent and at the University of Mainz is concerned with the question of defining the best interface for the "artificial booth mate". See the webpage of the Ergonomics for the Artifical Booth Mate project (EABM 2021) for preliminary results: https://www.eabm.ugent.be/survey/ (Accessed: 01.11.2021).

Intrinsic cognitive load (ICL) can be defined as the CL that is experienced by the subject while learning. It "depends on the number of elements that must be processed simultaneously in WM, and [this] in turn, depends on the extent of element interactivity of the materials or tasks that must be learned." (Van Merrienboer & Sweller 2005: 150). ICL thus increases when element interactivity increases. The experienced load depends on the task itself and its level of interactivity: the higher the interactivity of the task elements, the higher the ICL. The level of interactivity, in turn, depends on expertise: through the development of schemata, several interacting elements can be processed as a single input, thus reducing the experienced load. Interpreting may be considered as a process with a high level of interactivity. When multi-modal input is involved, such as in SI with digital terminological support, the interactivity is even higher. According to CLT, the intrinsic load of the task may be expected to increase (see also §3.4.2.1). Similarly to the field of learning, expertise in SI also leads to the development of schemata, which can prove useful to automatise several subprocesses involved in interpreting. As a consequence, the intrinsic load of the task may be lower for more experienced interpreters, especially if they have received training or enjoyed extensive practice in CASI. While the present study is not conducted within the expert-novice paradigm, the predictions of CLT for the intrinsic load produced by the task in question as a function of interpreters' expertise will be relevant for the discussion of results, especially in terms of their generalisability. Although the aspect of expertise is not included in Wickens's model (see §3.2), the total interference score may be seen as a theoretical quantification of intrinsic load as a function of element interactivity.

Extraneous cognitive load is a concept that refers to task design and presentation. Unlike intrinsic CL, extraneous CL is not dependent on the nature of the task to be performed, but rather on the way the task is presented. Given that intrinsic and extraneous CL are additive (Van Merrienboer & Sweller 2005: 150), in the presence of a high ICL, extraneous CL should be kept as low as possible, whereas in a lower load task, performance may not suffer from high extraneous load. If the intrinsic load of SI with terminology tools cannot be reduced, it may be possible to affect the total load imposed by the task by operating on the extraneous load determined by the tool interface or by the way information is visually organised in the digital glossary. In turn, differences in the load experienced when working with different tools may be traced back to differences in their interface, which may for instance be perceived as non conducive by experienced interpreters who have been using different tools for several years and may be one of the sources of resistance towards new tools among seasoned professionals. This "cognitive friction" (Cooper 2004: 19) may be the source of frustration and irritation, which has been shown to negatively affect CL in workplace studies on technology-assisted translation (e.g. Bundgaard et al. 2016, Teixeira & O'Brien 2019). A similar effect may reasonably be expected to occur also in technology-supported interpreting.

Finally, germane load is the mental effort that the learner or the subject exerts in order to perform a certain task. Germane load is subject-dependent and, like intrinsic load, can be expected to decrease with increased expertise. The concept of germane load is valuable as it highlights the role of individual preferences in interacting with the tools and points to the potentially beneficial effect of higher personalisation of support tools for interpreters, similarly to what has been suggested for translators (Taravella & Vielleneuve 2013). Recent approaches exemplified by Vogler et al.'s (2019) proposal of automatically predicting useful terminology to be displayed by ASR systems for interpreters may offer beneficial insights and practical solutions to positively intervene on germane load. Additionally, the notion of germane load as a function of competence emerges in the redundancy effect predicted by CLT, as will now be discussed in §3.4.2.1.

3.4.2 Attention splitting and audio-visual integration

As discussed above, CLT postulates that extraneous load is influenced by the way in which information is presented. The task of interpreting a speech simultaneously while being able to draw support from a digital terminology tool involves the processing of several streams of input (aural and visual): it is therefore useful to consider several additional principles which have been formulated within the framework of CLT and have received strong empirical support also within the field of TPR: the split-attention effect, the redundancy effect and the modality effect.

3.4.2.1 Split attention

The split-attention effect was identified by Tarmizi & Sweller (1988), who found that worked examples of geometry problems were more effective if the various sources of information (e.g. the diagram and the diagram description) were presented in an integrated fashion rather than spatially separated. This is because in the conventional mode of presentation, the various sources of information must be integrated for learning to occur, which strains WM. There is a positive split-attention effect if information processing is more effective when the sources of information are integrated in a single percept. Not only is spatial contiguity important to promote effective information processing, but so is temporal contiguity, as demonstrated by Sweller (2005) in a series of experiments on multimedia learning. As the time component is of the essence in SI, the temporal contiguity principle holds the potential to predict important effects on the timing of the terminological information presented on screen. In order to avoid or at least to reduce split-attention between the speaker's words and the terminological pair presented on the screen, it is essential that the term be found as quickly as possible by the interpreter when manual look-up is involved, and that the latency of the ASR system be kept as low as possible (see Montecchio 2021). At the same time, the information presented by the tool must remain visible long enough to avoid having to retain the visually-presented information in WM (see §3.1), which would cause attention splitting. The robustness of the split-attention effect has been corroborated by numerous empirical investigations (for a meta-analysis, see Ginns 2005) and has been applied and found support in studies on subtitle perception, which bears some similarities to technology-supported SI due to its multi-modality (on the positive effects of integrated subtitles, see for instance Fox 2018).

3.4.2.2 Redundancy and modality

An important addition to the split-attention principle came from a study conducted by Chandler & Sweller (1991). The study revealed that an important prerequisite for the split-attention effect to occur is that the information presented in an integrated format must not be redundant. On this basis, the redundancy principle postulates that having to integrate redundant information poses an unnecessary load on WM hindering information processing, as part of the processing capacity is devoted to the mental integration of the redundant sources of information. This understanding is also valuable for CASI. As discussed above (§3.4.1), experience affects the germane load of a task. In dealing with specialised terminology, provided that the aural information has been clearly perceived and correctly decoded by the interpreter, a term visually presented on screen may be perceived as redundant if effective terminological preparation has occurred and/or the term is available in the interpreter's LTM, or if strategies are applied to bypass the difficulty posed by the speaker's use of a specialised term. This may be expected to occur especially for terms automatically suggested by an ASR system, which currently does not discriminate between the terms presented (but see Vogler et al. 2019 for an alternative approach), as the interpreter has no control over what is shown on the screen. In other words, unnecessary multi-modal presentation of a stimulus term may impose additional extraneous load which may impair processing, rather than facilitate it by alleviating WM.

The split-attention effect operates on the extraneous load by reducing the strain imposed on WM. The modality effect arises from a different approach, i.e. expanding WM capacity. In alignment with Baddeley's (1990) model of WM, this may be achieved by dividing information processing between the subsystem devoted to processing auditory stimuli and the buffer devoted to visual stimuli. As for the split-attention effect, a positive effect of modality only occurs if the information presented across different modes is not redundant. A positive modality effect may occur in SI supported by an ASR system if the interpreter has not heard a term pronounced by the speaker or has not been able to decode it and the term is presented on the screen: in other words, if the system processes the term for the interpreter. Additionally, the visual presentation of terms on the screen may be beneficial due to the transient information effect, which occurs "when learning is reduced as a result of current information such as speech or animations being replaced by new" (Low & Sweller 2014: 242).

The modality effect has been formulated within studies in the field of learning psychology and instructional design, which have mainly considered the combination of images or graphs and of instructional cues in written or auditory format. As, according to the WM model by Baddeley and Hitch, verbal information is coded by the PL (see §3.1), the presentation of completely redundant verbal information in auditory and visual form may not alleviate WM by distributing information processing across two separate buffers. However, as observed by Seeber (2017), SI is a "noisy environment" (p. 464): a term presented in auditory and visual information may therefore not be perceived as entirely redundant. Rather, the multi-modal presentation may facilitate processing especially during comprehension through multi-modal integration (for a thorough discussion of multi-modal processing in SI, see Seeber 2017). However, as both the visual and the auditory stimuli are presented in the verbal code, there might be a negative trade-off due to interference, although multitasking may still be possible as the information is presented in different perceptual modalities, as predicted by Wickens (see §3.3).

3.4.3 Cognitive load as time-based resource sharing

Despite the structural differences in the models of (working) memory proposed by Baddeley and Hitch and Cowan (see §3.1), a notion shared by both theories is that of memory decay. Because of the inherent limitation of WM, due to the processing-retention trade-off, items temporarily stored in memory decay if they are not refreshed or attended to, which leads to performance deterioration. This is particularly relevant in multitasking, where information retention and processing compete for cognitive resources.

Barrouillet et al. (2004) look at CL in terms of the time allocated to the items that must receive attention in order to be processed. Their model reconciles previously held views that the inherent limitation of WM was dependent on the amount of cognitive resources available (a matter of resource-sharing) and other models which define WM spans as dependent on the duration of the processing component (and thus view it as a question of time-sharing, see Towse & Hitch 1995). Barrouillet and his colleagues posit that:

1. attention is required both by storage and by processing, and, being limited, it must be shared between the two;

2. when attention is switched away from retention, memory traces decay;

3. information retrieval from memory is constrained by a central bottleneck (Pashler 1998, Rohrer et al. 1998), which requires attention (and so maintenance suffers);

4. if processing involves retrieval tasks, attention sharing is time-based due to the aforementioned bottleneck, and can thus be viewed as rapid switching between processing and maintenance.

Barrouillet and colleagues define CL as the number of retrievals:time ratio for tasks in which retrievals are all of the same type and difficulty. Thus, CL can be measured as the time during which attention is captured. This understanding of CL may also be applied to translation and interpreting, which share similar processes of information retrieval from LTM for target text production. The availability of a system which takes care of information retrieval (in the form of a translation memory or of an ASR system for terminology) on the part of the translator and the interpreter may have beneficial effects on processing time and alleviate CL. If, however, processing of the visually presented information requires a considerable amount of attentional resources, attention may be diverted from retention of the auditory input, with potentially negative effects on task performance and, as predicted by the model, also in terms of processing speed.

3.5 Cognitive implications in interpreting

The models and theories discussed so far were developed within the field of cognitive and learning psychology. Due to the highly influential role played by these disciplines in the early development of research paradigms for Interpreting Studies (see Pöchhacker 2004: 61, Ferreira et al. 2015), the notions of WM, CL, attention allocation and resource sharing have found wide adoption in the theoretical and empirical inquiry into the black box of the interpreter's mind.

As discussed in the previous sections, the main criticisms towards the possibility of integrating digital support tools into the in-process phase of interpreting may be traced back to a view of interpreting primarily in terms of cognitive processing and specifically as a matter of resource sharing and attention allocation to several co-occurring tasks (see §2.3.4). Early models of the cognitive processes involved in SI approaching this activity from the perspective of multitasking have favoured a bird's eye-view of the issue. They have taken the valuable step of identifying relevant sub-processes involved in SI (Lederer 1981) and of underscoring the capacity constraints which affect multiple task performance (Kirchhoff 1976).

In the present study, I adopt a "micro-cognitive approach" (Muñoz & Martín 2020: 57) to the analysis of specific conditions under which SI occurs, investigating the effects of consulting digital terminological resources as a way to cope with specialised terms, common problem triggers in SI. In doing so, I will focus on the effects on the CL of the co-occurring tasks of interpreting and interacting with the computer.

Therefore, in the following sections, I discuss and compare two cognitive processing models of (simultaneous) interpreting which have approached the phenomenon primarily as a question of multitasking: Gile's Effort Model of SI and Seeber's Cognitive Load Model (CLM) of SI.

These models interpret issues surfacing in the interpretation as problems in the allocation of limited cognitive resources between competing tasks.

There are several reasons for choosing to focus on this subset of models over other cognitive, psycholinguistic and neurolinguistic/neurophysiological models of SI (see p. 3–5 in the Introduction). First, both Gile's and Seeber's models are cognitive models from the area of Cognitive Interpreting Studies which the present work is situated into and are grounded in the notions of cognitive psychology discussed in the previous sections of this chapter. Second, they have already been adopted as a theoretical reference in CAI research (see §2.4). Third, they allow modelling the interaction with external written traces (e.g. glossaries and transcripts of the ST) in addition to the internal interaction and competition between cognitive subprocesses. As such, they allow modelling several sources of cognitive load, both intrinsic and extraneous (see §3.4.1). Fourth, they both appear directly relevant to the present research object. Gile's Effort Model of SI incorporates specifically specialised terminology as a source of increased effort, whereas Seeber's CLM has already been applied and validated in studies on simultaneous interpreting with text, which shares many features with CASI (as discussed in §3.6), in particular in terms of the interpretation of specialised terminology. Finally, they lend themselves to being tested in a laboratory environment while allowing to study SI under relatively naturalistic conditions.

After illustrating and discussing the models, I motivate the theoretical framework chosen for the present empirical investigation and discuss its application to the present object of inquiry.

3.5.1 Gile's Effort Model of simultaneous interpreting

Gile (1988, 1997, 1999) developed his Effort Models (EM) to explain why errors, omissions and "infelicities" (EOIs, see Gile 2011, 2015), i.e. suboptimal rendition of the source speech, occur in interpreting. As specified by the author, the EMs should not be considered as "operational testing or calibrating" (Gile 1991b: 18) tools but were rather designed for the classroom to intuitively explain certain phenomena that can be observed in SI (Gile 2009: 188). For this reason, they have been regarded as a useful pedagogical tool. Nonetheless, the EMs have encountered the favour of many researchers and have been adopted as a conceptual framework "with explanatory and predictive potential on the level of actual interpreting performance" (Gile 1999: 2).

In developing his models, Gile refers to a key concept widely accepted in cognitive psychology and put forward by Shannon & Weaver (1949), i.e. that controlled processes are managed by an inherently limited system, developing further the considerations expressed by Kirchhoff (1976). Such is the case in interpreting, which involves several sub-processes. These operations are not automatic, but rather require the active allocation of limited cognitive resources. Through the development of interpreting expertise, however, some components of these inherently controlled operations can become automatic, freeing up more processing capacity and reducing the chances of EOIs.

Gile defines the sub-processes involved in interpreting as "efforts" and identifies:

- a listening and analysis effort (L), or more generally, a reception effort (R), as it was later renamed to account for visual perception during sign language interpreting and of additional visual inputs (e.g. PowerPoint presentations)

- a memorisation effort, i.e. the storage of the information to be processed in memory (M)

- a production effort, i.e. the delivery of the message in the target language (P), including self-monitoring

- a coordination effort (C) which is responsible for the allocation of the attentional resources and the successful concurrent performance of the above-mentioned sub-tasks

SI is thus defined as the sum of the three efforts:

$$SI = L \text{ (or R)} + M + P + C$$

Gile assumes that if the sum of the resources required by the different efforts does not exceed the sum of the attentional capacities available, then SI is feasible:

$$SI = R \text{ (the sum of attentional resources for each effort)} \leq A.$$

The same is true for each sub-process, which must not recruit "more than the specific capacity available to it" (Setton 2003). Otherwise, problems arise. It is important to clarify that the additivity of the efforts is not intended in the arithmetic sense, as the efforts also overlap and compete for resources (Gile 2009: 184, Gile 1999: 4).

The equation should not be seen as static either, but can rather vary during the interpreting process according to variations in task difficulty. In this respect, Gile (2008) introduces the notion of "local cognitive load" to indicate that overload may happen around occasional sources of difficulty.

Gile's EM of SI is integrated by the Tightrope Hypothesis (Gile 1999), i.e. the assumption that interpreters work close to saturation levels most of the time (Gile 2009: 198). Like tightrope walkers, interpreters must constantly strive to keep their balance between the individual sub-tasks which require careful coordination. According to Gile, EOIs therefore arise when the system is saturated as the interpreter experiences cognitive overload due to the inability to effectively deal with what Gile (1999: 157) defines as "problem triggers", e.g. proper names, specialised terms, numbers and enumerations, as they require increased cognitive resources, or because of suboptimal allocation of resources to the individual efforts. This is particularly true for novices, while expert interpreters may be better capable to effectively deal with problem triggers and may have better resource management, but are nonetheless constantly exposed to the risk of cognitive saturation.

A second addition to the effort models is the Gravitational Model of Language Availability (see also §1.2.3.1), which is useful to intuitively explain why specialised terminology may trigger overload or processing issues. Gile added this component based on the observation that the effortfulness of speech comprehension and production was influenced by the availability of "Units of Linguistic Knowledge". When words or expressions are used often, they are more readily available (they gravitate to the centre of the model). Otherwise, they tend to drift outwards, and their understanding and/or production is more effortful. According to the Gravitational Model, technical terms which cannot easily be retrieved

3 Simultaneous interpreting as a complex cognitive activity

from LTM may impose heightened attentional requirements on the listening effort (as the term may not be easily recognised and understood) as well as on the production effort. Interpreters may cope with such problem triggers by consulting electronic dictionaries or digital glossaries, although this may require time and attention (Gile 2009: 219).

Although reference is quite often made to "the" Effort Model to designate the EM of SI, Gile developed several effort models to provide an intuitive representation of the efforts involved in different modes of interpreting, e.g. SI with text, consecutive interpreting, interpreting from sign languages, and even remote interpreting. Where additional components seem to require considerable additional efforts on the part of the interpreter at the detriment of other efforts, Gile adds effort components to the equation, such as the human-machine interaction (HMI) effort for remote interpreting, a notion which may also be applied to SI with digital terminological support.

Despite the conceptual nature of the Effort Models, they have been adopted as a research framework in a number of studies. Most of these studies have provided support for the notion that the efforts are not automatic (Gumul 2018: 19) and that the human processing capacity is limited, a generally-accepted principle which is also at the core of Baddeley and Hitch's model of WM (Baddeley & Hitch 1974, see §3.1). Additionally, the findings by several studies (e.g. Gile 1999, Gumul 2018, Gile 2011, Matysiak 2001), including a recent ERP study by Koshkin et al. (2018) have been interpreted as support for the tightrope hypothesis.

Gile's Effort Models have been subjected to criticism by other interpreting scholars. For instance, Pym (2008) conducted an additional analysis of omissions in Gile's (1999) experiment stressing their functional role, which is not in contrast with the key principles of the model, but not explicitly included either. Other researchers have criticised the lack of temporal resolution of the model (Pöchhacker 2016). The harshest critic of the model is Seeber (2011), who focuses on the tightrope hypothesis. Seeber agrees that the tightrope hypothesis aptly describes cases in which the source speech presents specific sources of difficulty, such as high delivery rate, non-native accent or high information density. However, he observes that multitasking may very well be possible in interpreting, as commonly observed among professional interpreters, who, unlike budding interpreters, in some cases may have enough cognitive resources left to spare. The misunderstanding about the EM (e.g. Gile 2017b) probably originates from Seeber's view of the interpreting process from the perspective of cognitive psychology, which leads him to interpret the equation provided by Gile in the Effort Models as a reflection of Kahneman's (1973) single resource theory (see §3.3), or to equate the memory effort with WM and the coordination effort with Baddeley & Hitch's (1974) CE. Since the effort models present some parallels with key concepts of cognitive psychology[2], it is easy to understand where the misunderstanding stems from, as discussed by Gile (2009) himself. After all, similar interpretations of Gile's Effort Models can also be found among cognitive psychologists (Gile 2009).

Gile responded to these criticisms in subsequent and regular updates of the models (e.g. Gile 2016, 2017b, 2020). He observed that most criticism stems from the use of the models in empirical cognitive explorations of the interpreting process despite them having been conceived to provide a "holistic and intuitive" (Gile 2017b: 10) explanation of EOIs. The intended use of the models is to provide prospective interpreters with a functional explanation of why problems arise in interpreting, and to help them develop and reflect upon tactics and strategies to be used in interpreting (Gile 2020).

Nonetheless, Gile (2009: 205) claims that "the competition-between-Efforts principle is consistent with the theory of one central pool of processing capacity, not with the theory that there may be several pools that the Efforts can draw upon without there being interference with them". However, a multiple resource model does not negate interference. Rather, it offers a framework to differentiate between tasks which can be performed simultaneously without interference and tasks which interfere, and to describe the extent to which they do. If analysed from the perspective of theories formulated in cognitive psychology, it seems to me that Gile's (2009) "competition hypothesis" may also be explained by the interference of sub-tasks which draw from separate dimensions but share resources. This would be compatible with Wickens's model (§3.3). Indeed, empirical evidence taken as support of the tightrope hypothesis (Koshkin et al. 2018, Gumul 2018) mainly points to interference between efforts, but does not explore the structural reason for this interference. After all, the EM does not aim to provide an architectural explanation underlying information processing.

The notion that the co-existence of multiple "efforts" may increase capacity requirements (Gile 1999: 156) would also hold true within the framework of an architectural model assuming interference between tasks which share resources in some dimension (e.g. Wickens's multiple resource model, see §3.3). This is the case for SI, during which auditory-verbal resources are required both in the reception phase (Listening + Analysis Effort) and in the response phase (Production Effort). Additionally, Gile suggests that it might be useful to "develop 'tuning' or

---

[2]For instance, the non-automaticity of the sub-processes, the inherent limitation of the processing capacity, the idea of attention allocation and of task interference.

'scaling' rules for the quantification of processing capacity or time requirements for interpretation tasks" (Gile 1991b: 18). This may be achieved through the "demand vectors" proposed by Wickens (1976, 1984, 2002). Finally, the assumption that interpreters' resources are at risk of saturation most of the time has not yet received empirical support, as suggested by cases of perfect time-sharing (Schumacher et al. 2001, see also Seeber 2011). Gile concedes that "though the evidence supports the hypothesis of cognitive saturation, it does not necessarily show that such saturation occurs at global level" (Gile 2008: 61). Seeber & Kerzel's (2012) eyetracking study also found support for a local increase of CL, rather than a general increase of pupil dilation compared to the baseline. Note, however, that the tightrope hypothesis does not state how close interpreters supposedly come to saturation (Gile 2017a). Gile further observes that pupillometry can only capture instances of heightened load if the interpreter does not intervene to prevent it, and thus the risk of overload may not show in the data. It would be interesting to conduct further studies using other physiological measures (see §4.5 for an overview), for instance sensitive to stress, which is likely to be experienced when having to deal with problem triggers, and to verify whether this correlates with pupillary dilation.

To sum up, Gile's EMs interpret EOIs in the TT as evidence of the competition between efforts recruiting resources from a single pool of mental capacity. The models have had the merit of conceptualising the idea of the distribution of resources between concurring tasks through a series of components (the tightrope hypothesis, the gravitational model, and the competition-between-efforts principle) which have proved quite productive in training.

The main limitation of the models for the present exploration of CASI lies in the lack of components modelling the structural nature of the interference between tasks and explaining why, for instance, the human-machine interaction and the listening or the production effort may compete for resources. This level of detail appears, however, essential for interventions on the design of support tools aiming to reduce such interference.

Furthermore, the lack of a clear stance as to the models' grounding in cognitive psychology, coupled with unresolved issues preventing an unequivocal validation of the tightrope hypothesis, represent limitations for the models' application to experimental research aiming for an operational testing of its theoretical framework, which the present study aspires to do. For these reasons, I examine Seeber's CLM of SI in the following section and I illustrate the motivation for choosing the CLM as theoretical framework for the present study in §3.5.3.

3.5.2 Seeber's Cognitive Load Model of Simultaneous Interpreting

Unlike Gile, Seeber explicitly derives his model from cognitive psychology. He adapts Wickens's model of task interference to SI, while introducing some variations (Seeber 2007). First of all, he turns the three-dimensional model into a bi-dimensional model. This offers a double advantage. First, it enables to graphically represent all components of the model at once (some were "hidden" in the non-visible faces of the cube). Second, it reintroduces the general capacity, the pool of general resources postulated by Wickens, into the model, which did not previously fit into the cube. Seeber further expands the model by adding a Cognitive Resource Footprint (CRF), a visual representation of which resources are shared between the co-occurring tasks. Finally, he keeps Wickens's conflict matrix, with some modifications. Seeber uses this adaptation of Wickens's model, his own CLM, to represent and explore resource sharing during four language processing tasks: shadowing, sight translation, SI (Seeber 2007: 1383) and SI with text (Seeber 2017).

3.5.2.1 Cognitive Load Model of Simultaneous Interpreting

Seeber describes SI as a combination of two main tasks: 1) a listening and comprehension task and 2) a production and monitoring task. Listening and comprehension recruits auditory-verbal and cognitive-verbal resources at the perceptual-cognitive stage: conference interpreters receive the auditory stimulus, i.e. the source speech as pronounced by the speaker, and must analyse the verbal message for comprehension. In a more recent adaptation of the model (Seeber 2017), a visual-spatial component was added to account for the paraverbal information the interpreter perceives while interpreting (for visual information in interpreting, see also Seubert 2019). Interpreters then "respond" to this stimulus by delivering the message in the target language. At the same time, they must monitor their own rendition. The production and monitoring task thus demands auditory-verbal and cognitive-verbal resources at the perceptual-cognitive stage and additional vocal-verbal resources at the response stage.

Figure 3.2 represents the CRF of SI with visual input.

As described in §3.3, Wickens's model represents the level of dependence of a task on a resource by assigning demand vectors comprised between 0 (no dependence) and 2 (extreme dependence). Seeber postulates a demand vector of 1 for each of the concurring sub-tasks (resources), which in SI occur at both stages of processing (perception + cognition, responding), in both perceptual modalities (auditory and visual) and in the two processing codes (spatial and verbal).

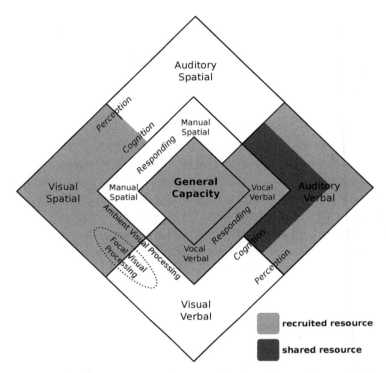

Figure 3.2: Cognitive resource footprint for SI with visual input (Seeber 2017: 468)

The revised model foresees three possible levels (0, 0.5, 1), where the use of half vectors serves to model complementarity between information sources (specifically between the auditory verbal and the visual spatial modalities/codes), while redundant information (see §3.4.2.2) within a stage is represented with a full (1) demand vector (Seeber 2017: 481).

The sum of the demand vectors and conflict coefficients thus assigned to SI is equal to a total interference score (TIS) of 11.6 (Figure 3.3).[3]

The application of the model to the three tasks of shadowing, sight translation and SI operationalises the hypothesis that SI requires the higher amount of individual resources as compared to the other tasks, as it involves more concurrent sub-processes, which results in the highest level of task interference.

The CLM of SI in its original version (without the inclusion of visual information) was tested by Seeber & Kerzel (2012) in an eyetracking experiment on the

---

[3]In the original model (Seeber 2007), the TIS was equal to 9. The higher score in the revised model (Seeber 2017) is determined by the addition of demands on visual-spatial resources due to the inclusion of paraverbal information provided by the speaker.

production & monitoring			listening comprehension							
			perceptual				cognitive		response	
		vector	0.5	∅	∅	0.5	0.5	0.5	∅	∅
	demand		visual spatial	visual verbal	auditory spatial	auditory verbal	cognitive spatial	cognitive verbal	response spatial	response verbal
perceptual	∅	visual spatial	0.8	0.6	0.6	0.4	0.7	0.5	0.4	0.2
perceptual	∅	visual verbal	0.6	0.8	0.4	0.6	0.5	0.7	0.2	0.4
perceptual	∅	auditory spatial	0.6	0.4	0.8	0.4	0.7	0.5	0.4	0.2
perceptual	1	auditory verbal	0.4	0.6	0.4	0.8	0.5	0.7	0.2	0.4
cognitive	∅	cognitive spatial	0.7	0.5	0.7	0.5	0.8	0.6	0.6	0.4
cognitive	1	cognitive verbal	0.5	0.7	0.5	0.7	0.6	0.8	0.4	0.6
response	∅	response spatial	0.4	0.2	0.4	0.2	0.6	0.4	0.8	0.6
response	1	response verbal	0.2	0.4	0.2	0.4	0.4	0.6	0.6	1.0

$$
\begin{aligned}
\text{Total interference score} &= \text{demand vectors} &+\ &\text{conflict coefficients}\\
&= (1+1+1+0.5+0.5+0.5+0.5) &+\ &(0.4+0.5+0.2+0.8+0.7+0.4\\
& &+\ &0.5+0.6+0.4+0.7+0.8+0.6) = 11.6
\end{aligned}
$$

Figure 3.3: Conflict matrix for SI with visual input (Seeber 2017: 469)

effect of asymmetric syntactical structures between English and German on the interpreter's CL. The authors applied the CLM to represent local variations in CL for verb-final sentences and symmetrical structures, predicting higher CL for asymmetrical structures. The CLMs effectively predict that "the interpretation of syntactically asymmetrical structures causes more CL than the interpretation of syntactically symmetrical structures towards the end of the sentence" (ibid., p. 238). The CLM may thus be used not only to model interference between tasks on a global level (i.e. listening and comprehension vs monitoring and production), but also to formulate more in-depth hypotheses on local CL.

Gieshoff (2018, 2021) conducted an experiment aimed at verifying whether seeing the speaker's lip movements during SI reduces CL. Inter alia, she used silent pause duration as an indicator of CL and found that silent pauses were shorter when the speaker's lips were visible. Her findings lend support to the hypothesis that auditory-verbal and visual-spatial information is integrated, as predicted by the CLM in alignment with abundant empirical evidence on multimodal integration (see §3.4.2.2). It should be noted that pupillometric data did not support the hypothesis, though Gieshoff interpreted larger pupils for the multimodal condition as an indicator of higher arousal rather than increased cognitive effort (Gieshoff 2018: 242).

Seubert (2019) also investigated the processing of visual information during SI with an exploratory eyetracking study conducted on a sample of 13 professional interpreters. The naturalistic research design, which favours the proximity to a real-life interpreting situation rather than a strict control of empirical variables, does not allow for an in-depth analysis of the cognitive interactions between different types of visual support with the interpreting process. Nonetheless, Seubert's research provides valuable observations, some of which offer support to the predictions of the CLM. In particular, the reported strategic behaviour of experienced professionals in dealing with different sources of visual input supports Seeber's hypothesis that strategies modulate the allocation of cognitive resources in order to avoid cognitive overload, and that the supportive or distracting potential of visual input depends, inter alia, also on the type of input processed. For instance, the observation that Seubert's test subjects devoted a high proportion of their visual attention to the speaker supports the hypothesis that paraverbal information may provide a valuable integration of the auditory channel. This is in line with Gieshoff's findings for lip movements, although in Seubert's experiment the speaker area of interest was much larger due to the situated nature of her experiment. It also aligns with the predictions of the CLM, but it should be noted that Seubert did not explicitly test such predictions. Her finding that informants' visual processing behaviour varied along with the (postulated) variations in CL during the interpreting session is also valuable. Before and after their interpreting turn, the interpreters' visual perceptual field appears to be larger than during the more cognitively demanding phases, which Seubert interprets as a higher amount of cognitive resources available for visual processing due to a lower CL (supporting Lavie's theory, as discussed in §3.2). This observation also supports the idea that the assumptions of the tightrope hypothesis (Gile 1999) may be valid more on a local level rather than on a global level, as pointed out in Seeber & Kerzel (2012).

3.5.2.2 Cognitive Load Model of SI with text

The addition of the visual-spatial component to the CLM does not include written information, which according to standard models of WM is processed in the PL, while gestures, lip movements and expressions are processed in the VSSP (see §3.1). To account for the processing of visual-verbal (written) information during SI, Seeber (2017) applied his model to a specific instantiation of SI with written information, i.e. SI with the full transcript of the speech (SIMTXT). For SIMTXT, the inclusion of the written text requires the addition of visual-verbal resources to the cognitive resource footprint (Figure 3.4).

In the conflict matrix, visual-verbal processing is added to the listening and comprehension phase and receives a full demand vector. The attribution of a demand vector of 1 reflects the duplication of aural information in written form. Hence, the total interference score is higher than for SI without written input (14.3), as can be seen from the expanded conflict matrix (Figure 3.5).

The application of Seeber's CLM of SIMTXT was adopted as a theoretical framework in a recent experiment by Seeber et al. (2020) and by Chmiel, Janikowski & Cieślewicz (2020). Seeber and colleagues report on an eyetracking experiment designed to test how attention is allocated to redundant written information during SI. The authors contrasted SIMTXT with reading while listening (RWL) as a control task. They found that interpreters attend to the visual-verbal support during their production, probably in order to "offload short term memory" (Seeber et al. 2020: 13), rather than exploiting redundancy effects to improve their comprehension. This is in line with Seeber's CLM which postulates the attribution of shared vectors to visual-spatial and auditory-verbal resource demands (i.e. for complementary information), and not for visual-verbal and auditory-verbal stimuli. In essence, their redundancy may require excessive effort for their integration to be possible in the listening and comprehension phase, but may prove beneficial during the production phase to assist with control processing.

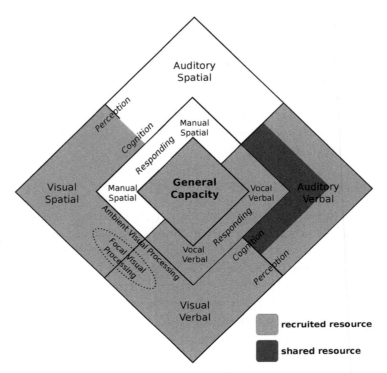

Figure 3.4: Cognitive resource footprint for SI with text (Seeber 2017: 471)

Chmiel, Janikowski & Cieślewicz (2020) investigated source language interference in an English to Polish SI and sight translation (ST) task. They measured the number of cognates, homographs and passive structures, in addition to time lag and total translation time as indicators of CL, adapting Seeber's CLM to operationalise their hypotheses. They observe that in ST the visual-verbal input is the only source of information, and thus its processing differs from SIMTXT and would deserve different values for the demand vectors and the conflict coefficient, though they do not explain what demand vector may be assigned for ST. Additionally, they propose a higher conflict coefficient for cognitive verbal vs response verbal demands in ST based on the inherent higher complexity of textual processing, but this contrasts with Wickens's observation that "the adjustment of conflict values should not be based on differences in single task demands, since these [are] captured by the single task analysis shell" (Wickens 2002: 170). Furthermore, in their adaptation, they do not mention removing the visual-spatial component, which Seeber (2017) had added to account for paraverbal information

production & monitoring			listening & reading comprehension							
			perceptual				cognitive		response	
		vector	0.5	1	∅	0.5	0.5	1	∅	∅
		demand	visual spatial	visual verbal	auditory spatial	auditory verbal	cognitive spatial	cognitive verbal	response spatial	response verbal
perceptual	visual spatial	∅	0.8	0.6	0.6	0.4	0.7	0.5	0.4	0.2
perceptual	visual verbal	∅	0.6	0.8	0.4	0.6	0.5	0.7	0.2	0.4
perceptual	auditory spatial	∅	0.6	0.4	0.8	0.4	0.7	0.5	0.4	0.2
perceptual	auditory verbal	1	0.4	0.6	0.4	0.8	0.5	0.7	0.2	0.4
cognitive	cognitive spatial	∅	0.7	0.5	0.7	0.5	0.8	0.6	0.6	0.4
cognitive	cognitive verbal	1	0.5	0.7	0.5	0.7	0.6	0.8	0.4	0.6
response	response spatial	∅	0.4	0.2	0.4	0.2	0.6	0.4	0.8	0.6
response	response verbal	1	0.2	0.4	0.2	0.4	0.4	0.6	0.6	1.0

$$
\begin{aligned}
\text{Total interference score} &= \text{demand vectors} && + \text{ conflict coefficients} \\
&= (1+1+1+0.5+1+0.5+0.5+1) && + (0.4+0.5+0.2+0.6+0.7+0.4 \\
& && + 0.8+0.7+0.4+0.5+0.6+0.4 \\
& && + 0.7+0.8+0.6) = 14.8
\end{aligned}
$$

Figure 3.5: Conflict matrix for SI with visual-verbal input (Seeber 2017: 472)

from the speaker. In ST, this component is not relevant. This would have probably resulted in an even lower TIS for ST than for SI. Their findings on time lag (longer for ST than for SI) did not elicit a unequivocal interpretation, as the external pacing in SI inherently affects time lag in SI. Additionally, total translation time was found to be longer in SI, which, contrary to their predictions, might point to higher CL in SI than in ST. Despite some limitations in the authors' adaptation of the model, the CLM proved a valuable tool for the formulation of hypotheses on SI with text.

In her 2019 experiment, Seubert also included written support material in the wide array of visual input presented to her test subjects. She did so by observing the interpreters' behaviour during the interpretation of citations, which they had not prepared beforehand (Seubert 2019: 198). Seubert reports that, when faced with longer text passages, 8 out of 11 interpreters averted their gaze from the speaker and the slide containing the quote. She interprets this as an indication of higher cognitive effort, which is corroborated by numerous hesitations and deficient content in the renditions (ibid., p. 209). This observation may lend support to the hypothesis that redundant information replicated across two different channels may lead to an increase in CL, which the CLM predicts. It is interesting to observe that for more isolated textual information, which only partially replicates the spoken input (e.g. the presentation table of contents, p. 199), the interpreters' gaze continuously switched from the speaker to the slides, which Seubert interprets as an indication that this type of visual support may be useful both for the planning and for the production and monitoring phase (p. 205). These findings partially contrasts with Seeber et al.'s (2020) findings that redundant textual support is used mainly in the production phase. It should be noted that Seeber's experiment was conducted in a laboratory setting under stringent variable control, which reduced the visual input to the speech transcript. In Seubert's experiment, the sheer amount of sources of visual information may have contributed to the perceptual overload which led the interpreters to avert their gaze and not to consult the slides containing the quotes. Her second observation that isolated information is consulted during both phases should be confirmed under more strict experimental conditions. However, I should mention that her findings were for a very specific type of support, i.e. a table of contents, which is different from a speech transcript and may therefore also require fewer plausibility checks on the part of the interpreters, as they may expect it to be a reliable source of information with fewer discrepancy than the written transcript compared to the spoken discourse. Different findings for different types of visual support further corroborate Seeber's observation that "although signal complementarity and signal redundancy appear to be important components of our natural environment, and we seem to have evolved to expect and rely on them, the way in which we process them may well depend on the composition of the signal" (Seeber 2017: 463). Conducting targeted studies on visual input during interpreting therefore seems motivated.

The analysis of Seeber's CLM and of relevant research in the area of simultaneous interpreting with visual support has highlighted how Seeber's conceptualisation of SI and SIMTXT may represent a more suited theoretical starting point for the present study than Gile's EMs (see §3.5.1). The following section reviews the main differences between the two models and illustrates the rationale behind the choice of Seeber's CLM for the present inquiry.

3.5.3 Discussion and choice of a model for the present work

The two models which have been in focus in the previous sections (§3.5.1, §3.5.2) represent SI essentially as a multitasking activity. They both postulate a limited attentional capacity constraining WM (though Gile refers to a more general "Memory Effort", see Gile 2009) and explicitly include the processing of textual information during SI (Gile 2009, 2020, Seeber 2017).[4] The textual component is pertinent to the present inquiry since terminology support is also presented in the visual-verbal modality and in part replicates the auditory input.

One important difference lies in Seeber's clear stance as to which framework he grounds his model in, i.e. Wickens's multiple resource theory. As such, his model is clearly rooted in cognitive psychology. As the present work is conducted within a cognitive processing paradigm adopting consolidated methods derived from TPR, which have in turn largely been adopted (and adapted) from cognitive psychology, choosing Seeber's CLM as the theoretical framework to operationalise my hypotheses seems the more coherent approach. Additionally, the model has been used to effectively predict a number of effects of interaction with visual-verbal input in SI (as discussed in §3.5.2.2) and to my knowledge, no empirical evidence has been found yet to contrast its assumptions. Though the initial model did not provide for facilitation effects due to crossmodal integration (Seeber 2007), Seeber's adaptation of Wickens's model through half-scores for the individual demand vectors allows to include such effects and to model hypotheses in this respect. In this sense, the CLM always posits higher or equal CL with the addition of further sub-tasks (e.g. interacting with a speech transcript or with a computer for terminology look-up), never lower.

---

[4]Although they are not the only models to do so. Other authors from different research paradigms have also included visual information in their models (for a review, see Seubert 2019).

Gile's Effort Model may be less strict in that in principle it allows to include facilitation effects by, for instance, combining auditory and visual processing in a single reception effort (see Gile 2009). If facilitation effects due to redundancy across different modalities were found (though, at present, this is not yet the case), the lower reception effort would leave more processing resources available for memory, coordination and production. However, it may be argued that, since aural and visual stimuli are processed separately, the elaboration of additional stimuli should be modelled as an extra effort, as suggests Gieshoff (2018: 74). This would require distributing attentional capacities across a higher number of sub-tasks, with fewer resources available for each task.

As for terms as problem triggers, they are discussed explicitly in Gile (2009) as potential causes of locally increased CL during SI. They may pose a higher load on the Reception Effort (if the term cannot be quickly recognised or identified) as well as on the Production Effort (if the target language equivalent is not available). As Wickens (2002) postulates a three-tier system for the allocation of demand vectors, it may theoretically be possible to postulate higher demands also within the framework of Seeber's CLM, either for the listening and understanding task or for the production task, or for both.

Despite the differences discussed above, evidence congruent with both accounts of multitasking during interpreting has been found (among recent studies, see for instance Chmiel, Janikowski & Cieślewicz 2020, Gieshoff 2021, Seeber et al. 2020). Yet, the two models have often been contrasted as antithetic, as stressed by Seeber (2011) himself. Approaching inquiries into CL from the perspective of cognitive psychology, Seeber views Gile's model as reflective of Kahneman's single resource theory, which contrasts with his CLM based on Wickens's multiple resource theory. As discussed above (§3.5.1), Gile does not support this interpretation of his model and further criticises the CLM as "not indicative of what actually happens in the booth" (Gile 2020: 9). In my view, the two models do not necessarily contradict each other. Rather, Gile's EM offers a broader, more holistic view of multitasking in SI. Seeber's CLM may, on the other hand, be seen as a micro-cognitive model of the interpreting process, rooted in the theories and findings of cognitive psychology and allowing for the formulation of fine-grained hypotheses on how the sub-components of interpreting may interfere with each other, and of why certain sub-components do so more than others.

As the present study contrasts the provision of terminological support through three different kinds of digital tools, this level of granularity may prove particularly suited to identifying specific sources of extraneous load and modelling their impact on the CL of CASI. Adopting a model of the interpreting process originating from a psychological model should further facilitate the interpretation of results in the present study in view of accepted theories stemming from cognitive psychology.

Additionally, Seeber's CLM presents several specificities:

1. It defines local CL as "a function of input and output features" (Seeber 2011: 189) in relation to the amount of parallel processing and the amount of time for which elements must be stored.

2. It shows how, while interpreters might indeed reach maximum CL locally, most of the time they work below this "red line".

3. It accounts for local variations in CL, which can be explored at a microscopic level. The output in SI is seen as the result of strategies aimed at managing the limits inherent to the task at hand and at saving elaboration capacity, as exemplified by his application of the model in the framework of an experiment investigating the impact of syntactical structure for the language pair German-English on CL in SI (Seeber 2011).

4. It is able to "account for the conflict potential posed by an overlap [of tasks] and the interference they cause" (Seeber 2011: 189).

5. It illustrates how the overall cognitive demands are affected by the different combinations of sub-tasks.

6. It offers a "first attempt at quantifying CL, relying principally on Wickens's demand vectors and conflict coefficients" (ibid.).

It is this level of granularity and flexibility of the model, already adapted to SI with text, which may represent the most valuable aspects of the CLM. Additionally, by postulating different demand vectors for a certain sub-task, it would be possible to further differentiate between diverse interpreting scenarios, predicting differences in the CL inherent to SI performed under different conditions and tracing them back precisely to the interference of defined sub-processes.

For the above-mentioned reasons, Seeber's framework is best suited to operationalise hypotheses on digital terminological support during SI through standard digital glossaries, CAI tools, and ASR-CAI hybrids.

3.6 A model of SI with digital terminology support

SI can be carried out in forms which add elements to its basic constellation of sub-tasks and resources recruited, as is the case for SI with text, or for assignments during which presentations are shown during speech delivery, an additional input that is also processed by the interpreter. What happens, then, when the interpreter searches for terminology in a glossary while interpreting simultaneously? Or when an interpreter is automatically prompted with terminology by an ASR system? Which cognitive resources are recruited, and in which of the four dimensions identified by Wickens? How much do said resources interfere with each other and why? As discussed in the previous sections (3.5.2), the CLM has been used to formulate hypotheses on "standard" SI (with visual input) and on SI with text. In order to formulate hypotheses around these questions, I propose to apply Seeber's CLM to SI with digital terminology support.

In previous publications (Prandi 2017, 2018), I had suggested an adaptation of Seeber's CLM to SI with digital glossaries, CAI tools and ASR based on the initial version of the model (Seeber 2007, 2011, Seeber & Kerzel 2012), as at the time of submission I was not yet aware of his more recent publication proposing an application of the model to SI with text (Seeber 2017). In my initial application of the CLM to SI with digital terminology support, I had not discussed the beneficial audio-visual integration effects due to the processing of paraverbal information provided by the speaker. The visual-spatial component had been included to account for visual search operations required in the case of morphological neighbours for target terms (Prandi 2018) and had therefore received a full demand vector. I will therefore revise and update my proposed application of the CLM to SI with digital glossaries, CAI tools and ASR based on the more recent expansion of the model (Seeber 2017).

3.6.1 Application of Seeber's CLM to SI with terminological support

Specialised terminology may not constitute a source of difficulty if the target language equivalent is readily available during the interpretation. In that case, the interpreter recruits cognitive resources to retrieve the equivalent from LTM. This may also result in higher CL, without, however, disrupting the rendition. Thorough preparation and terminological activation ahead of the assignment may help prevent impasses due to the use of specialised terminology. Indeed, assignment preparation, including terminological preparation, is considered an essential constituent of a successful interpreting performance, and is therefore often presented as a valuable strategy that interpreter trainees must learn to apply (e.g. Gile 2009). When the term cannot be retrieved from LTM, a series of coping tactics may be applied, such as paraphrasing, transcoding, generalising, and so forth (for an overview and discussion of different coping tactics, see Gile 2009). The progressive penetration of the digital medium in the interpreting profession, however, has made it relatively quick and easy to perform online queries in terminological resources, either peri-process or in-process. Glossaries are only one example of such resources, as mentioned in §1.2.3. For the scope of the present inquiry, I will focus on the consultation of terminological resources as a coping tactic (Gile 2009: 203) to deal with specialised terminology. I will do so by examining three potential types of digital support interpreters may utilise in order to cope with specialised terminology: digital glossaries, CAI tools, and ASR-CAI hybrids.

3.6.2 Manual terminology look-up

When terminology is manually looked up during SI, additional attentional resources are recruited. In order to search for a term in a digital glossary or a CAI tool database, the interpreter must perform several operations: (a) type a term or part thereof to query the database (and in most traditional digital glossaries, also click the enter key), (b) locate the relevant term on the page/in the list of terminological pairs, and (c) read the term and integrate it into the rendition. It should be noted that locating the term may not always require visual search in a digital glossary prepared, for instance, with Word or Excel or saved as a PDF. In all of these cases, all occurrences for the string searched may be highlighted, so the interpreter would need to visually identify the relevant term. However, if no orthographic neighbours are present in the glossary, only one term will be highlighted. The visual cue should attract the interpreter's visual attention through a bottom-up mechanism (see for instance Seubert 2019), rendering the identification of the target term more agile. Of course, much depends on the search settings chosen by the interpreters and on the strategies they adopt. For instance, one may select "search only whole words", to further reduce the number of results. For bigrams and trigrams, i.e. terms composed of more than one component, the number of results may depend on which element is searched. For instance, in a speech on nuclear energy, several types of reactors may be mentioned: if the glossary contains "boiling water reactor", "pressurised steam reactor" and "nuclear reactor" and the interpreter looks for "reactor", all three results will be highlighted and the interpreter may need to skip to the next occurrence or scroll down in the case of a multi-page glossary, whereas searching for "boiling" will only highlight one term and no further operations will be required. In a CAI tool such as InterpretBank, results which do not correspond to the search string are not displayed thanks to a dedicated search algorithm. However, visual search may still occur, as for digital glossaries, if several orthographic neighbours are shown on the screen.

However, InterpretBank poses three main advantages. First, it reduces the amount of visual input to be processed. Second, it does not require the user to position the cursor in the search field. This happens automatically in the Conference Mode: after a query, the programme is ready for the next search. If this operation has not been automatised by the interpreter, a digital glossary may cause the querying process to slow down, as the user has to prepare for the following query. Third, the search bar is cleared automatically after each query in InterpretBank, which is not the case for a standard digital glossary. Forgetting to clear the search bar at the end of a query may interfere with other sub-processes during the following query.

Using the CRF from the CLM as theoretical framework, there is first of all a "response" to the auditory stimulus during manual look-up. This recruits manual-spatial resources in addition to the vocal-verbal response, i.e. the interpreter's rendition. It seems correct to assign the terminology query to the production and monitoring stage as the manual query is conducted to support target language rendition. If the term has not been recognised, no manual query can be performed. Furthermore, visual-spatial resources are recruited at the perceptive-cognitive stage, to identify the term, while visual-verbal resources are required to read the term (Figure 3.6). SI with a glossary therefore shares something with sight translation and with SI with text, which also require visual-verbal resources during perception/cognition. As observed by Gieshoff (2018: 74–75), we may expect the glossary query to "interfere with the speech, the auditory stream, as both elements are verbal and cognitive-perceptual inputs".

The cognitive resource footprint of SI with manual look-up (digital glossary/ InterpretBank) illustrates the recruitment of additional resources (Figure 3.7). It should be noted that the CRF for SI with terminology look-up applies only to the instances in which a query occurs, and not to the entire interpreting task. When no query is performed, one can apply Seeber's CLM for SI. In sum, the CRF posits a recruitment of:

- the general capacity available for all tasks

- visual-verbal, visual-spatial and auditory-verbal resources at the perception and cognition stage

- manual-spatial, vocal-verbal and auditory-verbal resources at the production and monitoring stage

Thus, auditory-verbal and cognitive-verbal resources are recruited during both sub-tasks.

A comparison with the conflict matrix for "standard" SI (with visual input, Figure 3.3) highlights how manual terminology look-up during SI should produce a higher CL, not only because more resources are mobilised, but also because they are shared across a higher number of sub-tasks.

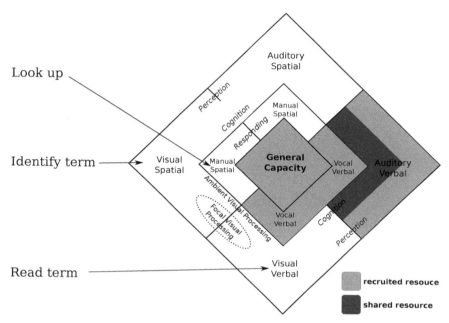

Figure 3.6: Additional cognitive resources recruited during SI with manual terminology lookup in a digital glossary or a CAI tool (Prandi 2018: 36)

As discussed above, however, CAI tools may offer a series of advantages which have the potential to partly reduce the additional load resulting from the interaction with the computer. This does not emerge from the CRF. In his model, Wickens (2002: 172) contemplates the use of three levels in the assignment of demand vectors to represent cases in which a sub-task recruits a certain resource to a high degree. Seeber applies this principle in the CLM of SI with visual input and of SIMTXT, where a demand vector of 0.5 is assigned in the case of multimodal integration due to beneficial modality effects (see §3.5.2.1 and §3.5.2.2). In theory, it could be possible to assign a higher demand vector, for instance 1.5, to further differentiate between the tools used for manual look-up, which may differ in the degree of recruitment both of visual-spatial resources and of manual-spatial resources at the production/monitoring stage. The different levels of recruitment of cognitive resources may thus be visually represented by the conflict matrices

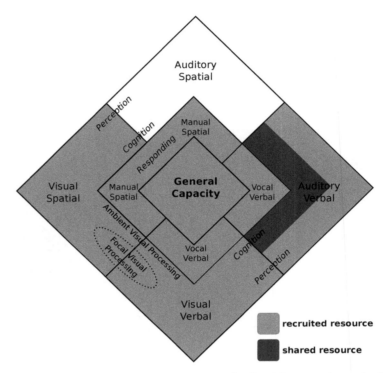

Figure 3.7: Cognitive Resource Footprint for SI with manual terminology lookup in a digital glossary or a CAI tool (Prandi 2018: 37)

of SI performed with the support of different tools, and could in turn result in higher total interference scores. At this stage, however, these remain theoretical speculations which need to be verified empirically.

3.6.3 Automatic terminology look-up

A CAI tool with ASR integration does not require active operation of the technological support by the interpreter. Specifically, the tool does not recruit manual-spatial resources. Nonetheless, visual-spatial and visual-verbal resources are recruited to locate and process the term visualised on the screen.

A further differentiation from tools with manual look-up lies in the potentially double advantage offered by speech recognition: the tool may support both comprehension and production processes. As observed by Pym (2011), technologies applied to translation and interpreting essentially externalises cognitive processes, acting as an external memory, or as a second brain. On the one hand, an ASR tool performs operations similar to those performed by the PL: it decodes the acoustic information and maps it against its internal lexicon, which results in "understanding", i.e. in the presentation of the term pronounced by the speaker on the screen. On the other hand, when coupled with an extraction tool, as is the case for the ASR integration in InterpretBank, it interacts with its "LTM" (the glossary) to retrieve the target-language equivalent. This is similar to the purpose of a translation memory, which retrieves pre-processed text segments facilitating the translator's work. Using an ASR tool may thus be valuable to facilitate terminology recognition during listening and, as for tools with manual look-up, to optimise the rendition of specialised terms during production.

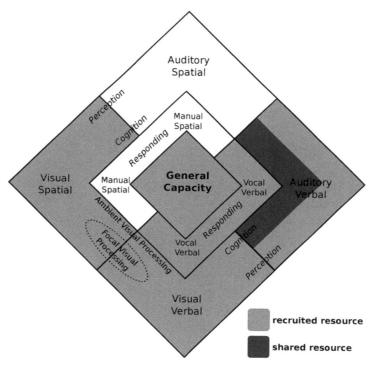

Figure 3.8: Cognitive Resource Footprint for SI with ASR support

The cognitive resource footprint for automatic terminology look-up during SI is represented in Figure 3.8. Of course, the advantage described above presupposes that the term recognition is successful. This is not the case in 100% of the cases with ASR: if the wrong term is recognised (for instance due to homophones or to a non-native accent), an imprecise or wrong suggestion, or a lack thereof, might go against the interpreter's expectations, resulting in irritation and thus potentially causing additional CL. Additionally, the system's latency also plays a role: long latencies lead to a drop in accuracy and fluency (for a dedicated analysis, see e.g. Montecchio 2021). Although current systems seem to perform sufficiently fast (Brüsewitz 2019), in real-life laptops do not always perform as expected and may become slow due to a number of reasons. If the term is not presented quickly enough on the screen, the potentially beneficial effect resulting from cross-channel redundancy may be hindered by a lack of temporal contiguity (see Mayer & Fiorella 2014): the tool's suggestions may be perceived as a distraction rather than as a facilitation (Van Cauwenberghe 2020).

A recent study by Chmiel, Janikowski & Lijewska (2020) has focused precisely on the issue of incongruence between auditory and written input, although in the framework of SI with text. The authors' findings indicate that when both auditory and written stimuli are presented, interpreters tend to focus on the visual modality. When the stimuli are incongruent, the visual modality interferes with the auditory input to the point that interpreters include incorrect units of information in their rendition – in this study, this happens especially for terms. Similar findings of imported errors from incorrect visual support for terms were also found in an experiment by Van Cauwenberghe (2020) on the provision of ASR support for specialised terminology. It is interesting that such effects were found not only for students (Van Cauwenberghe 2020), but also for professional interpreters. Chmiel, Janikowski & Lijewska (2020) also found that incongruent items tended to be fixated longer than congruent ones.

It may be argued that similar sources of irritation or distraction may also arise with manual terminology look-up: provided that the interpreters have correctly identified the term heard, they may not find it in the glossary, or may not find it quickly enough: in the case of very large glossaries, or if the interpreters have not had sufficient time to thoroughly prepare, this may not be a seldom occurrence. Even though they exceed the scope of the present study, the above-described scenarios are more than probable in real-life and would deserve further dedicated explorations, both in terms of their effect on cognition and on target-text production.

4 Measuring cognitive load

As pointed out in the literature, CL "cannot be observed and measured directly" (Chen 2017: 648). The reason for this is that CL is a multidimensional theoretical construct, the definition and nature of which are still debated both in the field of psychology, where it originated, and in Translation and Interpreting Studies (see §3.4). When aiming to estimate CL or to assess it empirically, researchers have therefore traditionally relied upon the observation and measurement of phenomena that arise as a consequence of high cognitive effort and reflect its variations (Paas et al. 2003, Ehrensberger-Dow et al. 2020). Several methods and measures have been adopted to this aim, good overviews of which are offered by Seeber (2013), based on Paas et al. (2003); Chen (2017), who also presents measures of workload, a construct derived from human workload studies; and Ehrensberger-Dow et al. (2020), who also report on innovative measures and thoroughly discuss their limitations. In this chapter, I review and discuss the methods and measures adopted in TPR for assessing CL as a key factor in the translation and interpreting process, in order to motivate and frame my methodological choices (§5.5.6).

Five main approaches may be identified in the measurement of CL or of the cognitive effort required by a particular task. The methods used to measure CL may be placed on a double continuum. On the one hand, methods may be divided according to the amount of intervention by the researcher. On the other hand, they may be classified by whether they require the active involvement of the experiment participant in providing cognitive-load related data, or whether this onus entirely falls on the researcher. This in turn reflects a more subjective versus a more objective type of measure. Due to inherent limitations of each type of measure, cognitive research often adopts a mixed-method paradigm, where several measures are combined "in a complementary fashion to elucidate the phenomenon of cognitive effort from different angles" (Ehrensberger-Dow et al. 2020: 222). For instance, performance measures may not provide reliable estimates of effort because a good or stable performance may mask the high mental effort invested to achieve this result. Combining this type of data with more direct measures of cognitive effort may unveil effects of a specific intervention on the load imposed by the task. As all methods present both advantages and potential drawbacks, as will be discussed in the following sections, a combination of methods represents a good way to maximise the potential of the individual methods while addressing their respective limitations (see §5.3).

4.1 Theoretical approaches

The first category of approaches for CL estimation comprises methods that do not require empirical experimentation and focus on the task, rather than on the task performer. They have been defined as analytical methods (Paas et al. 2003: 66) as they rely on a theoretical analysis of the task at hand conducted on the basis of models. Examples of this approach in interpreting research are Gile's Effort Models (1995, 2009) and Seeber's Cognitive Load Model of SI (2007, 2011) and of SI with text (Seeber 2017). Analytical methods rely on the analysis of task characteristics and are thus detached from individual performance. They represent an a-priori estimation of the CL generated by a particular task (Chen 2017: 647).

They may be useful in producing hypotheses to be tested empirically, especially in order to contrast the relative load imposed by similar tasks (see Seeber 2011, Seeber & Kerzel 2012). However, they may only provide an a-priori estimation of CL, not a direct measurement of cognitive or mental effort. Without experimental validation, they remain theoretical accounts of the postulated sources of CL for a task, and as a theory they are "unable to take into account individual differences" (Seeber 2013: 22).

4.2 Subjective approaches

Further on the continuum, subjective measures represent approaches which place the spotlight on the individual experience of the subject involved in the experiment. The adoption of subjective methods is based on the idea that "in an attempt of in-depth understanding and in order to find causal relationships, it is necessary to ask the subject" (Carl & Hansen 2011: 3). While this offers the advantage of highlighting individual differences and identifying phenomena not accounted for in theoretical models, it is open to "a possible contamination of data by memory and consciousness effects" (Seeber 2013: 19). Subjective measures rely on the active involvement of the participant in providing a personal estimate of the effort experienced during task performance, mainly through introspection, post-hoc questionnaires, retrospective interviews or think-aloud protocols (TAP) (ibid.).

Subjective data are often reflected in unidimensional or multidimensional psychometric rating scales (Chen 2017: 648). The latter can prove particularly useful in identifying the individual factors that may contribute to variations in CL. An example is represented by the NASA Task Load Index (NASA-TLX, Hart & Staveland 1988), widely used in mental workload research. It requires rating on six subscales measuring mental, physical and temporal demands, performance, effort and frustration, which can be altered or integrated depending on the research design. Chen (2017) identifies the NASA-TLX as a potentially useful asset in research on simultaneous and consecutive interpreting. An adaptation of this rating scale was recently applied by Gieshoff (2018) in combination with pupillometry measures and by Sun & Shreve (2014) in a study on translation difficulty. An important caveat of this approach is that the rating should be conducted immediately after task completion and "possibly be supplemented with cues (e.g., processed texts or recordings of the process) to facilitate recall" (Ehrensberger-Dow et al. 2020: 224).

As suggested by Gile & Lei (2020: 275), the inclusion of subjective methods in the research design, especially retrospection, may provide valuable clues for the interpretation of objective measures. A recent example is the adoption of retrospective questionnaires by Chmiel, Janikowski & Cieślewicz (2020) in a study on source language interference in sight translation and SI, which supported the research team in the interpretation of combined temporal measures and product analysis.

Subjective measures, however, present several disadvantages (see Ehrensberger-Dow et al. 2020). First, careful consideration is required in the choice of research devices to collect subjective data. In using questionnaires, one must consider that forced-choice questionnaires limit the subjects' reporting and might prime their answers, while open questions may be more difficult to process statistically. The issue of priming may also affect the outcomes of interviews due to the presence of the researcher, which may also reduce the participant's willingness to report experiences perceived as embarrassing, not noteworthy, or potentially undermining their perceived professionalism. This reluctance is an issue often encountered in studies involving professional interpreters as subjects. Retrospection must occur close to the experimental intervention to be effective, but this may significantly extend the experiment's duration and potentially result in fatigue effects. Finally, TAPs have the disadvantage of potentially slowing down the process due to the concurrent verbalisation and task performance (Jakobsen 2003). Additionally, only what is verbalised will become known to the researcher, while other important aspects may not emerge from studies only adopting subjective measures.

4.3 Performance measures

Performance measures combine the advantage of analysing and comparing individual performances with the measurement of objective parameters. In cognitive psychology, they have traditionally been applied using primary task measures, i.e. by measuring task performance, or by requiring the concurrent performance of a second task and measuring how its performance is affected by variations in the CL generated by the first (secondary task measures). In order to provide reliable indications of CL, experiments conducted using this approach require a stringent empirical design in order to avoid effects due to variables not controlled by the researcher (Seeber 2013: 20). This may require sacrificing some ecological validity to avoid uncontrolled effects. When high ecological validity is to be maintained, secondary task measures may be unsuitable, as they interfere with the main task (Ehrensberger-Dow et al. 2020: 227). A downside of using performance measures is that they often involve human raters, which may affect the degree of objectivity of these measures and requires strictly defined evaluation criteria.

In studies on translation and interpreting, the two most common aspects of performance analysed are accuracy and disfluencies, especially pauses. This is based on the assumption that performance suffers from heightened or excessive cognitive effort and that issues of cognitive resource management may therefore emerge on the linguistic surface.

4.3.1 Accuracy

As discussed in §1.1.2, accuracy has been identified as an important indicator of performance, both for translation and for interpreting. Accuracy may be assessed either holistically, i.e. on the global level of the text, or componentially (Tiselius 2015: 3), on an analytical level, i.e. by evaluating errors or omissions in individual components of the product (paragraphs, sentences, or words). A potential drawback of assessing the accuracy of the target text, be it written or oral, is that it is necessary to clearly define and describe the scale used for the evaluation. In some cases, the involvement of the researcher in the evaluation may contribute to reduce discrepancies between evaluators (Hansen 2009: 395–397). Studies conducted on the product of machine translation engines have addressed the limitations of human evaluation by adopting established taxonomies for word or phrase-based assessment of MT, for instance in the area of post-editing studies (e.g. Vardaro et al. 2019, Marzouk 2021).[1] Such taxonomies may, however, also

---

[1] The reader may refer to §1.1.2 for an overview of said evaluation frameworks.

be adopted to evaluate the product of human translations, particularly through a contrastive approach with the MT output. An example is the study by Carl & Buch-Kromann (2010) on the differences between student and professional translators. The study used BLEU scores and human evaluations to assess the accuracy and fluency of the target texts, combining performance measures with behavioural measures (eye movements and keystrokes, see §4.4).

Taxonomies of error types aimed at assessing the accuracy of the linguistic output in interpreting were proposed e.g. by Barik (1971), Altman (1994), Waden-sjö (1993: 2002) and Napier (2004, 2016). The dimensions of accuracy range from the word to the text level and the error and omission categories may reach a high level of granularity, but may also be very simple depending on the scope of the study. For instance, in a previous contribution (Prandi 2015a,b), I evaluated the accuracy of the terms interpreted with a simple dychotomic classification of "terms translated as per glossary" (yes/no).

An issue in the assessment of accuracy in interpreting, mostly operationalised in terms of errors and omissions, lies in the fact that the taxonomy tends to be modified or devised anew by each researcher. Therefore, "there are nearly as many error classification systems as there are empirical studies requiring an overall assessment of source–target correspondence" (Pöchhacker 2004: 143). A limitation of the application of widely used frameworks for the assessment of translation as discussed above is that they have not been explicitly formulated for the oral modality. Consequently, they need to be adapted for the evaluation of the interpreting performance. An example can be found in Xu (2015). In her doctoral thesis on corpus-driven preparation for interpreters, she incorporated, merged and redefined several error categories from BlackJack, MeLLANGE and SAE J2450. Her error categories included incorrect terms, omissions, inappropriate collocations, grammatical errors, pronunciation errors and semantic errors. The scoring rubric was used to assess the accuracy of interpretations for which students had prepared either following a traditional approach or using corpus-driven terminology extraction. In TPR, a popular evaluation framework used to measure the accuracy of the translated product is MQM (see §1.1.2). As will be discussed in §6.2.1, MQM and other standardised frameworks for quality evaluation in translation may also be adapted to interpreting (as in Xu 2015) and used as methods for accuracy measurement in the area of CAI.

4.3.2 Dysfluencies and pauses

In psycholinguistics, pauses in speech production have been investigated as correlates of cognitive effort (e.g. Goldman-Eisler 1972) and this association has been confirmed in a number of studies (e.g. Dragsted 2004, Lacruz et al. 2012, O'Brien et al. 2014, Kumpulainen 2015). In spoken discourse, interruptions in the speech flow may, however, also be adopted intentionally as a rhetorical device for emphasis or simply to draw breath. In addition, pause patterns (duration and frequency) tend to vary from each individual to the next (O'Brien 2006). Hence, the interpretation of pauses as indicative of cognitive processing or speech planning is not unequivocal, and is therefore often complemented by other measures in research on translation and interpreting. In SI, since the source speech unfolds continuously during the task, pauses may also suggest that the interpreter is waiting for more linguistic material from the speaker. Furthermore, the position of pauses in the rendition may also reflect an alignment of the interpreter's output to the speaker's rhetorical style.

Methodologically, measuring pauses also poses a number of difficulties, for instance in establishing what should be considered as a filled or silent pause and in determining the minimum duration of pauses. Current audio processing tools represent useful research aids as they allow to automatically identify silent pauses according to a set of criteria selected by the researcher. Other types of dysfluencies usually require manual tagging and counting (Gieshoff 2021: 185). This can make the analysis of dysfluencies other than silent pauses rather laborious. For this reason, depending on the amount of data, researchers may choose to investigate macro or micro-locations of pauses (Dragsted & Hansen 2008).

In interpreting, different levels of intentionality behind pause patterns emerge from studies comparing students and professional interpreters. Students' pauses tend to reflect hesitations and more effortful processing (e.g. Tissi 2001, Mead 2002, 2005). Conversely, experienced interpreters show more deliberateness in their pause patterns (see Cecot 2001, Ahrens 2005, 2007). Therefore, studies involving students as test subjects may find the analysis of pauses as indicators of cognitive effort useful. In a study comparing written translation and sight translation, Dragsted & Hansen (2009) calculated the number and duration of pauses to contrast text production patterns for interpreting and translation, suggesting that the inclusion of the oral modality in translator training may improve the output quality. A recent example of studies using pause patterns as correlates of CL is provided by Gieshoff (2018, 2021), who involved 14 interpreting students as her test subjects and used silent pauses to contrast SI with and without visible lip movements. Filled pauses (*uhm*) were analysed as indicators of cognitive effort in a corpus study by Plevoets & Defrancq (2016, 2018) and were found to correlate with the informational load of the input speech.

Pause-related metrics have also been successfully developed and implemented as indicators of cognitive effort in translation and post-editing (for a clear overview, see Lacruz et al. 2016). For instance, a study on the coordination of comprehension and production processes in translation by Dragsted & Hansen (2008) found that pauses indicate a coordination effort due to the transition between the two phases. In her study on post-editing, O'Brien (2006) found that pauses helped in the identification of a correlation between source text quality and post-editing effort (p. 17). In a study contrasting spoken translation (i.e. written translation obtained through target text dictation) and post-editing of MT, Carl, Lacruz, et al. (2016a) analysed the pause structure of target text production, finding a more coherent generation of translations when dictation was used. In research on the post-editing process, the two most widely used metrics are the average pause ratio (APR) and the pause-to-word ratio (PWR). Both were developed after O'Brien's (2006) influential work on post-editing, where she suggested a simple pause ratio measured as the total pause duration divided by the total duration of the post-editing task for a certain segment. The APR (O'Brien et al. 2014) is calculated as the average pause time divided by the average post-editing time per word for each segment. The APR was found to be reflective of cognitive effort, as the prediction that more numerous, shorter pauses may indicate more effortful post-editing was confirmed in a study on post-editing (Spanish to English) and later found not to be influenced by the pause threshold chosen (Lacruz et al. 2014). The PWR (ibid.) indicates the number of pauses divided by the number of source words per post-edited segment. This measure correlates strongly with APR as well as with other ratings of source quality (e.g. HTER, see Snover et al. 2006). This measure was further refined in Lacruz et al. (2018), where ranges of pauses of different lengths were considered in the analysis. Clusters of short monitoring pauses were found to correlate with cognitive effort during post-editing, suggesting that they might be indicative of monitoring processes.

4.4 Behavioural approaches

The collection of behavioural data, together with neurophysiological, hematic and cardiac correlates (see §4.5), occupies the other extreme of the objectivity continuum. Behavioural measures do not rely on the subjective evaluation by participants nor on the product-oriented evaluation of the performance, but rather on the measurement of phenomena arising in the translator's or interpreter's brain and body that have been empirically linked with cognitive activity (Jakobsen 2017: 22).

The higher degree of objectivity of these approaches represents a clear advantage compared to other measures: translation events may be measured and analysed to gain insight into the translation processes which guide the participant's behaviour. This fundamental assumption, underlying cognitive psychology and neuroscience, foregrounds the usefulness of empirical methods derived from these disciplines for the investigation of the translation and interpreting process. However, TPR has also developed its own additional measures and analysis tools to explore the translation process, hence the widespread adoption of mixed-method approaches in this research area.

In the following subsections, I discuss the main behavioural measures which have been adopted to evaluate the cognitive load and effort involved in various types of translation activity. Behavioural measures may be divided in the two overarching categories of measures of time and measures of eye movement.

4.4.1 Time-related measures

Both for translation and for interpreting, it is generally assumed that there exists a "rough correlation between time spent on translating a word or passage and the cognitive effort invested in solving a problem or in making a decision between competing solutions or strategies" (Jakobsen 2017: 30). Metrics based on the overall time required by the language processing task in question or by a sub-process thereof, or related to the transposition of individual elements of the source text into the target language may therefore provide useful and objective insights into the cognitive effort exerted by the participant. In research on written translation, post-editing and audio-visual translation, the use of time-based measures as indicators of the cognitive effort involved in producing a translation is facilitated by the use of keystroke logging, or key-logging, which enables a direct exploration of how the translation process unfolds over time. The advantage of the method is evident for the exploration of various types of translation activities, as testified by the development of dedicated tools, such as Scriptlog (Andersson et al. 2006), Translog and Translog-II (Jakobsen 2006), and Inputlog (Leijten & Van Waes 2013). However, key-logging may also hold the potential to gain further insight into time-related aspects of human-machine interaction during computer-supported or computer-mediated interpreting. An example may be the automatic recording of the user activity in CAI tools to produce log files which can be used for empirical analysis, as has been done in studies using InterpretBank (see Biagini 2015, Prandi 2015a,b, 2018).

With or without the support of key-logging, time measures have largely been employed in studies on interpreting as well as on translation. Two main types of time-based measures may be identified: on the one hand, speed-based measures, on the other, time-lag measures.

4.4.1.1 Speed and task time

The first subgroup of measures concerns the amount of time required to produce a unit of the target text or the entire target text. These measures are based on the assumption that difficult tasks tend to take longer than easier tasks (O'Brien 2008: 87). An example may be word production time (WPT), i.e. the total time required to produce a word in the target text in translation, including revisions (Carl, Lacruz, et al. 2016b: 3). Another example may be found in O'Brien (2008), where processing speed was measured to establish the cognitive effort involved in the translation of segments with the support of different levels of fuzzy matches in the TM of a CAT tool environment.

On a broader level, some study designs may obtain useful information by measuring the time required to perform the entire task. For instance, Jakobsen & Hvelplund (2008) compared "task time" in reading for comprehension, for translation, while interpreting and while translating. Chmiel, Janikowski & Cieślewicz (2020) measured "translation time" to compare SI and sight translation. This approach presents some limitations for interpreting, since especially SI is inherently constrained by the speaker's speech rate and because individual differences in the participants' delivery rate may be expected to play a role. Therefore, these factors should be taken into account when adopting overall measures of speed as indicators of effort.

4.4.1.2 Time lag: EVS and EKS

The second type of time-related measures focus on the time-span elapsing between the time of production of a specific element in the target text (written or oral) and its appearance or perception in the source text. Often described with the general term of "décalage" (Timarová 2015: 418), this time-span may represent different aspects of the process according to the object of investigation. Perhaps the two most widely adopted measures of this kind are the ear-voice span (EVS) in interpreting, especially simultaneous, and the eye-key span (EKS) in translation, which was derived from the first (Dragsted & Hansen 2008).

The EVS has been used not only to explore temporal aspects of the interpreting process (Pöchhacker 2004: 117), such as processing speed, but it has also been shown to provide a reliable indication of cognitive effort in SI (e.g. in Treisman 1965, Barik 1971, Shlesinger 1998, Timarová et al. 2011).

In interpreting, the duration of the EVS is taken as an indicator of cognitive effort: a shorter time required by the interpreter to produce the target-text equivalent of the source text, or of a specific source-text element, is generally understood as suggesting faster and, hence, less effortful processing. Timarová et al.

(2011) reviewed the various methods used to measure time lag in interpreting and compared EVS with EKS. The different methods used for the measurement of time-lag depend on the specific object of investigation, and can range from a broader and more surface-level analysis of EVS to establish reference values for SI, to a comparison of mean or median values across tasks or even to explore whether local variations in EVS reflect variations in cognitive processing. The most common approach is to measure time lag in number of seconds, but number of words has also been used.

In literature, the average EVS for professional conference interpreters has been identified as comprised between 2s and 4s (see for instance Barik 1973, Lederer 1978, Oléron & Nanpon 2002, Christoffels & De Groot 2004, Defrancq 2015, Timarová et al. 2011), though shorter and longer time lags have also been observed. It may even be negative "where true anticipation occurs" (Timarová 2015: 419). Overall, however, research has linked an EVS longer than 4s with a loss in accuracy (Lee 2002, 2003, Timarová et al. 2014). It is generally assumed that values longer than these point to processing issues on the part of the interpreter and may negatively affect the perception of quality, as they often result in long or frequent filled or silent pauses. However, the EVS has been found to vary both between and within tasks and to be influenced by external factors (e.g. the speaker's output rate, language combination) as well as by individual factors (e.g. the interpreter's own delivery rate, individual cognitive makeup, experience). For instance, professional interpreters have been found to have both longer (Moser-Mercer et al. 2000) and shorter EVS (Timarová et al. 2014) than trainees: this discrepancy might be interpreted as an indication that they are better able to adjust their décalage than interpreting students thanks to their expertise.

The interpretation of the EVS as indicative of cognitive effort is, therefore, not straightforward. This is particularly relevant when the EVS is not measured as a broad indicator of processing speed, but to contrast the speed of rendition of individual elements of the source text. Nonetheless, the EVS may be considered as a standard measure of cognitive effort in interpreting, and has been widely adopted in interpreting research, often in combination with further measures to address the already mentioned limitations.

The use of the EKS to investigate mental effort in translation has become possible thanks to the interfacing of key-logging and eyetracking (see §4.4.2), particularly with the development of dedicated data collection environments such as *Translog-II* (Jakobsen 2006). Thanks to the integration of a gaze-to-word mapping tool, Translog-II allows to effectively triangulate gaze data and participants' typing behaviour, which provides detailed insight into the unfolding of the translation, post-editing or subtitling process and offers valuable clues on the load imposed by the subprocesses involved and on the strategies guiding the user's choices. Studies using EKS have produced telling results on the underlying processes of translation. For instance, Dragsted (2010) identified two different translating styles typical of professional and budding translators. The first favour an integrated style, where comprehension, production and revision processes are strictly interlinked, as shown by the shorter EKS, comparable to that of simultaneous interpreters (an average 2.8s in her group of participants). The second tend to work sequentially, as shown by the longer EKS (7.2s on average), which indicates longer time elapsing between the comprehension and the translation of a specific text unit.

4.4.2 Eye movement measures and eyetracking

The measurement of movements of the eye and of other phenomena linked to the eye physiology is possible thanks to a technique called eyetracking. Put simply, eyetracking is "a technology for recording eye movements" (Jakobsen 2019: 398).

The adoption of the eyetracking methodology for cognitive inquiries into different translation activities rests on two fundamental theoretical tenets, subsumed in Just & Carpenter's (1980: 331) eye-mind hypothesis and immediacy assumption. The eye-mind hypothesis postulates that observable eye movements, i.e. physical manifestations of overt attention, are strictly linked with covert attention and cognitive processes. Therefore, the object of visual attention is assumed to be the object of cognitive attention (Hvelplund 2017: 250) and the measurement of eye movements can be indicative of concurring mental processes. According to the immediacy assumption, there is no "lag between what is being fixated [i.e. looked at for a period of time long enough to process it] and the hidden cognitive processes that take place inside the mind" (ibid.). The eye-mind assumption has however been challenged by the notion of mind drifting (see Posner 1980, Smallwood & Schooler 2006): it is possible for the mind to start wandering while looking at an object, a phenomenon commonly experienced in everyday life. This poses an important limitation on the eye-mind hypothesis, namely that this mind drifting cannot be observed nor measured, as it is not reflected in eye movements.

Additionally, it has been empirically demonstrated that there is a certain lag between the focus of visual attention and what is being cognitively processed at a given moment (Jakobsen 2019: 409). Essentially, the eyes "seem to behave somewhat like a dog on a leash held by the mind rather than there being a perfectly straightforward relationship" (Jakobsen 2017: 34). Nonetheless, as observed by Hvelplund (2014, 2017), while the researcher should be aware of these potential drawbacks, mind drifting during a cognitively taxing task such as translation is probably a rare occurrence. In interpreting, the probability of a cognitive shift of this kind can reasonably be assumed to be even more remote, particularly during SI due to the immediacy of the task. Owing to this, eye movements can reliably be interpreted as "correlates of cognitive processing in translation" and interpreting, as validated in neighbouring disciplines (Hvelplund 2014: 211).

Eyetracking has been used in several research areas, chiefly psychology, psycholinguistics and cognitive sciences as a way to empirically investigate human behaviour, cognition and attention (Hvelplund 2017: 248), and at a more basic level "to study the physiological mechanics of human eye movements" (Jakobsen 2019: 398). The potential of this technique, however, makes it suitable to the investigation of behaviour, cognition and attention allocation also in cognitively taxing activities such as translation and interpreting, as will be discussed in §4.4.2.3. In the following sections, I describe the equipment used in eyetracking and introduce the main measurements, with a focus on fixation-based and related metrics, as they have found wide application in TPR and in studies on human-computer interaction and may therefore also be applied to cognitive inquiries into interpreter-computer interactions.

4.4.2.1 Equipment and applications

The device used to produce a recording of where the eyes are looking is called eyetracker. What is recorded is not the image of the eye itself, but rather the reflection of infrared light on the cornea of the eye (Duchowski 2017: 54). The reflected light is recorded at a rate comprised between 30 and 2,000 Hz, which corresponds to 30 to 2,000 samples recorded per second (Jakobsen 2019: 399).

Different types of eyetracker are available, each presenting benefits and potential drawbacks. Head-mounted eyetrackers, for instance, often used in combination with chin rests, bite bars or forehead rests, allow for high quality data, as the precision of the eyetracker is enhanced by the steady position of the subject's head. On the other hand, it poses severe restrictions on the participants' freedom of movement, which may make this type of eyetracker unsuitable for certain types of research. On the other end of the spectrum are tracking eyeglasses, which offer the advantage of being very portable and of allowing researchers to take their investigation out of the laboratory, as they make it possible to record eye movements on several planes, i.e. on surfaces different from a computer monitor. These eyetrackers, however, have the limitation of allowing recordings only at slow speed (30 Hz). A compromise between the two is offered by stand-alone or attachable remote eyetrackers (see Ehrensberger-Dow 2014).

They are limited to the monitor they are integrated in or mounted on, but they are relatively unobtrusive as they do not require to be worn by the participant. At the same time, they allow for high-frequency recordings, essential due to the speed of eye movements, especially during translation (Jakobsen 2017: 36).

Despite its vast potential for the objective exploration of cognition and attention, the eyetracking methodology presents some limitations. First, it requires strict experimental conditions, as the lack of control of aspects such as light intensity or the participants' distance from the screen may affect data quality and results. Second, while a certain level of control can be achieved through a proper laboratory set-up (Rösener 2016), other aspects, particularly those linked to participants' characteristics and behaviour, may pose non-negligible issues to the researcher. A common example is the type of glasses or lenses worn by participants, which may create artefacts or impede the correct recording of eye movements. Finally, stress due to the experimental conditions cannot be ignored, although it may be contained by the use of remote eyetrackers which are less invasive and do not require a modification of the task being performed. Despite being contactless, however, they still require calibration, which makes the experimental condition more apparent. Nonetheless, as pointed out in the literature (e.g. Hvelplund 2014: 206, Hansen 2008: 390), stress may be perceived by participants due to the simple fact of being observed during task performance (the so-called white coat effect). While these potential drawbacks and external influencing factors cannot be eliminated entirely and should be considered during experimental design and data analysis, the advantages offered by eyetracking far outweigh its limitations, which explains its popularity in translation process research.

4.4.2.2 Fixation-based measures

Eyetracking allows to conduct several types of measurements. The most popular eyetracking measures are fixation-based measures and saccades, quick eye movements occurring between fixations (Poole & Ball 2005). From fixations and saccades, other metrics may be derived, for instance gaze measurements. Eyetracking also allows to collect additional types of data related to eye movements and eye physiology, such as blink rate and pupil size/dilation (see §4.5.3).

Due to the popularity of the eyetracking technique, a series of metrics have become established as the norm of reference for the investigation of translation in a cognitive framework, often borrowing from neighbouring disciplines. At the same time, TPR has offered further confirmation of the ability of certain indicators to account for specific variations in cognitive effort or in the allocation of attentional resources, and to measure the "number and patterns of translation process activities, the duration of and switches between activities, or the fluency in production" (Ehrensberger-Dow et al. 2020: 225).

In particular, fixation measures and measures derived therefrom have been widely used as dependent variables in TPR to determine the cognitive effort involved in the translation process, as they are more sensitive to linguistic factors (Staub & Rayner 2007). For this reason, as they will be relevant for the present inquiry, here I focus on these measures.[2]

Fixation-based measures provide useful indications concerning the "quality and intensity of cognitive attention in a task" (Jakobsen 2019: 402). A fixation is a period of time during which the eye remains stable (fixated) on a target, which is necessary for the ocular system to bring the object into focus (Duchowski 2017: 46). Its length is usually understood to be comprised between 200 and 300 ms in reading (Rayner 1998: 373, Holmqvist 2011: 381), but it "may be as long as several seconds" (Karsh & Breitenbach 1983, Young & Sheena 1975), and as short as 30–40ms (Holmqvist 2011: 413). In particular, the duration and number of fixations index the amount of cognitive attention on the fixated object or area of interest (AOI). At the same time, they indicate the intensity of cognitive effort required for the performance of a task, for instance for the processing of individual words or phrases in translation. In literature, longer or more numerous fixations have often been associated with "a deeper and more effortful cognitive processing" (Holmqvist 2011: 413, Hvelplund 2014: 212, Lacruz et al. 2016: 1214).

Among early measures, first fixation durations are particularly indicative of the amount of attention generated by an item, especially in reading when the area of interest is a single word (see Conklin et al. 2018: 124). Among late measures, fixation count and total gaze time, also defined as total fixation duration or total fixation time, are also used as indicators of attention and processing effort. If the interest is in how processing unfolds over time, time-related fixation measures may provide useful insights. Two widely used metrics of this kind are time to first fixation, which indicates how much time elapses before the AOI is fixated for the first time, and average fixation duration (Conklin et al. 2018: 129). Studies concerned with the focus of attention of a translator or of an interpreter may investigate gaze or fixation patterns to identify which area of the visual stimulus attracted the participant's attention (Ehrensberger-Dow et al. 2020).

In the following section, I present some examples of how the method and measures discussed above have been applied in TPR, with a focus on inquiries into

---

[2]A thorough description of eyetracking measures applicable to translation process research goes beyond the scope of the present contribution. For a comprehensive discussion, a useful reference may be found in Conklin et al. (2018).

interpreting. While the following overview has no ambition of completeness, it will contribute to highlight the role of eyetracking as a useful methodology for TPR.

4.4.2.3 Eyetracking in Translation Process Research

The wide application of eyetracking to the study of the translation process is due to its ability to offer objective, real-time measures of the mental processes involved in translation, often without requiring excessive manipulation of the task itself. In TPR, eyetracking measures have been widely adopted, often in combination with other behavioural measures as well as subjective and performance measures or with physiological methods such as PET or fMRI (see §4.5). Over the past twenty years, the eyetracking method has been used to study the cognitive processes underpinning translation, subtitling, post-editing and interpreting. The eyetracking technique has been applied to the exploration of a variety of aspects linked to the translation process and profession, such as "translation expertise, competence and experience, cognitive effort, reading in translation, human-computer and human-information interaction, metaphor processing, directionality, reception of translated material" (Hvelplund 2017: 251). As such, eyetracking research in translation and interpreting represents a relatively recent, albeit very productive innovation in Translation and Interpreting Studies.

Particularly relevant to the present contribution is the adoption of eyetracking as a research methodology to study the processing effort required by different translation tasks, specifically to explore how cognitive resources are allocated, distributed, and coordinated during translation or during specific translation subtasks (Hvelplund 2017: 254). A large body of research has adopted eyetracking to this aim. For instance, a number of studies have successfully investigated reading for and during translation with eyetracking, which has become a standard methodology in this field of research. Jakobsen & Hvelplund (2008) compared reading for comprehension, as preparation for translating, for sight translation and during translation. In addition to time on task, they analysed fixation counts, average fixation duration and gaze times, finding a constant progression in all of these metrics from the first to the last type of translation task. A similar experiment contrasting reading for comprehension, for oral summarisation and for sight translation conducted by Alves et al. (2012) found longer fixation durations for sight translation. Schaeffer & Carl (2014) measured translation effort in the production of the target-text equivalent for literal translations by measuring gaze and translation time, while in a comparable study, Dragsted (2012) analysed total reading time and number of fixations as indicators of translation effort.

To study interpreting, the eyetracking methodology has been adopted more extensively in research on modes of interpreting which involve a written and/or visual component (e.g. sight translation and consecutive interpreting) or for settings which require greater interaction (dialogue interpreting). It has recently seen a revival due to the low intrusiveness, high temporal resolution and relatively limited cost of eyetrackers, especially of the remote type, which interfere less with the interpreting process.

The first study applying eyetracking to interpreting comes from outside Interpreting Studies. McDonald & Carpenter (1981) used eyetracking to investigate how ambiguous phrases are interpreted and parsed in sight translation, comparing the comprehension and the target text production phase and including the mechanisms underlying the identification of errors during the task.

A series of studies adopting the eyetracking method followed, which focused on further testing the applicability of the method (in conjunction with fMRI) to the study of directionality in interpreting (Chang 2009), of sight translation performed by trainee interpreters (Chmiel & Mazur 2013) and professional interpreters (Hansen & Dragsted 2007), also in terms of "syntactic disruption and visual interference" in sight translation (Shreve et al. 2010). In these studies, fixation-based measures were used, often as a combination of several metrics, chiefly fixation duration and counts. An example is Dragsted & Hansen (2009) who combined these metrics with heatmaps and key-logging to contrast written and sight translation, elucidating differences in how interpreters and translators process the source text.

More recent studies using fixation durations are the one by Seubert (2019) on visual input in SI and by Seeber et al. (2020) on multimodal processing during SI with text. Seubert used fixation durations and gaze patterns to explore the effects of various sources of visual and written information on professional interpreters' attention allocation. Seeber et al. (2020) investigated visual attention measuring the proportion of fixations and mean dwell time on five areas of the written input (see also §3.5.2.2). Another application of eyetracking to research on interpreting lies in the use of pupillary measures, discussed in §4.5.3.

Eyetracking has not only been used to explore simultaneous or sight interpreting, but may also yield valuable insight into visual attention and cognitive load and effort in dialogue interpreting, characterised by a higher degree of interaction. A first step in this direction was recently taken by Tiselius & Sneed (2020), who used eyetracking glasses to collect data on the gaze patterns of experienced and inexperienced interpreters during dialogue interpreting. They suggest that gaze aversion during interpreting may index cognitive effort. In addition, the use of eyetracking may yield valuable information on how the note-taking process unfolds, as explored for instance by Kuang (2019).

Particularly interesting is the recent turn of eyetracking TPR towards an investigation of the interaction between translators and the tools they use as support for the translation task, from the consultation of digital resources such as websites and online terminological databases, to the use of CAT tools and translation workbenches during post-editing. As observed by Jakobsen (2019: 403), "a fascinating feature of gaze data is that they can be interpreted both as documentation of how well an interface design works, how well a translator interacts with a computer program, and as documentation of a translator's mental effort in carrying out a task". This characteristic of eyetracking measures may therefore prove useful to study the interaction between interpreters and CAI tools. Previous research has exploited eyetracking to this aim in studies on translation tasks of different kinds. An early example of this application is offered by O'Brien (2006), who used eyetracking to explore how the use of translation memories affects cognitive effort, finding that exact matches elicit the lowest effort, as indicated by pupil size. More recently, Alves et al. (2016) explored cognitive effort in post-editing tasks conducted in two different environments, i.e. with interactive and standard machine translation, using the metrics fixation count and fixation duration (average and median) as correlates of effort. Carl, Aizawa, et al. (2016) contrasted post-editing and translation dictation through speech recognition combining key-logging and time-based measures (e.g. translation duration, translation dictation duration) with gaze durations (see also Carl, Lacruz, et al. 2016a). In a study on the processes of error identification and correction in machine translated texts and post-edited machine translations, Vardaro et al. (2019) combined early measures (first fixation durations and first pass durations) and late measures (total reading time and regression path durations). Finally, in the area of audio-visual translation, Tardel et al. (2021) investigated cognitive effort by combining total fixation count, average visit duration, total reading time, relative attention to video and video replay time (p. 122).

4.5 Physiological measures

Additional methods have also been used to explore cognitive processing in written and oral translation, such as measures of "cardiac, hematic, electro-dermal, ocular, muscular and cerebral responses" (Seeber 2013: 25). Since they are based on the activation of the autonomic nervous system (Ehrensberger-Dow et al. 2020: 224), these measures are less subjective and are language independent, which increases comparability between studies. In addition, like gaze-related metrics, these measures are continuous, thus allowing for a detailed account of local variations of CL.

Some methods relying on physiological measures can, however, be rather intrusive and require expensive equipment as well as a high level of expertise by the researcher for their successful integration into the empirical design.

Because of their complexity, cost and intrusiveness, most psycho-physiological approaches have found rare application in studies on translation and interpreting. Nonetheless, physiological measures may substantiate claims about CL variations in translation and interpreting tasks because of their objectivity. In studies on CL in interpreting, physiological methods have mainly comprised measures of the brain, of the eye, and of the heart (Chen 2017: 649), which is why I focus on these metrics in the following sections.

4.5.1 Brain measures

Brain imaging methods comprise different techniques, either exploiting the electrical or magnetic activity of nerve cells (i.e. electroencephalography (EEG) and magnetoencephalography (MEG)) or hemodynamic changes in the brain (i.e. positron emission tomography (PET), functional magnetic resonance imaging (fMRI), and near-infrared spectroscopy (NIS)). Tommola et al. (2000) provide an accessible overview and discussion of the different methods. Research on the neurocognition of translation and interpreting has employed mostly the EEG, the fMRI and the PET methods.

For instance, Petsche et al. (1993) used electroencephalography (EEG) to identify which areas of the brain activate in SI and in shadowing. EEG is a non-invasive and affordable method, which provides excellent temporal resolution. When used to investigate the interpreting process, however, EEG presents an important limitation: because mandibular movements can generate artefacts, the tasks must be performed covertly, which may give rise to a series of effects unaccounted for and also prevent its combination with performance measures. Additionally, its spatial resolution is quite poor, a limitation which MEG does not have, although the issue of artefacts remains also with this method. Due to these limitations, the use of EEG has been more popular in studies on translation. Some examples are Oster's (2019) work on the translation of cognates or the extensive body of research by García (e.g. 2013, 2015, 2019).[3]

---

[3]An excellent introduction to neurocognitive inquiries into translation and interpreting is provided by García (2019).

Functional magnetic resonance imaging (fMRI) is also a non-invasive technique, which offers the opposite advantages and limitations compared to EEG: it can be useful for the localisation of brain functions due to its high spatial resolution, while its low temporal resolution and high sensitivity to head movements (including overt speech) limit its application to study interpreting, not least because the scanner environment is very noisy (Tommola et al. 2000). Nonetheless, research on the neural basis of interpreting has successfully utilised the method. Some examples are Hervais-Adelman et al. (2011, 2015) or research on directionality by Chang (2009) and Kalderon (2017). Kalderon used the method also to explore the effect of interpreting expertise in brain activation.

PET is a highly invasive method, as it requires the intravenous administration of radioactive ligands (Seeber 2013: 25). This may severely limit sample size. While its temporal resolution is limited, PET provides good spatial resolution and "seems to be the only one that allows the investigation of the entire multi-effort process of SI" (Tommola et al. 2000: 18). In Price et al. (1999), PET was used to compare translation and interpreting, while Rinne et al. (2000) and Tommola et al. (2000) used PET to compare speech shadowing and SI, including the effect of directionality on activation patterns.

4.5.2 Heart rate measures

Cardiac system measures such as heart rate, heart rate variability (i.e. variation in time intervals between consecutive heart beats, see Thayer et al. 2012), and blood pressure have been used to measure the impact of a variety of language processing tasks on stress (e.g. Klonowicz 1994, Korpal 2017, Kurz 2003). However, as higher stress experienced may signal increased cognitive effort, such measures may prove useful in explorations on mental effort in the translation and interpreting process.

Heart rate measures have been adopted to study the interpreting process, especially after what has been defined as the "psycho-affective turn in Interpreting Studies" (Korpal 2016: 298), i.e. a renewed interest for the role of psycho-affective factors in interpreting, for instance for aptitude testing (see also Chabasse 2009). As reported by Korpal (2016: 304), additional markers of stress used in interpreting research are skin conductance level (e.g. Kurz 2002, 2003), cortisol concentration (used in Blumenthal et al. 2006 and in AIIC 2002), and IgM levels (Moser-Mercer 2005), often used in combination with and integrated by subjective measures, such as self-reported measures of stress. In TPR, an example of the combination of multiple types of measures, including an extensive set of heart rate measures, can be found in Herbig et al. (2021), who explored how objective measures relate to the subjectively reported CL in MTPE.

4.5.3 Pupillary measures

Among physiological approaches, the collection of pupillometry data represents the least invasive and the more suited method to be applied to investigations of the interpreting process, in particular of SI, which, for its continuous and real-time nature, does not easily allow for the adoption of more invasive techniques, as discussed above.

Pupillary measures are also often used in the investigation of cognitive processes and attention. The pupil size and dilation, measured in millimetres, are taken to index the amount of processing effort exerted by a test subject to perform a certain task. The rationale behind the use of measures of pupil size and dilation in cognitive studies lies in the assumption that the diameter of the pupil reflects the difficulty of the task at hand or the working load posed by it (see for instance Hess & Polt 1964, Just & Carpenter 1993, Kahneman & Beatty 1966). The wider the pupil, the higher the difficulty and/or the working load. The interpretation of pupil measures is, however, far from being this straightforward, as the pupil has been found to contract and dilate in relation to a wide range of stimuli and psychological and affective states. The diameter of the pupil can be influenced not only by workload, but also by emotion and anticipation, fatigue, diabetes, age, pain and drugs (see Holmqvist 2011: 426 for a detailed discussion). However, some of these factors can be controlled experimentally, for instance by excluding participants with relevant pre-existing conditions or of a certain age group from data collection. To ensure good data quality, it is preferable to work with systems that have "a fixed distance between camera and eye" (Holmqvist 2011: 530). Remote eyetrackers may expose the researcher to the risk of introducing artifacts in the data. Most importantly, pupils react particularly to changes in luminance, which requires a stable source of light and a controlled environment during data collection. Ideally, the study design should include stimuli with equal brightness and contrast. A major complication in using pupillometry to investigate cognitive processing lies in the fact that pupillary responses do not occur immediately after stimulus presentation, but with a certain latency. Pupil dilation latency varies according to the stimulus presented, with latencies comprised between 150 and 400 ms for light stimuli or between 300 and 500 ms for interpreting, as found by Hyönä et al. (1995: 605) (see Hvelplund 2014: 215). This means that dilation data might refer to what the participant was processing before stimulus onset. For the aforementioned reasons, measures of pupil size and dilation are best analysed in combination with other metrics, and caution should be exercised when interpreting pupillary measures.

In the 90s, three groundbreaking studies sought to establish the feasibility of the application of pupillometry to the exploration of processing effort in SI (Tommola & Niemi 1986, Tommola & Hyönä 1990, Hyönä et al. 1995). As pupil diameter had been found to positively correlate with CL (the larger the pupil, the higher the load) during cognitive processes, including language comprehension, the researchers sought to establish whether pupillometry could be adopted as a diagnostic method to index variations in processing effort during interpreting. The choice of this physiological indicator was motivated by the fact that it was hypothesised to comply with the key requirements identified by Kahneman (1973): the ability to reflect load differences between and within tasks and between subjects. In other words, capturing differences in processing load during interpretation required an online, real-time and highly sensitive metric capable to co-vary with global and local variations in CL. In those first attempts at integrating this measure into the exploration of the interpreting process, pupillometry was used to compare listening (without comprehension testing), shadowing and SI into the participants' mother tongue (Tommola & Hyönä 1990) and, later, to investigate the effect of word difficulty and directionality on CL during SI (Hyönä et al. 1995). In the first study, the hypothesis was that SI would yield the largest average pupil diameter, followed by shadowing and listening. In the second experiment, pupil size was expected to be larger for the words classified as difficult to translate and for the repetition of words in the foreign language.

The intention behind these initial studies was rather of methodological nature. The results confirmed the adequacy of pupillometry as a method to investigate mental load during interpreting and related language tasks. Specifically, mean pupil size was found to be larger in the interpreting task. An order effect was also found, meaning that pupil dilation is larger at the beginning of the task. In the second experiment (Hyönä et al. 1995: 609), pupils were found to dilate on average by 0.40 mm during the translation of difficult words, while maximum dilation was found to be of 0.57 mm. Another important finding was that pupillary latency, i.e. the delay in pupillary response to a task, was between 300 and 500 ms (Hyönä et al. 1995: 605), which aligns with previously reported values (Beatty 1982, Hoeks & Levelt 1993). These pioneering studies paved the methodological way for the adoption of pupillometry in interpreting process research, showing its feasibility for the investigation of this cognitively-taxing task.

Pupillometry was recently adopted by Seeber & Kerzel (2012) and by Gieshoff (2018) to study, respectively, the effect of verb-final and verb-initial syntactical structures in German to English SI on local CL and of multimodal input presentation on mental workload in SI.

In their discussion of results, Seeber and Kerzel highlight an important aspect of the analysis of SI conducted under different conditions or on different source materials (as in the case analysed by the authors). While the differences in mean pupil diameter and dilation identified by Hyönä et al. (1995) were relatively large, which was to be expected due to the comparison of different tasks, when the comparison is made between the same task with more subtle modifications, the differences in pupil-based measures are likely to be less obvious. This was the case in Seeber and Kerzel's study, which found that pupils dilated by 3.996 and 4.048 mm while interpreting symmetrical and asymmetrical syntax respectively, as measured at the end of the task, i.e. in the temporal break between the stimuli sentences. This is an important methodological understanding, which should also be taken into account in the present study seeking to compare SI conducted with varying digital support for terminology look-up.

Gieshoff (2018) found an effect of audio-visual input (i.e. the presence of the speaker's video) on pupil size: its decrease was less marked than in the audio-only condition. On the other hand, background noise did not have an effect. She also found an effect of task, as she compared listening to interpreting. She found that pupil sizes decreased more largely in listening than in the SI task.

Results from the studies presented "illustrate the great potential of pupillometry as a method and [task-evoked pupillary responses] as a measure of cognitive load in simultaneous interpreting" (Seeber 2013: 27). However, the methodological challenges highlighted in the aforementioned studies underline how, despite its strengths, pupillometry requires a stringent experimental setup to allow the researcher to isolate stimulus responses. Additionally, pupillometry provides the best results when applied to isolated and short stimuli. When used over longer periods of time, local variations are averaged out and the technique does not offer useful insights into the underlying cognitive process (see for instance Schultheis & Jameson 2004).

The present chapter has reviewed the different methods and measures used to estimate CL in translation and interpreting. As discussed, all measures present advantages and disadvantages. A combination of several types of metrics may therefore prove beneficial to address the inherent limitations of each and maximise the benefits provided by the individual metrics. This is the approach commonly followed in TPR and it will also be adopted in the present study. The following chapter illustrates the methodology used in the experiment and discusses the measures chosen for data collection in §5.5.5.

5 Method

The present chapter illustrates and discusses the methodology used in the present study, which was conducted to compare the effects of digital terminological support tools on the product and process of SI. The research work comprised a pilot study and a main study.

The pilot study was aimed at validating the methodology. Its results, already published in Prandi (2017, 2018), and the adaptation of the design for the main experiment are discussed in §5.4.

In §5.5, the experimental materials and setup of the main study are presented. The results of the main study are presented and discussed in Chapter 6.

5.1 Research gap

As discussed in the literature review (§2.4), arguments in favour of and against the introduction of CAI tools and technologies such as ASR into the interpreting process are substantiated by empirical data only to a limited extent. The lack of data is accompanied by the lack of an empirically-validated research methodology for the combined collection and analysis of process and product data on SI with the support of digital tools. The existing empirical contributions have focused primarily on a product-oriented analysis through the collection of performance data. This currently represents a major barrier to the further development of empirical CAI research. Research has addressed the evaluation of terminological quality (Biagini 2015, Prandi 2015a,b, Van Cauwenberghe 2020) and, especially in the case of ASR support, the accuracy of number renditions (e.g. Defrancq & Fantinuoli 2021, Pisani & Fantinuoli 2021). Furthermore, most of these analyses have not expanded the focus beyond the unit of information for which support is offered, except for Biagini (2015) (who also considered whether glossary searches produced omissions or serious errors), Montecchio (2021) (who evaluated the impact on perceived fluency in addition to the accuracy of numerals rendition), and Frittella (2022), who conducted a qualitative evaluation of the interpretations of number-dense speeches. In some publications, subjective data were collected through retrospective questionnaires to gain further insight into the interaction with digital terminology support solutions (e.g. Defrancq & Fantinuoli

2021, Pisani & Fantinuoli 2021). To the best of my knowledge, no behavioural methods have been employed to date to substantiate these observations with more objective measures (as recommended e.g. by Hansen 2008: 391–392), such as time-lag or fixation-based metrics.

In addition to these methodological limitations, an evident research gap emerges. Research on CAI tools has focused mostly on the product, while the cognitive processes leading to specific phenomena in the target text have remained largely unexplored. The present contribution represents a first step in this direction by attempting a look into the cognitive inner-workings of CASI.

5.2 Hypotheses on cognitive load in SI with terminology look-up

As previously discussed (§3.4), CL should not be seen as a static construct, but rather as a variable that changes constantly during the interpreting task as a function of the cognitive resources recruited by the co-occurring tasks. For the scope of the present inquiry, I chose to focus my analysis on the effect of terminology look-up and of automatic terminological prompts on the CL experienced during SI. As highlighted in the previous sections, different digital solutions for the terminological support of the interpreter may be expected to have a different impact on cognitive effort and, from a product-oriented perspective, also on the terminological accuracy of the interpreter's rendition. In the context of the present contribution, I focus on the differences resulting from the adoption of a digital glossary, of a CAI tool (InterpretBank), and of ASR as terminological support in the booth.

On the basis of what has been discussed so far and as predicted by Seeber's CLM applied to CASI (see §3.5.2), it may be hypothesised that:

1. Tools which require manual terminology look-up (digital glossaries and standard CAI tools) may impose a higher CL due to the recruitment of additional manual-spatial resources during production and monitoring. Conversely, lower CL may be expected for ASR tools, which do not pose demands on manual-spatial resources. This should result in shorter EVS, shorter time on task, and shorter average fixation durations.

2. As the CAI tool InterpretBank provides a series of postulated advantages (see §3.6.2) compared to standard digital glossaries, the test subjects may be

able to identify the terms more quickly, at least when orthographic neighbours are shown on screen, resulting in shorter time to first fixation. Additionally, InterpretBank should impose a lower load on task coordination, as it does not require preparation for subsequent queries (see §3.6.2). This should result in a higher number of terms interpreted as per glossary and fewer serious errors and omissions compared to a digital glossary. It should also elicit more queries than a PDF glossary due to its posited higher user-friendliness and higher querying speed thanks to the incremental search.

3. ASR support may facilitate not only production, but also comprehension, due to beneficial redundancy effects (if temporal contiguity is ensured, see §3.4.2.1 and Seeber et al. 2020, Chmiel, Janikowski & Lijewska 2020). This should result in a higher number of terms interpreted as per glossary, and fewer serious errors and omissions compared to CAI tools and digital glossaries.

4. ASR support should reduce negative split attention effects (see §3.4.2.1) due to increased temporal contiguity and to the absence of manual look-up compared to CAI tools and digital glossaries, resulting in shorter fixation time on the tool area and promoting attentional focus on the speaker.

5.3 Research approach

The combination of product- and process-related data has been proposed as a means to improve TPR (Hansen 2007). As advocated for instance by Mellinger (2019), a product- and process-oriented perspective to the exploration of CAI appears necessary, if we are to advance our understanding of the impact of CAI tools on cognition in (simultaneous) interpreting and to develop tools truly tailored to the needs of interpreters and capable of addressing the inherent constraints of SI. In order to contribute to bridging the current research gap, both in terms of research object and of methodology, I therefore developed and tested a convergent mixed-method design for the investigation of the product and process of CASI with the support of different terminology look-up tools. The study adopts an experimental approach for the generation and collection of data under controlled laboratory conditions. The approach chosen is predominantly quantitative. Due to the complexity of the present object of study, "so much less convenient to study than language fixed in writing" (Pöchhacker 2004: 48), in the present contribution multiple types of quantitative data related to the CL generated by CASI are collected and combined, and are corroborated by qualitative data related to the participants' experience in the interaction with the tools.

The study adopts methods derived from the TPR framework and includes performance, subjective, and behavioural measures combined in order to address the inherent limitations of each method. The choice of measures was motivated by the review of the methods used to measure cognitive load and their application in TPR (see Chapter 4). Table 5.1 presents an overview of the metrics selected for the study and the type of data collected. The measures chosen are discussed in detail in §5.5.5.

Table 5.1: Metrics included in the main study, type (qualitative/quantitative) and category (subjective, performance, or behavioural)

Measure	Type	Category
Terminological accuracy	quantitative	performance
Errors/omissions	quantitative	performance
Inter-cluster pause duration	quantitative	behavioural
EVS	quantitative	behavioural
Glossary queries	quantitative	behavioural
Time to first fixation	quantitative	behavioural
Average fixation duration	quantitative	behavioural
Fixation time	quantitative	behavioural
Debriefing questionnaire	qualitative	subjective

The hypotheses concerning digital terminological support in the booth (§5.2) were explored using a within-subject design: in this way, as discussed in Lazar (2017: 65), "the impact of individual differences is effectively isolated and the expected difference can be observed with a relatively smaller sample size" (see also §5.5.1.1). A small-N design (Smith & Little 2018) need not necessarily be considered a limitation. In other disciplines, such as psychology, "there is a long history of research [...] employing small-N designs" (ibid., p. 2083). A small sample where multiple observations are performed on a limited number of participants may be even more informative than a large sample, as combining quantitative analysis with qualitative observations (e.g. from questionnaires) and exploring the same dataset through multiple metrics becomes more feasible. As a consequence, a researcher may be able to paint a more refined picture of the mechanisms underlying a specific process or observations made on the product. Considering that interpreter-machine interaction is still a largely unexplored topic in CAI, working with a small sample seems valid. As observed for instance by Hansen-Schirra & Nitzke (2020: 422), small-N studies "are valuable to build hypotheses for larger studies". The benefits of a small sample size have been recognised also in the area of human-computer interaction, where skilled participants are usually needed and cannot always be found easily (Lazar 2017: 65). At the time of the experiment, CAI tools and ASR in the booth were still a mirage for many interpreters and only included in training to a limited extent (Prandi 2020). When the use of CAI tools becomes more mainstream (and this may already be the case due to rapidly changing working conditions during the COVID-19 pandemic), it may be more feasible to recruit larger samples. In order to test the hypotheses of the present study, involving well-practiced participants was deemed more valuable than recruiting a large sample.

Whenever possible during the study, I strove to preserve ecological validity, i.e. "the naturalness of the investigated process" (Hansen 2008: 386). For this reason, real-life conditions were replicated insofar as they allowed for sufficient experimental control to be able to draw inferences from the collected data (see Spinner et al. 2013 for an empirically-based discussion on ecological validity in reading research, largely applicable to experiments on translation and interpreting). However, as addressed in §5.4.3, 5.4.4, 5.5.3, 5.5.6, it was necessary to limit the potential impact of confounding variables on results. Therefore, the stimuli were designed to reduce such impact (§5.4.3 and §5.5.3).

The review of the research conducted using eyetracking on translation and interpreting (see §4.4.2.3) shows that the technique may provide valuable insight into the mental processes at the core of translation and interpreting. In particular, the large body of TPR conducted using this technique, which has contributed to establishing a set of reference metrics taken to index cognitive load and effort, may prove especially valuable also for the present object of inquiry, which is why I opted to conduct an eyetracking study to address my research questions.

Since the present study is the first to explore SI with digital support for terminology from a preeminently cognitive perspective, it has an exploratory character and also aims at formulating further hypotheses in addition to providing initial findings on this complex research object.

5.4 Pilot study: Method and results

In order to test the methodology for the main study, a pilot study was conducted at the University of Mainz/Germersheim between May and July 2017. The experimental design combined process and product-oriented data collection methods. Its primary focus was the validation of the stimuli designed for data collection. In this section, I describe the experimental setup illustrating the stimuli used and analysing the participants' deliveries and queries performed. I then highlight the limitations identified in the approach chosen and discuss the modifications applied to the experimental design ahead of the main experiment.

5.4.1 Participants

For the pilot study, I was able to recruit six advanced students of the master's degree in conference interpreting of the University of Mainz/Germersheim. They had all received at least three semesters of instruction in simultaneous and consecutive interpreting and had English as their B (active) or C (passive) language. The sample was made up of three German natives (one male, two females) and three Italian natives (one female, two males). The two language combinations, comprising one Germanic and one Romance language, were chosen to ensure that the stimuli could be considered challenging independently of structural and linguistic similarities in the language pair, e.g. when cognates were included as stimuli. Participation in the study was voluntary and not remunerated, but compensated instead by allowing students to learn how to use a CAI tool which is not usually included in the regular interpreting curriculum. An additional benefit of participating in the study consisted in the added amount of practice hours with a laptop in the booth, which is rarely done systematically in class. This was, however, also a limitation, as students were required to schedule time for the practice sessions. This is probably the main factor contributing to the difficulties experienced during participant recruitment, a difficulty which was unfortunately also confirmed for the main study, as will be discussed in §5.5.1.

5.4.2 Test subjects' training

Before taking part in data collection, it was necessary to prepare participants in order to ensure that they were all equally proficient in the use of the three tools compared in the study, so that I could exclude this variable during data analysis. The individual disposition towards technology continues to play a role despite training, of course, but no subject preparation can change this highly personal factor. Nonetheless, it is certainly easier to exclude the variable of lack of tool expertise if the participants have gone through a dedicated training beforehand.

The students were therefore invited to attend a preliminary preparatory meeting during which they were instructed on the basics of terminology management for conference interpreters. The training had an explicit practical focus, as previous studies (Prandi 2015a,b) had highlighted the role of practice as more beneficial to familiarise the participants with the tool than a more theory-prone training. The preparatory meeting focused in particular on the search functions in Word, Excel and InterpretBank. The main difference between Word and Excel, both traditional tools for organising terminology, was that with Word participants could visualise all the results of a query in a column on the left hand-side of the screen, similarly to InterpretBank, but without the explicit optimisation for interpreters offered by InterpretBank. When working with Excel, they had to skip to the next occurrence manually. The five practice sessions that followed were organised to develop the ability to conduct queries while interpreting. All participants attended all practice sessions, which took place once a week for five weeks. During each session, their task consisted in interpreting three short speeches from English into their respective mother tongue (German or Italian) while using one of the tools to look up terminology. The order of the tools was changed at every session. The speeches used for the training were selected and adapted from the training material used in a previous study (Prandi 2015a,b), to which several authentic speeches were added that had been selected in order to ensure a certain progression from a more controlled to a more naturalistic practice environment. The topics chosen were medicine and biology. I prepared the glossary used for terminology look-up and made it available to all students for both language combinations and each tool, so that they all practised with the same material. The training was thus designed to guarantee equal practice time for each tool. It should be noted that I use the term "training" to indicate that practice was ensured before data collection. However, no specific input on the development of strategies for effective interpreter-machine interaction during SI was given.

After the last training session, the participants took a short proficiency test to verify whether they had all learned the basics of glossary querying with the three tools. The test consisted in a series of tasks to be performed with the tools and focused on the search function. Students were asked to record their screens while accomplishing the tasks. The screen recordings were later analysed: all students passed the test and could take part in data collection.

5.4.3 Materials

The speeches drafted for the pilot study were prepared based on a series of known effects and hypotheses related to features of oral speech perception and production and to linguistic and morphological characteristics of terms as stimuli. These considerations are described in the following subsections, while §5.4.3.6 illustrates the features of the speeches validated in the pilot study.

5.4.3.1 Speech rate and presentation

Speech rate is a prosodic factor which can be essential in determining the feasibility of the SI task. Especially excessively high input rates have been identified as a major stress factor in interpreting and may render the performance of SI impossible (e.g. Riccardi 2015). In SI, the ideal speech rate is comprised between around 95 and 120 wpm (Seleskovitch 1978, Gerver 1976, Seleskovitch 1978, Lederer 1981, Pio 2003, Seeber 2005). Therefore, for the experiment it was necessary to select a speech rate which would make looking up terminology during SI challenging, but not impossible. This was necessary to test the trade-off between looking up terminology and delivering an acceptable interpreting performance.

An additional aspect to consider was the mode of presentation. Pre-prepared, read-out speeches tend to be associated with a faster speaking rate and a less spontaneous intonation, which can make the input more difficult to process. However, as required by the experimental nature of the present study, it was necessary to ensure consistency between subjects and to use comparable speeches. Therefore, while it would be possible to have the speaker deliver a speech live to maintain higher ecological validity and collect data in a more naturalistic setting, in an experimental setting, video recordings can be a way of maintaining the necessary degree of control while at the same time approximating the mode of presentation of the source speech to real-life conditions. Additionally, video-recorded speeches are usual training material for interpreting students. Therefore, using a video-recorded read-out speech at a comfortable speaking rate was expected to be perceived by the participants as similar to their asynchronous training sessions in terms of speed and prosodic aspects.

5.4.3.2 Speech structure: Sentence processing

When designing the experiment, I was also faced with the challenge of presenting participants with clearly defined stimuli that could then easily be correlated with responses. At the same time, it was necessary to preserve a certain degree of ecological validity in order not to alienate the test subjects with a too unfamiliar task – a common challenge in the investigation of the interpreting process in a laboratory setting. While I am interested in analysing CL at a local level (see §3.4), presenting participants with individual terms to interpret without any context would have excluded the element of simultaneity from my study. This would have counteracted the very goal of my investigation, as it is the simultaneous performance of cognitive tasks that makes challenges and limitations arise which would otherwise not be noticeable when considering the individual tasks on their own. In contrast, using unedited speeches and conducting the analysis at the text level would have likely introduced an excessive amount of potentially confounding variables and made stimulus-response correlations difficult to identify. For these reasons, I aimed for highly controlled stimuli while at the same time trying to make the task as realistic as possible.

A useful reference was identified in Seeber & Kerzel's (2012) methodology. In their study on cognitive load effects in symmetric and asymmetric sentence structures in SI, they presented stimulus sentences embedded in sentence clusters, i.e. the critical (target) sentence is enclosed in a pre-critical (introductory) and a post-critical (continuation) sentence. This approach presents several advantages: it makes data analysis more efficient by allowing for a focus on the target sentences (i.e. the sentences including the stimulus-term); it promotes the creation of comparable speeches, as they all present the same structure; and finally, it provides participants with the impression that they are interpreting a continuous speech rather than isolated sentences.

In experimental research, the inclusion of filler items is essential to minimise unintended repetition effects due to noticeable patterns in the stimuli (see Conklin et al. 2018: 44–45, Keating & Jegerski 2015). In other words, if every sentence contained a stimulus, the participants may notice it and adjust their look-up strategy when working in the PDF or CAI condition. The terminological density may also be too high to allow for queries during the interpreting task and the participants may stop looking up terms altogether, which would defeat the purpose of the study. To avoid eliciting unwanted effects, the pre-critical (introductory) sentences and the post-critical (continuation) sentences would have to be superficially as similar as possible. Crucially, they would need to be highly comparable in terms of length, number of clauses and syntax (see Keating & Jegerski 2015: 16).

While one sentence between each stimulus and the next may have been sufficient to give participants some respite between two queries, the introduction of a continuation sentence was deemed useful to ascertain whether a glossary query may cause a trickle-down effect due to imported load (see Gile 2008), leading to severe errors and omissions in the following sentence. In studies on sentence processing, "the processing of a critical region in a sentence oftentimes continues or spills over onto the words immediately following the critical region" (Keating & Jegerski 2015: 6). This "spillover effect" (e.g. Rayner & Duffy 1986) is often noticeable not in the target region (i.e. the target sentence in this case), but rather in the spillover regions. Continuation sentences would therefore serve as a test-bed to verify whether coping with the stimulus term in the target sentence may lead to effects in the following textual material.

5.4.3.3 Compound processing

In English and German, all compounds are right-headed (Arcara et al. 2014, Semenza & Luzzatti 2014), while in Italian they can be either left- or right-headed (e.g. Ghiselli 2015). The morphological structure of the terms was expected to affect search behaviour. Since a word-length effect has been observed for acoustic understanding, i.e. shorter words have been found to be more difficult to process (e.g. Barton et al. 2014), short unigrams (monosyllabic or bi-syllabic) may have posed a difficulty for a glossary search. Therefore, if they had not been understood, they would offer less linguistic material to perform a query (which can be conducted also for incomplete words). However, as working memory span has been shown to increase for short words, if the stimuli were correctly understood they may have interfered less with the other subprocesses, since they would pose a lighter load on WM. Conversely, I expected longer terms to be easier to process acoustically. In particular, multi-word terms (bigrams and trigrams) would facilitate the glossary search by offering more linguistic material: for instance, participants may choose not to look for the first element of the term, but rather for one of the other elements (e.g. the modifier instead of the head of the compound expression). Additionally, compound expressions have been identified as an element of difficulty in SI (see Ghiselli 2015), and I therefore expected them to be looked up more often than unigrams.

5.4.3.4 Position of terms in the speeches

The position of the terms in the sentence was also expected to play a role. In reading research, sentence-final stimuli have been found to elicit longer fixations, which suggests higher cognitive load. This is known as the sentence wrap-up effect (Warren et al. 2009), which has been explained with the integration of sentence meaning with preceding and following context: at the end of the sentence, the reader receives all the necessary clues to correctly gauge the meaning of the sentence. It should be noted that this effect has been found not only for sentence-final stimuli, but also for clause-final stimuli. While the phenomenon has been studied mainly with reference to written textual processing, a similar effect has been found in the eyetracking study by Seeber & Kerzel (2012): verb-final sentences in German elicited significantly larger pupil dilations than verb-medial sentences in a study on SI from German into English. Similarly, a stimulus term placed at the end of the sentence may pose a higher strain on WM and result in CL possibly due to the need to store in memory previous units of information semantically or morphologically depending on the term. Furthermore, at the end of the target sentence, the interpreter would also have to start processing the following sentence: having to store the term in WM in addition to the previous information during the query and to finish interpreting the target sentence may increase the CL to the point of overloading or of resulting in serious issues or omissions in the continuation sentence. However, sentence-final stimuli offer the advantage of being preceded by more context than sentence-medial stimuli. This may facilitate semantic anticipation (e.g. Gile 2009). Hence, interpreters may be able to avoid a query altogether or apply the strategy of formulating their rendition with a less compromising syntactical structure, facilitating a seamless integration of the term after performing a query. For this reason, sentence-final stimuli may actually elicit lower additional load. If, on the other hand, the test subject does not anticipate that an unknown term requiring a glossary query is coming up, self-corrections may be necessary. This may be expected both for sentence-medial and sentence-final stimuli, resulting respectively in false starts and self-corrections or reformulations.

5.4.3.5 Frequency of the stimuli

Finally, the frequency of the stimuli used was expected to affect the participants' search behaviour. It was reasonable to expect that more frequent terms may have been known to the students and not require a query, whereas less frequent terms may have required glossary look-up. CAI tools are generally considered to be more user-friendly and to take up fewer cognitive resources than traditional glossary tools (see §2.4), thus allowing for a higher number of queries. In his study contrasting paper glossaries and InterpretBank, Biagini (2015) had found a higher number of terms searched in InterpretBank compared to the paper glossary condition. Introducing both frequent and infrequent terms as stimuli was expected to help explore the postulated advantages of CAI tools, which are designed to facilitate look-up. In particular, I hypothesised that participants would look up a higher percentage of no-query terms when working in the CAI condition due to a lower load on working memory (see §3.6.2, 5.2).[1]

5.4.3.6 Features of the speeches used in the pilot study

The design of the speeches was motivated by the considerations illustrated above and the intention to test how specific features of the speeches would affect the

---

[1]For the scope of the pilot study, the stimuli were not further controlled for linguistic aspects such as cognate status or level of concreteness, which can affect linguistic processing (see §1.1.1 for a discussion of the features of language for special purposes). These aspects were considered in the main study (see §5.5).

participants' performance and interaction with the tools. Additionally, the naturalistic base material was modified in order to control for potential confounding factors.

The speeches used for data collection were based on a corpus of speeches collected ad-hoc from the speech repository of the EU Directorate General for Interpretation[2] on the topics of energy sources. The speeches were on average 12 minutes long at an average speed of 122.26 words per minute (wpm). The speeches were read out by a male native speaker of British English and video recorded. Additionally, the speeches used as training materials ahead of the test were also presented in the same way. As the speaker was himself an interpreter trainer and conference interpreter, he was familiar with the use of pre-prepared material to deliver speeches for training purposes.

Each speech was made up of 36 sentence clusters, containing one stimulus each. Each sentence cluster was made up of:

1. An introductory sentence, which provides context but should not elicit glossary queries;

2. A target sentence containing the stimulus to be looked up;

3. A continuation sentence, with the same features and role of the introductory sentence.

Thus, each stimulus was separated from the following one by two filler sentences. Due to the presence of introduction and continuation sentences, each speech thus contained 66.7% noncritical sentences and 33.3% critical (target) sentences, as recommended in literature (e.g. Keating & Jegerski 2015: 17).

The structure was repeated throughout each speech. I report an example from Speech 1 to illustrate how the speeches were structured:

(1)   So we need to change this basic trend and this is why the urgency is there.
      In our policies, we should definitely address the need to improve *vehicle efficiency*.
      But there is still much more I can do, in many other areas, as you are aware.

(2)   At the EU level, there is another policy option that can help us.

---

[2]https://webgate.ec.europa.eu/sr/ (Accessed: 01.11.2021).

By focusing, for instance, on *woody biomass fuels*, we can truly make a difference.

They have the potential to help us respond to the challenges we're facing.

The stimuli introduced in the speeches present a set of features that were chosen to control for additional confounding variables. Each text contained 36 terms, one per target sentence. The terms were symmetrically grouped by morphological structure, by position in the sentence, and by necessity of a query based on their frequency.

Specifically, of the 36 terms, 12 were unigrams (e.g. "bioenergy"), 12 were bigrams, i.e. made up of two elements, usually noun-noun (e.g. "energy poverty") or adjective-noun compounds (e.g. "tidal barrage") and 12 were trigrams, in different combinations of adjectives and nouns (e.g. "pressurised water reactor"). For the above-mentioned reasons, I decided to control for the presence of multi-word and single word expressions in the speeches by equally distributing the stimuli across the three categories. In order to control for potential sentence-final effects and to test my hypotheses on anticipation, half of the terms were placed at the end of the sentence and half in the middle.

Finally, I divided the terms equally into terms requiring a query and terms for which a glossary search was not deemed to be necessary. The terms classified as requiring a glossary search were highly technical terms that do not belong to the 10,000 most common English terms as per their frequency in the Leipzig Corpora Collection (2012, 2016, 2021) corpora.

5.4.4 Procedure

At the time of the pilot study, the adoption of ASR as in-booth support had just been theorised for the first time (see Fantinuoli 2017b, Cavallo & Ortiz 2018). For this reason, and based on the results of the available inquiries into conference interpreters' terminological practices (see §2.3), the in-booth digital support solutions compared in the pilot study were Word glossaries, Excel glossaries and the CAI tool InterpretBank.

Data collection took place at the Translation and Cognition (TRA&CO) Center of the University of Mainz/Germersheim, the university's neurolinguistic laboratory dedicated to Translation Studies. Before the start of the experiments, the students were briefed about the structure of the study and signed a waiver on the collection and treatment of their data. They were informed that they could decline their consent to the use of their data at any time. They were informed about the interpreting task they were going to complete during the experiment and were told the topic of the speeches (renewables and other energy sources). I am aware that not having participants prepare ahead of the interpreting task does not reflect usual professional practice. Nonetheless, I decided to sacrifice this aspect of ecological validity in favour of a more controlled experimental design. Preparation is highly personal, depending on several variables, not least also on motivation, and attempting to control and standardise the test subjects' preparation time and thoroughness would have probably proved to be impossible. An additional reason for excluding preparation from the experiment was the need to ensure that participants would be presented with a sufficient number of stimuli to look up in the glossary. As a result, the number of queries is probably much higher in the experimental setting than in a real-life interpreting assignment, but having sufficient data points per participant was necessary considering the small sample, and essential to draw initial conclusions on the comparison of the three tools. The students were asked to approach the interpreting task as if they had to interpret at a real conference on renewable energy and had had little time to prepare, but a colleague had made available a glossary at the last minute. They were not explicitly encouraged to look up terms while interpreting, but were asked to consider the glossary simply as an aid that they could resort to when necessary.

I prepared the glossary, which contained 421 terms, i.e. all the specialised terminology included in the texts plus additional terms related to the topic in question. The same terms were available for each tool and language combination. The glossary, prepared in InterpretBank and then exported and converted into .xlsx and .docx files, presented a simple tabular structure which only included the term and its equivalent in the target language. It could be argued that interpreters' glossaries may also be more complex, containing additional information such as synonyms, definitions and collocations. Moreover, their structure and content are very personal, as they reflect the individual preparation style, preferences and strategies. Accounting for each of these variables would have been extremely complex empirically. Therefore, I chose to focus on the minimum common denominator for the test, i.e. the terminological pair.

During the experiment, participants interpreted three speeches from English into their A language, as they had done during the practice sessions. They used a different tool each time. The order of speeches and tools was randomised to avoid effects due to fatigue ensuing during the test (Spinner et al. 2013: 400, Keating & Jegerski 2015: 18) or to the individual speech/tool combination (Conklin et al. 2018: 42–43). The participants' glossary queries were collected automatically in the log file generated by InterpretBank after each trial and manually for the Word and Excel condition by reviewing the screen recordings.[3] The participants' interpretations were recorded with Audacity (2021) and then transcribed following the HIAT transcription conventions (Rehbein et al. 2004) in Partitur Editor, the transcription tool of the Exmaralda Suite (Schmidt & Wörner 2014).

5.4.5 Stimulus validation

The primary aim of the pilot study was verifying the validity of the a-priori classification of the stimuli in relation to glossary queries. In order to obtain sufficient data for a comparison between the Word, the Excel, and the CAI tool glossaries, it was necessary that the stimuli classified as requiring a query actually elicited a sufficient number of searches for all participants. While a certain degree of inter-subject variability should be expected, as each participant differs in terms of SI skills, world knowledge, and interpreting strategies, it was important for my classification to hold true at least in the majority of cases.

I therefore transcribed the students' deliveries and analysed them to verify:

- the total number of terms searched;

- the number of terms searched classified as requiring a query (QN);

- the number of terms searched classified as not requiring a query (NO QN).

As was to be expected, the percentage of terms searched classified as requiring a query varied considerably between participants, while it was quite similar for the terms not expected to elicit a query in the glossary. This percentage was similar for the German natives (PS1-01, PS1-02, PS1-03), although different terms were looked up. As can be seen in the graph below (Figure 5.1), one participant (PS1-06) looked up a considerably lower number of terms.

Additionally, it was important to verify which terms which had been classified as requiring a glossary search had not been looked up by any participant and vice versa. Out of 54 terms, five QN terms were not looked up in any case, while one NO QN term was looked up by all subjects. The terms in question would therefore require replacement or reclassification.

---

[3]During the pilot study, the eyetracking set-up used during the main study was also tested. Therefore, the gaze replay videos exported from the data analysis tool of the eyetracker (SMI BeGaze) were available and could be used to reconstruct the queries in the Word and Excel glossaries. However, during the pilot study, gaze data was not analysed. The eyetracking setup is therefore described and discussed in greater detail in §5.5.3 and §5.5.6.

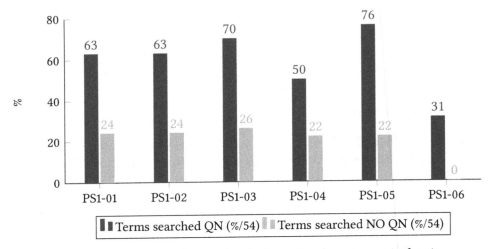

Figure 5.1: Percentage of terms searched per stimulus category in the pilot study. QN = query necessary, NO QN = no query necessary (Prandi 2018: 47)

5.4.6 Preliminary results

A thorough description of the results of the pilot study is reported in Prandi (2017, 2018), including a preliminary analysis of the strategies adopted during SI. While verifying hypotheses was not the main aim of the pilot study, I conducted a series of preliminary analyses on the transcribed interpretations to gain first insight into several expected phenomena in preparation for the main experiment. I first present the results of the analyses related to the stimuli classification and then continue with an analysis of product-related aspects.

5.4.6.1 Preliminary effects on search behaviour

As previously stated, the position of the stimuli was expected to affect the participants' search behaviour (see §5.4.3.4). Specifically, I expected the terms placed at the end of the sentence to result in more glossary queries than the terms in the middle of the sentence. In the small sample tested, sentence-final terms seemed to elicit more queries. This could be due to several reasons: first of all, participants could anticipate that a specialised term was going to come up based on the context and would prepare themselves to query the glossary. Additionally, it is possible that, anticipating the need for a glossary search, they would prefer a sentence structure in their delivery that would favour a search. This would certainly require the development of ad-hoc strategies to facilitate terminology look-up during SI and it could be argued that this would have been difficult for trainee interpreters. It may however be a behaviour likely to be observed in experienced interpreters who are highly proficient in the use of technology during SI. On the other hand, stimuli placed within the sentence could be more difficult to handle through a glossary query, as this would likely generate more noticeable disfluencies in the participants' rendition. It is possible that interpreters would therefore choose to use an alternative strategy, resulting in lower precision but in a more natural delivery and lower CL experienced.

In considering the morphological complexity of the terms (see §5.4.3.3), I could identify a prevalence in searches for unigrams belonging to the "NO QN" category. This could be due to the fact that querying the glossary for a unigram is more straightforward than for bi- or trigrams: either the term is understood and looked up, or it is not. In the case of bigrams and trigrams, there is an additional layer of decision as interpreters may first have to decide which element of the term should be looked up (provided that all components have been understood). This would require additional cognitive resources unless a dedicated strategy has previously been developed and automatised. Therefore, participants may choose to adopt a different approach altogether. For terms requiring a query, no clear trend could be identified.

5.4.6.2 Preliminary effects on accuracy

I also conducted additional observations on this preliminary data concerning the accuracy achieved when working with the three different tools. In the context of the present experiment, accuracy is adopted as a performance measure (see §4.3 and §4.3.1) to identify instances of cognitive effort in the interpreter-tool interaction, not as a component of quality to evaluate the target text. Accuracy is therefore operationalised as the fraction of terms translated as per glossary or with an equally acceptable term, which would indicate an effective use of the tool and/or limited cognitive effort exerted to produce the term.

The percentage of terms searched translated as per glossary was calculated and the results were analysed following a methodology already used in previous studies on CAI tool use in SI (Prandi 2015a,b, Biagini 2015). I classified the term renditions adapting a classification put forward by Wadensjö (1998) for interpreting (see §1.1.2). This framework was chosen for two main reasons. First, to promote comparability with previous studies. Second, because it adopts a broad categorisation and stresses the effectiveness of the rendition, which facilitates the operationalisation of accuracy as a correlate of effective interaction with the tool. For instance, as can be seen below, omissions and unacceptable renditions are grouped together as they both index unsuccessful or effortful queries. Other evaluation frameworks, such as MQM (see §1.1.2), also include accuracy and terminology as issue types, but they consider them as distinct dimensions.[4] These frameworks may prove very useful in studies aiming to assess the target text quality in CAI, especially if it has been specified that the interpreter should use the equivalent contained in the glossary, but this kind of analysis goes beyond the scope of the present experiment.

According to the framework chosen, terms could be classified as:

Close renditions: no information is lost, the rendition is precise, the term is translated with the glossary equivalent or an adequate synonym;

Acceptable renditions: some information is lost (e.g. through paraphrasing, the loss of an adjective in complex terms, a drop in register), but the general meaning is maintained;

Zero/unacceptable renditions: this category groups renditions that completely or largely deviate from the original (the content is different) and terms that were left untranslated.

I assigned a value of 2 to close renditions, of 1 to acceptable renditions and of 0 to unacceptable and zero renditions. As for the degree of terminological precision achieved with Word and Excel glossaries and with InterpretBank, inter-subject variability is high. Nonetheless, Excel seems to lead to the worst terminological performance, i.e. to more frequent unacceptable renditions or terms left untranslated. This is probably due to the fact that when working with Excel it is necessary to manually skip to the next result, while with the other tools the results are all visualised together. This might make queries in Excel excessively cumbersome and time-consuming. InterpretBank seems to perform slightly better than Word in this respect.

I also considered the terminological accuracy in relation to the term structure and found that InterpretBank leads to higher accuracy for unigrams in five cases out of six (with the exception of PS1-06, whose search behaviour however differed greatly from that of the other participants). My hypothesis was that InterpretBank would prove more effective, leading to higher accuracy, especially for complex terms (bigrams and trigrams). I did not find significant differences for bigrams and trigrams: queries with InterpretBank proved more effective than Word and Excel in half of the cases.

---

[4]Additionally, in MQM omission is included as a sub-dimension of accuracy separate from mistranslation, which does not fit into the present operationalisation of incorrect renditions.

The analysis of accuracy was conducted first at a microscopic level, that of terminology. However, a successful query that results in an accurately translated term may nonetheless require too much time and attention, thus leading to serious errors or even to the complete omission of information. I therefore expanded my analysis to the sentence level. The transcriptions were annotated following Barik's (1971) classification of omissions, additions and errors. Barik's classification is very fine-grained. I decided to adopt only three of the categories identified by the author, as lower-level errors may have been due to other factors and may have been exposed to a higher degree of subjectivity in their identification, especially since I did not involve a second rater at this stage. I annotated the renditions according to the following elements:

- substantial phrasing change (category E4 in Barik 1971);

- gross phrasing change (category E5 in Barik 1971);

- complete sentence omission (labelled M5).

Analysing partial omissions would certainly be interesting, but it would pose the methodological issue of defining units of information and of excluding the strategic use of omissions, which is difficult to evaluate post-hoc without involving the participants directly with a retrospective interview. Given the length of the experiment per participant (around 1.5 hours including the pre- and post-tests), I decided to reserve this analysis for future studies.

The renditions that did not present any issue or only minor issues (skipping omissions and mild phrasing changes) were grouped in a single category to streamline analysis. From this initial analysis, no clear trend could be identified. This is probably due to the variable number of terms searched, which made it difficult to compare performance between subjects.

5.4.7 Discussion of pilot study results

The pilot study overall validated the a-priori categorisation of the stimuli chosen for data collection. However, it highlighted a limitation of the initial design chosen for the experiment: given that only half of the stimuli introduced in the text were classified as requiring a glossary query due to their low frequency (i.e. 18 per condition, a total of 54), if participants only looked up a very limited number of terms, the data points collected for those participants would be too scarce to allow for a comparison with the rest of the sample. In order to overcome this limitation, I decided to replace the 54 stimuli classified as not requiring a query with less frequent, more specialised terms. This involved rewriting a considerable part of the speeches, but was nonetheless deemed necessary to ensure a more comparable search behaviour among participants.

As for the small effects observed for the stimuli position (see §5.4.3.4 for potential position effects on cognitive processing), it could be argued that the difference in search behaviour observed might be due to the terms chosen (e.g., cognate status, see also §5.5.3) rather than only to their position, even though the terms were equally distributed within the speeches (half were sentence-medial and half sentence-final). This is possible especially if one considers that only half of the terms in each position had been classified as requiring a query. This aspect could be further tested by switching the position of the stimuli used or by choosing a different set of terms. However, this would require a complete rewriting of the speeches, as in the present study the terms are not presented in isolation. Replacing the 54 stimuli classified as not requiring glossary look-up was expected to counterbalance this random effect.

Finally, while at the time of the pilot study ASR was still a hypothetical improvement of CAI tools, in the following months the first prototypes of ASR-CAI integrations started to appear (Fantinuoli 2017a, see §2.2.2). Word and Excel glossaries may be considered both as examples of "traditional" digital ways to organise and consult terminology for interpreters. Furthermore, they may be accidentally modified by participants during data collection, an unforeseen issue which occurred several times during the pilot study. For this reason, in the main experiment, I decided to prepare a tabular glossary and present it as a PDF file to overcome these limitations. I also added a mock-up of an ASR-CAI hybrid to include the most recent development in CAI technology, which I hypothesised to be the most cost-effective in terms of additional CL and degree of accuracy achieved in the interpretation (see §5.2).

To sum up, the pilot study represented a valuable step in the study design. The methodology developed and tested in the study is a novelty in the area of CAI research, especially in terms of the tools compared in the study, and of the rigour in the design of the materials used for data collection.

The pilot study was the first to specifically address solely digital support tools for terminology. Previous studies had either compared paper and digital glossaries (e.g. Biagini 2015) or focused on a single CAI tool explored through between-group designs (e.g. Prandi 2015a,b, Gacek 2015). The pilot study explored three different terminology support solutions, i.e. Word glossaries, Excel glossaries and CAI tools. The study also helped shed first light on the hypotheses guiding the present research work and refine the hypotheses, for instance by highlighting potential commonalities between Word and Excel glossaries, which informed the choice of the conditions to compare in the main study as discussed in §5.5.

The empirical validation of the methodology laid first ground for the collection of process and product data under controlled experimental conditions. The main methodological gain for the field consists in the development and validation of a new method of speech design (based on Seeber & Kerzel 2012). The level of control and the number of variables considered in the development of the speeches is unprecedented, as previous studies had worked with naturalistic materials without controlling for potential variables affecting the outcome. The usefulness of the methodology proposed in Prandi (2017, 2018) has been recognised by a number of recent studies, which have drawn on the methods presented in this section. For instance, a recent study by Van Cauwenberghe (2020) on ASR support for terminology explored the role of morphological complexity for the accuracy achieved by his participants. He also derived several aspects of his evaluation framework from the categories used in the pilot study. Investigating number renditions in ASR-supported SI, Frittella (2022) based the design of her speeches on the principles presented here.

Overall, the pilot study confirmed the validity of the design choices for the scope of the present research work, while at the same time highlighting weak spots in the design and supporting the optimisation of the methodology for the main experiment.

5.5 Main study: Rationale and method

This section describes the methodology and results of the main experiment conducted to compare the process and performance of SI with the support of traditional digital glossaries, CAI tools and CAI tools with integrated ASR.

5.5.1 Participants

In this section, I describe the recruitment process for the experiment, highlighting the challenges encountered and how they motivated my choice of research design. I further provide information on the demographics of the sample on which the experiment was conducted.

5.5.1.1 Participants recruitment

Like in the pilot study, participants were recruited among second-year students of the Master's Degree in Interpreting of the University of Mainz/Germersheim with German as their native language and English either as their B or their C language. This language combination was chosen because it is the most represented in the master's course and I thus hoped to reach a larger number of students to recruit for the experiment.

An e-mail was sent to the teaching staff of the English department, whom I asked to circulate the call among advanced interpreting students. I also asked for the collaboration of the student body representatives in circulating the e-mail and a leaflet containing the basic information about the experiment. Participants were also recruited through the University's Facebook groups, where the same information was posted in digital format. After a first round of e-mails sent during the Winter semester 2018/2019, which led to a few expressions of interest, a second round of e-mails was sent at the end of the Summer Semester 2019. Additionally, a recruitment e-mail was also sent to the University of Heidelberg, where I held a presentation of the study design and encouraged the students to take part in the study.

Participants were remunerated (€50) and received a three-month free InterpretBank license. In addition, they had the opportunity to attend a free course on a very relevant and topical subject not usually offered during regular instruction. Despite the considerable recruiting efforts, only 15 students expressed their interest in taking part in the study. Of the initial 15 students recruited, it was possible to collect data from nine students. Data by two students had to be discarded due to technical issues which emerged during data collection, one student could not be calibrated due to an eyesight condition, two resigned after having confirmed participation and one could not be tested due to the university facilities being closed in the wake of the COVID-19 pandemic.

The small size of the sample recruited highlights a certain lack of interest for the subject, probably due to a general lack of awareness of the existence of CAI tools and the increasing relevance they are gaining in the interpreting profession (see also Prandi 2020). Another aspect that certainly had a negative impact on participant recruitment was time. Due to the nature of my investigation, which presupposes a sufficient level of expertise in tool usage, training was necessary prior to data collection. The training required the availability of around one hour of time per training session, and it is possible that second-year students may not have had enough time in their busy schedule due to exam preparation. A similar experiment conducted recently on the simultaneous interpreting of numbers with ASR support (Defrancq & Fantinuoli 2021) did not foresee practice sessions prior to data collection, but it could be argued that for ASR, the interaction with the tool mainly consists in getting used to seeing terminological or, in Defrancq

& Fantinuoli's (2021) study, numerical suggestions on the screen while interpreting. The interaction with a PDF glossary or a CAI tool certainly requires more extensive training, the benefits of which had been identified in previous work on the topic (Prandi 2015a,b). Structured training on all three conditions was therefore considered essential to ensure that equal practice time be devoted to all three tools, a variable which could affect results.

Based on the considerations on small sample sizes outlined in §5.3, the speeches used for data collection contained a large number of stimuli, allowing numerous observations per participant. For each condition, participants were presented with 36 stimuli. The highest number of data points collected is for the ASR condition (36 for each participant, because the terms were shown automatically on the screen). For the two conditions which required an active search in the glossary (PDF and InterpretBank), the minimum number of data points per participant was 22.

5.5.1.2 Characteristics of the participants recruited

The final sample was made up of nine advanced interpreting students. Working with students was a choice of practical nature, since they had to be trained on the tools before the experiment and the equipment and facilities for data collection were available at the university (see §5.5.6). Additionally, having all been trained at the same institution and having received comparable amounts of training in SI, they may be considered a relatively homogeneous sample. The challenges in recruiting representative samples of professionals are well-known in TIS (e.g. Hansen-Schirra & Nitzke 2020). The main issue in working with students is that they "exhibit different cognitive processes and behavioural patterns than professionals, which might in turn affect the generalizability of the results" (ibid.). For this reason, care should be taken in generalising the results of the present study to the population of professional conference interpreters.

As will be described in more detail in §5.5.6, before collecting gaze data, I had my participants go through a series of tests to gain a more detailed picture of my sample. I measured their typing speed and the size of their English vocabulary (§5.5.1.2.4). I also asked them a series of questions to gauge their knowledge of the subjects of the speeches used during the experiment (§5.5.1.2.5).

With a view to provide a more nuanced picture of the sample at hand and identify additional confounding variables which may play a role in the interpretation of the experimental results, at the end of data collection I asked the participants to fill out the Translation and Interpreting Competence Questionnaire (TICQ) developed by Schaeffer et al. (2020). The main benefits offered by the tool consist in its easy customisation, its availability in four languages (English, German, Spanish and Chinese) and the fact that it can be administered online. As a quantitatively valid tool, its use has been advocated to promote greater comparability in T&I research (Schaeffer et al. 2020: 102). Only module A (demographics) and module C (interpreting competence) were administered in the online format. While compiling the questionnaire, some students informed me that they had either misinterpreted some questions or that they were uncertain on how the questions could be applied to their status of interpreting students.[5] This resulted in missing data for some questions and in a mismatch between the answers to several questions for the same test subject. Competence was not explicitly operationalised as a variable in the present study, and I was later informed that the interpreting competence score was still under development.[6] For these reasons, I do not report the total score here, but rather extrapolate from the questionnaire the answers which are related to my research questions and which may provide further insight into the make-up of my sample. These answers were also expected to provide useful additional qualitative data to interpret findings on the participants' interaction with the tools in the booth. I report relevant results in the sections below and then discuss the results of the pre-tests.

5.5.1.2.1 Demographics

The nine students recruited for the study were attending the Master's Degree in Conference Interpreting or the double Master's in Translation and Conference Interpreting at the time of the experiment. They had all received at least three semesters of instruction in simultaneous and consecutive interpreting. Seven were females, two were males (age M = 27.33 years, Mdn = 25). They were all native speakers of German; two of them were bilingual (with Arabic and Polish).

5.5.1.2.2 Language proficiency

In Module A3, the TICQ asks survey respondents to provide a self-rating of their knowledge of their L2 and L3 languages. In my sample, a small drawback consisted in the fact that two participants had indicated English as their L3, rather than as their L2. In the self-assessment question, no distinction is made between active and passive knowledge for L2, but only for L3. Therefore, if English had been selected as the participants' L3, the average rating was used. The mean self-reported value was 79.17 (on a scale from 0 to 100, SD = 7.71).

---

[5]For instance, the questions in section C2 concerning their professional experience.
[6]Schaeffer, personal communication (2021).

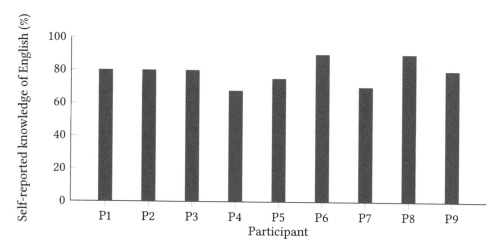

Figure 5.2: Bar plot of the self-reported knowledge of English (%). $M = 79.17$, SD = 7.71

5.5.1.2.3 Interpreting experience

No students identified themselves as conference interpreters, although some of them reported having some professional experience.

Their estimated décalage (Section C3.2 of the TICQ) was comprised between 2 and 3s ($M = 2.61$, SD = 0.48). A question present in the TICQ particularly relevant to my research desiderata concerned the strategies adopted to deal with an unknown term while interpreting. The preferred strategies was "Ask my partner", i.e. seeking help from the boothmate, followed by "Stalling" (Figure 5.3).

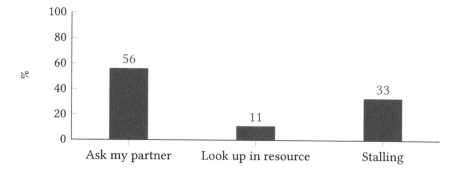

Figure 5.3: Preferred strategy to deal with unknown terms during interpretation

Only one participant indicated that they look up the term in their resources when they cannot recall it from memory, or they do not know its equivalent, which I found quite interesting considering the intensive training all students had attended prior to participating in the experiment and answering the TICQ. This might indicate that most of them prefer other, less demanding coping strategies in terms of attentional resources than performing a query in a digital glossary, which is probably considered an emergency tactic by most students in my sample. At the same time, the strategy of using an ASR-CAI hybrid to receive real-time terminology suggestions was not an available option for this question, which may have otherwise yielded different results.

5.5.1.2.4 Typing speed and English vocabulary size

The participants' typing speed was measured ahead of the experiment (in words per minute, wpm). In addition, I assessed the size of their English vocabulary using the online vocabulary test WordORnot (Center for Reading Research 2014). The test takes around four minutes and requires the participant to judge whether the words shown on the screen are actual English words or non-words. The final test score is an estimate of the participant's English vocabulary size. The results are illustrated in the graphs below (Figures 5.4 and 5.5).

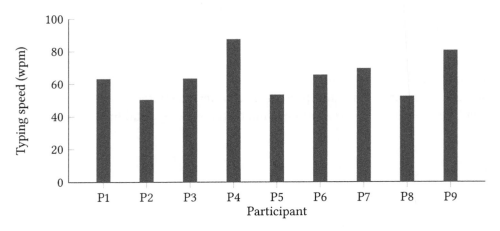

Figure 5.4: Typing speed of participants measured during the pre-test (wpm)

The participants' typing speed and the size of their English vocabulary was tested as these factors may have an impact on their search behaviour, in particular on the amount of terms looked up and on the amount of terms that they were

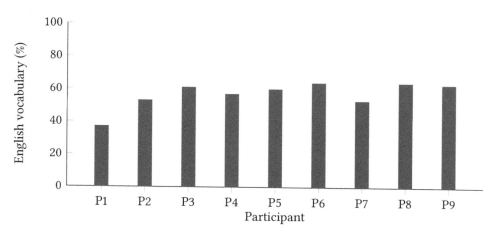

Figure 5.5: Estimated size of English vocabulary per participant (%)

able to find in the glossary. It should be noted that a correlation between these two factors and the search behaviour may not be straightforward, as a number of scenarios may arise: a fast typer may search a low percentage of terms if he or she has a wide English vocabulary, but the opposite may also be true, because he or she may choose to only look up the terms considered strictly necessary and to adopt alternative strategies, such as paraphrasing, which should be easier to adopt if one has high language flexibility. Nonetheless, I preferred to be on the safe side in order to consider also these aspects, if necessary.

5.5.1.2.5 Knowledge of speech topics

In addition to these data, participants had to answer a few questions which served a double purpose: to ascertain the participants' background knowledge of the topic of the speeches to interpret, which were different from the topics chosen for the training, and to provide the participants with at least a general overview of the speech topics. Not knowing the subject of the speeches may have caused additional stress ahead of the interpreting task. I first asked the participants to rate their knowledge of the key topics discussed in the speeches. As can be seen in Figure 5.6, no topic was completely unknown to the students, and moderate differences could be found between the students' knowledge about the six topics.

However, overall, none of the students considered themselves experts in the topic presented. Therefore, I could reasonably expect the students to look up a considerable number of terms during the experiment. Additionally, I verified the participants' terminological preparation on the topics in question. To this aim,

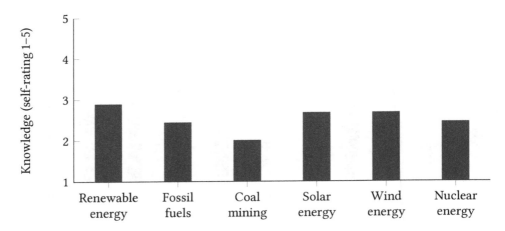

Figure 5.6: Self-ratings of knowledge of the main topics included in the speeches. Mean values for the sample on a scale from 1 (no knowledge) to 5 (expert knowledge)

I asked the students to write down three terms (with their German translation) which they associated with each of the six speech topics. I then checked which terms had been included and whether the students had indicated any term that was also present as a stimulus in the speeches. Of all the terms added by the participants, only four were similar or closely related to the stimuli selected. Of course, I cannot exclude that, just because a certain term was not mentioned during the briefing task, it was unknown to the student. Nonetheless, this task in the pre-test proved useful to verify which terms would first come to mind when thinking of a certain topic.

5.5.2 Participants' training

As in the pilot study, participants were required to attend a training course prior to data collection. The structure of the training was the same as during the pilot study, with the only difference that it was held online as a self-paced course. To this aim, I created an online course on the University's Moodle platform to which the study participants were enrolled after confirming their participation in the study. The introductory meeting was offered as a webinar that the students could attend live or watch later as a recording.

The online format of the training offered a double advantage: the participants could re-watch the recording as many times as necessary and they could more easily integrate the training in their schedules, with the additional option of re-peating practice sessions if they needed additional training. I had hoped that a more flexible and customisable training schedule would encourage participation in the study. Unfortunately, as described above, this was not the case.

In terms of the training content, the only modification introduced was the substitution of the Word and Excel glossaries with a PDF glossary, and the introduction of the ASR-CAI mock-up to account for a third generation of CAI tools which participants would likely be able to work with in their foreseeable future careers. The condition that equal practice time be ensured for each tool was also maintained for the main experiment. I made sure that the students had actually completed the five practice sessions by asking them to upload the recordings of their interpretations online. The students were able to proceed to the following training session only after completing the previous one. After the training had been completed, the participants were asked to take a short quiz to demonstrate their proficiency in the use of the tools. The questions were formulated in order to verify that the students had acquainted themselves with the user interface and were able to correctly operate the PDF tool and InterpretBank. All students passed the test and could hence take part in the data collection.

5.5.3 Materials

The speeches that the participants were asked to interpret during data collection were very similar to the ones used during the pilot study, with a few alterations. The speeches are reported in the Appendix.

First, as discussed in §5.4.7, the 54 stimuli which had previously been classified as not requiring a query were replaced with less frequent, more specialised terms. This required an almost complete rewriting of the speeches. Table 5.2 shows the distribution of terms in the final speeches.

It should be noted that the terms selected as stimuli do not represent all domain-relevant terms which could be of interest to interpreters. A domain-specific but highly frequent word could also elicit a glossary query. Ultimately, the terms were selected with the aim to generate sufficient data points for each participant.

As shown in Table 5.2, the ratio for each category (position and morphological complexity) was maintained also in the main experiment. All proper names and figures were removed from the text, as they could constitute further sources of difficulty in addition to specialised terminology (Gile 1995, 2009), which was in focus in the present study. Since the stimuli selected all had a very low frequency, they were expected to require a query in the glossary or a glance at the ASR suggestions in most cases. However, since the corpus of texts selected for the extraction of the stimuli was highly specialised, cognate facilitation effects may have occurred (Costa et al. 2000), for instance due to the prevalence of Latinisms,

Table 5.2: Distribution of terms for each speech in the main experiment. The morphological complexity and position of terms were equally distributed within the speeches.

Total	Morph. complexity		Position	
	Unigrams	12	End	6
			Middle	6
36	Bigrams	12	End	6
			Middle	6
	Trigrams	12	End	6
			Middle	6

which are frequent in specialised discourse (see §1.1). Since precedence was given to providing continuum by drafting entire speeches, it was not feasible to replace all cognate stimuli with non-cognates. Therefore, to control as much as possible for cognate facilitation effects, when a non-cognate translation was available, it was selected as target language equivalent for the glossary.

In addition, the cognate status of the stimuli across the three speeches used during the experiment was checked. To calculate the cognate status of the selected stimuli, I calculated the normalised Levenshtein ratio as:

$$\text{Levenshtein ratio} = 1 - \frac{\text{Levenshtein distance}}{\max(\text{length source}, \text{length target})}$$

The Levenshtein distance (Levenshtein 1966), i.e. the smallest number of deletions, additions and substitutions required to transform the source into the target string, is divided by the maximum length of the strings compared to account for word length. The formula above yields a score comprised between 1 (perfect cognate) and 0 (no overlap). A higher score indicates that fewer deletions, additions or transpositions are required to obtain the target term (Schepens et al. 2012).

The ANOVA of the normalised Levenshtein scores for the stimuli of each text was found to be non significant ($F(2, 105) = 0.243$, $p = 0.785$). On this basis, I did not expect cognate facilitation effects to significantly affect the participants' interaction with the support tools.

The speeches were recorded once again by the same speaker as in the pilot study. The structure made up of sentence clusters comprising an introductory, a target (T) sentence and a continuation (C) sentence was maintained. However,

in order to facilitate the analysis and isolate the effects of each stimulus on décalage and CL, I introduced a 5s pause between each sentence cluster and the next.
In literature, the average EVS for professional conference interpreters has been
identified as comprised between 2s and 6s (e.g. Barik 1973, Lederer 1978, Oléron
& Nanpon 2002, Christoffels & De Groot 2004, Timarová et al. 2011, Defrancq
2015), so a 5s pause was deemed sufficient. The average length of the speeches
used in the main experiment was 14'39", with an average WPM of 104.3 (164.4
average syllables per minute). As shown in Table 5.3, although the content of the
speeches varied, they were highly comparable in terms of length and speed.

To further verify whether the speeches were comparable, I analysed them using Coh-Metrix (McNamara et al. 2014). Coh-Metrix automatically computes a
series of indices of text cohesion and coherence which provide an estimation of
text difficulty and can be used both for written and for oral texts. The Flesch
Reading Ease Index (Flesch 1948), a common index of text readability, and the
SYNLE index, a reliable index of WM load (McNamara et al. 2014: 70), were considered as indices of difficulty. The texts were highly comparable also according
to these two indices. Therefore, the speech difficulty was not expected to affect
performance.

Table 5.3: Features of the speeches used in the main experiment. For
each speech, the table reports the duration, the number of words per
minute (wpm) and of syllables for minute (spm), the Flesch Reading
Ease score and the SYNLE score (left embeddedness, mean).

Speech	Duration	wpm	spm	Flesch Reading Ease	SYNLE
A	14'34"	105	165.8	59.92	3.57
B	14'46"	104	162.5	62.47	3.41
C	14'37"	104	164.9	61.35	3.71

While interpreting, the students could see both the video of the speaker and
the tool with the glossary on a split screen. The video was placed on the left
hand-side, the glossary on the right-hand side of the monitor. I decided to also
include the video of the speaker to reproduce a typical configuration of an SI task,
where the speaker is usually visible (see Seeber 2017). Additionally, visualising
the speaker video and the tool on screen may be compared to a typical RSI configuration (see §2.1.1), a setting in which the use of CAI tools, particularly with
ASR integration, may be envisaged in the near future. The speaker video was also
included for another purpose related to the hypotheses guiding the experiment:
since the video was expected to keep the participants' attention on the screen,

essentially serving as a fixation cross (Conklin et al. 2018), it would support the collection of gaze data when the participants were not interacting with the tools. This data proved useful in investigating effects on attention allocation during CASI (see §6.2.2.6).

5.5.4 Apparatus used for data collection

Gaze data was collected with an SMI red250 remote eyetracker mounted on an external desktop monitor. No chin rest or head support was used, although it would have improved data quality (Holmqvist 2011: 83), because it would have constricted the participants' head movements during speech and limited their ability to look at the keyboard while typing. The use of a head-mounted tracker and of a chin rest would have promoted more precision in the collection of gaze data (Conklin et al. 2018: 17), but it would have limited movement. The increased intrusiveness perceived may have caused greater stress. As pointed out by Hvelplund (2014: 206), "the [interpreter]'s eye movements may thus well be related to stress from not being able to look at what key is being pressed in addition to actual problem-solving activities arising from the [interpretation] itself".

The students' interpretations were recorded in Audacity with a microphone placed on the table, next to the participant. At the beginning of each video, whether with or without the ASR-CAI mock-up, I added a set of instructions that the participants were required to follow during data collection. Participants were instructed to wait until they would hear a loud "beep" coming from the computer before putting on their headphones. This acoustic marker was added to the recording to facilitate the synchronisation of the original speech with the interpretations. It was loud enough to be picked up by the microphone used to record the participants' deliveries.

5.5.5 Measures

Chapter 4 reviewed the main methods used to measure cognitive load and effort in translation and interpreting and highlighted how a combination of methods may represent a valuable experiment design choice to address the inherent limitations of each metric.

As introduced in §5.3 (see Table 5.1), the present study combined performance, behavioural, and subjective measures. It appears trivial to say that the measures selected for the main experiment are not the only measures which may be used to explore CASI from a cognitive processing standpoint. Conducting a comprehensive evaluation of how all measures of CL apply to the research object in question goes beyond the scope of the present study. For instance, in the experiment only duration-based eyetracking measures were used, while future studies may adopt additional metrics such as the number of fixations. Similarly, the only subjective measure used was a short qualitative questionnaire, but future research may, for instance, also test the use of cued retrospection to gain further insight into the CAI process. The present section provides the rationale for the selected metrics and describes how they were applied to the analysis of the data collected during the main experiment.

5.5.5.1 Performance measures

The study adopted the two performance measures included in the pilot study: terminological accuracy and number of errors and omissions.

5.5.5.1.1 Terminological accuracy

Assessing the terminological accuracy of terms consulted in the glossary or automatically prompted by ASR has become a standard measure in CAI research focused on terminology (e.g. Biagini 2015, Prandi 2015a,b), as one of the main claims of such applications is that their use may lead to greater target text (TT) accuracy.

To conduct the evaluation, I used the same three-level grading scale adopted in the pilot study. The three categories were defined as in the pilot study, i.e. a value of 2 would be assigned to "close renditions" (terms translated as per glossary or through a synonym), a value of 1 to acceptable renditions, and a value of 0 to wrong renditions or to an omission of the term which had not been replaced by a paraphrase. For the evaluation, the terms were presented to the raters in an Excel table. The terms were listed in isolation, not embedded in the respective utterance, in their order of appearance in the source speech and with their respective glossary equivalent. In order to facilitate the evaluation, adequate synonyms were listed (if available) next to the glossary equivalent. Next to the columns with the terms, the glossary equivalent and the synonyms, the participants' renditions were listed. Next to each participant's rendition, the raters could enter the accuracy scores. For this evaluation, the prosodic component was excluded (no audio recordings of the renditions were provided).

5.5.5.1.2 Errors and omissions

In analysing the quality of the deliveries, it is paramount to consider not only whether the stimulus term was correctly rendered, but also whether the glossary query occupied cognitive resources which could not be allocated to the processes of listening and processing of the adjacent units of information. It is theoretically possible that a correctly identified term co-occurs with contresens or the complete omission of target and/or continuation sentences, as discussed in §5.4.3.2. Therefore, in addition to the analysis of the terminological accuracy, I expanded the investigation to the sentence level. Since the individual interpreting skills also play a role, I chose to conduct the analysis at a more superficial level, only checking the presence of severe errors and complete omissions for the terms queried (in the InterpretBank and PDF glossary) and not venturing into a detailed analysis of other lower-level issues such as partial omissions in the interpreted sentences. This approach would require controlling for the individual interpreting competence and disambiguating between strategic and non-strategic omissions, additions and generalisations. These categories would be difficult to operationalise without subjective methods such as retrospective interviews, which I chose not to conduct because it would have further extended the duration of the experiment.

In analysing errors and omissions, I only considered the target and continuation sentences for which a glossary query had occurred. The goal was to establish whether a glossary query may result in an error or omission in the target or continuation sentence, which would indicate an interference between the two tasks. Therefore, I considered how the use of different tools affected this variable in order to answer the question: are there fewer complete omissions and severe errors when terms are presented on the screen automatically? Finally, in line with my hypotheses (see §5.2), I explored where the majority of errors and omissions occurred, whether in the target sentence or in the continuation sentence.

5.5.5.2 Behavioural measures

Six behavioural measures were included in the main experiment: glossary queries, EVS, inter-cluster pause duration (ICPD), time to first fixation, average fixation duration and fixation time.

5.5.5.2.1 Glossary queries

In order to gain a comprehensive picture of the test subjects' interactions with the tools during SI, I collected data pertaining to the queries performed in the PDF glossary and in InterpretBank. As will be discussed in §6.1.2.1, all participants fixated all stimuli terms on the screen, therefore the analysis focused on the tools with manual look-up.

This metric was included as its usefulness had been highlighted both by previous research (Prandi 2015a,b, Biagini 2015) and by the pilot study (see §5.4.7). The categories of terms analysed are reported in §6.1.2.1.

5.5.5.2.2 EVS

A widely-used indicator of CL in interpreting is the EVS, as discussed in §4.4.1.2. In the main experiment, I expected significant differences between tools in the EVS (see §5.2). This may point to a greater ease of use of the ASR-CAI mock-up compared to the CAI tool and the PDF glossary, and of the CAI tool compared to the PDF glossary.

In the main experiment, I calculated the EVS for the terms searched by the participants and compared it for the three tools, both for each participant and for the whole sample. The EVS was calculated as the begin time of stimulus translation minus the end time of stimulus utterance by the speaker. The availability of time stamps for individual words offered by the automatic transcription obtained with the Speechmatics tool (see §5.5.7.1) allowed overcoming a methodological challenge identified by Timarová et al. (2011: 155), i.e. the need to manually identify the beginning of the stimulus. Since this the timestamp was available automatically, the EVS could be measured with millisecond precision.

5.5.5.2.3 Inter-cluster pause duration (ICPD)

A short EVS may also suggest overall faster processing, but it does not measure it directly. Hence, I also analysed the duration of pauses between sentence clusters, i.e. between the last word of the continuation sentence pronounced by the speaker and the last word of the delivery pronounced by the participant for each sentence cluster. This may be considered as an additional measure of time lag and is geared towards a general analysis of how the speed of processing is influenced by the explanatory value of the tool used as support.

Since the speeches used in the main experiment presented a 5s pause between two sentence clusters (see §5.5.3), the ICPD may be used as an additional indicator of cognitive effort. More specifically, a long ICPD (of 5s or longer) may be interpreted as an indicator of fast processing.

5.5.5.2.4 Time to first fixation

The time to first fixation on the term AOI was expected to provide insight into the question of how the tool use affects the participants' speed in identifying the target term on the screen. SMI BeGaze provides the metrics "Time to first appearance" and "Entry time" for each AOI. The metrics, in ms, represent respectively the moment in which the AOI first becomes visible on the monitor and the start time of the first fixation to enter the AOI. For each participant and under each condition, I therefore calculated the mean time to first fixation for the term AOIs by subtracting the timestamp for "Time to first appearance" from the timestamp for "Entry time".

5.5.5.2.5 Average fixation duration on term and tool AOIs

Fixation duration has been traditionally used as an indicator of cognitive effort in the processing of the ST (see §4.4.2.2). In the present study, the focus was on the effort exerted by participants while interacting with the tools. The results therefore do not indicate how easy it is to interpret the target terms in different conditions but should rather be understood as an indication of the effort of human-machine interaction.

In each condition and for each participant, I calculated the average fixation duration on the term AOIs. Additionally, I also considered the duration of the fixations on the tool area.

5.5.5.2.6 Fixation time

In addition to the average fixation durations on the tool area, I also considered the total time spent fixating the speaker and the tool area. SMI BeGaze provides the metric "Fixation time", i.e. the "sum of the fixation durations inside the AOI" (SensoMotoric Instruments 2017a: 370). In the present study, the metric represents the amount of time spent processing the speaker video and the side of the screen where the tool was displayed. This metric was expected to provide information on how attention was allocated to the different sources of visual and visual-verbal information available to the participants, specifically on how much the tool distracted the participants from the speaker (see §5.2).

5.5.5.3 Subjective measure: The debriefing questionnaire

Only one subjective measure was included in the main experiment: a short post-hoc qualitative questionnaire. The questionnaire was kept short to avoid extending the duration of the already relatively long experiment. The inclusion of the debriefing questionnaire was expected to provide additional data to help frame the quantitative analysis and to highlight phenomena not emerging from the

quantitative analysis conducted with the above-mentioned performance and behavioural measures.

In the questionnaire, the participants were first asked to rank the speeches
from the easiest to the most difficult. This was done to check for potential effects due to the nature of the speeches interpreted and not to the other variables
controlled in the experiment. Additionally, the subjects were asked to rank the
tools from the most useful to the least useful and from the most distracting to the
least distracting. I also asked participants to include further details of which aspects of each tool they had found to be most useful and which most problematic.
This was expected to help identify the reasons behind their preference. Finally, I
explored their preferences as to the tool which they would bring with them into
the booth during future assignments.

5.5.5.4 A note on pupil size

In previous publications reporting on the envisaged methodology for the present
study Prandi (2017, 2018), I had postulated the inclusion of the metric "pupil size"
in addition to the measures discussed in the previous section and selected for the
main experiment.

Pupil size, or pupil diameter, was used in previous studies investigating the
interpreting process (see §4.5.3), both as an indicator of global cognitive load
generated by the task (e.g. Hyönä et al. 1995) and to explore local variations in
cognitive load as a response to specific features of the source speech (Seeber &
Kerzel 2012).

As discussed in §4.5.3, however, correlating variations in pupil size to variations in cognitive effort is not straightforward. There are a number of factors
which may influence the pupillary responses to the stimuli presented. This represents an important limitation for the adoption of pupillometry as a method to
explore cognitive load in interpreting.

The specific research object of the present investigation presents additional
limitations to the ones discussed in §4.5.3.

For instance, the way in which the terminological information was presented
in the PDF glossary and in the CAI tool may have resulted in higher arousal in the
participants than during the use of the ASR-CAI mock-up. In the PDF condition,
the participants could see a large number of terms on the screen. In the CAI
condition, the screen changed very quickly during the query. It is possible that
participants may have been more visually stimulated by the interfaces in the PDF
and the CAI condition due to the highly dynamic stimuli. Variations in pupil size

would therefore reflect different levels of arousal rather than higher or lower cognitive load.

Additionally, the ASR-CAI mock-up window was relatively empty: it was white most of the time apart from the moments in which the terms appeared. The higher screen luminance in this condition may have been expected to reduce the pupil size. This reduction in pupil size may therefore simply reflect a physiological reaction of the pupil to the brightness of the screen, not variations in cognitive effort. This is a common issue in human factors studies, for instance when participants interact with web pages (Holmqvist 2011: 530).

Finally, it should be noted that, in most studies on interpreting which adopted pupillometry to explore cognitive load (e.g. Hyönä et al. 1995, Seeber & Kerzel 2012), the informants were not interacting with visual stimuli. The only exception is the study by Gieshoff (2018). However, she was able to control for luminance across conditions and participants as the stimuli were not co-created by her participants, unlike in the present study for the two conditions which involve manual look-up.

For the limitations discussed above, I opted for a more cautious approach and chose not to include pupil size as a metric for the present study.

5.5.6 Procedure

The experimental design was very similar to the pilot study. I introduced several modifications and additional tests to round up and facilitate my subsequent data analysis. As described in §5.5.2, the main difference consisted in the replacement of the Word and Excel glossaries with a PDF glossary and the introduction of an ASR-CAI mock-up as the third condition. In the PDF glossary, the font size chosen was 16, as recommended in literature (e.g. O'Brien 2009: 261, Hvelplund 2014: 20, Conklin et al. 2018: 37). A large font size was also chosen for the InterpretBank glossary and for the ASR-CAI mock-up (see Figure 5.7).

The ASR-CAI mock-up was prepared following a previous study on the automatic speech recognition of numbers by Desmet et al. (2018), who had prepared a PowerPoint presentation containing all the numerals mentioned during the speech. I prepared a version of the recorded speech positioned on the left-hand side of the screen, as for the other conditions, while on the right-hand side of the screen, on a white background, I added the terms and their glossary equivalents shortly after they had been pronounced by the speaker.

This made it possible to simulate a constant system latency (ca. 1s) and ensure synchronisation between the speaker video and the ASR-CAI mock-up.

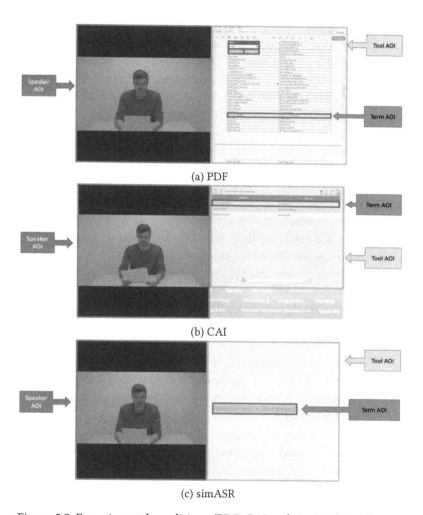

(a) PDF

(b) CAI

(c) simASR

Figure 5.7: Experimental conditions (PDF, CAI and simASR). In all conditions, the speaker was shown on the left hand-side of the screen, while the terminology was presented on the right. AOIs were placed on the speaker video, the tool area, and on each stimulus term.

As discussed in §5.5.3, only the terms present in the glossary were shown on the screen to simulate the behaviour of the ASR module, which uses the underlying glossary to identify relevant items in the generated transcription. The target language equivalents are those present in the glossary and which had been previously selected and validated during glossary creation. This architecture corresponds to the current state of the art for CAI tools (see §2.2.3 and §2.4).

The font and colour chosen were the same as in the only available prototype of this kind (InterpretBank with ASR). In the mock-up, only one term was shown at a time on the screen and it disappeared after 3000ms. I decided not to use the actual ASR integration in the CAI tool InterpretBank, but rather to simulate it, as I would be comparing two mature and stable systems (PDF glossary and InterpretBank) with a system still under development and which at the time of the experiment did not yet work optimally for terminology recognition. Mistakes in the use of the PDF glossary and InterpretBank would be due to suboptimal usage, not to system performance, unlike for the ASR-CAI hybrid. Additionally, using the real system could have resulted in different levels of performance, making it difficult to compare participants' data for this condition. While it would have been possible to simulate system failures experimentally, for instance by testing the real tool on the speaker's video, following this approach would have introduced yet another variable into the experimental set-up and further complicated data analysis. As this exceeds my research questions, I decided not to explore this facet of interpreter-tool interaction in the present experiment. Thus, the results for the ASR condition represent the ceiling performance that participants may achieve when using this kind of support. To denote that the ASR-CAI mock-up represents the best performance obtainable with an ASR-enhanced CAI tool, this condition will henceforth be defined as "simASR".

On the day of the experiment, participants were briefed on the structure of the experiment and signed a consent form for the collection and use of their data. They were informed that they would be able to revoke their consent at any time and that their data would be made anonymous for analysis. Participants were remunerated with €50 after the end of the experiment. Before interpreting, they went through a brief pre-test comprising a measurement of their typing speed and the size of their English vocabulary (see §5.5.1.2.4). Afterwards, they answered a series of questions to help them prepare for the interpreting task (see §5.5.1.2.5).

After the preliminary tests were completed, participants were asked to sit in front of the monitor where the stimuli were going to be presented. In the Tra&Co laboratory, a dedicated room is available for the collection of eyetracking data under stable light conditions. Participants were seated at a distance of around 60–65cm from the monitor. To keep the participants' position stable relative to the eyetracker and the monitor, a backpack was tied to the chair where they were sitting. They were asked to wear the backpack, which was adjusted in order not to restrict the participants' movements excessively, but to provide feedback if they shifted too close to the monitor. Nonetheless, a certain variation in their proximity to the screen was inevitable. Participants were seated on a chair without wheels to avoid them changing position during the experiment.

I explained what they were going to see on the monitor before the actual interpreting task would start and clarified any remaining doubts they may have on data collection. The microphone was placed on the table next to the participants to record their interpretation. Afterwards, the experiment was started.

The experiment was prepared in SMI Experiment Center (SensoMotoric Instruments 2017b). Participants were calibrated at the beginning of the experiment. A nine-point calibration was performed at the beginning of the experiment and then repeated at the start of each new trial. During lengthy recording sessions, drift can occur, i.e. a gradual loss of synchronisation between the participant's gaze and the recorded position on screen (see Hvelplund 2014: 210), which warrants a re-calibration between trials. After the calibration, a dry screen recording was run during which I prepared the speech and the tool on the participant's monitor. Then, the second screen recording started, for which gaze data was recorded.

I asked the participants to start the video and to follow the instructions on the screen. They would hear a loud "beep" coming from the computer and would then put on their headphones. I then asked participants to place their headphones on the desk in front of them at the end of each trial. To avoid fatigue effects, which can affect results (see Spinner et al. 2013: 400, Keating & Jegerski 2015: 18), I allowed participants to take a short break or drink a sip of water between trials. I then proceeded with the second and the third condition. In total, the eye-tracking part of the experiment lasted around one hour including breaks. Conklin et al. (2018) recommend not to exceed a duration of one hour of time for eyetracking studies.

As in the pilot study, the order of the speeches and of the tools were counterbalanced using a randomised Latin square design to minimise order effects (Conklin et al. 2018: 42–43). The impact of learning effects (e.g. Lazar 2017: 65) was minimised by the training attended by participants for all three conditions (see §5.5.2).

After the eyetracking section of the experiment was completed, I asked participants to answer some debriefing questions and sent them a link to fill out the TICQ questionnaire (see §5.5.1.2).

5.5.7 Data preparation

In this section, I illustrate how the data was prepared and systematised ahead of the analysis, the results of which are reported in §6.1.

5.5.7.1 Recordings

First, the audio recordings of the students' interpretations were cut in order to only contain the relevant material for the analysis. Due to the structure of the experiment prepared in SMI Experiment Center and in order to avoid accidental interference with the software during data collection, the recording had to be started in Audacity prior to the screen recording section of the experiment and therefore contained additional bits of audio. The trimming operation was not necessary for the original speeches, as they had been recorded prior to the experiment.

After trimming the recordings, the second step was aligning them with the original speech. In order to facilitate this step of the process, the original recording contained the auditory marker that was picked up also by the microphone used to record the students' renditions. After importing the two audio tracks into Audacity, the audio peak was identified in both audio tracks and used as a reference to align the source speeches and the renditions. In hindsight, a short and sharper sound would have been preferable, as it was sometimes difficult to identify the start of the peak, but the method proved nonetheless effective. Afterwards, the recordings of the students' interpretations were transcribed automatically using the commercial Speechmatics transcription service.[7] The transcripts thus generated were later corrected manually in order to remove any transcription error. As in the pilot study, the HIAT transcription conventions were followed (Ehlich & Rehbein 1976). Like other transcription systems, the Speechmatics ASR service provides the advantage of assigning time stamps to each word of the transcript, a feature which proved useful during data analysis. Even though the transcription was already available for the source speeches, they were nonetheless aligned using the dedicated feature also provided by the Speechmatics ASR service, in order to obtain time stamps for each word in the original speeches.

The third step consisted in importing the audio tracks and the relative transcriptions into the ELAN (2020) transcription software. For each audio recording, a dedicated track was added containing the aligned transcription. An additional dependent track was added for the interpretations: it contained only the stimulus

---

[7]https://www.speechmatics.com/ (Accessed 25.08.2020)

terms (source speeches) or their renditions by the test subjects. This facilitated the analysis, as it was possible to export each track separately, time stamps included. This was necessary to calculate the EVS between the terms pronounced by the speaker and the terms interpreted by the participants (see §6.1.2.2).

To calculate the pause length between the sentence clusters (see §6.1.2.3), the audio tracks and their transcriptions were imported into the transcription tool Partitur Editor (Schmidt & Wörner 2014),[8] which offers a feature to calculate pause length between two annotations automatically.

5.5.7.2 Areas of interest

The other set of data to be prepared consisted in the eyetracking recordings. There were a total of 27 recordings, three for each of the nine participants, who worked in the three different conditions (PDF, CAI, simASR).

The choice of areas of interest (AOIs) was motivated by my hypotheses concerning attention allocation under the three conditions (see §5.2). As I expected participants to be least visually (and cognitively) engaged in the simASR prompts and most focused on the glossary in the PDF condition, two large rectangle-shaped AOIs were placed on the main windows visualised by the participants: the speaker video and the tool window, to measure the time spent looking at the two areas of the screen. Additional AOIs were placed on the stimulus terms. For all AOIs, I used the hand-drawn method (see Hessels et al. 2016: 1695).

At this stage of analysis, I chose a large AOI for the speaker video, although it would be interesting to conduct more fine-grained inquiries exploring how visual attention is shared, for instance, between the speaker's lip movements (Gieshoff 2018, Seubert 2019) and gestures (Seeber 2012) and the glossary, i.e. between different sources of visual input. The stimulus term AOIs extended over the terminological pair. This was done in first instance for a practical reason: drawing separate AOIs on the source term and on the target term would have doubled the number of AOIs per stimulus. With nine participants each potentially processing a total of 108 terms (36 per speech), this would have resulted in a total of 1944 AOIs, of which 1296 would have had to be hand-drawn anew due to each participant's idiosyncratic search behaviour. Moreover, for moving terms (i.e. in the PDF and CAI condition), the AOIs would have been dynamic, requiring manual adjustment for intervening frames. Having double as many AOIs would also have doubled the amount of data to be analysed. To keep data analysis feasible, I opted for a larger AOI comprising both the source and the target term.

---

[8]www.exmaralda.org (Accessed 2021-07-13)

SMI BeGaze requires AOIs to be drawn post-hoc in the AOI Editor. This was necessary also because each participant worked with a different combination of speech and tool and because the term AOIs were determined by the participants' search behaviour. Because I had to use the screen recording component in Experiment Center and each participant conducted different queries in the glossary, data could not be collected for all participants on the same stimuli. To overcome this limitation, the AOIs for the elements shared by all participants (speaker video and tools) were created as global AOIs. The AOIs placed on the stimulus terms had to be created as local AOIs (i.e., not shared across participants), but each term received a code to facilitate the comparison across participants. The recording started slightly before the moment in which the students started the video of the original speech and the first 30 seconds of the recording contained the instructions for the participants. Therefore, the areas of interest placed on the speaker video and on the tool were activated (made visible) as soon as the speaker appeared on screen by adding a key frame. The same operation was repeated at the end of the speech, when the video ended and a second key frame was added when the AOIs were deactivated. In this way, the data was only analysed for the time window in which the AOIs were visible on the screen.

The same principle was followed while placing the AOIs on the terms presented automatically on the screen in the simASR condition: the AOI was activated as soon as the term appeared on screen and deactivated when it disappeared. It was not possible to standardise this step completely across all participants as the speech/tool combination was randomised, but I was nonetheless able to apply the AOI definitions for each video and tool for subsequent participants and merely had to adjust the timing.

The most challenging step consisted in drawing the AOIs on the stimulus terms looked up by the participants during the PDF and CAI trials. The two conditions presented similar issues, although the CAI condition was particularly complex. In principle, the same procedure was followed as for the simASR condition: the AOIs were placed on the terms searched and found in the glossary, activated as soon as they appeared and deactivated when they were no longer visible on screen.

Due to the nature of the PDF glossary, which showed a large amount of terms on screen at the same time, when two or more terms were alphabetically close to each other, several terms were already visible on screen while the first query was being performed. I had initially planned to activate the AOIs for all terms as soon as they were present on screen and to deactivate them once they were no longer visible. However, this would have resulted in AOIs visible on the screen for a very long time. As they would not represent the current stimulus, they would confuse the analysis. This would have also been problematic from a practical standpoint. Since the AOIs on the terms had to be placed manually for each individual term and participant, and the screen view could change multiple times due to intermediate searches before the stimulus term was mentioned by the speaker, the procedure could have been highly prone to human error, as each video frame would have had to be checked for the presence of stimuli not yet mentioned by the speaker.

The issue was even more evident in the CAI tool condition. Due to the progressive search, in InterpretBank the screen view can change numerous times before the user has completed the query. Therefore, it would have been necessary to verify which terms were present on the screen at each intermediate view and to check whether they were yet to appear in the speech, requiring an incommensurate amount of time. These factors would have made the whole procedure unfeasible and difficult to reproduce in future studies.

For this reason, for the PDF and CAI conditions, I decide to activate one AOI at a time, according to the stimulus term currently eliciting a response by the participant. Despite this necessary simplification, it was nonetheless indispensable to adjust the position of the AOI for each key frame in which the term changed position on the screen, and to ensure that the correct term was being tracked during the whole typing burst until the query was completed and the term reached its final position on the screen. The use of dynamic AOIs in SMI BeGaze makes it possible to track moving objects on the screen, but nonetheless requires manual adjustments for objects not moving smoothly, which was the case in the present study. It should be noted that the AOIs thus placed on the recording only reflect the cases in which the term searched was found by the tool.

In the following chapter, I illustrate the results and discuss them in relation to my hypotheses.

6 Results and discussion

The present chapter presents and discusses the results of the main experiment conducted following the methodology illustrated in Chapter 5. The results of the pilot study were already presented in §5.4.6. The data analysis is illustrated in §6.1. In §6.2, the results are interpreted and discussed against the hypotheses formulated in §5.2. §6.3 addresses the limitations of the study.

6.1 Results

The present section illustrates the results of the analysis of the data collected during the main experiment. The results are presented for each dimension analysed in the main study and explored through the measures introduced in §5.5.5. For an overview of the measures explored in the experiment, the reader may refer to Table 5.1 in §5.3.

6.1.1 Performance measures: Analysis

The first type of data analysed comprises the two product-related performance measures selected for the experiment (see §5.5.5.1): terminological accuracy and errors and omissions.

6.1.1.1 Terminological accuracy

The first metric analysed was the degree of terminological accuracy achieved for the PDF, the CAI, and the simASR condition. A total of 108 terms (36 for each speech) were evaluated by the author and by an experienced conference interpreter trainer working in the language pair English-German. The evaluation was conducted for all nine participants, for a total of 972 evaluations.

Before conducting the evaluation on the whole data set, I verified the adequacy of the grading scale by calculating Cohen's κ value on a sample of 22 terms (20% of all stimuli, which is a recommended amount in literature. See Mellinger & Hanson 2017: 326). Cohen's κ provides an indication of the level of agreement of two raters on the categories used for the evaluation. The maximum value achievable is 1, which indicates perfect agreement, while values below 0.6 are often considered problematic. This measure is more reliable and indicative of agreement than a mere calculation of the percentage of identical evaluations by two raters. The inter-annotator agreement calculated on the sample was substantial at 0.70 (see Landis & Koch 1977). This confirmed the adequacy of the definitions chosen to describe the three categories in the grading scale. The evaluation was then completed for the remaining stimuli and the percentage of terms for each category (0, 1, 2) was calculated for each subject. The percentages thus calculated were averaged between the two raters. The main discrepancies in the coding by the two raters was due to mispronunciations of the target terms, for which the first rater was more benevolent and assigned a value of 2 if the terms used were the ones presented in the glossary, while the second rater was stricter and usually assigned a code of 1 or 0. On the whole sample, the average intercoder agreement for the accuracy evaluation was nonetheless substantial ($\kappa = 0.77$).

6.1.1.1.1 Accuracy of terms searched

In this category, I considered the terminological accuracy achieved when terminology equivalents were suggested on screen, either automatically (simASR) or after a glossary query (PDF and CAI). This analysis should provide a first insight into how much the interaction with the tool interferes with the interpreting process and into how often a glossary query is successful and corresponds with an accurate rendition. If accuracy scores are high, this may provide a first indication that the integration of digital support into the SI process is feasible. This hypothesis requires, however, also the examination of errors and omissions co-occurring with searches in the glossary (see §6.1.1.2). In order to determine the effect of the tool on the degree of terminological accuracy achieved, the next category of terms (searched/found) will also be analysed.

For each participant and each tool, the bar charts below (Figures 6.1–6.3) illustrate the distribution of the three levels of terminological accuracy (0, 1, 2) for the terms searched in the glossary.

As expected, the best performance was achieved with simASR support: on average, 96.3% of terms received a score of 2, 2.62% a score of 1 and only 1.08% a score of 0. The aggregate mean value for the 2 and 1 scores was 98.92%, which indicates on average a very high degree of accuracy in the term renditions. This is to be expected, as for the simASR condition all stimulus terms were also "found" by the simulated tool. After a glossary query, the CAI tool led to a slightly worse performance (86.26% of terms obtained a score of 2 on average), followed by the

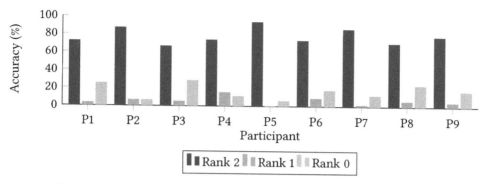

Figure 6.1: Accuracy scores for terms searched in the PDF condition

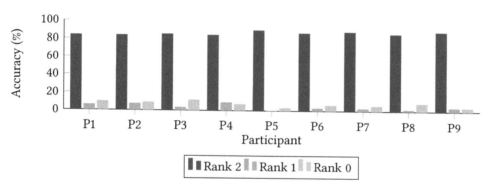

Figure 6.2: Accuracy scores for terms searched in the CAI condition

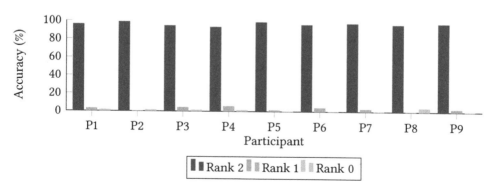

Figure 6.3: Accuracy scores for terms searched in the simASR condition

PDF tool (78.00% rated as close renditions, and a notable 16.36% were either un-translated or mistranslated). Overall, the terminological accuracy achieved with digital support was quite high, also in the PDF condition.

With reference to within-subject differences, a first inspection of the data showed a more nuanced picture, with cases in which greater accuracy (i.e. a higher percentage of 2 scores for terms) was achieved in the PDF condition than in the CAI condition, and fewer omissions or unacceptable translations were recorded for the PDF glossary than for the CAI tool.

I proceeded to verify whether the differences observed on the raw data between the scores achieved with the PDF glossary, the CAI tool, and the ASR-CAI mock-up were significant.

Since each participant was tested multiple times on the three conditions, I conducted a Friedman test. Choosing a non-parametric test seems appropriate, as the sample tested was small and the normality of distribution could not be assumed for all conditions. Non-parametric tests were chosen for the analysis also for the other metrics analysed in the study.

A Friedman test was conducted on the rank-transformed data for each of the categories of the grading scale. Since each participant worked in three conditions, ranks ranged between 1 (lowest value) and 3 (highest value), with the appropriate half scores in the case of ties.

For the terms searched, the difference between tools was not significant for the category "acceptable renditions" (score = 1): $\chi^2(2) = 3.182, p = 0.149$. A significant effect of tool was found for the category "close renditions" (score = 2), $\chi^2(2) = 14.89, p = 0.001$, and for the category "zero or unacceptable renditions" (score = 0), $\chi^2(2) = 16.22, p < 0.001$.

Post-hoc Wilcoxon signed-ranks tests with a Bonferroni correction were conducted for the significant categories, to identify which differences had led to the significant result. More close renditions were observed for the simASR condition (Mdn = 95.83%) than for the CAI condition (Mdn = 86.07%) and for the PDF condition (Mdn = 73.91%). This difference was statistically significant between the simASR tool and the PDF glossary ($p = 0.005$) and between the CAI tool and the simASR tool ($p = 0.005$). No statistically significant difference was observed between the PDF and the CAI condition ($p = 0.096$).

More 0 scores were assigned to terms searched in the PDF condition (Mdn = 17.19%) than in the CAI condition (Mdn = 7.14%) and in the simASR condition (Mdn = 1.39%). The Wilcoxon signed-ranks tests showed a statistically significant difference between the simASR and the PDF condition ($p = 0.004$) and between the simASR and the CAI condition ($p = 0.004$). A statistically significant difference was also observed between the PDF and the CAI condition ($p = 0.02$).

6.1.1.1.2 Accuracy of terms searched/found

The observations made for the terms looked up were confirmed by the analysis of
the accuracy scores for the terms searched/found in the glossary. In this case, the
differences between the tools were smaller and the results overall encouraging,
as the average percentage of terms rated as close renditions ranged from 91.35%
in the case of the PDF glossary to 96.30% for the ASR-CAI mock-up.

As for within-subject differences, the trend observed for the terms queried also
emerged at a first inspection of the data for the terms queried and found. Note
that for the simASR condition, all terms queried were also "found" (the ASR-CAI
mock-up did not contain recognition errors). However, the terms queried in the
PDF glossary and with the CAI tool may not be found. Thus, a query may not lead
to an accurately translated term. In order to explore this further, I repeated the
Friedman test also for the terms searched/found. The test yielded similar results
to those obtained for the terms searched. Significant differences between tools
were found for the categories "close rendition" ($\chi^2(2) = 7.52, p = 0.023$) and
"zero/unacceptable rendition" ($\chi^2(2) = 14.89, p = 0.001$).

Wilcoxon signed-ranks tests with a Bonferroni correction for repeated measures were conducted also for the terms searched/found in the glossary. After a
Bonferroni correction (3 comparisons), statistically significant differences were
found both for the category of close renditions and for the category of zero/
unacceptable renditions. In the "close renditions" category, a statistically significant difference was found only between the simASR and the PDF condition
($p = 0.026$). For the "zero/unacceptable renditions", a statistically significant difference was found between the CAI and the PDF condition ($p = 0.005$) and the
simASR and the PDF condition ($p = 0.005$).

6.1.1.2 Errors and omissions

The participants' interpretations were further analysed to explore how the interaction with the tools interfered with the subjects' interpreting performance on
a global level. In this analysis I considered two types of issues: severe errors and
complete omissions.

The following sections report the results of a series of tests conducted on the
data. I first considered all sentences (without distinguishing between target and
continuation sentences) and analysed the number of severe errors and complete
omissions occurring after a query. I then explored where the majority of errors
and omissions occurred, whether in the target sentence or in the continuation
sentence. Finally, I analysed how the tool used influenced the prevalence of errors
and omissions after a glossary query.

6.1.1.2.1 Evaluation framework

As for the analysis of the terminological accuracy, the assessment framework for errors and omissions was validated before proceeding with the evaluation. The level of intercoder agreement was calculated on a sample of sentences. The evaluation task included two subtasks: the identification of target and continuation sentences that contained a severe error, and the identification of sentences omitted in their entirety. The evaluation was conducted by the same raters as in §6.1.1.1. The sentences to be evaluated were presented in an Excel table. The original sentence and the rendition for each participant were juxtaposed, with an additional column for comments. For the scope of the present study, the participants' renditions were presented only in written format (but see e.g. Montecchio 2021 for an evaluation including effects on fluency).

The average Cohen's κ value was calculated for the first sample and was found to show moderate agreement ($\kappa = 0.50$). The inspection of the ratings assigned by the second evaluator showed that some sentences were marked as erroneous renditions, even though the only mistake consisted in the term used. At first, I had aimed to separate the evaluation of errors in the term renditions from the evaluation of the rest of the sentences. However, I realised that it would have been impossible to judge a sentence as "not erroneous" when the choice of term determined a complete upturning of the sentence meaning. Therefore, the evaluation task was defined as follows:

> "Please highlight in yellow the sentences that have been interpreted incorrectly (= the sentence does not make sense OR its meaning is entirely or largely different when compared to the original)".

This led to a higher number of sentences coded as erroneous, but also to substantial agreement between the raters after the evaluation was repeated on the sample and on the rest of the data set ($\kappa = 0.66$).

The reliability of the yes/no scale for omissions was very high (mean κ in the sample = 0.99), as was to be expected. The omitted sentences had been left blank in the evaluation table – the task merely consisted in confirming that the content of the sentences had been omitted, and was formulated as follows: "Please highlight in grey the sentences that were omitted completely (this might seem quite straightforward if the field is left blank ("/"), but there might be cases in which you feel that the "T" sentence already provides the information contained in the "C" sentence)".

On the whole data set, the agreement between the two raters was almost perfect, apart from one case in which the second rater did not code the continuation sentence as omitted because the sentence of the ST consisted in a reformulation of the preceding target sentence.

6.1.1.2.2 Global analysis

To start, I calculated the percentage of severe errors and complete omissions coinciding with a stimulus query. The values were calculated for each rater and then averaged. For this first global analysis, I did not consider the effect of the tool on the participants' performance. Rather, the objective was to explore how much the interaction with the tool resulted in evident issues in the participants' renditions.

In the whole sample, on average, around one sixth of all sentences including a term query led to severe errors (Mdn = 16.91%). Slightly more errors were committed in continuation sentences (Mdn = 16.67%) than in target sentences (Mdn = 13.50%), as shown by Figure 6.4.

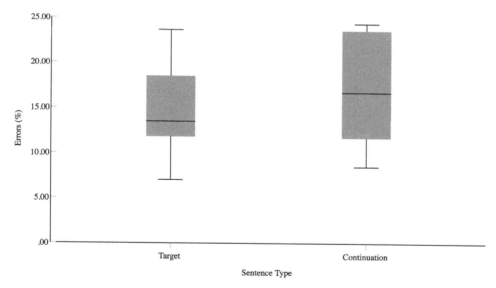

Figure 6.4: Boxplot of the percentage of errors in target and continuation sentences after a query. On average, more severe errors were committed in continuation sentences.

As for the number of omissions, a glossary query resulted in a complete omission of either the target or the continuation sentence (or both) in a limited number of cases (Mdn = 2.66%). More continuation sentences were omitted than target sentences (Mdn = 5.32 % vs. 1.05%, see Figure 6.5).

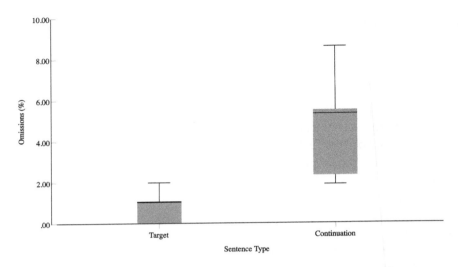

Figure 6.5: Boxplot of the percentage of omissions in target and continuation sentences after a query. On average, more continuation sentences were omitted completely.

Despite the apparent differences observed when considering the sample average, the bar plot of the data (Figure 6.6) showing each participant's performance did not suggest a common trend as to whether more errors were committed in target or continuation sentences. To confirm the lack of difference, I conducted a Mann-Whitney U test. As expected, the difference was not statistically significant ($U = 34.5, z = -0.53, p = 0.59$).

The bar plot did however show that all participants omitted more continuation sentences than target sentences. I therefore proceeded to verify whether the difference was significant. A Mann-Whitney U test confirmed that the difference was statistically significant ($U = 2.00, z = -3.41, p = 0.001$).

6.1.1.2.3 Effect of tool on errors and omissions: Terms searched

To verify how the individual tools affected the occurrence of severe errors and of complete omissions, I first analysed all cases in which a term query had been performed. As remarked for the analysis of the terminological accuracy (see §6.1.1.1), for the simASR condition, all terms searched were also "found".

As shown by Figure 6.7, fewer severe errors were committed under the simASR condition (Mdn = 11.11%). The worst performance was obtained with the PDF tool (Mdn = 19.85%), while in the CAI condition a glossary query yielded more severe errors than in the simASR condition, but less than in the PDF condition (Mdn = 15.28%).

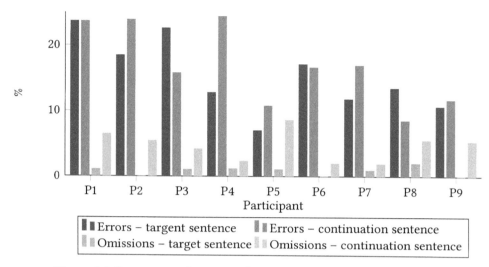

Figure 6.6: Percentage of errors and omissions in target and continuation sentences (Terms searched, mean value per participant)

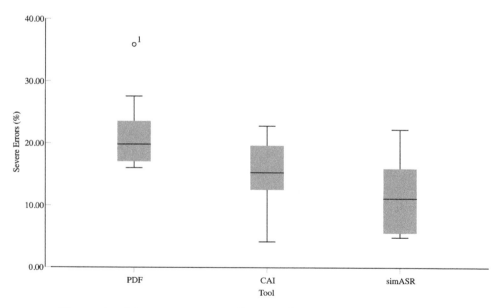

Figure 6.7: Mean percentage of errors for terms searched (Terms searched, mean value by tool)

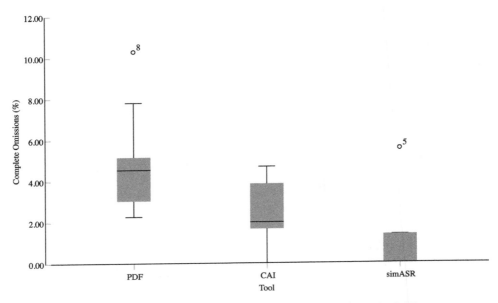

Figure 6.8: Mean percentage of omissions for terms searched (Terms searched, mean value by tool)

With reference to the number of sentences omitted completely due to the interaction with the tool (see Figure 6.8), the simASR yielded the best results (Mdn = 0.00% omitted sentences). Queries with the PDF glossary resulted in 4.55% (Mdn) omitted sentences, while the CAI tool led to better results (Mdn = 2.00%).

The bar plots in Figures 6.9 and 6.10 show the differences for each participant both for severe errors and completely omitted sentences.

To test whether the observed differences were significant, I conducted non-parametric Friedman's tests for the errors and omissions data. A non-parametric test was used since the omissions data were not normally distributed for the simASR condition and due to the limited sample size.

A significant difference was found for the effect of tools on the percentage of errors in the sentences for which a glossary query had been conducted ($\chi^2(2) = 8.00, p = 0.018$). The post-hoc Wilcoxon signed-ranks tests with a Bonferroni correction showed a statistically significant difference only between the simASR and the PDF condition ($p = 0.014$).

A statistically significant difference between tools was also found for the percentage of omitted sentences after a glossary query ($\chi^2(2) = 8.97, p = 0.011$). The post-hoc Wilcoxon signed-ranks tests with a Bonferroni correction showed a significant difference between the simASR and the PDF condition ($p = 0.010$).

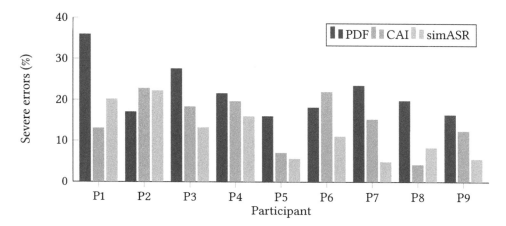

Figure 6.9: Mean percentage of errors for terms searched (Terms searched, mean value by tool per participant)

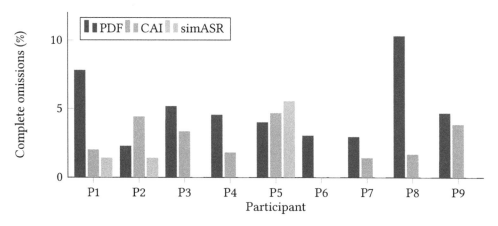

Figure 6.10: Mean percentage of omissions for terms searched (Terms searched, mean value by tool per participant)

6.1.1.2.4 Effect of tool on errors and omissions: Terms searched/found

To further the analysis, I explored whether there were differences between the tools in the percentage of severe errors and complete omissions after successful queries (terms searched/found).

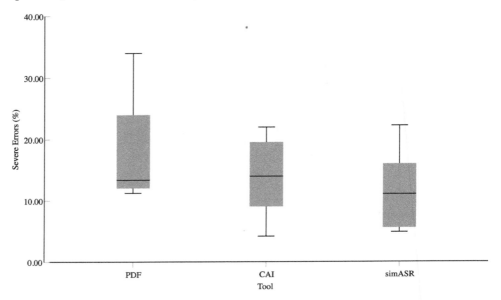

Figure 6.11: Mean percentage of errors for terms searched/found (Terms searched, mean value by tool)

For terms searched/found, the simASR results are the same as the ones reported in §6.1.1.2.3. As shown by Figure 6.11, slightly more severe errors were committed under the CAI condition (Mdn = 13.97%) than under the PDF condition (Mdn = 13.39%).

As for the number of sentences omitted completely despite a successful term query (Figure 6.12), the CAI tool yielded better results (Mdn = 1.92% omitted sentences) as compared to the PDF condition (3.70%).

The bar plots in Figures 6.13 and 6.14 show the differences for each participant both for severe errors and completely omitted sentences when the terms were searched/found in the glossaries.

As for the previous analyses on the data for the terms searched/found, I conducted two Friedman tests (for the errors and the omissions) to test for significance.

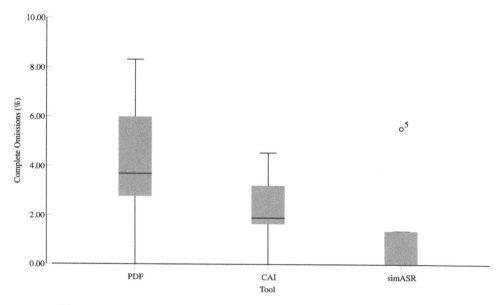

Figure 6.12: Mean percentage of omissions for terms searched/found (Terms searched, mean value by tool)

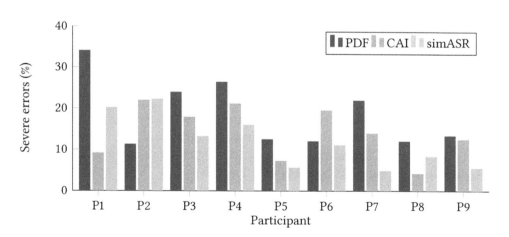

Figure 6.13: Mean percentage of errors for terms searched/found (Mean value by tool per participant)

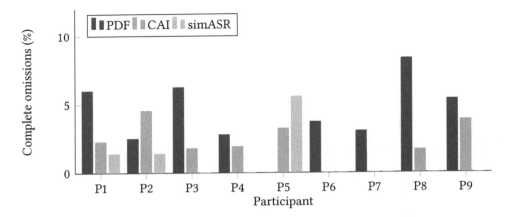

Figure 6.14: Mean percentage of omissions for terms searched/found (Mean value by tool per participant)

A significant difference was found for the effect of tools on the percentage of errors in the sentences for which a glossary query had been conducted ($\chi^2(2) = 6.88, p = 0.032$). The post-hoc Wilcoxon signed-ranks tests with a Bonferroni correction showed a significant difference between the simASR and the PDF condition ($p = 0.029$).

A statistically significant difference between tools was also found for the percentage of omitted sentences after a glossary query ($\chi^2(2) = 8.47, p = 0.014$). The post-hoc Wilcoxon signed-ranks tests with a Bonferroni correction showed a significant difference between the simASR and the PDF condition ($p = 0.014$).

6.1.2 Behavioural measures: Analysis

In addition to the two performance measures discussed in the previous sections, six behavioural measures were analysed. In this section, I report and discuss the results of the tests conducted on the glossary queries, on the two time-lag measures of EVS and ICPD, and on three gaze-related measures: time to first fixation, average fixation duration, and total fixation time.

6.1.2.1 Glossary queries

In order to gain a picture of the test subjects' interactions with the tools during SI, I collected data pertaining to the queries performed in the PDF glossary and in InterpretBank. For the CAI-ASR mock-up, no analysis was conducted, as in this condition no action was required from the participants.

In addition, the analysis of the glossary queries was used to test how the two criteria followed in the speech design, i.e. stimulus position in the sentence and morphological complexity (see §5.5.3), affected the participants' search behaviour. In this case, no distinction was made between the tools, as my goal was to verify whether my assumptions about potential effects of position or morphological complexity (see §5.5.5.2) would be supported by the analysis.

Based on a methodology already adopted in previous studies (Prandi 2015a,b, 2017, 2018), I therefore considered the following categories of terms:

- Terms searched by tool;

- Terms searched/found by tool;

- Terms searched by position (sentence-medial and sentence-final);

- Terms searched/found by position (sentence-medial and sentence-final);

- Terms searched by morphological complexity (unigrams, bigrams, trigrams);

- Terms searched/found by morphological complexity (unigrams, bigrams, trigrams).

6.1.2.1.1 Terms searched

This category represents the percentage of terms searched with each tool. Each speech contained 36 terms. For the CAI-ASR integration, the percentage was always 100%, since the terms were all automatically shown on the screen. For this category, it was therefore interesting to verify whether there was a difference in the percentage of terms looked up with the PDF glossary and with InterpretBank, since for both conditions participants were required to choose whether they wanted to conduct a glossary query or not. The simASR condition was therefore not considered in this analysis.

When considering the whole sample, slightly more terms were searched when working with the PDF glossary (Mdn = 88.89%) than with InterpretBank (Mdn = 83.33%), precisely in four cases out of nine. One participant looked up the same number of terms with both tools (83.33%). In another case (P7), all 36 terms were searched also when working with the CAI tool (see Figure 6.15).

A Wilcoxon signed-ranks test was conducted to test for significance. As expected, no statistically significant difference was found in the percentage of terms searched with the PDF and with the CAI tool ($T = 20.5$, $p = 0.67$).

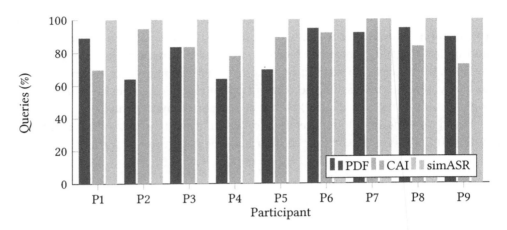

Figure 6.15: Percentage of terms searched in the PDF, CAI and simASR condition for each participant. The value is always 100% for the simASR condition.

6.1.2.1.2 Terms searched/found

One of the main indicators of how useful the tools prove as terminology support in the booth is the percentage of terms searched that were actually found by the tool. For this analysis, I did not consider whether the participant found the term in the glossary, but rather whether the term was visualised on the screen after having been looked up. It is possible that a term found by the tool may nonetheless be left untranslated or mistranslated if the participant was unable to localise it on the monitor.

Also in this case, the percentage is of course 100% for the ASR-CAI mock-up for all participants, so I only considered the PDF and the CAI tool in the analysis.

After a visual inspection of the data (see Figure 6.16), when comparing the percentage of terms searched/found by each tool, the CAI tool seemed to perform better than the PDF glossary for each participant.

I therefore decided to conduct further tests to verify whether the observed difference was significant. I conducted a Wilcoxon signed-ranks test to verify whether the observed difference was statistically significant. A non-parametric test was selected due to the small sample size. The results show a significant difference ($T = 45.00, p = 0.008$) between the CAI (Mdn = 96.88% successful queries) and the PDF condition (Mdn = 79.41% successful queries).

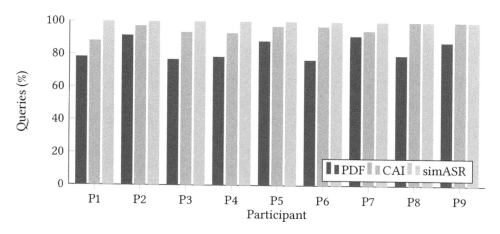

Figure 6.16: Percentage of terms searched/found in the PDF, CAI and simASR condition for each participant. The value is always 100% for the simASR condition.

6.1.2.1.3 Terms searched by position

In the speeches prepared for the experiment, the stimuli were distributed equally between terms in the middle of the sentence and terms at the end of the sentence.

At a first visual inspection of the data per participant, I did not identify a clear trend supporting either of the hypotheses formulated in §5.2, as in some cases the terms at the end of the sentence were looked up more often, while in others the opposite was true.

On average, however, the participants looked up more sentence-final terms (Mdn = 52.24%) than sentence-medial terms (Mdn = 47.76%), as shown by Figure 6.17.

A Mann-Whitney U test showed a statistically significant difference between the two conditions ($U = 5.00, z = -3.14, p = 0.002$).

6.1.2.1.4 Terms searched/found by position

In order to further explore whether the position of the terms may have affected the success rate of terminology look-up, I calculated the percentage of terms searched/found in each of the two positions (sentence-medial and sentence-final) for each participant. No clear trend could be identified between the PDF and the CAI tool after a visual inspection of the data.

For the participants, it was overall easier to find terms when they were placed at the end of the sentence (Mdn = 53.42%, sentence-medial terms: Mdn = 46.58%), as shown by Figure 6.18.

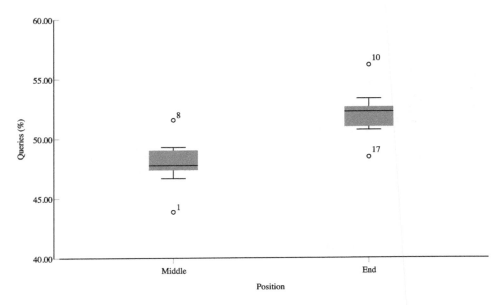

Figure 6.17: Percentage of terms searched according to their position in the sentence. More sentence-final terms were looked up than sentence-medial terms.

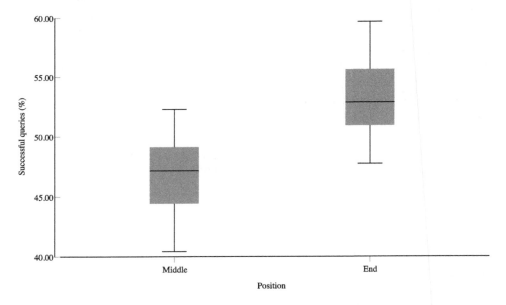

Figure 6.18: Percentage of terms searched/found according to their position in the sentence. More sentence-final terms looked up were found than sentence-medial terms.

A Mann-Whitney U test showed a statistically significant difference between the sentence-medial and the sentence-final terms ($U = 7.50, z = -2.915, p = 0.004$).

6.1.2.1.5 Terms searched by morphological complexity

I then considered whether the morphological complexity of the terms used as stimuli (see §5.5.3) may have had an impact on the participants' search behaviour.

The first category of terms analysed were the terms searched. The participants looked up more unigrams (Mdn = 34.33%) than bigrams and trigrams. More trigrams (Mdn = 33.33%) were looked up than bigrams (Mdn = 32.84%). However, the differences were small, as shown by the plotted data (Figure 6.19).

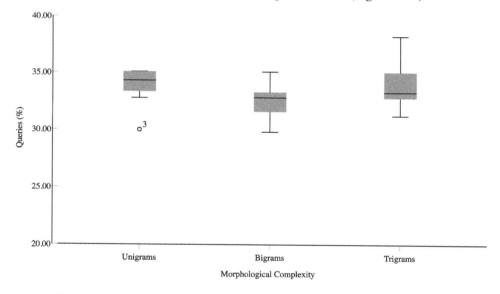

Figure 6.19: Percentage of terms searched according to their morphological complexity. Approximately the same percentage of unigrams, bigrams and trigrams were looked up.

A Kruskall-Wallis test revealed that the difference was not statistically significant ($H(2) = 2.41, p = 0.30$). In other words, the morphological complexity of the terms did not affect the number of terms looked up.

6.1.2.1.6 Terms searched/found by morphological complexity

In order to further explore my hypotheses on how term structure may affect the search behaviour and the success rate of the queries performed, I consider the percentage of uni-, bi- and trigrams searched/found with the PDF and the CAI tool, while I excluded the simASR condition for which the distribution was equal between the three categories.

In the sample, trigrams were the category of terms looked up that were found more often (Mdn = 36.21%), followed by bigrams (Mdn = 31.91%) and unigrams (Mdn = 31.03%), as shown by the boxplot in Figure 6.20.

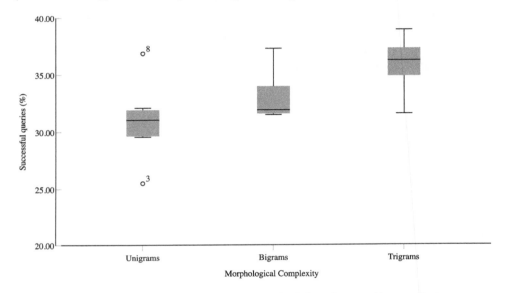

Figure 6.20: Percentage of terms searched/found according to their morphological complexity. Significantly more trigrams were found than unigrams.

I tested whether the observed difference was statistically significant using a Kruskal-Wallis non-parametric test as I had done for the terms searched. The difference was statistically significant ($H(2) = 11.85$, $p = 0.003$). Post-hoc Mann-Whitney tests with a Bonferroni correction revealed a statistically significant difference only between the number of unigrams and trigrams found in the glossary ($p = 0.002$). It appears that it was easier to find trigrams than it was to find unigrams.

6.1.2.1.7 Additional observations

A series of additional phenomena could be identified while reviewing the Gaze Replays for data preparation. Given the small sample size, it is possible that these phenomena are isolated occurrences, but I report them nonetheless as they may be useful in formulating additional hypotheses on SI with digital terminology support to be tested in future studies.

In four cases out of nine, a handful of terms (nine in total) were shown on the screen when the PDF and/or the CAI tool was used, even though they had not been looked up by the participants. In most cases, they were left untranslated or mistranslated, probably because they had not been seen. In 3 cases, the glossary equivalent was used, which would indicate that they had been seen by the participants. Even though this was a very rare occurrence during the experiment, it is interesting to notice that this could represent an additional advantage of using digital tools for terminology look-up. A dedicated experiment would be necessary to explore this aspect further.

When searching for terms, several participants could not find the term they were looking for as they did not know its spelling. This was shown by the repetition of the queries with different spellings of the same term. In some cases, the mistakes were quite naive and with all probability due to the participants having misheard the term. An experienced conference interpreter would probably have recognised that the term pronounced by the speaker was "fission", and not "fishing", especially in the context of a speech about nuclear energy. For other terms, such as "boule", which may have a complex spelling for non-native speakers of English, the difficulty is more understandable. This phenomenon further stresses the importance of preparation for effective terminology search during interpreting, as well as the role of CAI tools as digital aids and not as a replacement for preparation strategies.

Additionally, I observed several instances of terms queried which I had not selected as stimuli, such as "wheat", "power plant" and "coal". Nonetheless, they apparently represented additional difficulties for some participants. This might explain errors or omissions and in general the breakdown of the interpreting process even in sentences where no stimulus query had been performed.

6.1.2.2 Ear-voice span

For the PDF and CAI conditions, I only considered the terms which had been looked up and translated. The cases in which a search resulted in an omission of the term were not considered, as no relative time stamp was available. For the simASR condition, all terms were taken into consideration, as there were no cases of zero rendition for any participant in this condition.

As pointed out by Timarová et al. (2011), the EVS can vary considerably during an interpreting session and the average value is susceptible to minimum and maximum values. In my sample, I observed cases of very long EVS when compared to other values registered for the same participant. Therefore, for this analysis I report not only the average values, but also the median values, as suggested in Timarová et al. (2011).

The mean and median EVS varied considerably between subjects, which was to be expected as it can reflect different cognitive make-up, interpreting styles, strategies and reaction times. Nonetheless, all participants showed the same pattern, both for the mean and the median values: the EVS was consistently shorter when the simASR support was provided, followed by the CAI tool and the PDF (see Table 6.1). The difference appeared even more evident at the analysis of median instead of mean values.

To confirm whether the differences observed at a first inspection of the data were statistically significant, I proceeded with a series of tests. Data were not normally distributed as one participant had longer EVS than all other participants. Therefore, I opted for a non-parametric Friedman test on the rank-transformed data for the terms searched and searched/found in the PDF, CAI and simASR condition. Since the ranking was the same both for mean and median values and for the terms searched and searched/found, as the same pattern was observed for all participants, I conducted only one test.

The differences were statistically significant ($\chi^2(2) = 18.00, p < 0.001$). Pairwise comparisons were conducted post-hoc as Wilcoxon signed-rank tests with a Bonferroni correction. They confirmed that the difference in EVS length between each tool and the other two was statistically significant ($p = 0.009$ for all comparisons).

Considering the median values (see Figures 6.21, 6.22), which in this case seems more logical due to the higher values for P2 which bias the mean upwards, the average sample value seems to indicate that participants could gain 1.7s if they were working with the CAI tool as compared to a PDF glossary, and 1.2s when they used the ASR-CAI mock-up as compared to a standard CAI tool.

6.1.2.3 Inter-cluster pause duration

In calculating the mean and median ICPD (see Figure 6.23), I only considered the cases in which a search had been performed in the tool, while I omitted the cases in which the continuation sentence had been completely left out, as this would have shown a very long ICPD actually due to an omission.

Since the same group was tested multiple times on the three conditions, I ran a Friedman test to verify whether the differences in the ICPD were statistically significant. The Friedman test confirmed that the difference was statistically significant ($\chi^2(2) = 14.00, p = 0.001$).

Table 6.1: Mean and median EVS values (ms) for each condition, both for terms searched and for terms searched/found. The values are the same as for the simASR condition, as all terms were displayed on the screen.

	Terms searched					
Ptcpt	PDF		CAI		simASR	
	Mean	Median	Mean	Median	Mean	Median
1	5277	4339	3789	3800	2153	2045
2	7919	7210	6845	6560	3794	3089
3	5563	5068	4264	4000	2378	2445
4	5574	5290	3214	3003	1681	1567
5	5432	5495	5075	4168	2516	2065
6	5085	4690	3832	3300	1991	1875
7	4835	4200	3403	2719	2810	2505
8	5877	5070	2742	2605	1810	1490
9	4447	4210	3224	2860	1833	1650

	Terms searched/found					
Ptcpt	PDF		CAI		simASR	
	Mean	Median	Mean	Median	Mean	Median
1	5336	4351	3662	3782	2153	2045
2	7390	6950	6650	6350	3794	3089
3	5906	5114	4223	3886	2378	2445
4	5532	5270	3108	2982	1681	1567
5	5304	5208	4868	4166	2516	2065
6	5237	4860	3705	3250	1991	1875
7	4835	4200	3403	2719	2810	2505
8	5876	4785	2742	2605	1810	1490
9	4483	4210	3224	2860	1833	1650

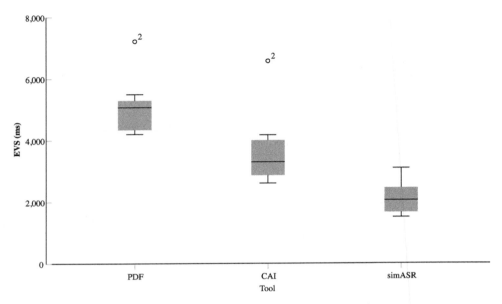

Figure 6.21: Median EVS for terms searched

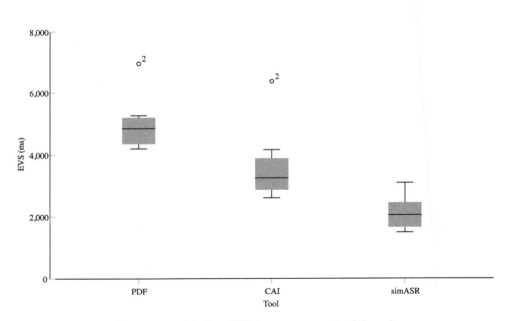

Figure 6.22: Median EVS for terms searched/found

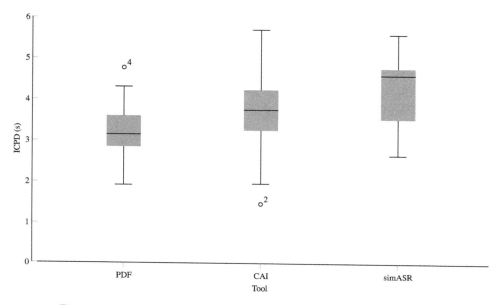

Figure 6.23: Boxplot of median ICPD (s) for each condition after a glossary query. A longer ICPD suggests faster processing of the preceding sentence cluster.

As I did for EVS, I also considered the median values of the ICPD. A Friedman test was conducted also on the median values and yielded similar results ($\chi^2(2) = 11.56, p = 0.003$).

By inspecting the data, I noticed that there were cases in which the average pause duration for the CAI tool was shorter than for the PDF, which I found quite surprising. With respect to the mean values, in one case the pause length was longer for the CAI tool than for the ASR mock-up (P4). I therefore also conducted post-hoc pairwise comparisons between the three conditions, both for the mean and the median values. The Wilcoxon signed-ranks tests with a Bonferroni correction for the mean values confirmed that the simASR ICPD was significantly longer (Mdn = 4.52s) when compared to the PDF (Mdn = 3.13s) condition ($p = 0.001$) or to the CAI (Mdn = 3.89s) condition ($p = 0.014$), but the same was not true for the other two conditions ($p = 1.00$).

If I consider the median values, a slightly different picture emerges. The differences in median ICPD were statistically significant only for the simASR tool (Mdn = 4.60s) compared to the PDF (Mdn = 3.15s) condition ($p = 0.003$). There was no statistically significant difference between the PDF and the CAI condition ($p = 1.00$) and between the CAI and simASR condition ($p = 0.055$). The median ICPD value for the CAI condition was 3.75s.

The same procedure was also followed for the pause durations between sentence clusters when terms had been found in the glossary[1], considering both the mean and the median values. Non-parametric tests were used also in this case due to the small sample size. A Friedman test returned significant differences for the mean values ($\chi^2(2) = 14.89$, $p = 0.001$) and for the median values ($\chi^2(2) = 11.56$, $p = 0.003$).

Post-hoc pairwise comparisons with Wilcoxon signed-ranks test with a Bonferroni correction yielded similar results to what had been observed for the searched terms. With concern to the mean values, the ICPD for the simASR condition (Mdn = 4.52s) were significantly longer ($p < 0.001$) than in the PDF condition (Mdn = 3.21s) and in the CAI condition ($p = 0.029$; Mdn CAI = 3.91s).

As for the median values (Figure 6.24), the simASR ICPD (Mdn = 4.60) was also significantly longer only as compared to the PDF condition ($p = 0.003$; Mdn PDF = 3.33s). The other two contrasts did not show statistically significant differences. The median ICPD value for the CAI condition was 3.72s.

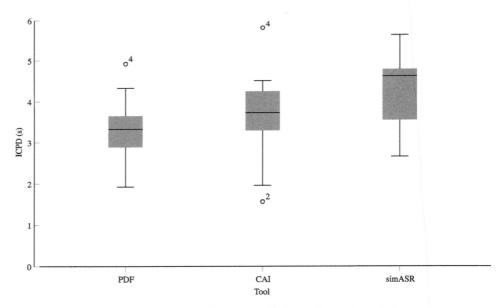

Figure 6.24: Boxplot of median ICPD (s) for each condition after a successful glossary query. A longer ICPD suggests faster processing of the preceding sentence cluster.

---

[1]As in the previous cases, the values for the simASR condition are the same.

6.1.2.4 Time to first fixation

To explore how fast the participants could identify the terms on the screen, I calculated the mean time to first fixation for the term AOIs for each participant under each condition. As for the previous metrics, I conducted a non-parametric Friedman test to establish whether the differences between the three conditions were statistically significant. The test showed a statistically significant difference ($\chi^2(2) = 13.56$, $p = 0.001$). Post-hoc Wilcoxon signed-rank tests with a Bonferroni correction showed statistically significant differences between the simASR and the PDF condition ($p = 0.018$) as well as between the ASR and CAI condition ($p = 0.018$). However, the difference between the CAI and the PDF condition ($p = 0.739$) was not significant.

6.1.2.5 Average fixation duration

In each condition and for each participant, I first calculated the average fixation duration for the term AOIs.

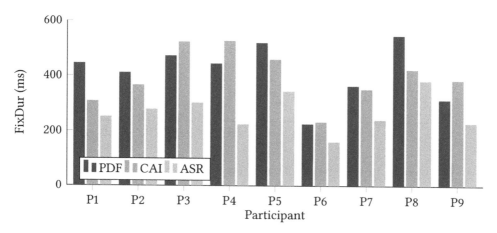

Figure 6.25: Mean fixation duration (ms) on the term AOIs for each participant and each tool

When data was available for both eyes, I averaged the mean values. After plotting the data (Figures 6.25 and 6.26), I noticed that the average fixation duration in the simASR condition seemed shorter than in the other two conditions for all participants. In some cases, shorter fixations were observed for the CAI condition and in others for the PDF condition. I therefore decided to verify whether the observed differences were statistically significant.

I used a Friedman test to test for significance. The test showed a significant difference between the three conditions ($\chi^2(2) = 13.56, p < 0.001$). Post-hoc pairwise contrasts with a Bonferroni correction for multiple comparisons indicate a significant difference between the simASR condition (Mdn = 250.04) and the PDF (Mdn = 441.51) condition ($p < 0.003$). A statistically significant difference ($p = 0.007$) was also observed between the simASR and the CAI condition (Mdn = 383.20). No statistically significant difference was found between the PDF and the CAI condition ($p = 1.00$).

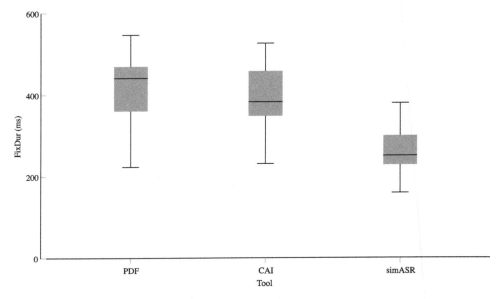

Figure 6.26: Mean fixation duration (ms) on the term AOIs for each tool

In addition to the average fixation durations on the term AOIs, I also considered the duration of the fixations on the tool area (Figures 6.27 and 6.28).

I computed the average duration of fixations on the tool AOIs for each participant and conducted a Friedman test to verify the statistical significance of the differences observed on the plotted data. The test showed a statistically significant difference in the average fixation durations on the tool area between the three conditions ($\chi^2(2) = 18.00, p < 0.001$). Pairwise comparisons conducted post-hoc showed a statistically significant difference ($p < 0.001$) for the simASR condition (Mdn = 247.35) as compared to the PDF condition (Mdn = 380.85). No statistically significant difference was found for the other contrasts (Mdn CAI = 314.85).

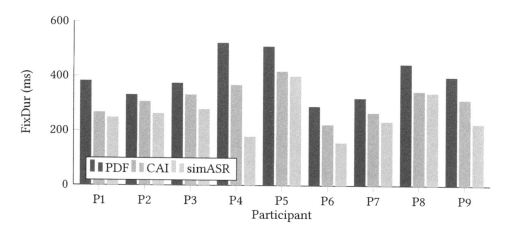

Figure 6.27: Mean fixation duration (ms) on the tool AOIs for each participant and each tool

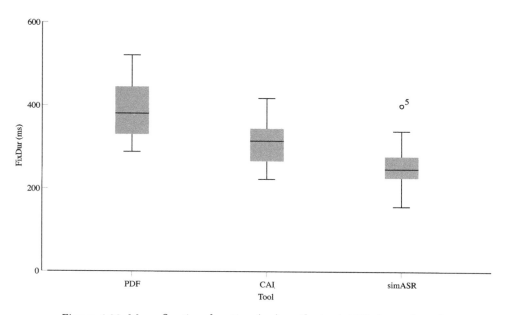

Figure 6.28: Mean fixation duration (ms) on the tool AOIs for each tool

6.1.2.6 Fixation time

The last gaze-related metric considered was the fixation time on the tool AOI and on the speaker AOI under the PDF, the CAI, and the simASR condition.

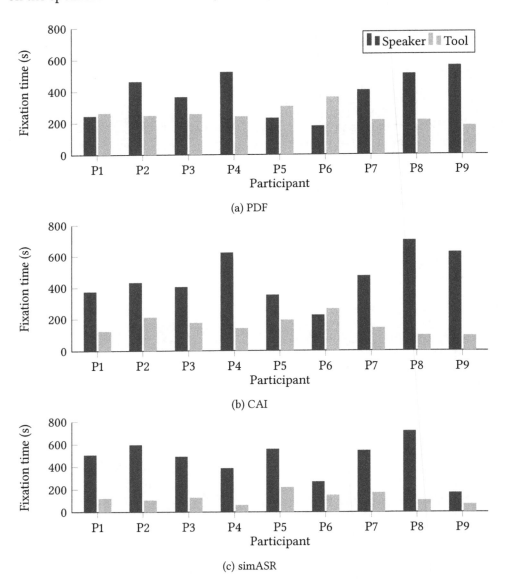

(a) PDF

(b) CAI

(c) simASR

Figure 6.29: Fixation time (s) on the speaker and tool area for each condition

The aim was to verify whether the participants spent a significantly different amount of time fixating the tool AOI as compared to the tool AOI under each condition.

The total fixation time was measured in seconds. I conducted a Mann-Whitney U test for each condition to verify my hypothesis that the effect of the tool would be greater for the simASR condition, i.e. that when working with the ASR-CAI mock-up, the participants spent significantly more time looking at the speaker than at the tool.

For the simASR condition, the difference in the time spent fixating the speaker AOI (Mdn = 503.00) and the tool AOI (Mdn = 118.00) was significant ($U = 1.00, z = -3.49, p < 0.001$). A statistically significant difference was also found for the CAI tool ($U = 1.00, z = -3.49, p < 0.001$) between the speaker (Mdn = 431.00) and the tool AOI (Mdn = 143.00). For the PDF condition, the median values for the speaker and tool AOIs were respectively 403.00s and 245.00s. The difference was not significant ($U = 20.00, p = 0.070$).

6.1.3 Subjective measure: The debriefing questionnaire

After data collection, participants were asked to answer a brief questionnaire designed to collect additional qualitative data to help frame the quantitative analysis.

To start, they were asked to rank the speeches from the easiest to the most difficult. Overall, the coal industry speech (speech C) was considered slightly more difficult, while the transmutation speech (B) was considered slightly easier, as can be seen in Figure 6.30.

However, in order to exclude speech difficulty effects, the order of the speeches and of the tools had been randomised. Therefore, I can exclude that the content of the speeches may have had a significant effect on the interpreting performance and on the interaction with the tools.

Additionally, participants were asked to rank the tools from the most useful to the least useful and from the most distracting to the least distracting.

As can be seen in Figure 6.31, the ASR-CAI mock-up was rated as the most useful and least distracting tool. The PDF glossary was considered the least useful and most distracting. As for the tool that participants would bring with them into the booth during a future assignment, most of them selected the ASR tool, two preferred the CAI tool and none indicated the PDF glossary as their preferred type of support.

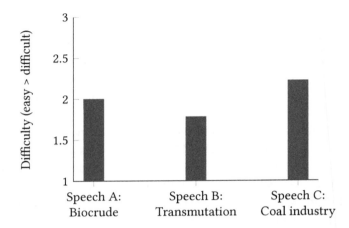

Figure 6.30: Bar plot of the participants' ratings of the perceived difficulty of the three speeches used in the main experiment (mean sample values)

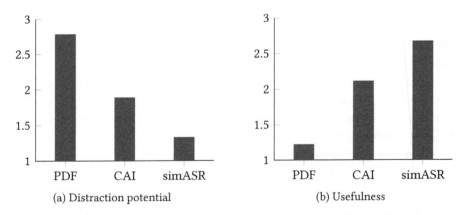

(a) Distraction potential

(b) Usefulness

Figure 6.31: Perceived distraction potential and usefulness of tools (mean sample values)

In Table 6.2, for each tool I report the characteristics identified as more useful and the key issues mentioned by the participants in descending order of frequency.

The most useful aspect of working with the PDF glossary was indicated as the possibility to see many entries at once.

As observed by one participant, this also provides the additional advantage of being able to identify a term in the glossary even though the spelling is unknown (provided that at least the first letter or sequence of letters has been typed correctly). Similar commentaries were also present in the responses (2 mentions) emphasising the usefulness of the alphabetical order, which facilitated a manual search whenever the spelling was unknown.

The program highlighted the first occurrence for the string searched. This was also considered as a useful visual aid in identifying the searched term. An additional helpful feature was identified in the ability of the program to search partial words and not only complete terms, which reduced the amount of time necessary for a search. In one case, no helpful features were mentioned, while in another case a participant laconically commented that "vocab[ulary]" was there.

As for the negative aspects of working with a PDF glossary, some comments reflect the other side of the coin of the features mentioned under "most useful". Very often (6 commentaries), reference is made to the need to navigate through the glossary if the first occurrence does not correspond to the term searched. This is a consequence of the fact that the results are not filtered out of the glossary, but rather highlighted in the body of the document. As stressed by one participant, this may prove distracting.

The way the search occurs within the document was also object of stark criticism. Here the main issues were identified in the need to clear the search field after each search, which may cause participants to lose precious time, and to click the enter key to start a search. Typing errors would also require a new search, as mentioned by two participants. These difficulties were summed up in the general commentary that "looking up words is cumbersome" in this modality.

Specular to this feedback is the description of the helpful and hindering aspects of the booth function of the CAI tool InterpretBank. The dynamic search, which shows first results already while typing and does not require to actively start the query, was mentioned as a positive feature in seven cases. The main positive consequence is that it is "not very time consuming". The same was also mentioned in relation to the fact that the search field is automatically cleared "after a few seconds", which makes it easy to "proceed to [the] next search". The ability of the tool to show fuzzy matches was also mentioned as a helpful characteristic.

Table 6.2: Most useful and most problematic aspects mentioned by participants in relation to the three conditions (PDF glossary, CAI tool, ASR-CAI mock-up). The number of mentions is indicated in brackets. Participants could indicate more than one aspect.

Tool	Most useful	Most problematic
PDF	Overview of terminology (4)	Distraction due to navigation in the file (6)
	Alphabetical order (2)	Search field not cleared automatically - time loss (5)
	Highlighting of results (2)	Traditional type of search (4)
	Search for parts of words (1)	Cumbersome (1)
	Terminology is available (1)	
	Nothing (1)	
CAI	Progressive search (7)	Distraction due to typing while speaking (4)
	Search field cleared automatically (4)	No correction of wrong spelling (2)
	Fuzzy search (2)	Too many/too few terms (1)
	Multiple results per query shown (2)	No assistance if term missed or misheard (1)
	Speed (1)	Nothing (1)
	Easier to use than PDF (1)	
ASR	No distraction due to typing (6)	Distraction / frustration if expected term not shown (7)
	Low latency (3)	Inability to search for terms not shown automatically (3)
	Easy to use (2)	High latency (1)
	No typing necessary (2)	Article not included (1)
	No time waste for queries (1)	
	Terminology support if term misheard (1)	
	Font/colour (1)	
	In-picture solution (1)	

Two general comments summarise the overall impression of InterpretBank, described as fast and easier to use than the PDF glossary. Despite the many points of praise, the CAI tool also presented several shortcomings. In four cases, participants pointed out that, despite the speed of the search, typing was nonetheless required, which interfered with their listening and proved distracting, although not as much as the PDF glossary. In one aspect the PDF glossary may provide an advantage: as pointed out by one student, when he/she had not correctly understood the term, he/she was not able to find it in the glossary. The CAI tool is thus less useful when a term had been misheard, unlike in the case of the PDF glossary which may allow the interpreter to search for terms on the page or by scrolling down.

In one case, no negative characteristics were mentioned in relation to the CAI tool.

As for the ASR-CAI tool, most participants agreed that the main advantage for the interpreter consisted in its very low distraction potential. Several respondents remarked that typing took up some of their attention and concentration, while being automatically prompted with terminological pairs during the interpreting task allowed them to stay fully focused on listening and interpreting, also because they did not have to identify the term in a list of potential candidates.

Another positive factor was the very low latency of the system in showing terms on the screen. Interestingly, one participant pointed out that, while the tool was fast, the terms could have sometimes "popped up earlier".

Other helpful features were the absence of typing from the human-machine interaction, the lack of time loss due to glossary queries, and the fact that the term was presented directly next to the speaker video.

An issue mentioned by several participants in relation to InterpretBank, partly addressed in the PDF glossary by the ability to search in the whole glossary, lies in the difficulty to find terms when their spelling is unknown. In some cases, students had the necessity to look up unknown terms which had not been shown on the screen. This was the main issue pointed out for the ASR-CAI tool.

This expectation and feeling of dependency on the tool is aptly, albeit rather naively expressed in one commentary: "in very few instances, I didn't understand a word from the original speech and the ASR didn't recognise it as [specialised] terminology and didn't translate it for me".

Finally, one participant remarked that the terminological equivalent shown on the screen by the ASR tool did not include the indication of the grammatical gender.

6.2 Discussion

In the present section, I discuss the hypotheses operationalised through Seeber's CLM (§3.5.2.2) and presented in §5.2 in light of the results presented in §6.1. The discussion concerns the effects of digital glossaries, CAI tools with manual look-up, and a mock-up, ASR-enhanced CAI tool on the process of SI.

These effects are explored by considering the performance, behavioural, and subjective measures adopted in the study (§5.5.5). This represents the basis for the validation of Seeber's CLM applied to CASI in §6.2.4. §6.3 concludes the chapter with a discussion of the limitations of the present study.

6.2.1 Performance measures

In the present study, data was collected using two performance measures (see §6.1.1):

- the degree of terminological accuracy achieved;

- the number of severe errors and complete omissions.

I will now discuss the results for each metric analysed.

6.2.1.1 Terminological accuracy

The use of digital terminology support solutions was expected to affect the terminological accuracy achieved during SI (see §5.2). Higher terminological accuracy would indicate lower cognitive effort required of the participants to operate the tool during SI (for the PDF and CAI condition) and to integrate the suggestions into their rendition. In particular, I expected significant differences between the three conditions. I proposed that the ASR tool would promote greater accuracy (see §5.2). Similarly, based on the postulated optimisation of the query function for CAI tools (see §3.6.2), I expected the use of the CAI tool to result in better terminological accuracy than the PDF glossary.

In the analysis, I first considered the accuracy achieved for all terms searched and I then focused on the terms searched/found. In considering all terms searched, i.e. both those which were found and those which were not found in the glossary, it appears that using an ASR-CAI tool as support may indeed promote more accurate renditions, both as compared to a traditional digital glossary and to a CAI tool with manual look-up. However, it should be noted that most close renditions resulted from successful queries. Therefore, discussing the category of close renditions when considering only the terms searched/found should be more revealing of the cognitive effort exerted by participants to integrate the suggestions into their renditions.

For the category of zero renditions, all tool contrasts showed statistically significant differences. In accordance with Seeber's CLM applied to technology-supported SI (see §3.6.2), I postulated that the CAI tool may interfere less than the PDF glossary with the production effort, even if a term was not found in the glossary. As a consequence, a CAI tool with manual look-up may allow the interpreter to use the available cognitive resources to at least produce an acceptable rendition of the term. On the other hand, I expected the PDF glossary to lead to a higher percentage of omitted terms due to a more complex human-machine interaction. The participants' ability to translate terms more accurately with a tool, independently of whether the query was successful or not, would suggest that lower cognitive effort is required to interact with said tool during SI. This would of course apply only to the two conditions requiring manual look-up, as under the simASR conditions all stimuli were shown on the screen. My hypothesis was confirmed, as the participants omitted or mistranslated fewer terms than with the PDF glossary not only when working under the simASR condition, but also under the CAI condition. Unsurprisingly, the fewest terms were omitted or mistranslated under the simASR condition. To sum up, the ASR-CAI mock-up seemed to perform better than the CAI tool and the PDF glossary, and the CAI tools seemed to interfere less with the SI process than the PDF glossary. This emerged especially from the relatively high percentage of terms left untranslated or mistranslated on average in the PDF condition (§6.1.1.1). These results suggest that, provided that no system failures occur, an ASR-enhanced CAI tool may promote more accurate renditions of specialised terminology and result in a lower percentage of omitted or misinterpreted terms as compared to a traditional digital glossary (in this case, in PDF format) and to a CAI tool with manual look-up.

The postulated differences in the terminological accuracy achieved with the three support systems were less evident for the successful queries (see §6.1.1.1). Data suggest that if a query is successful, the terminological quality achieved is similar for all solutions. What emerged from data analysis is, however, a superiority of bespoke tools for interpreters (be it standard or ASR-enhanced CAI tools) in preventing omissions or erroneous renditions of the specialised terms compared to a non-dedicated solution such as a digital glossary. The findings of the present study thus suggest that, even if a term is found in the PDF glossary, it may be more difficult to integrate it correctly into the rendition. One reason for this might be the fact that the target term is visually more difficult to identify on the screen (see §3.6.2).

Additionally, a first investigation of the transcriptions revealed that some students either misheard some stimuli (e.g. "peak plants" for "peatlands") or had difficulties looking up certain terms because they did not know how to spell them. This issue also emerged from the debriefing questionnaires (see §6.1.3 and the discussion in §6.2.3). This resulted in accuracy scores of 0 due to wrong renditions despite a glossary query, as the wrong term was looked up ("peak plants" instead of "peatlands", in my example) or to zero renditions, because the term was not found in the glossary. I could have excluded those stimuli from my analysis, as they represent a sub-category that had not been explicitly accounted for in the speech design. However, I decided to include them nonetheless since the ASR-CAI mock-up solved the problem for the students who interpreted the text with the support of this tool. This may represent an additional advantage when using CAI with integrated ASR, albeit more for certain languages (such as English) than for others, and only if the term is correctly recognised by the ASR module. This would support the idea that an ASR-CAI tool might reduce negative split-attention effects due to better temporal contiguity (see §3.4.2) and support both the production and monitoring and the listening and comprehension tasks (see §3.6.3). Van Cauwenberghe (2020) reached a similar conclusion, observing that an ASR tool might be useful especially in the interpretation of unknown unigrams (see also §6.1.1.1).

Overall, the results from the analysis of the terminological accuracy (both for terms searched and for terms searched/found) suggest that, when using an ASR tool for look-up, a higher degree of terminological accuracy can be achieved, especially as compared to a PDF glossary. Terms seem less likely to remain untranslated or to be mistranslated if they have been suggested by the ASR system. This is rather unsurprising and is in line with the positive results for the ASR tool observed by Van Cauwenberghe (2020: 105–109).

The relatively high percentage of terms searched with an accuracy score of 0 in the PDF condition may point, on the other hand, to greater difficulties in finding the terms in the glossary, as also suggested by the data on the glossary queries (see §6.1.2.1). This would indicate greater cognitive effort in operating the tool during SI. If the term is found, however, the differences between the tools may be less pronounced.

Using a CAI tool rather than a traditional digital glossary does not seem to offer a significant advantage in promoting more accurate renditions. It may be possible that the act of actively starting a query in the tool is what poses the real difficulty, while the fact that the search function is supposedly more efficient in the CAI tools only provides a limited advantage. After all, in order to perform a query, several cognitive operations must be performed ahead of typing, i.e. acoustically understanding the term in question, deciding to perform the query and, when the results are offered, identifying the term to be used. Most of these operations are not necessary when using the ASR tool: the term is recognised by the system (although this depends on the system performance); from a strategic point of view, the decision is not whether to look up the term, but rather whether to accept the suggestion and integrate it into the rendition; in the mock-up used, no selection of the term had to take place as previous results were deleted and the participant could only see the last term pronounced by the speaker.

However, the statistically significant difference found between the CAI tool and the PDF glossary for zero/unacceptable renditions (see §6.1.1.1.2) suggests that it was easier to find terms when working with a CAI tool and that once found, they are less likely to lead to terminological issues or omissions in the rendition.

The postulated usefulness of bespoke tools in improving terminological accuracy was suggested, among others, by Rütten (2007) and Will (2007, 2015) (see §1.2.3.2). Their hypothesis appears corroborated by the results of the present study, albeit rather for programs which do not require manually looking up terminology in the glossary during interpreting. This supports Fantinuoli's (2017b) intuition that including ASR in CAI tools may result in a considerable advancement in the usefulness of CAI tools in-process.

On the other hand, while feasible in most cases, the manual look-up operation does not always yield positive results, which supports the hypothesis that cognitive effort might be higher when more manual-spatial and more visual-spatial resources are recruited and interfere with the other subprocesses involved in SI. The suggestion that operating a software program during SI to look up terminology is incompatible with the other efforts (see §2.3.4) appears, however, rather unjustified. In sum, interpreters may find in CAI tools, especially with integrated ASR, useful support solutions for dealing with specialised terminology, while being advised that, just as their users, the tools remain fallible. This emerged also when considering the errors and omissions occurring in concomitance with a glossary query, as discussed in the following section.

6.2.1.2 Errors and omissions

The analysis of severe errors and complete omissions was conducted first by considering general trends in the sample and by also exploring differences resulting from the type of support used. As for the distinction between target and continuation sentences, my expectation was that while performing the query, the participants may have sufficient cognitive resources to retain in memory the content of the original target sentence but may not be able to dedicate enough resources to processing the continuation sentence while at the same time finishing to deliver the content of the previous sentence. Therefore, I expected more errors and omissions to occur in continuation sentences (see §5.2).

Statistical analysis only partially supported my hypotheses. The study participants omitted more continuation sentences than target sentences. This is consistent with the hypothesis formulated above that attentional resources may be sufficient to process the content of the target sentence while a term was shown on the screen (simASR condition) or searched in the glossary (PDF and CAI condition), but may prove insufficient to also process the contents of the continuation sentence. Surprisingly, there was no statistically significant difference in the number of severe errors performed in target and continuation sentences. This is probably due to the fact that my participants had not prepared on the speech topics. However, it suggests that interacting with a terminology tool during SI is a non-trivial task, which may produce issues throughout the interpretation. This may point to a trade-off between the level of terminological accuracy and overall acceptability of the rendition when a terminology support tool is used during SI, and may also suggest that the interaction with the tool may in some cases excessively interfere with the other SI subprocesses, resulting in evident issues in the rendition.

One interpretation of the spillover effect for omissions observed in the sample may be the notion of exported load put forward by Gile (2008): even though the issue does not occur in the sentence containing the target term, problems may arise later in the rendition. Since in my study the speeches used presented a high terminological density and the study design prompted the participants to look up a high percentage of the stimulus terms, the decisive element might be the number of queries performed. It is possible that under more naturalistic conditions, with less dense speeches, the number of omitted or erroneously interpreted sentences may be lower. At the same time, these findings also underline the importance of preparation, which cannot be replaced by the mere availability of target language equivalents for the specialised terminology contained in the speech. Being able to look up a term in a glossary or visualising it on a monitor is no guarantee of a successful rendition of the sentence in which the term is embedded. Similar issues have been also found in MTPE, where it has been suggested that post-editors may focus "more on the microlevel of the text than on the macro-level/the overall text." (Čulo et al. 2017: 197).

In addition to this global analysis, I also considered the effect that the different tools had on the number of severe errors and complete omissions during CASI. With reference to the number of errors and omissions coinciding with a glossary query, my hypothesis was that a lower percentage of severe errors and entirely omitted sentences would occur under the simASR condition as compared to the CAI and to the PDF condition. This is because I expected the ASR-CAI mock-up to interfere less with the SI process. The same was expected to occur for the CAI condition as compared to the PDF condition (see §5.2).

Already at a first examination of the data considering all stimuli sentences (see §6.1.1.2), the use of simASR as support for terminology seemed to interfere the least with the overall interpreting process, as fewer errors and omissions were observed for this condition in the sample average. With reference only to the sentences for which the participants performed a query, additional trends emerged. In all sentences (both target and continuation), a term query or an automatic suggestion on the screen led to severe errors in 16.11% of cases on average. This result may suggest that in most cases it was possible for the participants to look up a term in the glossary (or attend to the automatic suggestion on the screen) and still produce an acceptable sentence in the target language. The fact that the ASR-CAI mock-up, on average, led to a lower percentage of severe errors after a query also supports the hypothesis of lower interference, although there were notable exceptions and the same trend could not be observed for all participants.

As for the effect of the tool used on the number of erroneous or omitted sentences in target and continuation sentences, the only statistically significant difference observed was between the PDF and the simASR condition: fewer errors and omissions were observed in the simASR condition than in the PDF condition. It hence seems that the participants were better able to integrate into their rendition terms suggested automatically than terms which they had looked up in the PDF glossary. Using an ASR-CAI tool may therefore not only help translating the target term correctly (see §6.2.1), but also effectively rendering the utterance containing the specialised term.

The CAI tool also seemed to lead to an overall better performance than the PDF glossary, but the differences observed were not statistically significant. No statistically significant differences were observed also between the simASR and the CAI tool. These results are rather surprising, but it is possible that on larger samples, smaller effects may indeed be found. It should also be noted that the analysis of errors and omissions was conducted from a rather broad perspective. This may explain why the only statistically significant differences observed were between the tool expected to yield the best performance (i.e., the ASR-CAI mock-up) and the tool expected to yield the worst results (i.e. the PDF glossary).

To my knowledge, the only other study which analysed the number of omissions in addition to terminological accuracy for CASI is Biagini (2015). However, different from the present study, Biagini considered both partial and complete omissions, and reported values for the number of terms searched, found and correctly interpreted which did not lead to an omission. The results were not particularly encouraging, as only between 23.5% and 43.3% of terms (M = 33.43%) correctly interpreted did not lead to an omission. In the present study, the fact that only 2.14% (on average, range = 0.00%–4.55%) of correctly identified terms coincided with a complete omission when the CAI tool was used is a rather positive result. Of course, the two values are not directly comparable, as different categories of terms and different types of omissions were considered.

Additionally, Biagini's (2015) experimental material did not present the same level of control as the speeches adopted in the present experiment, and it therefore cannot be excluded that the features of the speeches used, or the type and distribution of stimuli terms, may have impacted the result. It should also be noted that, in the present study, the values may have been higher if partial omissions had been included (see §5.5.5.1).[2]

The results of the analysis of both terminological accuracy (§6.2.1.1) and errors and omissions warrants a methodological reflection. The inclusion of a broader-level analysis beyond the term level highlighted phenomena which would have otherwise not emerged. It therefore appears highly valuable to include this type of evaluation in studies concerned with the impact of CAI tools on interpreters' cognitive effort. While terminological accuracy and errors and omissions were examined in the present study as indicators of cognitive effort, accuracy scores (for terms, but also and especially for numbers) have often been approached from the perspective of quality (e.g. in Defrancq & Fantinuoli 2021). Without a more holistic analysis of the rendition, it seems unjustified to equate improved terminological accuracy (or improved numeral precision) with an overall improvement in the quality of the rendition. For studies investigating the quality of SI, it might therefore be useful to adopt evaluation frameworks which go beyond the assessment of individual elements of the rendition. Translation process research on CAT tools and MT or MTPE has used evaluation frameworks involving multiple elements of quality, such as MQM (see §4.3.1). Using frameworks such as these, provided that they are adapted to the unique features of interpreting, may offer a standardised methodology which would in turn also improve the comparability of studies on CAI. In light of the technological turn (Fantinuoli 2018b) in interpreting, adopting a standardised methodology for quality evaluation may also

---

[2]This observation of course applies not only to the CAI tool with manual look-up also used in Biagini (2015), but also to the PDF glossary and to the ASR-CAI mock-up.

help compare the quality of CAI not only with traditional SI, but also with MI, as has been done in TPR (e.g. Vardaro et al. 2019) using MQM to evaluate the quality of both NMT and human post-editing of MT.

Additionally, it appears useful to also perform qualitative, rather than exclusively quantitative, analyses of the interpreters' performance with CAI tool support, as suggested by Frittella (2022) for numbers, and similarly to the adoption of a "communicative approach" to analyse MI (Fantinuoli & Prandi 2021). An approach of this type may also promote greater awareness on the part of interpreters of the role played by the tool and may help prevent effects such as those observed by Van Cauwenberghe (2020: 123) of unnecessary self-corrections after visualising automatic term equivalent suggestions on the monitor during SI. Self-corrections of this kind were observed anecdotally also in the present study, and suggest an excessive reliance on the tool, which was noted also in the first studies on the topic (e.g. Biagini 2015, Prandi 2015a,b).

6.2.2 Behavioural measures

Six behavioural measures were adopted in the study (see §5.5.5.2):

- number of terminological queries performed under the three conditions;

- the EVS for the terms searched and searched/found;

- the inter-cluster pause duration;

- time to first fixation on term AOIs;

- average fixation duration on term AOIs and tool AOIs;

- fixation time on tool and speaker AOIs.

The results of the analysis of the term queries provide insight into the interpreter-machine interaction and, to a more limited extent, into the technical effort involved in CASI. The two time-lag measures, i.e. EVS and ICPD, are indicators of the speed of processing. The three gaze-related metrics provide information as to the cognitive effort experienced under the three conditions and about attention allocation during SI with digital terminological support.

6.2.2.1 Terminological queries

Since the simASR condition did not involve active glossary look-up, the results of the analysis of the terminological queries may only provide insight into the differences between digital glossaries (PDF condition) and CAI tools with manual look-up. Based on the results of the pilot study and the findings in Biagini's (2015) study comparing paper glossaries and CAI tools, my hypothesis was that the CAI tool would elicit more queries due to its hypothesised ease of use and higher querying speed thanks to the incremental search (see §5.2).

When considering the percentage of terms searched (see §6.1.2.1), the results do not support my hypothesis. The percentage of terms searched in the PDF and the CAI tool did not differ significantly. This may suggest that the querying process in a PDF or in a CAI tool is more similar than expected in terms of effort (see §3.6.2 and §5.2), despite the postulated optimisation of the querying process in the CAI tool. It is, however, also possible that the extensive pre-test practice enjoyed by the study participants may have helped them improve their ability to perform manual queries while interpreting, even if the PDF was not optimised for this scope. Additionally, the informants may already have been used to looking up terminology in traditional digital glossaries during their regular interpreting classes.

Another aspect to consider is the nature of the materials used for data collection. The speeches developed for the experiment were highly terminology-dense, which may explain the similar percentage of looked-up terms under the two conditions. Furthermore, the lack of preparation on the topic in all likeliness contributed to the overall high number of queried terms. The percentage of term queries may, however, yield more interesting results in designs including a preparation phase, as was the case in Biagini (2015) or Prandi (2015a,b). For instance, Prandi had found a relatively high inter-subject variability in the percentage of queries performed with InterpretBank. Low percentages were due to the fact that only the essential terms were looked up and probably also due to the effective domain-specific and terminological preparation of the students involved in the experiment. Note, however, that in that first exploratory study students worked in pairs and sometimes did not look up terms themselves while interpreting.

A more useful indicator of effort in the present experiment may be the percentage of terms searched/found (see §6.1.2.1). In this respect, the statistically significant difference between the percentage of terms correctly displayed under the PDF and the CAI condition suggests that using a CAI tool may provide an advantage when manually searching for terminology as compared to a PDF glossary. In other words, an interpreter wishing to conduct manual queries in a digital glossary may be better advised to choose a dedicated CAI tool than a non-bespoke solution. The positive results for the CAI tool are in line with Prandi's (2015a, 2015b) findings that a relatively high percentage of queries performed with InterpretBank were successful.

As for the impact of the position and morphological complexity of the terms on the participants' search behaviour, the results were mixed. The position of the terms within the sentence seemed to influence the number of terms looked-up and found in the speech. The fact that significantly more sentence-final terms were looked up and found supports my hypothesis that participants may be better able to anticipate a query and prepare for it if the term is at the end of the sentence (see §5.2). This result also supports the experimental design choice to control for the terms position in the speeches (see §5.4.3).

As for the morphological complexity and the postulated effects of length, the findings from the present study did not paint a unitary picture. Slightly more unigrams were searched on average in the sample, which would support my hypothesis that participants may be more inclined to look up shorter terms because the process may be more immediate. This result is also in line with the results of the pilot study. These results could, however, also be due to a number of additional reasons, even to the very terms chosen for the experiment. The small differences observed were not significant, which suggests that the morphological complexity of the terms did not seem to affect the participants' search behaviour. However, significantly more trigrams were found than unigrams. This would support my hypothesis that the more elements a term offers, the more likely it is for a term to be found in the glossary, because the interpreter has more material to exploit for the search. This is in line with evidence from studies on the length effect on auditory processing, as discussed in §3.1. These results are also in line with Van Cauwenberghe's (2020) findings that unigrams tended to be interpreted with the glossary equivalent significantly more often than other categories of morphological complexity (bigrams – pentagrams). Although the distribution of terms was not balanced in his speeches (only two pentagrams were present), he also reached the conclusion that especially short and unknown unigrams may pose a challenge to the interpreter (ibid., p. 119–120). This is consistent with the significantly lower number of unigrams than trigrams found by the participants of the present study. To sum up, these findings suggests that an ASR-CAI tool may provide valuable support especially for short and unknown terms.

If the findings discussed above are confirmed by examinations on larger samples, the analysis of how the morphological complexity affects the search behaviour may provide useful insights as to the strategies to adopt when using digital tools with manual look-up, as suggested in Prandi (2018). However, the strategic aspect of CASI appears relevant not only when manual look-up is involved, but also when terms are automatically displayed in an ASR-CAI tool, as literature has shown that interpreters find processing multi-word terms challenging, as discussed in §5.4.3.3. It would be interesting to explore whether the ability of interpreters to correctly integrate a suggestion provided by an ASR-CAI tool varies as a function of the morphological complexity of the terms adopted as stimuli. If it does, this would further motivate the choice to control for the variable "morphological complexity", as was done in the present study.

Overall, controlling for the position and morphological complexity of the stimulus terms included in the speeches appears a valuable design choice to consider also in future studies.

6.2.2.2 EVS

As a traditional metric used to explore cognitive effort, the EVS (see §4.4.1.2) was also included as a behavioural measure. Two categories of terms were analysed: the terms searched and the terms searched/found, i.e. first all glossary queries and then only successful queries. Note that also in this case, the two categories of terms coincided for the simASR condition (see §6.1.2.2). Additionally, in order to calculate the EVS, only those queries for which the term had been translated could be taken into consideration.

For both categories, I expected the average EVS to be shorter for the simASR condition, followed by the CAI tool and the PDF glossary (see §5.2). The results presented in §6.1.2.2 would lend support to my hypothesis of lower cognitive effort when participants interpreted with the support of an ASR-CAI integration: once the terms have been visualised, they may be integrated more quickly into the rendition. This would speak in favour of the integration of ASR technology into CAI tools for live terminology support during interpreting.

It should also be noted that when the ASR-CAI mock-up was used, the average EVS for terms was in the lower range of EVS observed in interpreters (around 2s, see §4.4.1). This is rather unsurprising, as the latency for the ASR-CAI mock-up had been intentionally kept short, in line with the findings by Montecchio (2021) that a high latency for an ASR tool may hinder a successful interpretation, and with Van Cauwenberghe's (2020) observation that the latency was sufficiently short when a real ASR tool was used, rather than a mock-up such as in the present experiment.

More interesting is the fact that the EVS was close to the higher end of average EVS values for the PDF condition. The five-second pause between sentence clusters was an artefact introduced for the purpose of the experiment, as detailed in §5.4.3. It therefore appears that in a real-life situation, an EVS of around five seconds, such as that observed for the PDF condition, may result in an even higher number of severe errors and complete omissions than were observed in the present experiment. For the CAI tool, the median EVS was also rather long (3.3s). Therefore, queries might be possible with this type of support, but nonetheless lead to errors or omissions in the rendition. Overall, this suggests that using an ASR tool may help prevent issues related to a long EVS and help keep décalage short.

Using the EVS as a measure of cognitive effort with ASR support, however, presents an evident limitation: in virtue of the fact that no manual query is required, the ASR tool is inherently faster. However, the EVS length may also be influenced by the syntactic structure chosen by the interpreter. It is possible that, under the simASR condition, the interpreter might choose a structure closer to that of the ST because the target language equivalent immediately becomes available. When a PDF glossary or a CAI tool with manual look-up is used, however, the interpreter may choose to restructure the target sentence to gain precious time during which to conduct the search. A longer EVS for the PDF or the CAI condition may therefore also suggest that the term was integrated into the interpreted sentence later down the line, and not necessarily that it took participants more time to find the term equivalent in the glossary. Differences in EVS may therefore be due not only to how fast the term can be found, but also to strategic choices made by the interpreter. Which of the two hypotheses applies remains unclear and should be further investigated. It is possible that a combination of both factors may contribute to the EVS length. Investigating whether interpreters choose specific syntactic structures to accommodate for a glossary query may also provide useful indications as to the best strategic approach to adopt when performing a query during SI.

As for the postulated advantage provided by the CAI tool over the PDF glossary, the significantly shorter EVS for the stimulus terms (see §6.1.2.2) shows that the interpreting process may indeed be quicker with the CAI tool. This result, in addition to the significantly lower percentage of term omissions or misinterpretations for the CAI tool as compared to the PDF glossary (see §6.1.1.2), represents an additional argument in favour of the use of a bespoke tool for interpreters. Especially in the case of a very fast and/or dense speech for which shortening the décalage may be a useful coping tactic, the CAI tool may therefore offer a non-negligible advantage compared to the PDF tool, while an ASR-CAI tool may be the best choice of all.

Although subject to the limitations discussed above, especially as concerns the ASR tool, the EVS may indeed be seen as a valuable indicator of how the use of a digital glossary, of a CAI tool with manual look-up and of an ASR-CAI tool affects the speed of processing in SI, which in turn reflects the effort exerted by the interpreter.

The two hypotheses formulated above as to the differences in EVS length also highlight the different dimensions of the cognitive effort experienced in CASI and reflect the make-up of the cognitive load imposed by the CASI task. As discussed in §3.4, there is an intrinsic load imposed by the interpreting task which is compounded by the extraneous load imposed by the individual tools. Similarly to the post-editing effort (see Krings 2001), the effort exerted by the interpreter during CASI may therefore be described as CAI effort, comprising both the technical effort required to interact with the tool, the cognitive effort required to adjust one's own rendition to the interaction with the tool, and the temporal effort deriving from the time required to find the term equivalent in the glossary. Considering all three sub-efforts, the CAI effort may reasonably be expected to be lower with the support of an ASR tool than with a CAI tool or a non-bespoke digital glossary.

6.2.2.3 ICPD

The inter-cluster pause duration (ICPD, see §6.1.2.3), was used in the analysis as an additional indicator of cognitive effort. Since the silent pause introduced between two sentence clusters was always 5s long in the source text, I consider an ICPD of 5 or more seconds in the participants' delivery as indicative of a faster interpreting process. On the other hand, cluster-to-cluster spans shorter than 5s should be indicative of higher cognitive effort, or, at least, of a slower interpreting process. The closer to 0, the more complex the task and, presumably, the higher the cognitive effort. If the search requires a lot of time, it is possible that the subject will have to use most of the 5s silent pause to finish interpreting the passage. A longer pause would therefore indicate a more seamless integration of the term into the interpreted sentence, i.e. a more efficient interaction with the tool, and a shorter décalage.

On this basis, my hypothesis was that pauses between clusters in the renditions would be longer for the simASR condition than in the CAI and the PDF conditions (see §5.2). For the other two conditions, on the other hand, I expected mean pause duration to be shorter, which would indicate a longer décalage, i.e. the need to use all or part of the silence between clusters to finish interpreting. I however expected the ICPD to be shorter for the PDF condition than for the CAI condition.

Overall, data show that, when using the simASR tool, the interpreting process was quicker, i.e. the décalage was shorter, and the participants could keep up better with the speaker than when working with a PDF glossary.

On the other hand, the hypothesis that the CAI tool may interfere less than the PDF glossary with the production effort in SI, but more than in the simASR condition, did not find support from the analysis of inter-cluster pause duration. As reported in §6.1.2.3, significant differences were found only between the ASR-CAI mock-up and the PDF condition, but not between the CAI tool and the PDF glossary and between the CAI tool and the simASR tool. On the basis of these results, I may only affirm that the simASR seems to slow down the interpreting process less than a traditional digital glossary. It also appears that the CAI tool with manual look-up did not significantly slow down the interpreting process more than under the simASR condition.

I do not have an explanation for the discrepancy between the results for the EVS and the ICPD. As observed for the analysis of errors and omissions, these discrepancies may indeed be due to the small sample size. A qualitative analysis of the TT or a quantitative analysis of partial omissions in the TT may help qualify these findings. This goes beyond the scope of the present contribution. It would also be interesting to use other pause metrics, such as silent pauses as in Gieshoff (2021), as an indicator of cognitive effort, either in place or in addition to the metrics used in the present experiment.

6.2.2.4 Time to first fixation on term AOIs

As predicted by Seeber's CLM (see §3.6.3), the simASR tool should facilitate the fast individuation of the term on the monitor, since the terms were displayed in isolation in the mock-up. The ASR-CAI integrations already available experimentally, such as the one offered by InterpretBank (Fantinuoli 2017a), display the results in progressive order of appearance, with the most recently found term at the top of the list. If the interpreters are aware of this, they will probably be prepared to only look in that area of the tool window. Therefore, I suppose that results would be similar if a real tool of this kind was used rather than a mock-up like in my experiment. This remains, however, a hypothesis which should be tested experimentally.

The CAI tool presents the advantage of showing results while the query is in progress, which should promote a faster individuation of the target term than in the PDF condition. Additionally, in the version used for the experiment, the CAI tool InterpretBank by default shows a maximum of nine results on the screen, and the search stops after at least five terms have been found for the query.[3] This was expected to further facilitate the individuation of the term on the screen and to reduce negative effects deriving from a visual search for the target term equivalent, as discussed in §3.6.2.

When using the PDF glossary, the participants could visualise the entire glossary page. In some cases, for instance for the terms on the last page of the glossary, fewer terms were shown, which would make it easier to identify the term searched for. This was a limitation which did not emerge in the pilot study. However, only a limited number of stimuli terms were present on the last page. In most cases, I expected participants to require more time to identify the term on the page due to having to sort through the large amount of visual material (see §5.2).

The results presented in §6.1.2.4, i.e. the significantly shorter times to first fixation for the simASR condition as compared to the PDF and CAI condition, are rather unsurprising. However, contrary to my expectation, the supposed advantage provided by the CAI tool was not confirmed by statistical testing. This is interesting, especially because many participants had identified as the most problematic aspects for the PDF glossary the lack of filtering among the results and the need to navigate in the document to find the correct equivalent. Only one participant had commented that the CAI tool had offered too many results after a query (see §6.1.1).

Caution should however be exercised in interpreting these results as an indication that the CAI tool may not provide an advantage over the PDF glossary. When a CAI tool is used, it is possible that the term may be displayed on the monitor earlier than for the PDF glossary. This might explain why the time to first fixation was longer than expected under the CAI condition. This hypothesis seems justified considering that the EVS for the CAI condition was significantly shorter than for the PDF condition (see §6.2.2.2). It is therefore possible that the CAI tool was indeed able to find the target term faster than the PDF glossary, which would be an encouraging result.

The participants who had identified the term on the screen with greater delay when working with the CAI tool may simply have continued typing even though the target term was already visible on the monitor. This may indicate that interpreters may actually need to type less than they think is necessary when working with a CAI tool. At the same time, these results may also suggest that, in the phase between the start and the end of the query, the intermediate results may be more difficult to process. The search behaviour of the individual participants

---

[3]This option was removed in later InterpretBank versions.

certainly is an important factor: for instance, touch typing may promote greater focus on the monitor and a quicker identification of the term equivalents.

6.2.2.5 Average fixation duration on term and tool AOIs

Due to the lack of a manual query with the ASR-CAI mock-up, I hypothesised that the simASR condition would require lower (technical) effort than the PDF and the CAI condition (see §5.2). In turn, I also expected that using the CAI tool would result in more limited additional effort than the PDF due to the progressive search. The progressive search was expected to facilitate the interpreter-tool interaction, resulting in an easier integration of the querying process into the interpreting process. The metrics of average fixation duration on the term and tool AOIs were expected to provide insight as to these hypotheses, specifically with reference to the cognitive effort experienced in processing the terms under the three conditions during SI and in interacting with the different tools.

The results for the average fixation duration on the term and tool AOIs partially support these hypotheses. The analysis of fixation durations on the term AOIs (see §6.1.2.5) showed significant differences between the simASR and the other two conditions and non-significant differences between the PDF glossary and the CAI tool. The significantly shorter fixation durations on the term AOIs found for the simASR condition as compared to the two other conditions lend support to my hypothesis that processing the term may be easier (and faster) when terminology is automatically presented on the screen.

However, the fact that no significant difference was found between the PDF glossary and the CAI tool for this metric may point to a higher degree of recruitment of cognitive resources by the CAI tool than expected, specifically of visual-spatial resources (see §3.6.2). My hypothesis is that this may be due to the need to visually identify the term in a list of results also when working with the CAI tool, despite the number of results being smaller than in the PDF condition.

The significant difference in the duration of fixations on the tool area (see §6.1.2.5) also supports the hypothesis that the ASR tool may recruit fewer attentional resources than the PDF glossary. The shorter fixations on the simASR area may be seen as an indication of a lower level of cognitive engagement with the tool.

However, the fact that no statistically significant differences were found for the fixations on the CAI tool area as compared to the other two conditions suggests that the CAI tool may not always be less distracting than the PDF tool, and not always more distracting than the ASR tool. It is possible that this may depend on the number of results displayed on the screen after a CAI tool query:

for some terms, the query may yield only one result (similarly to the simASR condition); for others, there may be a rather long list of terms (similarly to the PDF condition).

Overall, a lower degree of attentional resources recruited by a terminology support solution may be expected to promote focused attention on the speaker (see §3.4.2). In other words, the interpreter might have felt the need to monitor the simASR tool significantly less than the PDF glossary. Using an ASR tool in particular may help monitor (e.g. Schaeffer et al. 2019) the primary source of information (the speaker video). The metric fixation time, discussed below, may help gain further insight into this hypothesis.

6.2.2.6 Fixation time on tool and speaker AOIs

The metric fixation time, i.e. the total duration of fixations, on the tool and speaker AOIs (see §6.1.2.6), was expected to provide additional information about participants' monitoring of the tools as well as about the distribution of attention (see §3.4.2) between the speaker and the support tool. Due to the postulated lower degree of engagement with the tool in the simASR condition, I expected the participants to spend significantly more time processing the video stimulus in this condition than in the CAI and PDF condition, and, in turn, to spend more time looking at the speaker in the CAI condition than in the PDF condition (see §5.2). In other words, in the simASR condition, they would be better able to monitor the speaker and focus their attention on the speaker video, while they would need to monitor the tool the least.

The results of the analysis for this metric (see §6.1.2.6) support my hypothesis. Specifically, these results may be interpreted as evidence that, in the PDF condition, attention was more equally distributed between the speaker and the tool, which suggests that the tool required a considerable amount of attentional resources from the participants which could not be devoted to the speaker video. In turn, in the simASR and CAI conditions, it was probably easier for the participants to intentionally divide their attention between the speaker and the tool and to focus more on the speaker, particularly in the simASR condition.

Considering that the tool area only provided term equivalents, participants should ideally only attend to the tool when such information is provided or when they actively seek it during SI. In the PDF condition, however, the participants split their attention more between the speaker and the tool than in the CAI condition, and in some cases fixated more on the tool than on the speaker. The significant differences observed when comparing the duration of fixations on the tool

AOIs and the total fixation time on the speaker AOI and the tool AOI support the choice of an ASR tool over a solution requiring manual look-up.

Despite the advantage which the ASR-CAI mock-up seemed to provide over the other solutions, it should be noted that all terminology support tools may cause a negative split attention effect during SI. Yet, thus far potential split attention effects do not seem to have been taken into consideration in the design of CAI tools, with and without integrated ASR. It still remains to ascertain how the placement of the information on the screen affects attention allocation during SI. Both the Booth Mode of InterpretBank (Defrancq & Fantinuoli 2021) and the SmarTerp prototype (Frittella 2022) present terms, numbers and named entities in separate areas or columns. If a negative split attention effect is identified which can be traced back to the current tool interfaces, it would be interesting to assess whether alternative interfaces can be designed in order to reduce said effect. For instance, solutions along the lines of what has been proposed through integrated subtitles (Fox 2018) may be explored: improving not only the temporal but also the spatial contiguity (see §3.4.2) for ASR tools might help reduce their extraneous load (see §3.4.1). This, however, remains a hypothesis. Nonetheless, for the sake of CAI tool usability, it seems necessary to test different modes of display and determine their impact on the interpreting process and product.

6.2.3 Subjective measure: The debriefing questionnaire

In addition to the quantitative measures discussed above, a questionnaire was administered to the participants at the end of the experiment to collect qualitative data. The answers to the debriefing questionnaire (see §6.1.3) allow to further qualify and disambiguate the results of the quantitative analysis discussed above.

The participants were asked to rank the tools according to how useful and how distracting they proved during the experiment. I expected the ASR-CAI tool to be ranked as most useful and least distracting, and the PDF glossary to be ranked as least useful and most distracting (see §5.2). My hypothesis was supported. Overall, the participants' answers support the hypothesis that the PDF glossary may require more attentional resources than the CAI tool, and that the ASR tool may be preferable both to the PDF glossary and to the CAI tool. It is however interesting to note that two out of nine participants would bring the CAI tool and not the ASR tool into the booth. Let us therefore discuss the most useful and most problematic aspects pointed out by the participants, as they may represent useful indications for the optimisation of CAI tools and ASR tools.

With reference to the PDF glossary, participants appreciated being able to see several entries at once. This would explain why the fixation time was particularly high on the PDF area: they may have looked at the glossary also when they were not looking for a term, for example during the breaks between sentence clusters. It could be argued that this aspect depends on the way the glossary is organised, on the height of the rows and on the font size, but it seems logical that the presentation of vocabulary one page at a time favours an overview of the terminology. This might also explain why there was no significant difference in the number of queries between the PDF and the CAI tool, as discussed in §6.2.2.1: some participants may not have needed to query the glossary for certain stimuli because they could already see the target term on the monitor. This is however likely to have occurred in a limited number of cases, since the number of queries was overall relatively high.

Something similar applies to the alphabetical order, a feature which participants also appreciated as it helped them identify the terms on the screen. The alphabetical order is, however, not a prerogative of a PDF, Word or Excel glossary. Therefore, the alphabetical order may be considered as a useful feature per se. It may, however, be relevant mostly when little to no preparation is possible, or in general when the interpreters have not had time to study the glossary in detail, such as in the present experiment. Other glossary structures may be more effective under different conditions.

The participants also appreciated being able to scroll the page down to look for terms as an alternative to using the search bar. However, this is likely to require a conspicuous amount of time and might only prove useful in emergency situations. This is supported by the fact that most participants highlighted that the PDF might be distracting and cumbersome: the number of terms displayed on the screen at the same time may indeed prove overwhelming. As for the CAI tool, most participants underlined that the dynamic search and the automatic clearing of the search field make the querying process less time-consuming than in the PDF glossary.

In this respect, it is necessary to remind the reader that, although the progressive (dynamic) search, the automatic clearance of the search field and the fuzzy search are specific to InterpretBank and not available in the PDF tool, a manual query without automatic clearance of the search field and without fuzzy results can also be performed with the CAI tool. If those settings had been selected for InterpretBank, the participants' commentaries for the two conditions would have probably been very similar. Since the aim was to compare three solutions which allow for different ways for the human interpreter to interact with the machine, the search settings which correspond to the most commonly selected features for the CAI tool InterpretBank and which constitute its main element of distinction were selected.

I found it interesting that, even though only several terms are shown in the CAI tool after a query, they may nonetheless be too numerous for the user to be able to identify the target term under the time pressure inherent to SI, as pointed out by some participants.

Finally, the simASR tool was often described as not particularly distracting, specifically because no typing was required, unlike in the CAI and in the PDF condition.

Replacing typing with ASR has after all been found beneficial for the translation process (e.g. Carl, Lacruz, et al. 2016a). The fact that the attitude of most participants towards the simASR tool was overall positive might seem to contrast with a certain adversity to MT observed among translators (see §2.3.4). The ASR-CAI tool mocked-up in the present study, however, is not based on the use of MT, but rather on a combination of an ASR module with an extraction module. The results presented on the monitor had therefore already been validated through the creation of an ad-hoc glossary. In theory, however, it would be possible to use MT without having prepared a glossary beforehand, similarly to the creation of automatic interlingual subtitles (e.g. Dessloch et al. 2018). If a tool of this kind was used to provide support to interpreters during SI, it is possible that similar negative attitudes to the ones found for translators may also be found for interpreters.

Indeed, a certain level of distrust has already been suggested in studies using real tools instead of mock-ups, which, although a glossary was used as the basis for the terminology extraction, may not always display the expected result (see Van Cauwenberghe 2020).

Furthermore, while the fact that the human-machine interaction is minimal in the simASR condition and is therefore expected to improve concentration and reduce time loss, it results in an important limitation. When interpreters work with an ASR tool, they are unable to influence the queries performed by the tool and to actively query the glossary when an unknown term is not suggested automatically, as pointed out by some participants. This unfulfilled expectation may also lead to stress or distraction, as it may require reformulating the TT or re-evaluating the strategy chosen to deal with the lack of an available equivalent for the term in question. Interpreters may therefore experience the same "cognitive friction" (O'Brien et al. 2017, Cooper 2004: 19) observed in translators working with CAT tools and MT outputs.

It should be noted that the differences in cognitive engagement and distraction potential observed between the tools may also be due to the user interface. The simASR tool was relatively bare, while more elements were present in the CAI tool and especially in the PDF glossary. This aspect could have been accounted for by developing three tools ad-hoc for the experiment only differing in the search algorithm (not progressive, progressive, and automatic) and in the display of results, with no difference in terms of user interface, brightness (through the use of grey tones in the UI, for instance), etc. Such a solution, while more time consuming in the experiment preparation phase, would have allowed to pin-point the source of difference between the tools with greater certainty, and to address the limitations discussed for the metric pupil size (see §4.5.3).

Nonetheless, even if the PDF tool attracted more attention and thus proved more distracting due to its UI, this would represent an additional argument in favour of the simplification of the UI of CAI tools, whether with or without ASR integration, to reduce the distraction potential of digital support tools for interpreters. TPR has addressed the issue of the distraction caused by the interface of CAT tools and MT (e.g. O'Brien et al. 2017). Studies have been dedicated to the optimisation of the UI of CAT tools and PE environments (e.g. Moorkens & O'Brien 2016). It appears fundamental to also address the ergonomics of CAI tools, both with and without ASR integration, to maximise their support potential while reducing the extraneous load (see §3.4.1) deriving from suboptimal interfaces. A first step in this direction has been taken through the EABM (2021) project, which seeks to explore potential user preferences through questionnaires (see also §3.4). It appears necessary to explore this research question further to determine the impact of the tools' interface on the CASI process and at the same time improve the tools' usability.

By the same token, future experiments may also address the type of information presented by ASR tools. At present, most prototypes of an ASR integration into a CAI tool present the terms in isolation, devoid of any additional information. While this is easily modifiable and does not constitute an insurmountable obstacle in the use of the tool, it is also true that both traditional digital glossaries and most CAI tools easily allow the user to add columns or fields for accessory information, such as the column "Booth Info" in InterpretBank, which the user can choose to make visible in the conference modality. This feature may also be integrated into ASR-supported CAI tools, as suggested by one participant in the questionnaire.

Unsurprisingly, participants appreciated the low latency of the simASR tool, as the mock-up had been specifically prepared with this characteristic. As such, students experienced an ideal ASR-CAI integration, while real solutions may not perform as well as in the experimental setting. Although the results for the systems currently available are encouraging, especially for numbers (e.g. Defrancq & Fantinuoli 2021), latency remains an essential factor, not to be underestimated in the design and use of ASR tools (see Montecchio 2021). It was surprising to see that one participant mentioned "high latency" as a negative side of the simASR tool, as the latency was the same for all terms. My hypothesis is that in some cases, the participant in question may have preferred to know the equivalent faster in order to effectively integrate it into the syntactic structure chosen to formulate the TT.

One aspect in which the ASR tool is undoubtedly superior to the other two solutions is the assistance provided by the tool when a term has been misheard or not heard by the interpreter, due to the phonological interference experienced during SI (Díaz-Galaz & Torres 2019), or simply because the term is unknown. This had emerged also during the analysis of how the morphological structure of the terms influenced the number of queries (see §6.2.2.1). An ASR engine should provide useful support in this cases, provided that the SR performs well, which may not always be the case due to the characteristics inherent to oral speech.

6.2.4 Validation of the CLM applied to computer-assisted SI

The present study was motivated by the intention to explore how various types of in-booth technological support for terminology affect the process of simultaneous interpreting. The hypotheses on the differences in human-machine interaction and the resulting cognitive effort between traditional digital glossaries, CAI tools with manual terminological lookup and ASR-enhanced CAI tools were formulated using Seeber's Cognitive Load Model of SI illustrated in §3.6. The present section validates the model in light of the results of the experiment discussed in the previous sections.

Based on Seeber's CLM of SI (2011, 2017), the three solutions were expected to differ mainly in the degree of recruitment of manual-spatial resources at the response stage (i.e. while interacting with the tool to find the stimulus term) and of visual-spatial resources at the perceptive-cognitive stage (for the identification of the equivalent on the monitor). In particular, it was hypothesised that the PDF glossary might recruit a higher degree of resources during the query (manual-spatial resources at the response stage during the production and monitoring task), as well as for the identification of the term equivalent on the monitor (visual-spatial resources, also during the production and monitoring task) (see §3.6.2 and §5.2).

CAI tools were also expected to recruit manual-spatial and visual-spatial resources, but also to facilitate the querying process due to the progressive search and to support the identification of the term equivalent by displaying only the relevant terms on the screen (see §3.6.2).

Finally, it was speculated that the simASR tool would recruit no additional attentional resources at the response stage during production and monitoring, as the terms were displayed automatically on the monitor. The simASR tool was also not expected to recruit visual-spatial resources for the identification of the term on the screen during the production and monitoring phase.

The findings of the experiment support the assignment of different demand vectors to model the differences in the level of resource recruitment for the different tools. In particular, the significantly lower number of terms found for the PDF tool as compared to the CAI tool, lends support to the hypothesis that using a traditional digital glossary may be more cognitively taxing than a bespoke solution. If the querying process is successful, it stands to reason that the additional effort interferes less with the production effort in the interpretation. Hence, assigning a lower demand vector (1) to the CAI tool than to the PDF tool (2) for the manual-spatial resources recruited during the response stage appears justified.

Due to the lack of significant differences in the time to first fixation between the PDF and the CAI condition (see §6.2.2.4), I may assign a demand vector of 2 to the CAI tool for the recruitment of visual-spatial resources in the receptive-cognitive stage, thus equating it to the PDF glossary (the ASR tool would receive a value of 1). However, these results contrast with the significant difference between the PDF and the CAI condition found for the EVS, as discussed above (§6.2.2.2), which would justify a demand vector of 1 for the CAI tool. As observed in §6.2.2.4, the findings for the CAI condition may be biased by the fact that I used the timestamp of the first moment in which the term AOI becomes visible on screen as a reference to calculate the time to first fixation. A significant difference may indeed be found if the end of the query was taken as a reference point instead. From an operational point of view, this might, however, prove problematic for the CAI condition, because participants may continue to type after having already found the term on the screen. The first fixation may therefore fall outside of the time span considered for the analysis. Due to the inconsistency between these findings, the assignment of a demand vector of 1 for visual-spatial resources in the CAI condition remains but a tentative conclusion, which may be further explored in future studies.

The facilitation effect postulated for the multimodal presentation of the terms (visual-verbal and auditory-verbal modality) for the simASR condition is supported by the responses to the questionnaire. These findings also corroborate Seeber's proposal to model facilitation effects in the CLM. In particular, they support the choice to model the interaction with the ASR-CAI mock-up together with the listening and comprehension task (Seeber 2017: 472), which the multimodal presentation facilitated in the experiment. Here, a parallel may be drawn with the role of the visual trace of the TT in translation (see Schaeffer et al. 2019). In translation, being able to see the TT may help monitoring the writing process and the translation choices. In interpreting, it may support the transcoding of the

ST as well as the monitoring of the rendition of the TT, albeit with the limitation of individual terms.

The use of different demand vectors to model different levels of resource recruitment appears useful within the context of the present experiment and is in line with the role of these components in Wickens's (2002) original model. Seeber made a different use of the demand vectors both in the early and in the later version of his models. As discussed in the literature review (see §3.5.2), in his application of the model the demand vectors can only take a value of 0 or 1, or of 0.5 to model facilitation effects for multimodal integration.

This double role of the demand vectors appears rather difficult to reconcile in a single model. One might therefore follow two approaches. The first would consist in modelling multimodal and multicue integration and the level of resource recruitment in two separate models: one CLM of resource integration and interference, i.e. Seeber's application of Wickens' model as in Seeber (2017), and one CLM of resource recruitment in SI, i.e. my application of the model as in Prandi (2017, 2018) and in the present work. The second approach might consist in expanding Wickens' model to include an additional layer of vectors: demand vectors as in Wickens' original model, and integration vectors as in Seeber's application of the model. To avoid doubling the demand vectors for multiple cues, which would take a full demand vector (1), it might be possible to sum the integration vectors as proposed by Seeber (2017) and to sum "the average demand, across all resources, within a task (and [to sum] over both tasks)", as originally intended by Wickens (2002: 171).

Figures 6.32, 6.33 and 6.34 represent the CLM applied to SI under the PDF, CAI and simASR condition following the second approach of combining demand and integration vectors.

As discussed in the previous sections, there are several unanswered questions as to the level of resource recruitment and sub-task interference in CASI. Future studies conducted on larger samples might help provide answers which may lead to a further refinement of the model.

6.3 Limitations

The main contribution of the present work lies in the methodology developed for the study of technology support for specialised terminology in simultaneous interpreting. Nonetheless, the study presents some limitations, which I discuss in this section, before providing my concluding remarks, reflecting on the methodological, practical and didactic implications of my findings, and addressing potential avenues for further research in this relatively new domain.

	listening comprehension & reading							
	perceptual				cognitive		response	
vector	1	Ø	Ø	1	1	1	Ø	Ø
vector	0.5	Ø	Ø	0.5	0.5	0.5	Ø	Ø
	visual spatial	visual verbal	auditory spatial	auditory verbal	cognitive spatial	cognitive verbal	response spatial	response verbal
visual spatial	0.8	0.6	0.6	0.4	0.7	0.5	0.4	0.2
visual verbal	0.6	0.8	0.4	0.6	0.5	0.7	0.2	0.4
auditory spatial	0.6	0.4	0.8	0.4	0.7	0.5	0.4	0.2
auditory verbal	0.4	0.6	0.4	0.8	0.5	0.7	0.2	0.4
cognitive spatial	0.7	0.5	0.7	0.5	0.8	0.6	0.6	0.4
cognitive verbal	0.5	0.7	0.5	0.7	0.6	0.8	0.4	0.6
response spatial	0.4	0.2	0.4	0.2	0.6	0.4	0.8	0.6
response verbal	0.2	0.4	0.2	0.4	0.4	0.6	0.6	1.0

Figure 6.32: Conflict matrix for the PDF condition

6.3.1 Participants and choice of experimental design

An important limitation for the generalisability of the experimental findings lies in the small population of participants that could be recruited for the study. As discussed in §5.5.1, despite clear efforts devoted to the recruitment of participants, I was only able to include nine students in the study, mostly due to a lack of time and, probably, interest on their part, and on a series of unforeseen factors. The small sample size clearly limits my ability to generalise the results of the present study to the population of interpreting students. To counteract this limitation, a within-subjects design was chosen for the experiment. As my aim was to compare simultaneous interpreting with different types of glossary support, a within-subject, repeated measures design allowed me to work with a smaller

			listening comprehension & reading							
			perceptual				cognitive		response	
demand	integr.	vector	1	∅	∅	1	1	1	∅	∅
		vector	0.5	∅	∅	0.5	0.5	0.5	∅	∅
			visual spatial	visual verbal	auditory spatial	auditory verbal	cognitive spatial	cognitive verbal	response spatial	response verbal
perceptual	1? 1	visual spatial	0.8	0.6	0.6	0.4	0.7	0.5	0.4	0.2
	1 1	visual verbal	0.6	0.8	0.4	0.6	0.5	0.7	0.2	0.4
	∅ ∅	auditory spatial	0.6	0.4	0.8	0.4	0.7	0.5	0.4	0.2
	1 1	auditory verbal	0.4	0.6	0.4	0.8	0.5	0.7	0.2	0.4
cognitive	1 1	cognitive spatial	0.7	0.5	0.7	0.5	0.8	0.6	0.6	0.4
	1 1	cognitive verbal	0.5	0.7	0.5	0.7	0.6	0.8	0.4	0.6
response	1 1	response spatial	0.4	0.2	0.4	0.2	0.6	0.4	0.8	0.6
	1 1	response verbal	0.2	0.4	0.2	0.4	0.4	0.6	0.6	1.0

(left outer label: production & monitoring)

Figure 6.33: Conflict matrix for the CAI condition

sample wherein each participant acted as his or her own control group. This decision proved particularly helpful, as recruitment of participants was more complex than anticipated. As the participants were randomly selected among advanced students of the master course in conference interpreting of the University of Mainz and showed, among other aspects, different levels of command of the English language and different typing speeds, I feel quite confident that the trends observed in the sample were not due to the individual characteristics of the participants, but would probably also be found in a larger sample.

Nonetheless, a within-subject design also presents some limitations, in particular due to a potential increase in Type 1 error due to repeated tests in statistical analysis. I took this into account in the choice of inferential statistics and by applying corrections when necessary.

			listening comprehension & reading							
			perceptual				cognitive		response	
demand	vector		1	1	Ø	1	1	1	Ø	Ø
	integr. vector		0.5	1	Ø	0.5	0.5	1	Ø	Ø
			visual spatial	visual verbal	auditory spatial	auditory verbal	cognitive spatial	cognitive verbal	response spatial	response verbal
production & monitoring — perceptual	Ø Ø	visual spatial	0.8	0.6	0.6	0.4	0.7	0.5	0.4	0.2
	1 1	visual verbal	0.6	0.8	0.4	0.6	0.5	0.7	0.2	0.4
	Ø Ø	auditory spatial	0.6	0.4	0.8	0.4	0.7	0.5	0.4	0.2
	1 1	auditory verbal	0.4	0.6	0.4	0.8	0.5	0.7	0.2	0.4
cognitive	Ø Ø	cognitive spatial	0.7	0.5	0.7	0.5	0.8	0.6	0.6	0.4
	1 1	cognitive verbal	0.5	0.7	0.5	0.7	0.6	0.8	0.4	0.6
response	Ø Ø	response spatial	0.4	0.2	0.4	0.2	0.6	0.4	0.8	0.6
	1 1	response verbal	0.2	0.4	0.2	0.4	0.4	0.6	0.6	1.0

Figure 6.34: Conflict matrix for the simASR condition

Additionally, learning, boredom and fatigue effects may also represent issues not to be underestimated in within-subject designs. While boredom was not considered as a potential issue given the difficult task at hand[4], even more complex when performed by students, learning and fatigue may have posed important limitations.

In particular, it is possible that a certain practice effect may have ensued within-task and also from the first trial to the last. Specifically, it is possible that the students may have noticed the recurrence of the 5s pause between each continuation and introductory sentence. This may have caused them to intentionally

---

[4]Although students may have been less motivated to perform well compared to an exam situation or to a real interpreting assignment. However, I can reasonably assume that a low level of motivation would have affected all trials equally.

slow down or interrupt their rendition of the source speech while looking up terms, as they were aware of the fact that they could catch up with the speaker in the short break between clusters. For this reason, the EVS measured cannot be generalised as the average EVS of students working with PDF, CAI or ASR glossaries during SI, as it is possible that different values may be observed in a more naturalistic setting with less controlled speeches.

I had taken the learning effect into account and attempted to exclude it from the equation by training the participants ahead of data collection. If students had developed strategies to work with the individual tools, this would have already happened before testing and not during the experiment. However, it is possible that the fixed structure of the speeches may have promoted a certain practice effect within-task, as the test speeches were made up of collated sentence clusters, unlike the practice speeches which were more naturalistic in nature. Nonetheless, if a learning effect occurred, it would have occurred for all three treatments. The fact that there was a significant difference in the EVS between the three conditions seems to suggest that the type of tool used to prompt the participant with specialised terminology did affect the speed of integration of the term into the rendition. It would be interesting to further explore this instance in more naturalistic settings and also while manipulating the speaker's delivery speed, as presentation rate has been proven to influence the interpreter's ear-voice lag (see Barik 1973, Lee 2002).

As for fatigue, it is inevitable that students may have felt more tired at the end of the testing session. The trials lasted around 20 minutes each, of which 14 were occupied by the very demanding interpreting task. Given the high number of terms looked up on average in the PDF and CAI condition, it would have probably been sufficient to limit the length of each speech to around 10 minutes, in order to replicate the average duration of an interpreting exercise. I had controlled for a potential order effect experimentally by randomising the speech-tool combinations. It is interesting to notice that performance evaluations and accuracy scores were higher for the simASR condition across the board, even though in some cases the simASR treatment had been the last in the experiment. In my opinion, this might suggest that, even in situations of increased fatigue, the type of support provided by an ASR tool may help promote a high quality delivery, at least in terms of terminological accuracy and adherence to the source text in terms of informational content.

Finally, it should be stressed that, as in most other studies available on the topic (see §2.4), the experiment was conducted on students. Therefore, my findings cannot be generalised to the population of interpreters, for which the experiment outcomes may (or may not) have been very different.

6.3.2 Use of simulated ASR

The results for the simASR condition speak in favour of the adoption of CAI tools with integrated ASR as compared to traditional digital glossaries and CAI tool with manual look-up. Particularly, a tool with integrated ASR poses the advantage of reducing the additional cognitive load generated by manually querying the glossary for terminology. Nonetheless, it is important to remind the reader that, in the present experiment, the absolute ceiling performance of an ASR-enhanced CAI tools was simulated. This implied mocking-up a system with perfect precision and recall, excluding potential system failures from the experimental design. As discussed in §5.5.6, this was a conscious choice. It was taken to avoid further complicating an already highly complex experimental setup within the context of a study which presents an exploratory character and which mostly aims to offer a methodological contribution to the field of CAI research.

In light of these considerations, it is not possible to extrapolate the findings of the experiment to real-life CAI tool without hypothesising that system failures, which are bound to occur, may have a negative impact on interpreters' cognitive processing and their interaction with CAI tools. In some instances, it may even prove counterproductive to adopt an ASR-enhanced CAI tool during SI, precisely because even high-performing systems may offer sub-optimal support under certain conditions. On the one hand, this will require further research to explore the effects of system failures on SI, both from a process- and from a product-related perspective. On the other hand, increasing interpreters' AI literacy may assist them in selecting the right tool for the job and in adjusting their expectations towards AI-enhanced tools, thus contributing to making their use of said tools more effective.

6.3.3 Priming

When working with a glossary, be it in PDF format, in a CAI tool, or even printed on paper, it is possible that additional terms may be visualised while looking for another term simply because they are on the same page or because they appear in the list of results. In those cases, it is possible that for said terms a priming effect occurs: the interpreter may identify said terms faster when she looks them up after having already viewed them on screen. In the present experiment, a number of terms had already been displayed on the screen during previous queries. Priming may have determined shorter times to first fixation and shorter fixation durations for these terms.

Despite this limitation, in the present study I chose not to include this subset of terms in the analysis. This decision was made for reasons of practicality, as discussed in §5.5.7, but it would have certainly been interesting to explore this further. For instance, a sample of terms likely to have been primed may have been analysed for all participants. The first step would have consisted in the identification of the terms that had been looked up by all participants, for each of the three speeches and for both the PDF and the CAI condition. If the simASR tool was used, only one term was shown at a time, so no priming could have occurred. The next step would have consisted in reviewing the gaze replays for the participants working with the PDF glossary. When using a PDF glossary, it is possible to visualise terms occurring later in the speech only if they are alphabetically close to the term currently being looked up. With a CAI tool, it is more probable for terms to be visualised on screen even though they are mentioned later in the speech, for example because one of the elements making up the term contains the letter sequence typed by the test subject. Therefore, the PDF condition should be selected as the reference for the identification of the sample of terms (searched/found in the glossary) likely to have been primed. Finally, additional AOIs may be drawn on top of the regular AOIs to keep the two analyses separate.

While I did not consider this aspect in the analysis of gaze data, I may reformulate my conclusions as follows: even though the use of a traditional digital glossary or of a standard CAI tool may facilitate the identification of terms on the screen, the ASR integration nonetheless promotes a faster identification of the term on the monitor. However, it is possible that some of the differences observed between the PDF and the CAI tool may be explained by the priming effect rather than only by the different search mechanism.

6.3.4 Eyetracking methodology

The present study was the first to explore the cognitive implications of SI with CAI support with the eyetracking methodology in combination with more established methods focusing on the product of technology-supported SI, such as the analysis of terminological accuracy and errors and omissions in the rendition. In addition to the priming effect discussed above (§6.3.3), the collection of gaze data presented some methodological challenges, which have in part limited my interpretation of the experiment outcomes.

The first challenge is linked with the activation and deactivation of the areas of interest on the stimulus terms. In the PDF and CAI condition, in several occasions, the previous stimulus term was still visible on screen when the next term was pronounced by the speaker. To facilitate my analysis, I decided to deactivate the previous term as soon as the query for the new stimulus had been started by the participant. This was a necessary, albeit arbitrary decision, but which was applied to all stimuli in the same way. It would certainly be interesting to explore the gaze behaviour of the participants in situations in which both terms are visible on screen. However, this would have exceeded the scope of the present study, which is why I chose to exclude this aspect from my analysis. It should be noted, however, that in some cases the terms disappeared from the monitor soon after the delivery of the sentence cluster in question had been rendered in the target language. This was due either to the participant actively clearing the search field immediately after the query to prepare for the next search, or to the participant having looked up another term unknown to them, which I had not selected as stimulus (see §6.1.2.1.7). This may explain shorter total fixation times on the term AOIs and even shorter fixation durations for some participants (see §6.1.2.5).

The second limitation is linked with the fact that, in the PDF and CAI conditions, the AOIs could only be placed on the terms which had been found in the glossary. This aspect of my experimental design made it impossible to use eyetracking to explore the cognitive impact of a failed query, which may have yielded interesting results.

Additionally, the metric "time to first fixation", which I used to contrast the recruitment of visual-spatial resources in the three conditions, is limited in its ability to compare tools with different query mechanisms, such as in this case. The first fixation on the term in the simASR condition is likely to coincide with processing, while the first fixation on terms in the other two conditions may only reflect the individuation of the term on the screen (§6.1.2.4). For this reason, I did not adopt the metric "first fixation duration", as identifying the first duration reflecting cognitive processing of the term would have probably resulted in mere guesswork.

Despite some limitations, the use of the eyetracking methodology in this field of interpreting studies seems promising and may reveal aspects of human-machine interaction with CAI tools still unexplored with different methods.

7 Conclusion

The present study set out to explore the impact of digital terminology support tools on the SI process. Through an experimental contribution comparing traditional digital glossaries, CAI tools with manual look-up and ASR-enhanced CAI tools, the study addressed two main limitations in current CAI research: the almost exclusive focus on the product of CASI and the lack of a validated methodology for the exploration of the CASI process. Building upon previous research conducted on the topic, I explored the impact of the different support solutions on the SI process through product-related measures, but I also analysed the usefulness of additional process-based measures. The present study was therefore the first to adopt a mixed-method approach for the exploration of the cognitive processes of CASI, deriving its methods from TPR, and exploring assumptions on the impact of CAI tools on the process of SI through a systematic approach.

Chapter 1 introduced the topic of terminology in conference interpreting and described the relevance of terminology as a quality factor. Additionally, it reviewed conference interpreters' habits for terminology preparation pre-assignment and for terminology look-up during the assignment emerging from several surveys conducted on the topic.

After reviewing the main technologies applied to interpreting, Chapter 2 broadened the analysis to supporting technologies for terminology work, with a focus on the most recent development in this field: CAI tools with and without ASR support. The chapter reviewed current CAI research and discussed open questions not yet addressed in scholarship.

As the main aspect of innovation of the present doctoral work consisted in the exploration of technology-supported SI cognition, Chapter 3 discussed interpreting from a cognitive standpoint. The chapter illustrated and contrasted relevant theoretical models derived from cognitive psychology and Interpreting Studies and previously applied to experimental research on the interpreting process with CAI tools and multimodal input. Seeber's CLM of SI with text was applied to the present research object to illustrate the hypothesised differences in the cognitive impact of tools under the three conditions contrasted during the experiment.

Chapter 4 discussed the various approaches adopted in Interpreting Studies and TPR to measure CL, discussing the benefits and shortcoming of theoretical approaches as well as subjective, performance, behavioural and physiological methods.

In Chapter 5, I defined the research gap addressed by the experimental contribution and formulated the hypotheses on CL in CASI. Additionally, I motivated the selection of the metrics analysed in the experimental contribution and illustrated the methodology of the experiment conducted to verify my hypotheses. I first presented the method and objectives of the pilot study carried out to validate the stimuli and methodology adopted in the main experiment. I then discussed the main experiment, going into the details of the participants' training, of the materials and apparatus used and of data collection and preparation.

Chapter 6 presents and discusses the results of the analyses of the experimental data, which overall support the research hypotheses. The chapter also illustrates the main lacunae of the study.

In this final chapter, I offer some reflections on the methodological, didactic and practical implications of the findings of the present study and suggest potential areas of exploration to be addressed in future studies on the relatively new field of computer-assisted (simultaneous) interpreting. §7.1 presents the methodological implications for future studies on this topic. In §7.2, I address the implications for the inclusion of CAI tools with and without integrated ASR in the interpreting curriculum. §7.3 discusses practical implications for the development and improvement of bespoke support tools for conference interpreters. §7.4 concludes the work by suggesting potential avenues for future CAI research.

7.1 Methodological implications

The main contribution of the present study lies in the development of an experimental methodology for the exploration of the CASI process. As described in Chapters 5 and 6, the research object was investigated through the combination of multiple methods for the collection of primarily quantitative data.

Building on a previous study which had highlighted the importance of training for effective in-process interaction with CAI tools (Prandi 2015a,b), the pilot study and the main experiment were preceded by a training phase. The choice to switch to an online training may prove particularly useful also in future studies, as it has the potential to reach a higher number of participants while at the same time allowing for a more personalised and flexible, self-paced training process, both in terms of the frequency and of the integration of the training into the subjects' schedule. The online format may also allow for an easier integration of the participants' training into the study design as compared to face-to-face training.

As for the stimulus material used in the experiment, the preparation of the speeches turned out to be highly time-consuming. Nonetheless, the result is a set of highly controlled, highly comparable speeches which may be used to further explore the cognitive implications of human-machine interaction during interpreting, for instance in terms of coping tactics adopted during interpreting. In light of the current lack of uniform methods and validated materials for the investigation of the CASI process and product, it is my hope that this material will prove useful also for future studies in the field.

With reference to the study design, the adoption of a mixed-method approach appears promising. This approach allowed me to link observations derived from the product-based measures (term accuracy, errors and omissions) with the findings from process-related measures derived from TPR. This represents a step forward as compared to previous studies which had adopted only product-based metrics. In addition, the choice to combine several metrics allowed for a deeper understanding of the process of SI with digital terminological support, bringing to light a series of phenomena which would have otherwise remained unknown.

The inclusion of multiple measures and methods commonly adopted in TPR to study the translation and interpreting process proved beneficial. Further work is however necessary to refine the measures used and identify additional useful metrics for the investigation of CASI.

Following this approach is however likely to produce a large amount of data which requires extensive preparation, thus complicating the analysis. Future studies may therefore choose to focus on individual aspects which the present work has touched upon.

The choice of a within-subject design proved valuable to cope with the limited number of participants available. In particular, it allowed for the use of inferential statistics even on a limited population of participants, improving the reliability of the results presented. Larger samples, however, would provide greater confidence in the results.

A between-subject design, despite requiring accurate participant selection to ensure sample homogeneity, may ensure even greater comparability in the stimuli used and lend further support to some tentative observations formulated in the present contribution. However, until the use of CAI tools becomes mainstream, it is possible that between-subject designs with sufficiently large samples may be difficult to adopt and that within-subject designs may constitute a more practical choice. Additionally, it may be considered unethical to only provide training to one group, so this should be taken into consideration especially for studies involving students. Furthermore, if we are to establish which tools may best support interpreters during interpreting while interfering the least with the other subprocesses involved in SI, intra-subject explorations may indeed represent a more adequate design choice to address our research questions.

Since a few institutions have already introduced CAI tools into their curricula, studies involving larger populations of student participants would represent a valuable contribution. However, an important limitation of the present study and of previous CAI research lies in the almost exclusive involvement of trainee interpreters in the experiments, as discussed in §6.3.1. Hence, it appears necessary to also include professional conference interpreters in studies on technology-enhanced interpreting.

7.2 Didactic implications

The outcome of the present study presents a series of implications for training, especially because the sample population involved in the experiment and in the pilot study was made up of student interpreters.

To start, the study explored the possibility to train students on the tool functionalities through distance-learning. I see potential for the development of e-learning modules on this topic. In light of the still limited inclusion of CAI tools into the training of 21st century interpreters, online training may represent an efficient way to promote the development of new digital skills despite bureaucratic or logistic limitations. Especially the logistic limitations which have emerged significantly in the wake of the COVID-19 pandemic may be partly addressed by distance training. However, it should be remarked that, for the present experiment, no didactic intervention aimed to promote the students' effective use of CAI tools was included in the training module: the participants' training mostly included self-directed practice sessions. Our currently still limited understanding of the CAI process and of the impact of CAI tool use on the product of SI represents an important limitation for CAI tool training. Nonetheless, as not only training, but also research has had to address the logistic limitations imposed by the pandemic, using online modules may be useful if participants are only to gain sufficient practice in the experimental task ahead of data collection.

Anecdotal observations conducted on the students' interaction with the different support tools during the experiment (see §6.1.2.1.7) highlighted a sometimes ineffective approach to the use of the tools, emerging for instance as repeated queries or as queries performed for terms of which the spelling was unknown. These phenomena, combined with a certain over-reliance on the tools observed in the present and previous studies (e.g. Prandi 2015a,b, Van Cauwenberghe 2020), would suggest that training may not only be necessary to develop the required practical skills in operating the tools in the booth, but also as concerns the strategic dimension of the in-booth interaction with CAI tools. In particular, it appears important that students and professionals know the technologies behind ASR-enhanced CAI tools and be able to adjust their expectations on the systems and adopt effective coping tactics in case of system failure.

In light of the above, I believe that training should also address the benefits and shortcomings of each type of solution also from a strategic standpoint, i.e., in terms of how the tool selected may affect the process and product of interpreting. An example is the positive, although unsurprising, effect on the EVS observed for the ASR mock-up (§6.2.2.2). As IS literature has found that adjusting the décalage may be an effective tactic to cope with very dense or fast speeches (e.g. Gile 2009), the choice between an ASR-enhanced and a CAI tool with manual look-up may also be motivated by reasons of this kind. At the same time, in §6.2.2.2, I had formulated the hypothesis, which remains to be tested in future studies, that a faster integration of the term into the rendition may also coincide with a syntactic structure closer to the original. For some language pairs, this may result in a less fluent or idiomatic delivery. This, however, also remains to be explored in future research. Overall, I believe that it would be beneficial to discuss the implications of the choice of one tool over other solutions not only in terms of its potential impact on the delivery, but also of its interference with the other cognitive subprocesses of interpreting.

The strategic dimension of human-tool interaction may also be addressed at a deeper level, for instance in terms of the query strategy to adopt during interpreting for manual look-up. In my study, trigrams were the category of terms that were found more easily in the PDF and CAI condition, presumably because participants had more linguistic material to use for the query (see §6.2.2.1). On the other hand, participants had more difficulties in finding unigrams. Trainers may therefore draw the students' attention to this aspect by pointing out effective querying strategies also oriented to the morphology of the terms.

Despite the potential for accuracy improvement with support tools, the presence of errors and omissions highlighted the crucial role of preparation in SI. Therefore, guided in-booth experience with the tool may also prove useful to stress the importance of the pre-assignment phase and to ensure a more effective interaction with the tool.

Finally, in light of the severe errors and complete omissions observed despite the high level of terminological accuracy achieved, trainers may want to raise awareness on the trade-off between the support provided by the machine and the additional effort inherent to human-machine interaction during SI.

The suggestions outlined above are not intended to be exhaustive, but were presented as a means of illustration of the potential implications of CAI research for training. At present, these suggestions remain hypotheses based on the observations conducted in the present study. For all its limitations, however, the present contribution highlighted several issues which, if corroborated by further studies, may offer important implications not only for professional practice, but also for training. If we are to prepare interpreting trainees to effectively use CAI tools in their professional career, it appears necessary to conduct further research to gain a deeper understanding on the impact of CAI tools on the process and product of SI, and to align training with the findings of CAI research.

7.3 Practical implications

The findings from the present study, which are in line with similar experiments conducted on ASR-enhanced CAI tools for the in-booth prompting of numbers, may have important implications also for the future development of support technologies for interpreters. If the ASR module does not fail, as was tested in the context of the present experiment, it seems to provide a superior type of support to the trainee interpreter, with the lowest additional cognitive effort and the highest degree of accuracy observed. Against this background and in light of the considerable advances in AI, in particular in the performance of ASR engines, it is safe to assume that AI-enhanced, third generation CAI tools may represent the in-booth support tool of choice for a large number of interpreters in the future.

In response to a question in the debriefing questionnaire, some students had highlighted the inability to perform manual queries when needed in the simASR condition as a shortcoming of the system. Therefore, while it seems reasonable to focus on the development of ASR-enhanced CAI tools in the near future, i. e. requiring no active search in the glossary by the interpreter, hybrid systems may also be explored as an option to reconcile the benefits of automatic support with the need to actively query the glossary under certain circumstances.

However, some of the benefits observed for the ASR-CAI mock-up may have originated from the specific user interface and terminology presentation mode chosen for the experiment. Both the present study and previous research have highlighted potential pitfalls in interpreter-tool interaction, such as irritating or distracting features, which may be addressed by interventions on the tools' UI design. Valuable steps in this direction have been taken in TPR to explore the origins of the cognitive friction experienced by translators using CAT tools. CAI research may derive useful methods and insight from this area of TPR, thus informing the design of future tools.

7.4 Future work

In addition to the tentative conclusions formulated in the previous sections, several aspects have emerged from the present study which deserve to be further explored in future research.

One area of research may focus on the impact of the performance of the ASR engine on the product and process of SI. Previous studies have identified the risk of over-reliance on the tool (Prandi 2015a,b, Defrancq & Fantinuoli 2021, Van Cauwenberghe 2020). At the same time, Defrancq & Fantinuoli (2021: 87) reported a potentially beneficial psychological effect deriving from the perception of the ASR tool as a "safety net". Both aspects also emerged from the debriefing questionnaire administered to my participants post-study. However, in my experiment, no system failures were simulated for the simASR tool. Explicitly introducing this variable in future studies may provide further insight into the psychological and practical impact of system failures when ASR is provided in the booth.

The questionnaire adopted in the study only explored the reception of the tools at a broad level. Nonetheless, it was useful to generate a series of hypotheses, which may be further tested in future explorations of the research object. If CAI tools become a staple in the standard toolkit of conference interpreters, large-scale questionnaires may be used to further explore the reception of such tools and identify potential shortcomings to be addressed by developers and trainers. First steps in this direction have been taken[1], but there are still a lot of aspects which deserve further exploration, and which may be investigated in future studies focused on the CAI process.

A third avenue, only briefly touched upon in the pilot study, may investigate how the provision of CAI support in the booth affects the tactics used to cope with specialised terminology. In particular, future studies may explore the impact of preparation on the interaction with the tool in the booth, also with the goal to establish which strategies may lead to the best outcome in terms of the trade-off between terminological accuracy and overall quality of the rendition.

Additionally, it should be noted that CAI research has thus far mostly focused on the simultaneous mode. With a few exceptions (e.g. Wang & Wang 2019), consecutive interpreting has not yet been in focus. However, it may be hypothesised that the technologies deployed to support the SI process may also prove valuable for the consecutive mode. Further research appears necessary to determine the impact of supporting technologies on the process and product of consecutive in-

---

[1]See for instance the EABM (2021) project.

terpreting, and to establish validated methodologies for the exploration of this research object.

Finally, future studies may choose to explore the adoption of other metrics for the investigation of the product and process of SI with CAI tools, with and without integrated ASR. For instance, the analysis of the quality of the interpreters' output may be conducted using a more comprehensive framework going beyond the broad categories of grave error and complete omission chosen for the present study. As discussed in §6.2.1.2, the adaptation of established and standardised quality evaluation frameworks, as has been done for instance in research on human translation and post-editing, may offer a more nuanced picture of the impact of live in-booth support on the quality of SI.

Furthermore, it would certainly be interesting to include metrics centred around the presentation of the interpreted texts, such as prosody and pause patterns, and to include final users in the evaluation. In addition to cognitive effort, the stress experienced in working with in-process support tools may also be investigated, ideally with a combination of physiological measures and subjective measures.

Despite having produced a growing amount of research in recent years, the area of Interpreting Studies focusing on CAI is still in its infancy. The present study was conceived at a time when ASR support for interpreters was just starting to emerge. Since then, the application of technology to interpreting has experienced a quantum leap, and an increasing technologisation of the profession may reasonably be expected in light of the increasing uptake of technology by interpreters over the past few years, further accelerated by the recent pandemic. The increasing sophistication and capabilities of technology thanks to the advances in AI may equally be expected to further promote the permeation of technology into the interpreting profession. Despite its focus on a specific set of technological solutions, it is my hope that the methodological contribution offered by the present study may prove valuable for further explorations on technology applied to interpreting, a research subject which is bound to become increasingly relevant for the interpreting profession in the near future, but which currently remains still largely unexplored.

Appendix A: Speech A

(1) Commissioner, thank you once again for inviting me to today's conference.
    I would like to start my speech by providing some information about *biocrude*.
    At present, the efforts to produce it are still limited, but things are changing.

(2) Before talking about its production, let me address some of its chemical properties.
    Perhaps the most interesting one is the fact that this kind of fuel has a low *flash point*.
    This is very important because it means that less energy is required to produce it.

(3) I believe we should support research in this field, because the advantages don't end here.
    One should also mention that its *pour point* is also much lower than for other fuels.
    But this conference is not about chemistry, so let's move on to the next point.

(4) Now, of course the production of this fuel is quite complex, as is often the case.
    It first undergoes what is known as *hydrotreating*, which is quite common in this industry.
    After that, the fuel is ready to be used in transport instead of more harmful ones.

(5) To make the production of this fuel possible, various devices have been developed.
    A good example is the *bubbling fluidized bed*, which has a pretty long history.
    It is quite clear, however, that we need to pursue many options in terms of technology.

(6)   These kinds of devices I have just talked about come with some disadvantages.
The biggest one is that they require an *inert carrier gas* to operate, unlike other devices.
This might lead to a series of issues in terms of quality of the end product.

(7)   There are other options that make our transport sector less harmful to the environment.
By focusing, for instance, on *woody biomass fuels*, we can truly make a difference.
They have the potential to help us respond to the challenges we're facing.

(8)   These fuels can be used in road, railroad and also aviation transportation.
A real breakthrough in the transport sector could be represented by *water splitting*.
Luckily, there are already many different types of clean fuels that can be used in transport.

(9)   As you can imagine, the production of these fuels involves very advanced technologies.
New technologies are replacing *plug flow reactors*, which present some issues.
And I think that producing clean fuel shouldn't harm the environment.

(10)   I don't want to bore you too much, so I'm not going to name all kinds of clean fuel.
However, I would like to provide you with a good example: *rapeseed methyl ester.*
I know this name may sound intimidating, but it's actually just fuel.

(11)   Clean fuels are obtained through different processes and with different methods.
Of the two main ways to obtain them, the most innovative one is *transesterification.*
It's however a rather complicated chemical process, so I won't go into too much detail.

(12)   I would like to mention, however, that this process presents a lot of advantages.
For instance, it makes it possible to reuse materials such as *spent bleaching earths.*
This shows that simple materials can be used to produce clean fuel.

(13)   Fuel of this kind can be obtained, for example, through a process that extracts oil from seeds.

       At the end of this process, we have a *residue cake*, which is what is left after seeds are crushed.

       Depending on its characteristics, this residue can then be used as a fertiliser or to feed animals.

(14)   But what are the resources we can use to produce these kinds of fuels?

       The first category involves, for instance, *short rotation coppice*.

       Let me give you some more information before moving on to the other two categories.

(15)   These resources are used to produce more efficient and less harmful fuels.

       Fuels of this sort are still quite new and can be derived, for example, from *switchgrass*.

       The new technologies used in this field are expected to help expand production as well.

(16)   The second category involves resources that are derived from the resources in the first category.

       These resources can be obtained chemically, as is the case for *black liquor*.

       They can, however, also be produced using physical or biological processes.

(17)   This means that we have a lot of different methods at our disposal.

       Let me just briefly mention *pulping*, which will be further discussed this afternoon.

       I am sure my colleagues will be able to tell you something more about it.

(18)   Unfortunately, we don't have much time to address this topic in particular.

       I would like, however, to mention *liquid rosin*, which I know a bit more about.

       Unlike the resource I mentioned before, it is the result of a natural process.

(19)   The third category is nothing special as it involves all kinds of waste from human activities.

       Another good example I forgot to give you for the first category is *corn stover*.

       As you can see, it is possible to use very common materials to produce fuel.

(20) There are, however, also other sources from which clean fuels can be derived, such as wheat.
To this aim, wheat must undergo two different processes, the first of which is called *milling*.
This simply means that the cereal is cut into much smaller pieces.

(21) After undergoing this first process, the second phase begins.
An important stage of this process is *kilning*, which occurs under controlled conditions.
So far, I've been talking about clean fuels mainly used in the transport system.

(22) There is however another field I would like to describe in more detail.
A good alternative to coal, which can be used for heating purposes, is *lignocellulosic solid biomass*.
The gas obtained from it can also be used to generate electricity.

(23) There are two main processes used to produce the necessary resources for clean heating.
The first one is called *gasification* and what we obtain through it can also be used for cooking.
The gas can, however, also be converted to electricity or used for other applications.

(24) To perform this process, various devices can be used, although some are preferable.
Among these systems, the *entrained flow gasifier* is an interesting device.
It is preferred because it has a lower impact on the environment.

(25) After the process, the gas is filtered and can be used to generate power more efficiently.
Sometimes, however, the efficiency of the process can be lower due to *elutriation*.
This is why it is very important to focus on devices that limit this issue.

(26) Many African countries are already trying to find clean alternatives to traditional coal.
One of these is the production of *green charcoal*, which looks to be very promising.
It is an environmentally friendly alternative to traditional charcoal, derived from vegetation.

(27) There has been a lot of media coverage about the negative consequences on the environment.
One of the first things that can be done to prevent them is investing in *soil amendment*.
The negative impact of uncontrolled production is, unfortunately, quite wide-ranging.

(28) Luckily, there are various methods and tools that we can use to counteract such effects.
Let me briefly talk about *biochar* – not a new invention, but a very useful one.
It can endure in soil for many years and has many potential benefits.

(29) On the one hand, it can be used to improve the fertility of our soils.
On the other hand, however, it may also play an important part in *carbon sequestration*.
This is true especially when coupled with other processes and measures.

(30) We have witnessed improvements in many sectors and many countries.
In the transportation sector there has been an increase in the use of *carbon sequestration*.
This technology makes trains more efficient and is good for the environment.

(31) To produce gas, research and development is exploring new possibilities.
In order to maximise production, researchers are working on *steam methane reforming*.
This process comes with a lot of advantages, even though it is quite expensive.

(32) Despite the advantages, the process I just mentioned comes with some challenges.
One of these is something called *coking*, which might have negative effects on production.
Additionally, the whole process is still considered quite costly and impractical.

(33) We all know that we must also start looking elsewhere if we want to protect the environment.
We need to keep investing in *tidal barrages*, for example, which are proving to be a valid alternative.
By investing in this new sector, my country had an annual export of several billion euros a year.

A Speech A

(34) Let me conclude my speech by describing how we can harvest the energy of ocean waters.
The most famous system used to obtain this kind of energy is probably *ebb generation.*
I guess all of us have heard about it before, so I don't need to explain this further.

(35) We can, however, also capture the energy derived from ocean waves.
For instance, we can use *point absorber buoys* in order to generate electricity.
This is, however, only one of the four most common approaches and technologies.

(36) Over the past few years, new technological solutions have entered the market.
Experts have already been working to develop *oscillating water columns.*
This is, however, still not enough, so Europe must keep investing to bring about real change. Thank you.

Appendix B: Speech B

(1) Ladies and gentlemen, today I will talk about a topic that is very dear to me.

I will be talking about *transmutation*, a process used to generate nuclear energy.

It is rather complicated, so I promise not to go into too much detail.

(2) Some of you may have already heard this term before, although in a different context.

It described the transformation of *base metals* into gold attempted by alchemists.

I find the history of this word very fascinating, but let's not digress.

(3) I'm sure you will agree with me that nothing in life is without consequences.

Let's think about what happens when we build a *storage dam*.

It is for sure useful to generate electricity, but also negatively impacts the environment.

(4) This is true also for nuclear energy, which generates a lot of waste of different types.

To start, I'd like to mention *depletalloy*, which was long considered unusable.

It is only mildly radioactive, but is not, however, the only type of waste we get.

(5) After its extraction, the raw material containing uranium is crushed into sand.

The useful material is then removed and we are left with *mill tailings*.

They can be carried by the wind and enter our waters, which is not a desirable outcome.

(6) This is a complicated topic, because even apparently safe materials can be radioactive.

Even though we're talking about small amounts, this is true also for *shale*.

But this is something that will be addressed by other speakers later today.

(7) Luckily, however, in this industry there are also less problematic types of waste.
You might have guessed that I'm referring to *spent nuclear fuel*.
Even though it can no longer be used directly, it can be repurposed.

(8) So as you can see, even in this controversial sector there's a positive side of the coin.
Industry is focusing on *mixed oxide fuel*, which is already widely used.
Who would have thought that recycling was possible in this sector, too?

(9) One of the main advantages of this fuel is that it's pretty easy to manufacture.
It is not used all over the world, but in some countries it powers *breeder reactors*.
This certainly doesn't solve the problem, but at least reduces the amount of waste.

(10) Not all waste is equally dangerous and can be classified into three groups.
After initial treatment, some waste can be mixed with *blast furnace slag*.
This is, however, not a solution feasible for the most dangerous material.

(11) Let's take a look at the other two categories that I haven't discussed yet.
The first one isn't very interesting, while an example for the second is *cladding*.
A problem, however, still remains: at some point you have to get rid of the waste.

(12) And this is where things get tricky; this is what causes concern.
What makes people think twice is especially the issue of *nuclear waste disposal*.
The waste can indeed remain radioactive for thousands of years.

(13) There are, however, solutions to this problem, but not all of them are good.
The first one is burying the waste in so-called *deep geological repositories*.
But who would want to have these near where they live?

(14) I am quite sure no one would, and that's why so many people are against this type of energy.
And the waste has to go through *vitrification* beforehand, so the process is actually not so easy.
So as you can see, things are actually not quite as easy as they might seem at first.

(15) What I just mentioned isn't, however, the only solution we could adopt.
One additional potential solution is storing the waste in *boreholes*.
But because of its costs and impact on the environment, this is not implemented.

(16) Some scientists have already come up with very creative solutions.
It may actually be possible to transport the waste into space using *mass drivers*.
The necessary technology is not there yet, but it might be available in the future.

(17) As you all know, the waste cannot be eliminated completely.
This is the reason why *dry cask storage* is often used in this field.
This system comes in various designs, some of which can also be used for transportation.

(18) Research is constantly looking for new solutions to the issues I'm discussing today.
One such solution is simply storing the waste products in *salt domes*.
Some, however, criticise this solution because they consider it dangerous.

(19) Another problem is what to do with the plants once they are no longer active.
Among the solutions to this problem, *entombment* is just one of the many possibilities.
It is the least used option because it is very complex and requires continuous surveillance.

(20) After a plant has been shut down, some issues must still be solved.
Even with no reactions, some *decay heat* remains, which is very dangerous.
For this reason, many people tend to discard the subject very quickly.

(21) The answer to all these issues lies in the process I'm talking about today.
It should not be confused with the process called *fission*, which produces the waste.
That process is the one used to create the atomic bomb, such as that of Hiroshima.

(22) And then of course there's another process that we all know and learnt about at school.
The reaction I'm talking about naturally occurs in stars and is called *fusion*.

It is the process that takes place in the Sun, at extremely high temperatures.

(23) This process can produce energy with a virtually unlimited supply of fuel. For this and other reasons, *tritium breeding* is already being tested and demonstrated.
As you can see, the process I'm discussing is feasible and can help get rid of the waste.

(24) It cannot, however, solve the problem completely, so we must keep looking for alternatives.
Let me just mention, for instance, *airborne wind turbines*, which have proven to be very useful.
It may not sound like it, but I am in favour of this kind of technology, too.

(25) And I particularly appreciate the investments that have been made into it. This has made possible to develop *nacelles* made from more sustainable materials.
This would also reduce costs and make the technology accessible to more countries.

(26) I was reading about this the other day and I have to say things look very promising.
The reduction in the costs for *onshore wind* is just one factor in favour of this source of energy.
Nonetheless, huge progress has been made in the sector we're discussing today.

(27) Part of this progress is linked with the possibility of using it for other applications.
Many countries today are discussing the need to promote *cogeneration*. Though not very widespread, this concept has already been applied in various industry sectors.

(28) It has significant potential and could open up many new markets in the mid and long term.
Partnerships between the public and private sector are underway in the field of *desalination*.
Through this process, the same plant can be used to produce fresh water as well as energy.

(29) This is not only good for our communities, but especially for the environment.

In fact, we can make full use of *brackish water* thanks to this process. This is relevant for the Middle East, which will probably invest in the sector we're discussing today.

(30) I believe that if we truly want to protect the environment, we must be flexible and open.
We cannot get rid of *peaker plants* because they are still needed.
But I think focusing on new approaches can really help us take the next step.

(31) And this is true not only for clean energy, but also for traditional solutions.
Governments should start setting aside funds for *fast burst reactors.*
The technology is already there, but developing it further would help cut costs too.

(32) On the other hand, technology is also needed to make sure the plants can last years.
That is why research is essentially focused on long-lived components, such as the *reactor vessel.*
This component is not replaced regularly, so it's essential to ensure it can stand the test of time.

(33) I really believe that in the energy sector technology is the key and can help solve many current issues.
The industry is working on *organically moderated reactors* to reach isolated markets.
The first prototypes are already available, but there's still much to be done in this sector.

(34) Technology will really be essential to shape the future of the sector that we're talking about today.
At the moment, for example, *pressurised water reactors* are the most widespread kind.
There is only a handful of countries where this is not the case.

(35) They are very stable because they tend to produce less power as temperatures increase.
The second most widespread kind is the *boiling water reactor.*
These reactors tend to have uniform designs and are very similar to one another.

(36)   In order to improve sustainability and safety, research is trying to offer new solutions as well.

Among the designs currently available, the *molten salt reactor* is one of the most promising.

I won't go into detail about this, but I hope my speech helped clarify any doubts. Thank you.

Appendix C: Speech C

(1) Ladies and gentlemen, let me give you some information about the coal industry.

The vast majority of the world's electricity is generated using the *vapour power cycle*.

The main source of heat used in this process is coal, used to generate steam.

(2) Its use is likely to continue in certain regions of our planet, even if it's very polluting.

Organic material derived, for instance, from *peatlands*, can also be used as fuel.

We should, however, be very careful when we use natural resources.

(3) Mother nature is truly very generous, even though we often forget it.

When we think of the existence of *carbon sinks*, this becomes immediately clear.

But let's move on to explaining how the cycle I'm talking about works.

(4) I guess part of the audience will already be familiar with this, but I'll just describe it briefly.

First of all, a large *grinder* turns the coal that has been transported to the plant into a very fine powder.

This step is necessary to make sure that all the coal is burnt to maximize the production of heat.

(5) Unfortunately, this cycle requires a lot of water, so it's not good for the environment.

Before moving on to the next step, the water can be transported to a *feedwater heater*.

This additional step in the cycle increases the efficiency of the system.

(6) It can, however, also lead to a pretty big issue, which shouldn't be forgotten.

Serious damage can be caused to the plant if the water doesn't go through a *deaerator*.

It comes in very different types, but they all serve the same purpose.

(7) Let's now move on to describing the other steps and elements of the cycle.
     After the first step, the coal ends up in a *boiler*, where it is burnt.
     This way, the coal provides heat to the power plant, which is used to produce steam.

(8) I know the audience isn't made up of engineers, so I won't be too technical.
     However, I think I should also mention the importance played by the *boiler steam drum*.
     It's exciting to see so much technical progress being made in this respect.

(9) In the cycle I'm describing, there are also optional steps the steam can go through.
     For instance, the steam can enter a *superheater*, which can be pretty small or very big.
     The main advantage of using it is that it reduces the consumption of water.

(10) There are, of course, also clean ways of generating energy using steam.
     This requires using different technologies, such as the one involving *flash steam*.
     Nonetheless, coal is still widely used and this comes with huge environmental issues.

(11) So focusing on coal to generate energy is not a feasible solution, and let me tell you why.
     Coal has the most substantial *carbon footprint* of all fuels.
     For this reason, this source of energy will have to be used less and less.

(12) As you can see, what this industry is promoting is not a real solution.
     I cannot deny that there are ways to reduce its impact, like using *baghouses*.
     But it still remains a messy business and a pretty complex one.

(13) So before discussing the desirable alternatives, let's try to understand it better.
     Among the different methods used to extract coal, we can mention *longwall mining*.
     It is the one that makes best use of the natural resources present underground.

(14) As we all know, coal is not readily available on the surface.
      In order to reach it, the *overburden* must first be removed.
      This is done mechanically nowadays, but this wasn't the case in the past.

(15) Not all of the coal is used to produce heat and, ultimately, electricity.
      Part of it can be used in other industries, for example in the case of
      middlings.
      This is, however, a totally different topic, so let's move on.

(16) The coal doesn't reach the plant immediately; its journey is a bit longer.
      In order to remove all impurities, the coal must first reach a *coal handling
      plant.*
      This increases its value and at the same time lowers its transportation
      costs.

(17) To achieve better quality, the coal must undergo a series of processes to
      be purified.
      One such process requires *dense medium separation* to discard useless
      material.
      There are many different types of it, but we don't need to name them.

(18) I'm really just trying to give you an idea of the complexity of this
      industry.
      Coal contains water, so a *screen bowl centrifuge* can be used to remove it.
      The good thing about this process is that water can also be recycled.

(19) When it comes to this industry, however, there are really a lot of negative
      aspects.
      Let's think, for instance, of the many lethal accidents caused by *firedamp.*
      This industry is extremely dangerous for the workers, as I'm sure you all
      know.

(20) Using coal to generate electricity also has a devastating impact on the
      environment.
      Let me just mention the amount of *flue ash* that contaminates our waters.
      And we all know how precious water is, especially in today's world.

(21) Plants using coal as fuel are also the biggest water polluters, at least in
      my country.
      Every day, these plants dump millions of litres of *sullage* into rivers and
      lakes.
      So it's quite clear that we need to use clean sources of energy, like that of
      the sun.

(22)   Solar energy is within the reach of individuals and small businesses.
It is expected to play a major role in the future *power generation mix*.
There have been a lot of developments in this field, so let's discuss them.

(23)   First of all, research is focusing on improving some components of the
system.
For instance, industry seems to be increasingly in favour of *negatively
doped wafers*.
This is by far the best choice available on the market, because it's the
most efficient.

(24)   They are, however, still quite expensive, because there are only a few
manufacturers.
The recent introduction of *interdigitated back contacts* has made things
easier.
They make the cells more efficient and easier to place closer together.

(25)   It is also very important that storage is efficient and nothing goes to
waste.
This has been made possible with the creation of batteries with better
float life.
There is a wide range of devices used to harvest the energy of the sun.

(26)   They are usually classified into three generations, depending on the basic
materials used.
The first generation uses *crystalline silicon*, the material most commonly
used in this industry.
This is a mature technology that currently dominates the market and is
in mass production.

(27)   Despite being an advanced technology, its costs can be reduced through
improvements in materials.
Manufacturing also plays a role, for example when it comes to the
production of *boules*.
This is however not the only technology available on this market at the
moment.

(28)   After many years of research and development, a new technology is
beginning to be deployed.
The second generation focuses on another kind of technology called *thin
film*.
It could potentially provide lower-cost electricity than first generation
cells.

(29) Three primary types of this kind of cells have been commercially developed, using different materials.

The most widely known type is based on *amorphous silicon*, which has pretty good efficiency.

Then there are other technologies, some of which are still in the early stage of development.

(30) I'm going to talk about three of the four technologies of the third generation.

The first of these new technologies are the so-called *concentrating photovoltaic systems*.

They offer a pretty high level of efficiency, which is even higher in experimental settings.

(31) Let's now move on to another solution that is part of third generation technology.

I'm talking about *evacuated tube collectors*, which use low-cost materials.

They are also simple to manufacture, but their performance can degrade over time.

(32) Then there are a number of innovative technologies, all very promising.

Good examples of those technologies are the ones that rely on *superlattices*.

Now I'm not going to into detail about this, because it's rather complicated.

(33) It is beside the point I want to make, but I think it's always interesting to know what's out there.

Another type of these new, third generation technologies is based on *quantum dots*.

These are very small particles that can conduct electricity and are used in other fields too.

(34) Finally, there are some ideas that haven't yet been developed fully.

Some of those have a huge potential, like *solar updraft towers*.

They have been criticised in the past, but could become increasingly relevant.

(35) A very positive thing about this technology is that it is very versatile.

Let's think for example of *floating solar arrays*, which can be installed on water.

They represent a new development and make this technology more accessible.

(36)   There are many positive aspects when it comes to these technologies. The most evident one is that they allow us to easily reach *socket parity*. So as you can see this is a good alternative to coal, which we should focus on in the future. Thank you.

References

Ahrens, Barbara. 2005. Prosodic phenomena in simultaneous interpreting: A conceptual approach and its practical application. *Interpreting: International Journal of Research and Practice in Interpreting* 7(1). 51–76. DOI: 10.1075/intp.7.1.04ahr.

Ahrens, Barbara. 2007. Pauses (and other prosodic features) in simultaneous interpreting. *FORUM: Revue internationale d'interprétation et de traduction / International Journal of Interpretation and Translation* 5(1). 1–18. DOI: 10.1075/forum.5.1.01ahr.

AIIC. 2002. *Interpreter workload study: Full report.* https://aiic.org/document/468/AIICWebzine_FebMar2002_7_AIIC_Interpreter_workload_study_full_report_WLS_Full_Report.pdf.

Altman, Janet. 1994. Error analysis in the teaching of simultaneous interpretation: A pilot study. In Sylvie Lambert & Barbara Moser-Mercer (eds.), *Bridging the gap: Empirical research in simultaneous interpretation*, 25–48. Amsterdam: John Benjamins. DOI: 10.1075/btl.3.05alt.

Alves, Fábio, Adriana Pagano & Igor da Silva. 2012. Towards an investigation of reading modalities in/for translation: An exploratory study using eye-tracking data. In Sharon O'Brien (ed.), *Cognitive explorations of translation*, 175–196. London: Bloomsbury.

Alves, Fábio, Karina Sarto Szpak, José Luiz Gonçalves, Kyoko Sekino, Marceli Aquino, Rodrigo Araújo e Castro, Arlene Koglin, Norma B. de Lima Fonseca & Bartolomé Mesa-Lao. 2016. Investigating cognitive effort in post-editing: A relevance-theoretical approach. In Silvia Hansen-Schirra & Sambor Grucza (eds.), *Eyetracking and applied linguistics*, 109–142. Berlin: Language Science Press. DOI: 10.17169/langsci.b108.296.

Ammon, Ulrich. 2011. *The dominance of English as a language of science.* Berlin: De Gruyter Mouton.

Andersson, Bodil, Johan Dahl, Kenneth Holmqvist, Jana Holsanova, Victoria Johansson, Henrik Karlsson, Sven Strömqvist & Åsa Wengelin. 2006. Combining keystroke logging with eye-tracking. In Luuk Van Waes, Marielle Leiten & Christophe Neuwirth (eds.), *Writing and digital media*, 45–72. Leiden: Brill.

References

Apfelbaum, Birgit & Cecilia Wadensjö. 1997. How does a verbmobil affect conversation? Discourse analysis and machine-supported translatory interaction. In Christa Hauenschild & Susanne Heizmann (eds.), *Machine translation and translation theory*, 93–122. Berlin: De Gruyter Mouton.

Arcara, Giorgio, Carlo Semenza & Valentina Bambini. 2014. Word structure and decomposition effects in reading. *Cognitive Neuropsychology* 31(1-2). 184–218. DOI: 10.1080/02643294.2014.903915.

Arntz, Reiner & Heribert Picht. 1982. *Einführung in die übersetzungsbezogene Terminologiearbeit*. Hildesheim: Georg Olms Verlag.

Atkinson, Richard C. & Richard M. Shiffrin. 1968. Human memory: A proposed system and its control processes. In Kenneth W. Spence & Janet Taylor Spence (eds.), *The psychology of learning and motivation: Advances in research and theory*, vol. 2, 89–195. New York: Academic Press.

Atkinson, Richard C. & Richard M. Shiffrin. 1971. The control of short-term memory. *Scientific American* 225(2). 82–90. DOI: 10.1038/scientificamerican0871-82.

Audacity Team. 2021. *Audacity®: Free audio editor and recorder*. https://audacityteam.org/ (17 March, 2021).

Baddeley, Alan D. 1975. Word length and the structure of short-term memory. *Journal of Verbal Learning and Verbal Behavior* 14(6). 575–589. DOI: 10.4324/9781315111261-11.

Baddeley, Alan D. 1990. *Human memory: Theory and practice*. Needham Heights: Allyn & Bacon.

Baddeley, Alan D. 2000. Short-term and working memory. In Endel Tulving & Fergus I. M. Craik (eds.), *The Oxford handbook of memory*, 77–92. New York: Oxford University Press.

Baddeley, Alan D. 2012. Working memory: Theories, models, and controversies. *Annual Review of Psychology* 63(1). 1–29. DOI: 10.1146/annurev-psych-120710-100422.

Baddeley, Alan D. & Graham Hitch. 1974. Working memory. In Gordon H. Bower (ed.), *Psychology of learning and motivation*, vol. 8, 47–89. New York: Academic Press.

Baddeley, Alan D., Graham Hitch & Philip T. Quinlan. 2018. Is the phonological similarity effect in working memory due to proactive interference? *Journal of Experimental Psychology: Learning, Memory, and Cognition* 44(8). 1312–1316. DOI: 10.1037/xlm0000509.

Baddeley, Alan D., Giuseppe Vallar & Barbara Wilson. 1987. Sentence comprehension and phonological memory: Some neuropsychological evidence. In Max Coltheart (ed.), *Attention and performance 12: The psychology of reading*, 509–529. Hillsdale: Lawrence Erlbaum Associates, Inc.

Baigorri-Jalón, Jesús. 1999. Conference interpreting: From modern times to space technology. *Interpreting: International Journal of Research and Practice in Interpreting* 4(1). 29–40. DOI: 10.1075/intp.4.1.05bai.

Barik, Henri C. 1971. A description of various types of omissions, additions and errors of translation encountered in simultaneous interpretation. *Meta: Journal des Traducteurs/Meta: Translators' Journal* 16(4). 199–210. DOI: 10.7202/001972ar.

Barik, Henri C. 1973. Simultaneous interpretation: Temporal and quantitative data. *Language and Speech* 16(3). 237–270. DOI: 10.1177/002383097301600307.

Barrouillet, Pierre, Sophie Bernardin & Valérie Camos. 2004. Time constraints and resource sharing in adults' working memory spans. *Journal of Experimental Psychology: General* 133(1). 83–100. DOI: 10.1037/0096-3445.133.1.83.

Barton, Jason J. S., Hashim M. Hanif, Laura Eklinder Björnström & Charlotte Hills. 2014. The word-length effect in reading: A review. *Cognitive Neuropsychology* 31(5-6). 378–412. DOI: 10.1080/02643294.2014.895314.

Beatty, Jackson. 1982. Task-evoked pupillary responses, processing load, and the structure of processing resources. *Psychological Bulletin* 91(2). 276–292. DOI: 10.1037/0033-2909.91.2.276.

Behl, Holly. 2013a. *The paperless interpreter experiment: Part I.* http://www.precisolanguage.com/2013/01/paperless-interpreter-part-i/ (3 July, 2021).

Behl, Holly. 2013b. *The paperless interpreter experiment: Part II.* http://www.precisolanguage.com/tag/consecutive-interpreting/ (3 July, 2021).

Berber-Irabien, Diana. 2010. *Information and communication technologies in conference interpreting.* Tarragona: Universitat Rovira i Virgili. (Doctoral dissertation).

Biagini, Giulio. 2015. *Glossario cartaceo e glossario elettronico durante l'interpretazione.* Trieste: Università di Trieste. (MA thesis).

Bilgen, Baris. 2009. *Investigating terminology management for conference interpreters.* Ottawa: University of Ottawa. (MA thesis).

Blancafort, Helena, Béatrice Daille, Tatiana Gornostay, Ulrich Heid, Claude Méchoulam & Serge Sharoff. 2010. TTC: Terminology extraction, translation tools and comparable corpora. In *14th EURALEX International Congress*, 263–268. Leeuwarden.

Blancafort, Helena, Ulrich Heid, Tatiana Gornostay, Claude Méchoulam, Béatrice Daille & Serge Sharoff. 2011. User-centred views on terminology extraction tools: Usage scenarios and integration into MT and CAT tools. In *Tralogy I. Métiers et technologies de la traduction: Quelles convergences pour l'avenir?*, 1–10.

References

Blumenthal, Pamela, Thomas W. Britt, Jason A. Cohen, James McCubbin, Nathan Maxfield, Erica B. Michael, Philip Moore, Loraine K. Obler, Petra Scheck, Teresa M. Signorelli & Thomas S. Wallsten. 2006. Stress effects on bilingual language professionals' performance. *International Journal of Bilingualism* 10(4). 477–497. DOI: 10.1177/13670069060100040501.

Braun, Peter, Burkhard Schaeder & Johannes Volmert (eds.). 2014. *Internationalismen II: Studien zur interlingualen Lexikologie und Lexikographie*. Berlin: Max Niemeyer Verlag. DOI: 10.1515/9783110911978.

Braun, Sabine. 2019. Technology and interpreting. In Minako O'Hagan (ed.), *The Routledge handbook of translation and technology*, 271–288. London: Routledge.

Broadbent, Donald E. 1958. *Perception and communication*. Oxford: Pergamon Press.

Brüsewitz, Nora. 2019. Simultandolmetschen 4.0: Ist automatische Spracherkennung der nächste Schritt? In Wolfram Bauer & Felix Mayer (eds.), *Proceedings of Übersetzen und Dolmetschen 4.0.: Neue Wege im digitalen Zeitalter*. Berlin: BDÜ Fachverlag.

Bruya, Brian & Yi-Yuan Tang. 2018. Is attention really effort? Revisiting Daniel Kahneman's influential 1973 book *Attention and effort*. *Frontiers in Psychology* 9. 1–10. DOI: 10.3389/fpsyg.2018.01133.

Bühler, Hildegund. 1986. Linguistic (semantic) and extra-linguistic (pragmatic) criteria for the evaluation of conference interpretation and interpreters. *Multilingua* 5(4). 231–235. DOI: 10.1515/mult.1986.5.4.231.

Bundgaard, Kristine, Tina Paulsen Christensen & Anne Schjoldager. 2016. Translator-computer interaction in action: An observational process study of computer-aided translation. *The Journal of Specialised Translation* 25. 106–130.

Cabré Castellví, Maria Teresa. 1998. Do we need an autonomous theory of terms? *Terminology* 5(1). 4–19. DOI: 10.1075/term.5.1.03cab.

Cabré Castellví, Maria Teresa. 2003. Theories of terminology: Their description, prescription and explanation. *Terminology: International Journal of Theoretical and Applied Issues in Specialized Communication* 9(2). 163–199. DOI: 10.1075/term.9.2.03cab.

Campo, Ángela. 2005. The politics of scientific and technical translation. *Newsletter of the Canadian Association for Translation Studies* 18(1).

Canali, Sara. 2018. *Utilizzo del riconoscimento vocale come supporto durante l'interpretazione simultanea dei numeri*. Roma: Università degli Studi Internazionali di Roma. (MA thesis).

Carl, Michael, Akiko Aizawa & Masaru Yamada. 2016. English-to-Japanese translation vs. dictation vs. post-editing: Comparing translation modes in a multilingual setting. In *Proceedings of the tenth international conference on language resources and evaluation (LREC'16)*, 4024–4031. Portorož: European Language Resources Association (ELRA). https://aclanthology.org/L16-1635 (25 May, 2021).

Carl, Michael & Matthias Buch-Kromann. 2010. Correlating translation product and translation process data of professional and student translators. In *Proceedings of the 14th annual conference of the European Association for Machine Translation*, 1–8. Saint Raphaël: European Association for Machine Translation. https://aclanthology.org/2010.eamt-1.14 (24 July, 2021).

Carl, Michael & Gyde Hansen. 2011. Digital humanities and empirical human translation process research: Past, present and future perspectives. In Bente Maegaard (ed.), *Conference proceedings: Supporting digital humanities, Copenhagen 17–18 November 2011*, 1–7. Croatia: Croatian National Corpus.

Carl, Michael, Isabel Lacruz, Masaru Yamada & Akiko Aizawa. 2016a. *Comparing spoken and written translation with post-editing in the ENJA15 English à Japanese Translation Corpus*. Paper presented at the 22nd Annual Meeting of the Association for Natural Language Processing, 1–4. Sendai: NLP 2016.

Carl, Michael, Isabel Lacruz, Masaru Yamada & Akiko Aizawa. 2016b. *Measuring the translation process*. Paper presented at the 22nd Annual Meeting of the Association for Natural Language Processing, 1–4. Sendai: NLP 2016.

Cavallo, Patrizia & Luis Eduardo Schild Ortiz. 2018. Computer-assisted interpreting tools (CAI) and options for automation with automatic speech recognition. *Tradterm* 32. 9–31. DOI: 10.11606/issn.2317-9511.v32i0p9-31.

Cecot, Michela. 2001. Pauses in simultaneous interpretation: A contrastive analysis of professional interpreters' performances. *The Interpreters' Newsletter* 11. 63–85. http://hdl.handle.net/10077/2448 (24 July, 2021).

Center for Reading Research, Ghent University. 2014. *Wordornot*. http://vocabulary.ugent.be/ (14 September, 2021).

Chabasse, Catherine. 2009. *Gibt es eine Begabung für das Simultandolmetschen? Erstellung eines Dolmetscheignungstests mit Schwerpunkt Simultandolmetschen* (Beiträge zur Translationswissenschaft 4). Berlin: SAXA Verlag.

Chandler, Paul & John Sweller. 1991. Cognitive load theory and the format of instruction. *Cognition and Instruction* 8(4). 293–332. DOI: 10.1207/s1532690xci0804_2.

Chang, Chieh Ying. 2009. *Testing applicability of eye-tracking and fMRI to translation and interpreting studies: An investigation into directionality*. London: Imperial College London. (PhD Thesis). http://hdl.handle.net/10044/1/11409 (25 June, 2021).

Chen, Sijia. 2017. The construct of cognitive load in interpreting and its measurement. *Perspectives* 25(4). 640–657. DOI: 10.1080/0907676X.2016.1278026.

Chernov, Ghelly V. 1979. Semantic aspects of psycholinguistic research in simultaneous interpretation. *Language and Speech* 22(3). 277–295. DOI: 10.1177/002383097902200308.

Chernov, Ghelly V. 1994. Message redundancy and message anticipation in simultaneous interpreting. In Sylvie Lambert & Barbara Moser-Mercer (eds.), *Bridging the gap: Empirical research in simultaneous interpretation*, 139–153. Amsterdam: John Benjamins. DOI: 10.1075/btl.3.13che.

Chesterman, Andrew. 2016. *Memes of translation: The spread of ideas in translation theory*. Amsterdam: John Benjamins. DOI: 10.1075/btl.123.

Chiaro, Delia & Giuseppe Nocella. 2004. Interpreters' perception of linguistic and non-linguistic factors affecting quality: A survey through the world wide web. *Meta: Journal des Traducteurs/Meta: Translators' Journal* 49(2). 278–293. DOI: 10.7202/009351ar.

Chmiel, Agnieszka, Przemysław Janikowski & Anna Cieślewicz. 2020. The eye or the ear? Source language interference in sight translation and simultaneous interpreting. *Interpreting: International Journal of Research and Practice in Interpreting* 22(2). 187–210. DOI: 10.1075/intp.00043.chm.

Chmiel, Agnieszka, Przemysław Janikowski & Agnieszka Lijewska. 2020. Multimodal processing in simultaneous interpreting with text: Interpreters focus more on the visual than the auditory modality. *Target: International Journal of Translation Studies* 32(1). 37–58. DOI: 10.1075/target.18157.chm.

Chmiel, Agnieszka & Iwona Mazur. 2013. Eye tracking sight translation performed by trainee interpreters. In Catherine Way, Sonia Vandepitte, Reine Meylaerts & Magdalena Bartłomiejczyk (eds.), *Tracks and treks in translation studies*, 189–205. Amsterdam: John Benjamins. DOI: 10.1075/btl.108.10chm.

Cho, Eunah, Christian Fügen, Teresa Herrmann, Kevin Kilgour, Mohammed Mediani, Christian Mohr, Jan Niehues, Kay Rottmann, Christian Saam, Sebastian Stüker & Alex Waibel. 2013. A real-world system for simultaneous translation of German lectures. In *Proc. Interspeech 2013*, 3473–3477. DOI: 10.21437/Interspeech.2013-612.

Christoffels, Ingrid K. & Annette M. B. De Groot. 2004. Components of simultaneous interpreting: Comparing interpreting with shadowing and paraphrasing. *Bilingualism: Language and Cognition* 7(3). 227–240. DOI: 10.1017/S1366728904001609.

Conklin, Kathy, Ana Pellicer-Sánchez & Gareth Carrol. 2018. *Eye-tracking: A guide for applied linguistics research*. Cambridge: Cambridge University Press. DOI: 10.1017/9781108233279.

Cooper, Alan. 2004. *The inmates are running the asylum: Why high tech products drive us crazy and how to restore the sanity*. Indianapolis: Sams.

Corpas Pastor, Gloria & Lily May Fern. 2016. *A survey of interpreters' needs and practices related to language technology.* Technical paper. https://www.researchgate.net/publication/303685153_A_survey_of_interpreters%5C%27_needs_and_practices_related_to_language_technology (24 July, 2021).

Costa, Albert, Alfonso Caramazza & Nuria Sebastian-Galles. 2000. The cognate facilitation effect: Implications for models of lexical access. *Journal of Experimental Psychology: Learning, Memory, and Cognition* 26(5). 1283–1296. DOI: 10.1037/0278-7393.26.5.1283.

Costa, Hernani, Gloria Corpas Pastor & Isabel Durán Muñoz. 2014a. Technology-assisted interpreting. *MultiLingual 143* 25(3). 27–32. https://multilingual.com/articles/technology-assisted-interpreting/ (24 July, 2021).

Costa, Hernani, Gloria Corpas Pastor & Isabel Durán Muñoz. 2014b. A comparative user evaluation of terminology management tools for interpreters. In *Proceedings of the 4th international workshop on computational terminology (Computerm)*, 68–76. Dublin: Association for Computational Linguistics & Dublin City University. DOI: 10.3115/v1/W14-4809.

Costa, Hernani, Gloria Corpas Pastor & Isabel Durán Muñoz. 2015. An interpreters' guide to selecting terminology management tools. In *NATO Conference on Terminology Management*. Brussels.

Cowan, Nelson. 1988. Evolving conceptions of memory storage, selective attention, and their mutual constraints within the human information-processing system. *Psychological Bulletin* 104(2). 163–191. DOI: 10.1037/0033-2909.104.2.163.

Cowan, Nelson. 2009. Sensory and immediate memory. In William P. Banks (ed.), *Encyclopedia of consciousness*, 327–339. Amsterdam: Elsevier. DOI: 10.1016/B978-012373873-8.00048-7.

Čulo, Oliver, Silvia Hansen-Schirra & Jean Nitzke. 2017. Contrasting terminological variation in post-editing and human translation of texts from the technical and medical domain. In Gert De Sutter, Marie-Aude Lefer & Isabelle Delaere (eds.), *Empirical translation studies: New methodological and theoretical traditions*, 183–206. Berlin: De Gruyter Mouton.

Darling, Stephen, Richard J. Allen & Jelena Havelka. 2017. Visuospatial bootstrapping: When visuospatial and verbal memory work together. *Current Directions in Psychological Science* 26(1). 3–9. DOI: 10.1177/0963721416665342.

Darling, Stephen & Jelena Havelka. 2010. Visuospatial bootstrapping: Evidence for binding of verbal and spatial information in working memory. *Quarterly Journal of Experimental Psychology* 63(2). 239–245. DOI: 10.1080/17470210903348605.

References

Darò, Valeria & Franco Fabbro. 1994. Verbal memory during simultaneous interpretation: Effects of phonological interference. *Applied Linguistics* 15(4). 365–381. DOI: 10.1093/applin/15.4.365.

Darò, Valeria. 1994. Non-linguistic factors influencing simultaneous interpretation. In Sylvie Lambert & Barbara Moser-Mercer (eds.), *Bridging the gap: Empirical research in simultaneous interpretation*, 249–271. Amsterdam: John Benjamins. DOI: 10.1075/btl.3.20dar.

Darò, Valeria. 1997. Experimental studies on memory in conference interpretation. *Meta: Journal des Traducteurs/Meta: Translators' Journal* 42(4). 622–628. DOI: 10.7202/002484ar.

De Merulis, Gianpiero. 2013. *L'uso di InterpretBank per la preparazione di una conferenza sul trattamento delle acque reflue: Glossario terminologico e contributo sperimentale.* Forlì: Università di Bologna. (MA thesis).

Defrancq, Bart. 2015. Corpus-based research into the presumed effects of short EVS. *Interpreting: International Journal of Research and Practice in Interpreting* 17(1). 26–45. DOI: 10.1075/intp.17.1.02def.

Defrancq, Bart & Claudio Fantinuoli. 2021. Automatic speech recognition in the booth: Assessment of system performance, interpreters' performances and interactions in the context of numbers. *Target* 33(1). 73–102. DOI: 10.1075/target.19166.def.

Déjean Le Féal, Karla. 1980. Die Satzsegmentierung beim freien Vortrag bzw. beim Verlesen von Texten und ihr Einfluss auf das Sprachverstehen. *Sprache und Verstehen* 1. 161–168.

Déjean Le Féal, Karla. 1981. Lectures et improvisations: Incidences de la forme de l'énonciation sur la traduction simultanée. *Fremdsprachen* 1(81). 29–32.

Déjean Le Féal, Karla. 1990. Some thoughts on the evaluation of simultaneous interpretation. In David Bowen & Margareta Bowen (eds.), *Interpreting: Yesterday, today, and tomorrow*, 154–160. Binghamton: John Benjamins. DOI: 10.1075/ata.iv.27lef.

de Saussure, Ferdinand. 1959. *Course in general linguistics.* New York: Philosophical Library.

Desblache, Lucile. 2001. *Aspects of specialised translation.* Paris: La Maison du Dictionnaire.

Desmet, Bart, Mieke Vandierendonck & Bart Defrancq. 2018. Simultaneous interpretation of numbers and the impact of technological support. In Claudio Fantinuoli (ed.), *Interpreting and technology*, 13–27. Berlin: Language Science Press. DOI: 10.5281/zenodo.1493291.

Dessloch, Florian, Thanh-Le Ha, Markus Müller, Jan Niehues, Thai-Son Nguyen, Ngoc-Quan Pham, Elizabeth Salesky, Matthias Sperber, Sebastian Stüker, Thomas Zenkel & Alexander Waibel. 2018. Kit lecture translator: Multilingual speech translation with one-shot learning. In Zhao Dongyan (ed.), *Proceedings of the 27th International Conference on Computational Linguistics: System Demonstrations*, 89–93. Santa Fe: Association for Computational Linguistics.

Deutsch, J. Anthony & Diana Deutsch. 1963. Attention: Some theoretical considerations. *Psychological Review* 70(1). 80–90. DOI: 10.1037/h0039515.

Díaz-Galaz, Stephanie & Alejandro Torres. 2019. Comprehension in interpreting and translation: Testing the phonological interference hypothesis. *Perspectives* 27(4). 622–638. DOI: 10.1080/0907676X.2019.1569699.

Donovan, Clare. 1990. *La fidélité en interprétation*. Paris: Université de la Sorbonne Nouvelle/Paris III. (Doctoral dissertation).

Dragsted, Barbara. 2004. *Segmentation in translation and translation memory systems: An empirical investigation of cognitive segmentation and effects of integrating a TM system into the translation process* (Ph.D. series 2004). Copenhagen: Samfundslitteratur.

Dragsted, Barbara. 2010. Coordination of reading and writing processes in translation: An eye on uncharted territory. In Gregory M. Shreve & Erik Angelone (eds.), *Translation and cognition*, 41–62. Amsterdam: John Benjamins. DOI: 10.1075/ata.xv.04dra.

Dragsted, Barbara. 2012. Indicators of difficulty in translation: Correlating product and process data. *Across Languages and Cultures* 13(1). 81–98. DOI: 10.1556/Acr.13.2012.1.5.

Dragsted, Barbara & Inge Gorm Hansen. 2008. Comprehension and production in translation: A pilot study on segmentation and the coordination of reading and writing processes. In Susanne Göpferich, Arnt Lykke Jakobsen & Inger M. Mees (eds.), *Looking at eyes: Eye-tracking studies of reading and translation processing* (Copenhagen Studies in Language), 9–29. Frederiksberg: Samfundslitteratur.

Dragsted, Barbara & Inge Gorm Hansen. 2009. Exploring translation and interpreting hybrids. The case of sight translation. *Meta: Journal des Traducteurs/Meta: Translators' Journal* 54(3). 588–604. DOI: 10.7202/038317ar.

Drechsel, Alexander. 2004. *Computereinsatz beim Dolmetschen in Ausbildung und Praxis: Ein Beitrag zur Dolmetschdidaktik*. Leipzig: Universität Leipzig. (MA thesis).

Drechsel, Alexander & Joshua Goldsmith. 2016. Tablet interpreting: The evolution and uses of mobile devices in interpreting. In Hannelore Lee-Jahnke & Martin Forstner (eds.), *CIUTI-forum 2016*. Geneva.

Drewer, Petra & Donatella Pulitano (eds.). 2019. *Terminologie: Epochen–Schwerpunkte–Umsetzungen.* Berlin: Springer.

Duchowski, Andrew T. 2017. *Eye tracking methodology: Theory and practice.* London: Springer.

EABM. 2021. *Survey - Ergonomics for the artificial boothmate.* https://www.eabm.ugent.be/survey/ (13 August, 2022).

Ehrensberger-Dow, Maureen. 2014. Challenges of translation process research at the workplace. *MonTI: Monografías de Traducción e Interpretación.* 355–383. DOI: 10.6035/MonTI.2014.ne1.12.

Ehrensberger-Dow, Maureen, Michaela Albl-Mikasa, Katrin Andermatt, Andrea Hunziker Heeb & Caroline Lehr. 2020. Cognitive load in processing ELF: Translators, interpreters, and other multilinguals. *Journal of English as a Lingua Franca* 9(2). 217–238. DOI: 10.1515/jelf-2020-2039.

Ehlich, Konrad & Jochen Rehbein. 1976. Halbinterpretative Arbeitstranskriptionen (HIAT). *Linguistische Berichte* 45. 21–41.

Ehrensberger-Dow, Maureen & Sharon O'Brien. 2015. Ergonomics of the translation workplace: Potential for cognitive friction. *Translation Spaces* 4(1). 98–118. DOI: 10.5922/2225-5346-2019-1-3.

Eisenrieth Dokumentations GmbH. 2010. *Flashterm.* https://www.flashterm.eu/en/ (13 August, 2021).

ELAN. 2020. Version 5.9. https://archive.mpi.nl/tla/elan (13 August, 2022).

Eriksen, Barbara A. & Charles W. Eriksen. 1974. Effects of noise letters upon the identification of a target letter in a nonsearch task. *Perception & Psychophysics* 16(1). 143–149. DOI: 10.3758/BF03203267.

European Parliament, DG Translation. 2019. *Live speech to text and machine translation tool for 24 languages.* https://etendering.ted.europa.eu/cft/cft-display.html?cftId=5249 (14 September, 2021).

Fabbro, Franco & Laura Gran. 1994. Neurological and neuropsychological aspects of polyglossia and simultaneous interpretation. In Sylvie Lambert & Barbara Moser-Mercer (eds.), *Bridging the gap: Empirical research in simultaneous interpretation,* 273–318. Amsterdam: John Benjamins. DOI: 10.1075/btl.3.21fab.

Fantinuoli, Claudio. 2006. Specialized corpora from the web and term extraction for simultaneous interpreters. In Marco Baroni & Silvia Bernardini (eds.), *Wacky! Working papers on the web as corpus,* 173–190. Bologna: CEDIB.

Fantinuoli, Claudio. 2012. *InterpretBank: Design and implementation of a terminology and knowledge management software for conference interpreters.* Germersheim: University of Mainz. (Doctoral dissertation).

Fantinuoli, Claudio. 2016. InterpretBank. Redefining computer-assisted interpreting tools. In João Esteves-Ferreira, Juliet Macan, Ruslan Mitkov & Olaf-Michael Stefanov (eds.), *Proceedings of the Translating and the Computer 38 Conference in London*, 42–52. Geneva: Editions Tradulex.

Fantinuoli, Claudio. 2017a. Computer-assisted preparation in conference interpreting. *Translation & Interpreting* 9(2). 24–37. DOI: 10.12807/ti.109202.2017.a02.

Fantinuoli, Claudio. 2017b. Speech recognition in the interpreter workstation. In João Esteves-Ferreira, Juliet Macan, Ruslan Mitkov & Olaf-Michael Stefanov (eds.), *Proceedings of the 39th Conference Translating and the Computer*, 25–34. Geneva: Editions Tradulex.

Fantinuoli, Claudio. 2018a. Computer-assisted interpreting: Challenges and future perspectives. In Gloria Corpas Pastor & Isabel Durán-Muñoz (eds.), *Trends in e-tools and resources for translators and interpreters*, 153–174. Leiden: Brill. DOI: 10.1163/9789004351790_009.

Fantinuoli, Claudio. 2018b. Interpreting and technology: The upcoming technological turn. In Claudio Fantinuoli (ed.), *Interpreting and technology*, 1–12. Berlin: Language Science Press. DOI: 10.5281/zenodo.1493289.

Fantinuoli, Claudio. 2019. The technological turn in interpreting: The challenges that lie ahead. In Wolfram Baur & Felix Mayer (eds.), *Übersetzen und Dolmetschen 4.0: Neue Wege im Digitalen Zeitalter*, 334–354. Berlin: BDÜ Fachverlag.

Fantinuoli, Claudio, Giulia Marchesini, David Landan & Lukas Horak. 2022. KUDO Interpreter Assist: Automated real-time support for remote interpretation. In João Esteves-Ferreira, Ruslan Mitkov, Maria Recort Ruiz, Olaf-Michael Stefanov, David Chambers, Juliet Margaret Macan & Vilelmini Sosoni (eds.), *Proceedings of the 43th Conference Translating and the Computer*, 68–77. Geneva: Editions Tradulex.

Fantinuoli, Claudio & Maddalena Montecchio. 2022. Defining maximum acceptable latency of AI-enhanced CAI tools. *arXiv preprint*. DOI: 10.48550/arXiv.2201.02792.

Fantinuoli, Claudio & Bianca Prandi. 2018. Teaching information and communication technologies: A proposal for the interpreting classroom. *Transkom* 11(2). 162–182.

Fantinuoli, Claudio & Bianca Prandi. 2021. Towards the evaluation of automatic simultaneous speech translation from a communicative perspective. In *Proceedings of the 18th International Conference on Spoken Language Translation*, 245–254. Bangkok: Association for Computational Linguistics.

References

Ferreira, Aline, John W. Schwieter & Daniel Gile. 2015. The position of psycholinguistic and cognitive science in translation and interpreting. In Aline Ferreira & John W. Schwieter (eds.), *Psycholinguistic and cognitive inquiries into translation and interpreting*, 3–15. Amsterdam: John Benjamins. DOI: 10.1075/btl.115.01fer.

Flesch, Rudolph. 1948. A new readability yardstick. *Journal of Applied Psychology* 32(3). 221–233. DOI: 10.1037/h0057532.

Floros, Georgios. 2003. *Kulturelle Konstellationen in Texten: Zur Beschreibung und Übersetzung von Kultur in Texten*. Tübingen: Gunter Narr.

Folaron, Debbie. 2019. Technology, technical translation and localization. In Minako O'Hagan (ed.), *The Routledge handbook of translation and technology*, 203–219. London: Routledge.

Fox, Wendy. 2018. *Can integrated titles improve the viewing experience? Investigating the impact of subtitling on the reception and enjoyment of film using eye tracking and questionnaire data* (Translation and Multilingual Natural Language Processing 9). Berlin: Language Science Press. DOI: 10.5281/zenodo.1180721.

Frittella, Francesca Maria. 2022. CAI-tool supported SI of numbers: A theoretical and methodological contribution. *International Journal of Interpreter Education* 14(1). 32–56. DOI: 10.34068/ijie.14.01.05.

Gacek, Michael. 2015. *Softwarelösungen für DolmetscherInnen*. Wien: Universität Wien. (MA thesis).

García, Adolfo M. 2013. Brain activity during translation: A review of the neuroimaging evidence as a testing ground for clinically-based hypotheses. *Journal of Neurolinguistics* 26(3). 370–383. DOI: 10.1016/j.jneuroling.2012.12.002.

García, Adolfo M. 2015. Translating with an injured brain: Neurolinguistic aspects of translation as revealed by bilinguals with cerebral lesions. *Meta: Journal des Traducteurs/Meta: Translators' Journal* 60(1). 112–134. DOI: 10.7202/1032402ar.

García, Adolfo M. 2019. *The neurocognition of translation and interpreting*. Amsterdam: John Benjamins. DOI: 10.1075/btl.147.

García Becerra, Olalla. 2016. Survey research on quality expectations in interpreting: The effect of method of administration on subjects' response rate. *Meta: Journal des Traducteurs/Meta: Translators' Journal* 60(3). 542–556. DOI: 10.7202/1036142ar.

García de Quesada, Mercedes. 2011. Terminologie. In Angela Collados Aís, Emilia Iglesias Fernández, E. Macarena Pradas Macías & Elisabeth Stévaux (eds.), *Qualitätsparameter beim Simultandolmetschen: Interdisziplinäre Perspektiven*, 219–251. Tübingen: Gunter Narr.

Garzone, Giuliana. 2006. *Perspectives on ESP and popularization.* Milano: CUEM.

Gerver, David. 1976. Empirical studies of simultaneous interpretation: A review and a model. In Richard W. Brislin (ed.), *Translation: Applications and research*, 165–207. New York: Gardner Press.

Gerzymisch-Arbogast, Heidrun. 1996. *Termini im Kontext: Verfahren zur Erschließung und Übersetzung der textspezifischen Bedeutung von fachlichen Ausdrücken.* Tübingen: Gunter Narr.

Ghiselli, Serena. 2015. *Le sfide traduttive dei sintagmi nominali con modificatori in posizione prenominale nell'interpretazione simultanea dall'inglese in italiano: Uno studio sul corpus EPIC.* Forlì: Università di Bologna. (MA thesis).

Gieshoff, Anne Catherine. 2012. *Aus 92 wird zwölf: Zahlen im Simultandolmetschen.* Germersheim: University of Mainz. (MA thesis).

Gieshoff, Anne Catherine. 2018. *The impact of audio-visual speech input on work-load in simultaneous interpreting.* Germersheim: Johannes Gutenberg-Universität Mainz. (Doctoral dissertation). DOI: 10.25358/openscience-2180.

Gieshoff, Anne Catherine. 2021. The impact of visible lip movements on silent pauses in simultaneous interpreting. *Interpreting: International Journal of Research and Practice in Interpreting* 23(2). 168–191. DOI: 10.1075/intp.00061.gie.

Gile, Daniel. 1988. Le partage de l'attention et le "Modèle d'efforts" en interprétation simultanée. *The Interpreters' Newsletter* 1. 4–22. http://hdl.handle.net/10077/2132 (24 July, 2021).

Gile, Daniel. 1990. L'évaluation de la qualité de l'interprétation par les délégués: Une étude de cas. *The Interpreters' Newsletter* 3. 66–71. http://hdl.handle.net/10077/2156 (24 July, 2021).

Gile, Daniel. 1991a. A communicative-oriented analysis of quality in nonliterary translation and interpretation. In Mildred L. Larson (ed.), *Translation: Theory and practice, tension and interdependence*, 188–200. Binghamton: John Benjamins. DOI: 10.1075/ata.v.19gil.

Gile, Daniel. 1991b. The processing capacity issue in conference interpretation. *Babel: Revue internationale de la traduction / International Journal of Translation* 37(1). 15–27. DOI: 10.1075/babel.37.1.04gil.

Gile, Daniel. 1995. *Regards sur la recherche en interprétation de conférence.* Lille: Presses universitaires de Lille.

Gile, Daniel. 1997. Conference interpreting as a cognitive management problem. In Franz Pöchhacker & Miriam Shlesinger (eds.), *The interpreting studies reader*, 163–176. London: Routledge.

Gile, Daniel. 1999. Testing the effort models' tightrope hypothesis in simultaneous interpreting: A contribution. *HERMES: Journal of Language and Communication in Business* 23. 153–172. DOI: 10.7146/hjlcb.v12i23.25553.

Gile, Daniel. 2008. Local cognitive load in simultaneous interpreting and its implications for empirical research. *FORUM: Revue internationale d'interprétation et de traduction / International Journal of Interpretation and Translation* 6(2). 59–77. DOI: 10.1075/forum.6.2.04gil.

Gile, Daniel. 2009. *Basic concepts and models for interpreter and translator training.* Amsterdam: John Benjamins.

Gile, Daniel. 2011. Errors, omissions and infelicities in broadcast interpreting: Preliminary findings from a case study. In Cecilia Alvstad, Adelina Hild & Elisabet Tiselius (eds.), *Methods and strategies of process research*, 201–218. Amsterdam: John Benjamins. DOI: 10.1075/btl.94.15gil.

Gile, Daniel. 2015. Effort models. In Franz Pöchhacker (ed.), *Routledge encyclopedia of interpreting studies*, 135–137. Oxon: Routledge.

Gile, Daniel. 2016. *The effort models: Clarifications and update.* (Presentation). DOI: 10.13140/RG.2.1.4221.7849.

Gile, Daniel. 2017a. Biases in critical reading of TIS literature. *Tradução em Revista* 23. 1–19. DOI: 10.17771/PUCRio.TradRev.32213.

Gile, Daniel. 2017b. *The effort models clarifications.* (Presentation). DOI: 10.13140/RG.2.2.21975.27049.

Gile, Daniel. 2020. *2020 update of the effort models and gravitational model.* (Presentation). DOI: 10.13140/RG.2.2.24895.94889.

Gile, Daniel & Victoria Lei. 2020. Translation, effort and cognition. In Fábio Alves & Arnt Lykke Jakobsen (eds.), *The Routledge handbook of translation and cognition*, 263–278. London: Routledge.

Ginns, Paul. 2005. Meta-analysis of the modality effect. *Learning and Instruction* 15(4). 313–331. DOI: 10.1016/j.learninstruc.2005.07.001.

Godefroy, Olivier, Philippe Azouvi, Philippe Robert, Martine Roussel, Didier LeGall, Thierry Meulemans & Groupe de Réflexion sur l'Evaluation des Fonctions Exécutives Study Group. 2010. Dysexecutive syndrome: Diagnostic criteria and validation study. *Annals of Neurology* 68(6). 855–864. DOI: 10.1002/ana.22117.

Goldman-Eisler, Frieda. 1972. Segmentation of input in simultaneous translation. *Journal of Psycholinguistic Research* 1(2). 127–140. DOI: 10.1007/BF01068102.

Goldsmith, Joshua. 2017. A comparative user evaluation of tablets and tools for consecutive interpreters. In João Esteves-Ferreira, Juliet Macan, Ruslan Mitkov & Olaf-Michael Stefanov (eds.), *Proceedings of the 39th Conference Translating and the Computer*, 40–50. Geneva: Editions Tradulex.

Goldsmith, Joshua & Josephine Christine Holley. 2015. *Consecutive interpreting 2.0: The tablet interpreting experience.* Geneva: University of Geneva. (MA thesis).

Görög, Attila. 2014a. Quality evaluation today: The dynamic quality framework. In João Esteves-Ferreira, Juliet Macan, Ruslan Mitkov & Olaf-Michael Stefanov (eds.), *Proceedings of the 36th Conference Translating and the Computer*, 155–164. Geneva: Tradulex.

Görög, Attila. 2014b. Quantifying and benchmarking quality: The TAUS Dynamic Quality Framework. *Tradumàtica: tecnologies de la traducció* 12. 443–454.

Gumul, Ewa. 2018. Searching for evidence of Gile's effort models in retrospective protocols of trainee simultaneous interpreters. *Między oryginałem a przekładem* 24(4(42)). 17–39. DOI: 10.12797/MOaP.24.2018.42.02.

Halliday, Michael A. K. & James R. Martin. 2003. *Writing science: Literacy and discursive power*. London: Routledge.

Hamidi, Miriam & Franz Pöchhacker. 2007. Simultaneous consecutive interpreting: A new technique put to the test. *Meta: Journal des Traducteurs/Meta: Translators' Journal* 52(2). 276–289. DOI: 10.7202/016070ar.

Hansen, Gyde. 2007. Ein Fehler ist ein Fehler ... oder?: Der Bewertungsprozess in der Übersetzungsprozessforschung. In Gerd Wotjak (ed.), *Quo vadis Translatologie?*, 115–131. Berlin: Frank & Timme.

Hansen, Gyde. 2008. The dialogue in translation process research. In *Translation and cultural diversity: Selected proceedings of the XVIII FIT world congress 2008*, 386–397. Shanghai: Foreign Languages Press.

Hansen, Gyde. 2009. Some thoughts about the evaluation of translation products in translation process research. In Inger M. Mees, Susanne Göpferich & Fábio Alves (eds.), *Methodology, technology and innovation in translation process research: A tribute to Arnt Lykke Jakobsen* (Copenhagen Studies in Language), 389–402. Frederiksberg: Samfundslitteratur.

Hansen, Inge Gorm & Barbara Dragsted. 2007. Speaking your translation: Exploiting synergies between translation and interpreting. In Franz Pöchhacker, Arnt Lykke Jakobsen & Inger M. Mees (eds.), *Interpreting studies and beyond: A tribute to Miriam Shlesinger* (Copenhagen Studies in Language 35), 251–274. Frederiksberg: Copenhagen Business School Press.

Hansen-Schirra, Silvia. 2012. Nutzbarkeit von Sprachtechnologien für die Translation. *Transkom* 5(2). 211–226. (24 July, 2021).

Hansen-Schirra, Silvia & Jean Nitzke. 2020. Translation, the process–product interface and cognition. In Fábio Alves & Arnt Lykke Jakobsen (eds.), *The Routledge handbook of translation and cognition*, 415–432. London: Routledge.

Hansen-Schirra, Silvia, Jean Nitzke & Katharina Oster. 2017. Predicting cognate translation. In Silvia Hansen-Schirra, Oliver Čulo & Sascha Hofmann (eds.), *Empirical modelling of translation and interpreting*, 23–39. Berlin: Language Science Press. DOI: 10.5281/zenodo.1090944.

References

Hart, Sandra G. & Lowell E. Staveland. 1988. Development of NASA-TLX (Task Load Index): Results of empirical and theoretical research. In Peter A. Hancock & Najmedin Meshkati (eds.), *Human mental workload* (Advances in Psychology 52), 139–183. Amsterdam: Elsevier. DOI: 10.1016/S0166-4115(08)62386-9.

Heid, Ulrich & Anita Gojun. 2012. Term candidate extraction for terminography and CAT: An overview of TTC. In Ruth Vatvedt Fjeld & Julie Matilde Torjusen (eds.), *Proceedings of the 15th Euralex International Congress*, 585–594. Oslo: Reprosentralen, UiO.

Herbig, Nico, Santanu Pala, Antonio Krügera & Josef van Genabitha. 2021. Multimodal estimation of cognitive load in post-editing of machine translation. In Tra&Co Group (ed.), *Translation, interpreting, cognition: The way out of the box*, 1–32. Berlin: Language Science Press. DOI: 10.5281/zenodo.4545029.

Hervais-Adelman, Alexis Georges, Barbara Moser-Mercer & Narly Golestani. 2011. Executive control of language in the bilingual brain: Integrating the evidence from neuroimaging to neuropsychology. *Frontiers in Psychology* 2. 1–8. DOI: 10.3389/fpsyg.2011.00234.

Hervais-Adelman, Alexis Georges, Barbara Moser-Mercer, Christoph M. Michel & Narly Golestani. 2015. fMRI of simultaneous interpretation reveals the neural basis of extreme language control. *Cerebral Cortex* 25(12). 4727–4739. DOI: 10.1093/cercor/bhu158.

Hess, Eckhard H. & James M. Polt. 1964. Pupil size in relation to mental activity during simple problem-solving. *Science* 143(3611). 1190–1192. DOI: 10.1126/science.143.3611.1190.

Hessels, Roy S., Chantal Kemner, Carlijn van den Boomen & Ignace T. C. Hooge. 2016. The area-of-interest problem in eyetracking research: A noise-robust solution for face and sparse stimuli. *Behavior Research Methods* 48(4). 1694–1712. DOI: 10.3758/s13428-015-0676-y.

Hoberg, Felix. 2021. Dialogue-oriented evaluation of Microsoft's skype translator in the language pair Catalan-German. In Tra&Co Group (ed.), *Translation, interpreting, cognition: The way out of the box*, 67–77. Berlin: Language Science Press. DOI: 10.5281/zenodo.4545035.

Hoberg, Felix. 2022. *Informationsintegration in mehrsprachigen Textchats: Der Skype Translator im Sprachenpaar Katalanisch-Deutsch* (Translation and Multilingual Natural Language Processing 17). Berlin: Language Science Press. DOI: 10.5281/zenodo.5902971.

Hoeks, Bert & Willem J. M. Levelt. 1993. Pupillary dilation as a measure of attention: A quantitative system analysis. *Behavior Research Methods, Instruments, & Computers* 25(1). 16–26. DOI: 10.3758/BF03204445.

Holmqvist, Kenneth. 2011. *Eye tracking: A comprehensive guide to methods and measures*. Oxford: Oxford University Press.

Hvelplund, Kristian Tangsgaard. 2011. *Allocation of cognitive resources in translation: An eye-tracking and key-logging study* (PhD series 10.2011). Frederiksberg: Samfundslitteratur.

Hvelplund, Kristian Tangsgaard. 2014. Eye tracking and the translation process: Reflections on the analysis and interpretation of eye-tracking data. *MonTI: Monografías de Traducción e Interpretación*. 201–223. DOI: 10.6035/MonTI.2014. ne1.6.

Hvelplund, Kristian Tangsgaard. 2017. Eye tracking in translation process research. In John W. Schwieter & Aline Ferreira (eds.), *The handbook of translation and cognition*, 248–264. Hoboken: Wiley Online Library.

Hyönä, Jukka, Jorma Tommola & Anna-Mari Alaja. 1995. Pupil dilation as a measure of processing load in simultaneous interpretation and other language tasks. *The Quarterly Journal of Experimental Psychology* 48(3). 598–612. DOI: 10.1080/14640749508401407.

Jacquemot, Charlotte, Emmanuel Dupoux & Anne-Catherine Bachoud-Lévi. 2011. Is the word-length effect linked to subvocal rehearsal? *Cortex* 47(4). 484–493. DOI: 10.1016/j.cortex.2010.07.007.

Jakobsen, Arnt Lykke. 2003. Effects of think aloud on translation speed, revision, and segmentation. In Fábio Alves (ed.), *Triangulating translation: Perspectives in process oriented research*, 69–95. Amsterdam: John Benjamins.

Jakobsen, Arnt Lykke. 2006. Research methods in translation: Translog. In Eva Lindgren & Kirk P. H. Sullivan (eds.), *Computer keystroke logging and writing* (Studies in writing 18), 95–105. Oxford: Pergamon Press.

Jakobsen, Arnt Lykke. 2017. Translation process research. In John W. Schwieter & Aline Ferreira (eds.), *The handbook of translation and cognition*, 19–49. Hoboken: John Wiley & Sons, Ltd. DOI: 10.1002/9781119241485.ch2.

Jakobsen, Arnt Lykke. 2019. Translation technology research with eye tracking. In Minako O'Hagan (ed.), *The Routledge handbook of translation and technology*, 398–416. London: Routledge.

Jakobsen, Arnt Lykke & Kristian Tangsgaard Hvelplund. 2008. Eye movement behaviour across four different types of reading task. *Copenhagen Studies in Language* 36. 103–124.

Jia, Ye, Michelle Tadmor Ramanovich, Tal Remez & Roi Pomerantz. 2022. Translatotron 2: High-quality direct speech-to-speech translation with voice preservation. In Kamalika Chaudhuri, Stefanie Jegelka, Le Song, Csaba Szepesvari, Gang Niu & Sivan Sabato (eds.), *Proceedings of the 39th international conference on machine learning*, 10120–10134. Baltimore: PMLR.

Jia, Ye, Ron J. Weiss, Fadi Biadsy, Wolfgang Macherey, Melvin Johnson, Zhifeng Chen & Yonghui Wu. 2019. Direct speech-to-speech translation with a sequence-to-sequence model. In *Proc. interspeech 2019*, 1123–1127.

Jiang, Hong. 2013. The interpreter's glossary in simultaneous interpreting: A survey. *Interpreting: International Journal of Research and Practice in Interpreting* 15(1). 74–93. DOI: 10.1075/intp.15.1.04jia.

Jiang, Hong. 2015. *A survey of glossary practice of conference interpreters.* https://aiic.org/document/950/AIICWebzine_2015_Issue66_5_JIANG_A_survey_of_glossary_practice_of_conference_interpreters_EN.pdf (24 July, 2021).

Just, Marcel A. & Patricia A. Carpenter. 1980. A theory of reading: From eye fixations to comprehension. *Psychological Review* 87(4). 329–354. DOI: 10.1037/0033-295X.87.4.329.

Just, Marcel A. & Patricia A. Carpenter. 1993. The intensity dimension of thought: Pupillometric indices of sentence processing. *Canadian Journal of Experimental Psychology/Revue canadienne de psychologie expérimentale* 47(2). 310–339. DOI: 10.1037/h0078820.

Kageura, Kyo & Elizabeth Marshman. 2019. Terminology extraction and management. In Minako O'Hagan (ed.), *The Routledge handbook of translation and technology*, 61–77. London: Routledge.

Kahneman, Daniel. 1973. *Attention and effort.* Englewood Cliffs: Prentice-Hall.

Kahneman, Daniel & Jackson Beatty. 1966. Pupil diameter and load on memory. *Science* 154(3756). 1583–1585. DOI: 10.1126/science.154.3756.1583.

Kalderon, Eliza. 2017. *Neurophysiologie des Simultandolmetschens: Eine fMRI-Studie mit Konferenzdolmetschern.* Germersheim: Johannes Gutenberg-Universität Mainz. (Doctoral dissertation). DOI: 10.25358/openscience-4538.

Kalina, Sylvia. 1998. *Strategische Prozesse beim Dolmetschen: Theoretische Grundlagen, empirische Fallstudien, didaktische Konsequenzen.* Tübingen: Gunter Narr.

Kalina, Sylvia. 2005. Quality assurance for interpreting processes. *Meta: Journal des Traducteurs/Meta: Translators' Journal* 50(2). 768–784. DOI: 10.7202/011017ar.

Kalina, Sylvia. 2006. Zur Dokumentation von Maßnahmen der Qualitätssicherung beim Konferenzdolmetschen. In Carmen Heine, Klaus Schubert & Heidrun Gerzymisch-Arbogast (eds.), *Text and translation: Theory and methodology of translation*, 253–268. Tübingen: Gunter Narr.

Kantowitz, Barry H. & James L. Knight. 1976. On experimenter-limited processes. *Psychological Review* 83(6). 502–507. DOI: 10.1037/0033-295X.83.6.502.

Karsh, Robert & Francis W. Breitenbach. 1983. Looking at looking: The amorphous fixation measure. In Rudolph Groner, Christine Menz, Dennis F. Fisher

& Richard A. Monty (eds.), *Eye movements and psychological functions: International views*, 53–64. Hillsdale: Erlbaum.

Keating, Gregory D. & Jill Jegerski. 2015. Experimental designs in sentence processing research: A methodological review and user's guide. *Studies in Second Language Acquisition* 37(1). 1–32. DOI: 10.1017/S0272263114000187.

Kilgarriff, Adam, Vít Baisa, Jan Bušta, Miloš Jakubíček, Vojtěch Kovář, Jan Michelfeit, Pavel Rychlỳ & Vít Suchomel. 2014. The Sketch Engine: Ten years on. *Lexicography* 1. 7–36. DOI: 10.1007/s40607-014-0009-9.

Kirchhoff, Hella. 1976. Simultaneous interpreting: Interdependence of variables in the interpreting process, interpreting models and interpreting strategies. In Franz Pöchhacker & Miriam Shlesinger (eds.), *The interpreting studies reader*, 110–119. London: Routledge.

Klonowicz, Tatiana. 1994. Putting one's heart into simultaneous interpretation. In Sylvie Lambert & Barbara Moser-Mercer (eds.), *Bridging the gap: Empirical research in simultaneous interpretation*, 213–224. Amsterdam: John Benjamins. DOI: 10.1075/btl.3.16klo.

Kopczynski, Andrzej. 1994. Quality in conference interpreting: Some pragmatic problems. In Mary Snell-Hornby, Franz Pöchhacker & Klaus Kaindl (eds.), *Translation studies: An interdiscipline*, 189–198. Amsterdam: John Benjamins.

Köpke, Barbara & Teresa M. Signorelli. 2012. Methodological aspects of working memory assessment in simultaneous interpreters. *International Journal of Bilingualism* 16(2). 183–197. DOI: 10.1177/1367006911402981.

Korpal, Paweł. 2016. Interpreting as a stressful activity: Physiological measures of stress in simultaneous interpreting. *Poznań Studies in Contemporary Linguistics* 52(2). 297–316. DOI: 10.1515/psicl-2016-0011.

Korpal, Paweł. 2017. *Linguistic and psychological indicators of stress in simultaneous interpreting* (Outstanding WA dissertations 12). Poznań: Wydawnictwo Naukowe UAM.

Koshkin, Roman, Yury Shtyrov, Andriy Myachykov & Alex Ossadtchi. 2018. Testing the efforts model of simultaneous interpreting: An ERP study. *PLOS ONE* 13(10). 1–18. DOI: 10.1371/journal.pone.0206129.

Kosma, Alexandra. 2007. Le fonctionnement spécifique de la mémoire de travail en traduction. *Meta: Journal des Traducteurs/Meta: Translators' Journal* 52(1). 22–28. DOI: 10.7202/014716ar.

Krings, Hans P. 2001. *Repairing texts: Empirical investigations of machine translation post-editing processes*. Kent: Kent State University Press.

Kuang, Huolingxiao. 2019. Computerized note-taking in consecutive interpreting: A pen-voice integrated approach towards omissions, additions and reconstructions in notes. In Michael Carl & Silvia Hansen-Schirra (eds.), *Proceedings of the second MEMENTO workshop on Modelling Parameters of Cognitive Effort in Translation Production*, 18–19. Dublin: European Association for Machine Translation.

Kumpulainen, Minna. 2015. On the operationalisation of 'pauses' in translation process research. *The International Journal for Translation & Interpreting Research* 7(1). 47–58. DOI: ti.106201.2015.a04.

Kurz, Ingrid. 1989. Conference interpreting: User expectations. In Deanna L. Hammond (ed.), *Coming of age: Proceedings of the 30th annual conference of the American Translators Association*, 143–148. Medford: Learned Information.

Kurz, Ingrid. 1993. Conference interpretation: Expectations of different user groups. *The Interpreters' Newsletter* 5. 13–21. http://hdl.handle.net/10077/4908 (24 July, 2021).

Kurz, Ingrid. 1994. A look into the "black box": EEG probability mapping during mental simultaneous interpreting. In Mary Snell-Hornby, Franz Pöchhacker & Klaus Kaindl (eds.), *Translation studies: An interdiscipline. Selected papers from the Translation Studies Congress, Vienna, 1992*, 199–208. Amsterdam: John Benjamins. DOI: 10.1075/btl.2.25kur.

Kurz, Ingrid. 1996. *Simultandolmetschen als Gegenstand der interdisziplinären Forschung*. Wien: WUV-Universitätsverlag.

Kurz, Ingrid. 2002. Physiological stress responses during media and conference interpreting. In Giuliana Garzone & Maurizio Viezzi (eds.), *Interpreting in the 21st century: Challenges and opportunities*, 195–202. Amsterdam: John Benjamins. DOI: 10.1075/btl.43.19kur.

Kurz, Ingrid. 2003. Physiological stress during simultaneous interpreting: A comparison of experts and novices. *The Interpreters' Newsletter* 12. 51–67. http://hdl.handle.net/10077/2472.

Lacruz, Isabel, Michael Carl & Masaru Yamada. 2018. Literality and cognitive effort: Japanese and Spanish. In *Proceedings of the Eleventh International Conference on Language Resources and Evaluation (LREC 2018)*, 3818–3821.

Lacruz, Isabel, Michael Carl, Masaru Yamada & Akiko Aizawa. 2016. *Pause metrics and machine translation utility*. Paper presented at the 22nd Annual Meeting of the Association for Natural Language Processing, 1–4. Sendai: NLP 2016.

Lacruz, Isabel, Michael Denkowski & Alon Lavie. 2014. Cognitive demand and cognitive effort in post-editing. In *Proceedings of the 11th Conference of the Association for Machine Translation in the Americas*, 73–84. Vancouver: Association for Machine Translation in the Americas. https://aclanthology.org/2014.amta-wptp.6 (24 July, 2021).

Lacruz, Isabel, Gregory M. Shreve & Erik Angelone. 2012. Average pause ratio as an indicator of cognitive effort in post-editing: A case study. In Sharon O'Brien, Michel Simard & Lucia Specia (eds.), *Workshop on post-editing technology and practice*, 1–10. San Diego: Association for Machine Translation in the Americas. https://aclanthology.org/2012.amta-wptp.3 (24 July, 2021).

Lambert, Sylvie. 1988. Information processing among conference interpreters: A test of the depth-of-processing hypothesis. *Meta: Journal des Traducteurs/Meta: Translators' Journal* 33(3). 377–387. DOI: 10.7202/003380ar.

Landis, J. Richard & Gary G. Koch. 1977. The measurement of observer agreement for categorical data. *Biometrics* 33(1). 159–174. DOI: 10.2307/2529310.

Laplace, Colette. 1994. *Théorie du langage et théorie de la traduction. Les concepts-clefs de trois auteurs: Kade (Leipzig), Coseriu (Tübingen), Seleskovitch (Paris)*. Paris: Didier Érudition.

Läubli, Samuel & David Orrego-Carmona. 2017. When Google Translate is better than some human colleagues, those people are no longer colleagues. In João Esteves-Ferreira, Juliet Macan, Ruslan Mitkov & Olaf-Michael Stefanov (eds.), *Proceedings of the 39th Conference Translating and the Computer*, 59–69. Geneva: Editions Tradulex.

Lavie, Nilli. 1995. Perceptual load as a necessary condition for selective attention. *Journal of Experimental Psychology: Human Perception and Performance* 21(3). 451–468. DOI: 10.1037/0096-1523.21.3.451.

Lavie, Nilli. 2000. Selective attention and cognitive control: Dissociating attentional functions through different types of load. In Stephen Monsell & Jon Driver (eds.), *Control of cognitive processes: Attention and performance XVIII*, 175–194. Cambridge: MIT Press.

Lavie, Nilli. 2005. Distracted and confused? Selective attention under load. *Trends in Cognitive Sciences* 9(2). 75–82. DOI: 10.1016/j.tics.2004.12.004.

Lavie, Nilli. 2010. Attention, distraction, and cognitive control under load. *Current Directions in Psychological Science* 19(3). 143–148. DOI: 10.1177/0963721410370295.

Lavie, Nilli, Aleksandra Hirst, Jan W. De Fockert & Essi Viding. 2004. Load theory of selective attention and cognitive control. *Journal of Experimental Psychology: General* 133(3). 339–354. DOI: 10.1037/0096-3445.133.3.339.

Lazar, Jonathan. 2017. *Research methods in human computer interaction*. Cambridge: Elsevier.

Lederer, Marianne. 1978. Simultaneous interpretation: Units of meaning and other features. In David Gerver & H. Wallace Sinaiko (eds.), *Language interpretation and communication*, 323–332. Boston: Springer.

Lederer, Marianne. 1981. *La traduction simultanée: Expérience et théorie.* Paris: Minard Lettres Modernes.

Lee, Tae-Hyung. 2002. Ear voice span in English into Korean simultaneous interpretation. *Meta: Journal des Traducteurs/Meta: Translators' Journal* 47(4). 596–606. DOI: 10.7202/008039ar.

Lee, Tae-Hyung. 2003. Tail-to-tail span: A new variable in conference interpreting research. *FORUM: Revue internationale d'interprétation et de traduction / International Journal of Interpretation and Translation* 1(1). 41–62. DOI: 10.1075/forum.1.1.03lee.

Leijten, Mariëlle & Luuk Van Waes. 2013. Keystroke logging in writing research: Using Inputlog to analyze and visualize writing processes. *Written Communication* 30(3). 358–392. DOI: 10.1177/0741088313491692.

Leipzig Corpora Collection. 2012. English web text corpus (United Kingdom) based on material from 2012. In *Leipzig corpora collection. Dataset.* https://corpora.uni-leipzig.de/?corpusId=eng-uk_web_2012 (24 May, 2022).

Leipzig Corpora Collection. 2016. English news corpus based on material from 2016. In *Leipzig corpora collection. Dataset.* https://corpora.uni-leipzig.de?corpusId=eng_news_2016 (26 May, 2022).

Leipzig Corpora Collection. 2021. English Wikipedia corpus based on material from 2021. In *Leipzig corpora collection. Dataset.* https://corpora.uni-leipzig.de?corpusId=eng_wikipedia_2021 (26 May, 2022).

Levenshtein, Vladimir I. 1966. Binary codes capable of correcting deletions, insertions and reversals. *Soviet Physics Doklady* 10(8). 707–710. https://nymity.ch/sybilhunting/pdf/Levenshtein1966a.pdf (24 August, 2021).

Logie, Robert H. 1995. *Visuo-spatial working memory.* London: Psychology Press.

Logie, Robert H. 2016. Retiring the central executive. *Quarterly Journal of Experimental Psychology* 69(10). 2093–2109. DOI: 10.1080/17470218.2015.1136657.

Lommel, Arle, Aljoscha Burchardt, Maja Popović, Kim Harris, Eleftherios Avramidis & Hans Uszkoreit. 2014. Using a new analytic measure for the annotation and analysis of MT errors on real data. In *Proceedings of the 17th annual conference of the European Association for Machine Translation*, 165–172. Dubrovnik: European Association for Machine Translation. https://aclanthology.org/2014.eamt-1.38 (24 July, 2022).

Lommel, Arle, Hans Uszkoreit & Aljoscha Burchardt. 2014. *Multidimensional quality metrics (MQM) definition.* http://www.qt21.eu/mqm-definition/ (24 May, 2021).

Low, Renae & John Sweller. 2014. The modality principle in multimedia learning. In Richard Mayer (ed.), *The Cambridge handbook of multimedia learning*, 227–

246. Cambridge: Cambridge University Press. DOI: 10.1017/CBO9781139547369.012.

Lu, Sara A., Christopher D. Wickens, Julie C. Prinet, Shaun D. Hutchins, Nadine Sarter & Angelia Sebok. 2013. Supporting interruption management and multimodal interface design: Three meta-analyses of task performance as a function of interrupting task modality. *Human Factors: The Journal of the Human Factors and Ergonomics Society* 55(4). 697–724. DOI: 10.1177/0018720813476298.

Mack, Gabriele & Lorella Cattaruzza. 1995. User surveys in simultaneous interpretation: A means of learning about quality and/or raising some reasonable doubts. In Jorma Tommola (ed.), *Topics in interpreting research*, 37–49. Turku: Centre for Translation & Interpreting, University of Turku (Finland).

Marrone, Stefano. 1993. Quality: A shared objective. *The Interpreters' Newsletter* 5. 35–41. http://hdl.handle.net/10077/14664 (5 August, 2021).

Martin, Reg. 2014. *Glossary assistant.* http://swiss32.com (13 August, 2021).

Martínez, Silvia Montero & Pamela Faber. 2009. Terminological competence in translation. *Terminology: International Journal of Theoretical and Applied Issues in Specialized Communication* 15(1). 88–104. DOI: 10.1075/term.15.1.05mon.

Marzouk, Shaimaa. 2021. German light verb construction in the course of the development of Machine Translation. In Tra&Co Group (ed.), *Translation, interpreting, cognition: The way out of the box*, 47–66. Berlin: Language Science Press. DOI: 10.5281/zenodo.4545033.

Massaro, Dominic W. 1978. An information-processing model of understanding speech. In David Gerver & H. Wallace Sinaiko (eds.), *Language interpretation and communication*, 299–314. Boston: Springer US. DOI: 10.1007/978-1-4615-9077-4_26.

Matysiak, Anna. 2001. *Controlled processing in simultaneous interpretation: A study based on Daniel Gile's Effort Models.* Poznan: University of Poznan. (MA thesis).

Mauri, Daniele. 2021. *QEMI-C: An ad hoc corpus for quality evaluation of machine interpreting.* Germersheim: University of Mainz. (MA thesis).

Mayer, Felix. 2019. Terminologiearbeit und Terminographie. In Petra Drewer & Donatella Pulitano (eds.), *Terminologie: Epochen–Schwerpunkte–Umsetzungen*, 83–93. Berlin: Springer.

Mayer, Richard E. & Logan Fiorella. 2014. Principles for reducing extraneous processing in multimedia learning: Coherence, signaling, redundancy, spatial contiguity, and temporal contiguity principles. In Richard Mayer (ed.), *The Cambridge handbook of multimedia learning*, 279–315. Cambridge: Cambridge University Press. DOI: 10.1017/CBO9781139547369.015.

References

McDonald, Janet L. & Patricia A. Carpenter. 1981. Simultaneous translation: Idiom interpretation and parsing heuristics. *Journal of Verbal Learning and Verbal Behavior* 20(2). 231–247. DOI: 10.1016/S0022-5371(81)90397-2.

McLeod, Peter. 1977. A dual task response modality effect: Support for multiprocessor models of attention. *Quarterly Journal of Experimental Psychology* 29(4). 651–667. DOI: 10.1080/14640747708400639.

McNamara, Danielle S., Arthur C. Graesser, Philip M. McCarthy & Zhiqiang Cai. 2014. *Automated evaluation of text and discourse with Coh-Metrix.* New York: Cambridge University Press.

Mead, Peter. 2002. Exploring hesitation in consecutive interpreting: An empirical study. In Giuliana Garzone & Maurizio Viezzi (eds.), *Interpreting in the 21st century: Challenges and opportunities*, 73–82. Amsterdam: John Benjamins. DOI: 10.1075/btl.43.08mea.

Mead, Peter. 2005. Methodological issues in the study of interpreters' fluency. *The Interpreters' Newsletter* 13. 39–63. http://hdl.handle.net/10077/2469 (24 August, 2021).

Meak, Lidia. 1990. Interprétation simultanée et congrès médical: Attentes et commentaires. *The Interpreters' Newsletter* 3. 8–13. http://hdl.handle.net/10077/2148 (24 August, 2021).

Mellinger, Christopher D. 2019. Computer-assisted interpreting technologies and interpreter cognition: A product and process-oriented perspective. *Tradumàtica: tecnologies de la traducció* 17. 33–44. DOI: 10.5565/rev/tradumatica.228.

Mellinger, Christopher D. & Thomas A. Hanson. 2017. *Quantitative research methods in translation and interpreting studies.* London: Routledge.

Mertin, Elvira. 2006. *Prozessorientiertes Qualitätsmanagement im Dienstleistungsbereich Übersetzen.* Berlin: Peter Lang.

Mikkelsen, Hans Kristian. 1991. Arntz, Reiner/Heribert Picht: Einführung in die Terminologiearbeit. Hildesheim, Zürich, New York: Georg Olms Verlag 1989. 344 Seiten. *Hermes* 6. 161–173.

Miller, George A. 1956. The magical number seven, plus or minus two: Some limits on our capacity for processing information. *Psychological Review* 63(2). 81–97. DOI: 10.1037/h0043158.

Mizuno, Akira. 2005. Process model for simultaneous interpreting and working memory. *Meta: Journal des Traducteurs/Meta: Translators' Journal* 50(2). 739–752. DOI: 10.7202/011015ar.

Montecchio, Maddalena. 2021. *Defining maximum acceptable latency of ASR-enhanced CAI tools. Quantitative and qualitative assessment of the impact of*

ASR latency on interpreters' performance. Germersheim: University of Mainz. (MA thesis).

Moorkens, Joss & Sharon O'Brien. 2015. Post-editing evaluations: Trade-offs between novice and professional participants. In *Proceedings of the 18th annual conference of the European Association for Machine Translation*, 75–81.

Moorkens, Joss & Sharon O'Brien. 2016. Assessing user interface needs of post-editors of machine translation. In Dorothy Kenny (ed.), *Human issues in translation technology*, 109–130. London: Taylor & Francis.

Moser, Barbara. 1978. Simultaneous interpretation: A hypothetical model and its practical application. In David Gerver & H. Wallace Sinaiko (eds.), *Language interpretation and communication*, 353–368. Boston: Springer.

Moser, Peter. 1995. *Survey on expectations of users of conference interpretation*. Vienna: SRZ Stadt + Regionalforschung.

Moser, Peter. 1996. Expectations of users of conference interpretation. *Interpreting: International Journal of Research and Practice in Interpreting* 1(2). 145–178. DOI: 10.1075/intp.1.2.01mos.

Moser-Mercer, Barbara. 1992. Banking on terminology: Conference interpreters in the electronic age. *Meta: Journal des Traducteurs/Meta: Translators' Journal* 37(3). 507–522. DOI: 10.7202/003634ar.

Moser-Mercer, Barbara. 1997. Process models in simultaneous interpretation. In Christa Hauenschild & Susanne Heizmann (eds.), *Machine translation and translation theory*, 3–18. Berlin: De Gruyter Mouton. DOI: 10.1515/9783110802474.3.

Moser-Mercer, Barbara. 2005. Remote interpreting: The crucial role of presence. *Bulletin Suisse de Linguistique Appliquée* 81. 73–97. https://core.ac.uk/download/20649880.pdf (24 August, 2021).

Moser-Mercer, Barbara, Ulrich Frauenfelder, Beatriz Casado & Alexander Künzli. 2000. Searching to define expertise in interpreting. In Birgitta Englund Dimitrova & Kenneth Hyltenstam (eds.), *Language processing and simultaneous interpreting: Interdisciplinary perspectives*, 107–132. Amsterdam: John Benjamins. DOI: 10.1075/btl.40.09mos.

Mudersbach, Klaus. 1999. Die holistische Betrachtung von Fachtexten und deren Übersetzung. In Heidrun Gerzymisch-Arbogast, Daniel Gile, Juliane House & Annely Rothkegel (eds.), *Wege der Übersetzungs- und Dolmetschforschung*, 13–42. Tübingen: Gunter Narr.

Muñoz Martín, Ricardo & Celia Martín de León. 2020. Translation and cognitive science. In Fábio Alves & Arnt Lykke Jakobsen (eds.), *The Routledge handbook of translation and cognition*, 52–68. London: Routledge. DOI: 10.4324/9781315178127-5.

References

Napier, Jemina. 2004. Interpreting omissions: A new perspective. *Interpreting: International Journal of Research and Practice in Interpreting* 6(2). 117–142. DOI: 10.1075/intp.6.2.02nap.

Napier, Jemina. 2016. *Linguistic coping strategies in sign language interpreting.* Washington: Gallaudet University Press.

Navigli, Roberto, Michele Bevilacqua, Simone Conia, Dario Montagnini & Francesco Cecconi. 2021. Ten years of BabelNet: A survey. In *Proceedings of the Thirtieth International Joint Conference on Artificial Intelligence*, 4559–4567. Montreal: International Joint Conferences on Artificial Intelligence Organization. DOI: 10.24963/ijcai.2021/620.

Navigli, Roberto & Simone Paolo Ponzetto. 2012. BabelNet: The automatic construction, evaluation and application of a wide-coverage multilingual semantic network. *Artificial Intelligence* 193. 217–250. DOI: 10.1016/j.artint.2012.07.001.

Norman, Donald A. 1968. Toward a theory of memory and attention. *Psychological Review* 75(6). 522–536. DOI: 10.1037/h0026699.

O'Brien, Sharon. 2006. Pauses as indicators of cognitive effort in post-editing machine translation output. *Across Languages and Cultures* 7(1). 1–21. DOI: 10.1556/Acr.7.2006.1.1.

O'Brien, Sharon. 2008. Processing fuzzy matches in translation memory tools: An eye-tracking analysis. In Susanne Göpferich, Arnt Lykke Jakobsen & Inger M. Mees (eds.), *Looking at eyes: Eye-tracking studies of reading and translation processing* (Copenhagen Studies in Language), 79–102. Frederiksberg: Samfundslitteratur.

O'Brien, Sharon. 2009. Eye tracking in translation process research: Methodological challenges and solutions. In Inger M. Mees, Fábio Alves & Susanne Göpferich (eds.), *Methodology, technology and innovation in translation process research*, 251–266. Copenhagen: Samfundslitteratur.

O'Brien, Sharon. 2012. Translation as human–computer interaction. *Translation Spaces* 1. 101–122. DOI: 10.1075/ts.1.05obr.

O'Brien, Sharon, Laura Winther Balling, Michael Carl, Michel Simard & Lucia Specia (eds.). 2014. *Post-editing of machine translation: Processes and applications.* United Kingdom: Cambridge Scholars Publishing.

O'Brien, Sharon, Maureen Ehrensberger-Dow, Megan Connolly & Marcel Hasler. 2017. Irritating CAT tool features that matter to translators. *HERMES: Journal of Language and Communication in Business* 56. 145–162. DOI: 10.7146/hjlcb.v0i56.97229.

Ogden, Charles Kay & Ivor Armstrong Richards. 1923. *The meaning of meaning: A study of the influence of language upon thought and of the science of symbolism.* New York: Harcourt, Brace & World.

Oléron, Pierre & Hubert Nanpon. 2002. Research into simultaneous translation. In Franz Pöchhacker & Miriam Shlesinger (eds.), *The interpreting studies reader*, 43–50. London: Routledge.

Olohan, Maeve. 2008. Scientific and technical translation. In Mona Baker & Gabriela Saldanha (eds.), *Routledge encyclopedia of translation studies*, 246–249. London: Routledge.

Olohan, Maeve. 2013. Scientific and technical translation. In Carmen Millán & Francesca Bartrina (eds.), *The Routledge handbook of translation studies*, 425–437. London: Routledge.

Orlando, Marc. 2010. Digital pen technology and consecutive interpreting: Another dimension in notetaking training and assessment. *The Interpreters' Newsletter* 15. 71–86. http://hdl.handle.net/10077/4750 (24 August, 2021).

Orlando, Marc. 2014. A study on the amenability of digital pen technology in a hybrid mode of interpreting: Consec-simul with notes. *Translation & Interpreting* 6(2). 39–54. DOI: 10.12807/ti.106202.2014.a03.

Oster, Katharina. 2019. *Lexical activation and inhibition of cognates among translation students*. Germersheim: Johannes Gutenberg-Universität Mainz. (Doctoral dissertation). DOI: 10.25358/openscience-3748.

Paas, Fred, Juhani E. Tuovinen, Huib Tabbers & Pascal W. M. Van Gerven. 2003. Cognitive load measurement as a means to advance cognitive load theory. *Educational Psychologist* 38(1). 63–71. DOI: 10.1207/S15326985EP3801_8.

Padilla, Francisca, Maria Teresa Bajo & Pedro Macizo. 2005. Articulatory suppression in language interpretation: Working memory capacity, dual tasking and word knowledge. *Bilingualism: Language and Cognition* 8(3). 207–219. DOI: 10.1017/S1366728905002269.

Paone, Matteo Domenico. 2016. *Mobile Geräte beim Simultandolmetschen mit besonderem Bezug auf Tablets*. Vienna: University of Vienna. (MA thesis).

Papagno, Costanza, Alessandro Comi, Marco Riva, Alberto Bizzi, Mirta Vernice, Alessandra Casarotti, Enrica Fava & Lorenzo Bello. 2017. Mapping the brain network of the phonological loop. *Human Brain Mapping* 38(6). 3011–3024. DOI: 10.1002/hbm.23569.

Pashler, Harold E. 1998. *The psychology of attention*. Cambridge: MIT Press.

Pavel, Silvia & Diane Nolet. 2001. *Handbook of terminology*. Gatineau: Minister of Public Works & Government Services Canada.

Petsche, Hellmuth, Susan C. Etlinger & Oliver Filz. 1993. Brain electrical mechanisms of bilingual speech management: An initial investigation. *Electroencephalography and Clinical Neurophysiology* 86(6). 385–394. DOI: 10.1016/0013-4694(93)90134-H.

Pignataro, Clara. 2012. Terminology and interpreting in LSP conferences: A computer-aided vs. empirical-based approach. In Cynthia J. Kellett Bidoli (ed.), *Interpreting across genres: Multiple research perspectives*, 125–140. Trieste: EUT Edizioni Università di Trieste.

Pio, Sonia. 2003. The relation between ST delivery rate and quality in simultaneous interpretation. *The Interpreters' Newsletter* 12. 69–100. http://hdl.handle.net/10077/2475 (3 April, 2022).

Pisani, Elisabetta & Claudio Fantinuoli. 2021. Measuring the impact of automatic speech recognition on number rendition in simultaneous interpreting. In Caiwen Wang & Binghan Zheng (eds.), *Empirical studies of translation and interpreting: The post-structuralist approach*, 181–197. London: Routledge. DOI: 10.4324/9781003017400.

Plevoets, Koen & Bart Defrancq. 2016. The effect of informational load on disfluencies in interpreting: A corpus-based regression analysis. *Translation and Interpreting Studies* 11(2). 202–224. DOI: 10.1075/tis.11.2.04ple.

Plevoets, Koen & Bart Defrancq. 2018. The cognitive load of interpreters in the European Parliament: A corpus-based study of predictors for the disfluency uh(m). *Interpreting: International Journal of Research and Practice in Interpreting* 20(1). 1–28. DOI: 10.1075/intp.00001.ple.

Pöchhacker, Franz. 1994. *Simultandolmetschen als komplexes Handeln*. Tübingen: Gunter Narr.

Pöchhacker, Franz. 2001. Quality assessment in conference and community interpreting. *Meta: Journal des Traducteurs/Meta: Translators' Journal* 46(2). 410–425. DOI: 10.7202/003847ar.

Pöchhacker, Franz. 2004. *Introducing interpreting studies*. 1st ed. Amsterdam: John Benjamins.

Pöchhacker, Franz. 2011. Simultaneous interpreting. In Franz Pöchhacker (ed.), *Routledge encyclopaedia of interpreting studies*, 381–382. London: Routledge.

Pöchhacker, Franz. 2015. *Routledge encyclopedia of interpreting studies*. London: Routledge.

Pöchhacker, Franz. 2016. *Introducing interpreting studies*. 2nd ed. London: Routledge.

Poole, Alex & Linden J. Ball. 2005. Eye tracking in human-computer interaction and usability research. In Claude Ghaoui (ed.), *Encyclopedia of human-computer interaction*, 211–219. Pennsylvania: Idea Group.

Popovic, Maja. 2011. Hjerson: An open source tool for automatic error classification of machine translation output. *The Prague Bulletin of Math and Linguistics* 96. 59–68. DOI: 10.2478/v10108-011-0011-4.

Posner, Michael I. 1980. Orienting of attention. *Quarterly Journal of Experimental Psychology* 32(1). 3–25. DOI: 10.1080/00335558008248231.

Postle, Bradley R. 2006. Working memory as an emergent property of the mind and brain. *Neuroscience* 139(1). 23–38. DOI: 10.1016/j.neuroscience.2005.06.005.

Prandi, Bianca. 2015a. *L'uso di Interpretbank nella didattica dell'interpretazione: Uno studio esplorativo.* Forlì: Università di Bologna. (MA thesis). https://amslaurea.unibo.it/id/eprint/8206 (24 August, 2021).

Prandi, Bianca. 2015b. The use of CAI tools in interpreters' training: A pilot study. In *Proceedings of the 37th Conference Translating and the Computer*, 48–57. London: AsLing.

Prandi, Bianca. 2017. Designing a multimethod study on the use of CAI tools during simultaneous interpreting. In João Esteves-Ferreira, Juliet Macan, Ruslan Mitkov & Olaf-Michael Stefanov (eds.), *Proceedings of the 39th Conference Translating and the Computer*, 76–88. Geneva: Editions Tradulex.

Prandi, Bianca. 2018. An exploratory study on CAI tools in simultaneous interpreting: Theoretical framework and stimulus validation. In Claudio Fantinuoli (ed.), *Interpreting and technology*, 29–59. Berlin: Language Science Press. DOI: 10.5281/zenodo.1493293.

Prandi, Bianca. 2020. The use of CAI tools in interpreter training: Where are we now and where do we go from here? *inTRAlinea Special Issue: Technology in Interpreter Education and Practice.* 1–10.

Price, Cathy J., David W. Green & Roswitha von Studnitz. 1999. A functional imaging study of translation and language switching. *Brain* 122(12). 2221–2235. DOI: 10.1093/brain/122.12.2221.

Pym, Anthony. 2008. On omission in simultaneous interpreting: Risk analysis of a hidden effort. In Gyde Hansen, Andrew Chesterman & Heidrun Gerzymisch-Arbogast (eds.), *Efforts and models in interpreting and translation research: A tribute to Daniel Gile*, 83–105. Amsterdam: John Benjamins. DOI: 10.1075/btl.80.08pym.

Pym, Anthony. 2011. What technology does to translating. *Translation & Interpreting* 3(1). 1–9.

Rayner, Keith. 1998. Eye movements in reading and information processing: 20 years of research. *Psychological Bulletin* 124(3). 372. DOI: 10.1037/0033-2909.124.3.372.

Rayner, Keith & Susan A. Duffy. 1986. Lexical complexity and fixation times in reading: Effects of word frequency, verb complexity, and lexical ambiguity. *Memory & Cognition* 14(3). 191–201. DOI: 10.3758/BF03197692.

Rehbein, Jochen, Thomas Schmidt, Franziska Watzke & Annette Herkenrath. 2004. Handbuch für das computergestützte Transkribieren nach HIAT. *Arbeiten zur Mehrsprachigkeit* B(56). 1–79.

Riccardi, Alessandra. 2005. On the evolution of interpreting strategies in simultaneous interpreting. *Meta: Journal des Traducteurs/Meta: Translators' Journal* 50(2). 753–767. DOI: 10.7202/011016ar.

Riccardi, Alessandra. 2015. Speech rate. In Franz Pöchhacker (ed.), *Routledge encyclopaedia of interpreting studies*, 397–399. London: Routledge.

Rinne, Juha O., Jorma Tommola, Matti Laine, Bernd J. Krause, D. Schmidt, Valtteri Kaasinen, Mika Teräs, Hanni Sipilä & Marianna Sunnari. 2000. The translating brain: Cerebral activation patterns during simultaneous interpreting. *Neuroscience Letters* 294(2). 85–88. DOI: 10.1016/S0304-3940(00)01540-8.

Rodríguez, Nadia & Bettina Schnell. 2009. A look at terminology adapted to the requirements of interpretation. *Language Update* 6(1). 1–5.

Rodríguez, Susana, Roberto Gretter, Marco Matassoni, Daniele Falavigna, Álvaro Alonso, Oscar Corcho & Mariano Rico. 2021. SmarTerp: A CAI System to Support Simultaneous Interpreters in Real-Time. In *Proceedings of the Translation and Interpreting Technology Online Conference TRITON 2021*, 102–109. Shoumen: INCOMA Ltd. DOI: 10.26615/978-954-452-071-7_012.

Rohrer, Doug, Harold Pashler & Jason Etchegaray. 1998. When two memories can and cannot be retrieved concurrently. *Memory & Cognition* 26(4). 731–739. DOI: 10.3758/BF03211393.

Rosado, Tony. 2013. *Note taking with iPad: Making our life easier.* (Blog article). http://rpstranslations.wordpress.com/2013/05/28/note-taking-with-ipad-making-our-life- (3 July, 2021).

Rösener, Christoph. 2016. Eye tracking and beyond: The dos and don'ts of creating a contemporary usability lab. In Silvia Hansen-Schirra & Sambor Grucza (eds.), *Eyetracking and applied linguistics*, 143–163. Berlin: Language Science Press. DOI: 10.17169/langsci.b108.297.

Roy, Cynthia B. 1996. An interactional sociolinguistic analysis of turn-taking in an interpreted event. *Interpreting: International Journal of Research and Practice in Interpreting* 1(1). 39–67. DOI: 10.1075/intp.1.1.04roy.

Roy, Cynthia B. 2000. *Interpreting as a discourse process.* Oxford: Oxford University Press.

Rütten, Anja. 2000. *Terminologieprogramme für Dolmetscher.* Saarbrücken: Universität des Saarlandes. (MA thesis).

Rütten, Anja. 2004. Why and in what sense do conference interpreters need special software? *Linguistica Antverpiensia, New Series – Themes in Translation Studies* 3. 167–178. DOI: 10.52034/lanstts.v3i.110.

Rütten, Anja. 2007. *Informations- und Wissensmanagement im Konferenzdolmetschen* (Sabest: Saarbrücker Beiträge zur Sprach- und Translationswissenschaft 14). Frankfurt am Main: Peter Lang.

Rütten, Anja. 2008. Zielgerichtet und effizient Wissen managen. *MDÜ* 1. 22–25.

Rütten, Anja. 2011. Translation-Memory-Systeme: Auch für Dolmetscher? *MDÜ* 5. 42–43.

Rütten, Anja. 2012a. From desk to booth: TMs for interpreters. *MultiLingual* 23. 43–47.

Rütten, Anja. 2012b. Pragmatik in der Informations- und Wissensarbeit von Konferenzdolmetschern. In Barbara Ahrens, Silvia Hansen-Schirra, Monika Krein-Kühle, Michael Schreiber & Ursula Wienen (eds.), *Translationswissenschaftliches Kolloquium II, Beiträge zur Übersetzungs- und Dolmetschwissenschaft, Köln/Germersheim*, 261–271. Frankfurt/Main: Peter Lang.

Rütten, Anja. 2013. Terminologiesysteme im Dolmetscheinsatz. *eDITion* 1. 25–28.

Rütten, Anja. 2017. Terminology management tools for conference interpreters: Current tools and how they address the specific needs of interpreters. In João Esteves-Ferreira, Juliet Macan, Ruslan Mitkov & Olaf-Michael Stefanov (eds.), *Proceedings of the 39th Conference Translating and the Computer*, 98–103. Geneva: Editions Tradulex.

Rütten, Anja. 2018. Can interpreters' booth notes tell us what really matters in terms of information and terminology management? In *Proceedings of the 40th Conference Translating and the Computer*, 132–144. London: AsLing.

SAE International. 2001. *SAE J2450: Translation quality metric.* Warrendale: Society of Automotive Engineers.

Salevsky, Heidemarie. 1987. *Probleme des Simultandolmetschens. Eine Studie zur Handlungsspezifik.* Berlin: Akademie der Wissenschaften der DDR.

Sand, Peter. 2003. *Manage your terminology with Interplex.* https://aiic.org/document/541/AIICWebzine_Dec2003_3_SAND_Manage_your_terminology_with_Interplex_EN.pdf (24 June, 2021).

Sand, Peter. 2010. *The new Interplex: Glossaries made fast and easy.* https://aiic.org/document/813/AIICWebzine_Winter2011_5_SAND_The_new_Interplex_glossaries_made_fast_and_easy_EN.pdf (25 June, 2022).

Scarpa, Federica. 2010. *La traduction spécialisée: Une approche professionnelle à l'enseignement de la traduction.* Ottawa: University of Ottawa Press.

Schaeffer, Moritz & Michael Carl. 2014. Measuring the cognitive effort of literal translation processes. In *Proceedings of the EACL 2014 workshop on humans and computer-assisted translation*, 29–37. Gothenburg: Association for Computational Linguistics. DOI: 10.3115/v1/W14-0306.

References

Schaeffer, Moritz, Sandra L. Halverson & Silvia Hansen-Schirra. 2019. "Monitoring" in translation: The role of visual feedback. *Translation, Cognition & Behavior* 2(1). 1–34. DOI: 10.1075/tcb.00017.sch.

Schaeffer, Moritz, David Huepe, Silvia Hansen-Schirra, Sascha Hofmann, Edinson Muñoz, Boris Kogan, Eduar Herrera, Agustín Ibáñez & Adolfo M. García. 2020. The Translation and Interpreting Competence Questionnaire: An online tool for research on translators and interpreters. *Perspectives* 28(1). 90–108. DOI: 10.1080/0907676X.2019.1629468.

Schepens, Job, Ton Dijkstra & Franc Grootjen. 2012. Distributions of cognates in Europe as based on Levenshtein distance. *Bilingualism: Language and Cognition* 15(1). 157–166. DOI: 10.1017/S1366728910000623.

Schjoldager, Anne. 1995. An exploratory study of translational norms in simultaneous interpreting. Methodological reflections. In Franz Pöchhacker & Miriam Shlesinger (eds.), *The interpreting studies reader*, 301–311. London: Routledge.

Schmidt, Thomas & Kai Wörner. 2014. EXMARaLDA. In Jacques Durand, Ulrike Gut & Gjert Kristoffersen (eds.), *The Oxford handbook of corpus phonology*, 402–419. Oxford: Oxford University Press.

Schultheis, Holger & Anthony Jameson. 2004. Assessing cognitive load in adaptive hypermedia systems: Physiological and behavioral methods. In Paul M. E. De Bra & Wolfgang Nejdl (eds.), *Adaptive hypermedia and adaptive web-based systems*, 225–234. Berlin: Springer.

Schumacher, Eric H., Travis L. Seymour, Jennifer M. Glass, David E. Fencsik, Erick J. Lauber, David E. Kieras & David E. Meyer. 2001. Virtually perfect time sharing in dual-task performance: Uncorking the central cognitive bottleneck. *Psychological Science* 12(2). 101–108. DOI: 10.1111/1467-9280.00318.

SDI München. 2007. Detaillierte Angaben zur Projektarbeit von Studierenden des SDI München. *MDÜ* 3. 26–36.

SDL. 2008. *Terminology: An end-to-end perspective: SDL research paper.* (Blog article). http://www.sdl.com/en/globalization-knowledge-centre/research_results/terminology-an-end-to-end-%20perspective.asp (1 November, 2021).

Seeber, Kilian G. 2005. Temporale Aspekte der Antizipation beim Simultandolmetschen komplexer SOV-Strukturen aus dem Deutschen. *Bulletin Suisse de Linguistique Appliquée* 81. 123–140.

Seeber, Kilian G. 2007. Thinking outside the cube: Modeling language processing tasks in a multiple resource paradigm. In *Interspeech 2007*. Antwerp.

Seeber, Kilian G. 2011. Cognitive load in simultaneous interpreting: Existing theories—new models. *Interpreting: International Journal of Research and Practice in Interpreting* 13(2). 176–204. DOI: 10.1075/intp.13.2.02see.

Seeber, Kilian G. 2012. Multimodal input in simultaneous interpreting: An eye-tracking experiment. In Lew. N. Zybatow, Alena Petrova & Michael Us-taszewski (eds.), *Proceedings of the 1st International Conference TRANSLATA, Translation & Interpreting Research: Yesterday - today - tomorrow, May, 2011, Innsbruck*, 341–347. Frankfurt am Main: Peter Lang.

Seeber, Kilian G. 2013. Cognitive load in simultaneous interpreting: Measures and methods. *Target: International Journal of Translation Studies* 25(1). 18–32. DOI: 10.1075/target.25.1.03see.

Seeber, Kilian G. 2017. Multimodal processing in simultaneous interpreting. In John W. Schwieter & Aline Ferreira (eds.), *The handbook of translation and cognition*, 461–475. Hoboken: Wiley. DOI: 10.1002/9781119241485.ch25.

Seeber, Kilian G., Laura Keller & Alexis Georges Hervais-Adelman. 2020. When the ear leads the eye: The use of text during simultaneous interpretation. *Language, Cognition and Neuroscience* 35(10). 1480–1494. DOI: 10.1080/23273798.2020.1799045.

Seeber, Kilian G. & Dirk Kerzel. 2012. Cognitive load in simultaneous interpreting: Model meets data. *International Journal of Bilingualism* 16(2). 228–242. DOI: 10.1177/1367006911402982.

Seel, Norbert M. (ed.). 2012. *Encyclopedia of the sciences of learning*. New York: Springer.

Seleskovitch, Danica. 1976. Interpretation, a psychological approach to transla-tion. In Richard W. Brislin (ed.), *Translation: Applications and research*, 92–116. New York: Gardner Press.

Seleskovitch, Danica. 1978. Language and cognition. In David Gerver & H. Wal-lace Sinaiko (eds.), *Language interpretation and communication*, 333–341. Berlin: Springer.

Semenza, Carlo & Claudio Luzzatti. 2014. Combining words in the brain: The processing of compound words. Introduction to the special issue. *Cognitive Neuropsychology* 31(1-2). 1–7. DOI: 10.1080/02643294.2014.898922.

SensoMotoric Instruments. 2017a. *Begaze manual. Version 3.7*. http://www.humre.vu.lt/files/doc/Instrukcijos/SMI/BeGaze2.pdf (17 March, 2021).

SensoMotoric Instruments. 2017b. *Experiment center Version 3.7*.

Setton, Robin. 1999. *Simultaneous interpretation: A cognitive-pragmatic analysis*. Amsterdam: John Benjamins.

Setton, Robin. 2003. Models of the interpreting process. In Angela Collados Aís & José Antonio Sabio Panilla (eds.), *Avances en la investigación sobre inter-pretación*, 29–89. Granada: Editorial Comares.

Seubert, Sabine. 2019. *Visuelle Informationen beim Simultandolmetschen: Eine Eyetracking-Studie*. Berlin: Frank & Timme.

References

Shannon, Claude E. & Warren Weaver. 1949. *The mathematical theory of communication*. Champaign: University of Illinois Press.

Shlesinger, Miriam. 1998. Corpus-based interpreting studies as an offshoot of corpus-based translation studies. *Meta: Journal des Traducteurs/Meta: Translators' Journal* 43(4). 486–493. DOI: 10.7202/004136ar.

Shlesinger, Miriam. 2000. *Strategic allocation of working memory and other attentional resources in simultaneous interpreting*. Ramat Gan: Bar-Ilan University. (Doctoral dissertation).

Shreve, Gregory M., Isabel Lacruz & Erik Angelone. 2010. Cognitive effort, syntactic disruption, and visual interference in a sight translation task. In Gregory M. Shreve & Erik Angelone (eds.), *Translation and cognition*, 63–84. Amsterdam: John Benjamins. DOI: 10.1075/ata.xv.05shr.

Simons, Daniel J. & Christopher F. Chabris. 1999. Gorillas in our midst: Sustained inattentional blindness for dynamic events. *Perception* 28(9). 1059–1074. DOI: 10.1068/p281059.

Smallwood, Jonathan & Jonathan W. Schooler. 2006. The restless mind. *Psychological Bulletin* 132(6). 946–958. DOI: 10.1037/0033-2909.132.6.946.

Smith, Philip L. & Daniel R. Little. 2018. Small is beautiful: In defense of the small-N design. *Psychonomic Bulletin & Review* 25(6). 2083–2101. DOI: 10.3758/s13423-018-1451-8.

Snover, Matthew, Bonnie Dorr, Rich Schwartz, Linnea Micciulla & John Makhoul. 2006. A study of translation edit rate with targeted human annotation. In *Proceedings of the 7th Conference of the Association for Machine Translation in the Americas: Technical Papers*, 223–231. Cambridge: Association for Machine Translation in the Americas.

Spinner, Patti, Susan M. Gass & Jennifer Behney. 2013. Ecological validity in eye-tracking: An empirical study. *Studies in Second Language Acquisition* 35(2). 389–415. DOI: 10.1017/S0272263112000927.

Staub, Adrian & Keith Rayner. 2007. Eye movements and on-line comprehension processes. In M. Gareth Gaskell (ed.), *The Oxford handbook of psycholinguistics*, 326–342. Oxford: Oxford University Press. DOI: 10.1093/oxfordhb/9780198568971.013.0019.

Steurs, Frieda, Iulianna van der Lek-Ciudin & Tom Vanallemeersch. 2017. How translators work in real-life: SCATE observations. In *Translating for Europe forum*. Brussels. http://ccl.kuleuven.be/scate/TEF.pdf (10 November, 2021).

Stewart, Craig, Nikolai Vogler, Junjie Hu, Jordan Boyd-Graber & Graham Neubig. 2018. Automatic estimation of simultaneous interpreter performance. In *Proceedings of the 56th annual meeting of the Association for Computational Lin-*

guistics (Volume 2: Short Papers), 662–666. Melbourne: Association for Computational Linguistics.

Stoll, Christoph. 2009. *Jenseits simultanfähiger Terminologiesysteme: Methoden der Vorverlagerung und Fixierung von Kognition im Arbeitsablauf professioneller Konferenzdolmetscher.* Trier: Wissenschaftlicher Verlag Trier.

Stoll, Christoph. 2010. The Heidelberg model of simultaneouus interpreting. *T21N: Translation in Transition.* 1–26.

Stroop, John Ridley. 1935. Studies of interference in serial verbal reactions. *Journal of Experimental Psychology* 18(6). 643–662. DOI: 10.1037/h0054651.

Stuss, Donald T. & Michael P. Alexander. 2007. Is there a dysexecutive syndrome? *Philosophical Transactions of the Royal Society B: Biological Sciences* 362(1481). 901–915. DOI: 10.1098/rstb.2007.2096.

Sun, Sanjun & Gregory M. Shreve. 2014. Measuring translation difficulty: An empirical study. *Target: International Journal of Translation Studies* 26(1). 98–127. DOI: 10.1075/target.26.1.04sun.

Sweller, John. 2005. The redundancy principle in multimedia learning. In Richard Mayer (ed.), *The Cambridge handbook of multimedia learning*, 159–168. Cambridge: Cambridge University Press. DOI: 10.1017/CBO9780511816819.011.

Taravella, Anne Marie & Alain O. Vielleneuve. 2013. Acknowledging the needs of computer-assisted translation tools users: The human perspective in human-machine translation. *The Journal of Specialised Translation* 19. 62–74.

Tardel, Anke. 2021. Measuring effort in subprocesses of subtitling: The case of post-editing via pivot language. In Michael Carl (ed.), *Explorations in empirical translation process research*, 81–110. Cham: Springer International Publishing. DOI: 10.1007/978-3-030-69777-8_4.

Tardel, Anke, Silvia Hansen-Schirra, Silke Gutermuth & Moritz Schaeffer. 2019. Automatization of subprocesses in subtitling. In *Proceedings of the second MEMENTO workshop on Modelling Parameters of Cognitive Effort in Translation Production*, 19–20. Dublin: European Association for Machine Translation. https://aclanthology.org/W19-7010 (24 June, 2021).

Tardel, Anke, Silvia Hansen-Schirra, Moritz Schaeffer, Silke Gutermuth, Volker Denkel & Miriam Hagmann-Schlatterbeck. 2021. Attention distribution and monitoring during intralingual subtitling. In Tra&Co Group (ed.), *Translation, interpreting, cognition: The way out of the box*, 145–162. Berlin: Language Science Press. DOI: 10.5281/zenodo.4545043.

Tarmizi, Rohani A. & John Sweller. 1988. Guidance during mathematical problem solving. *Journal of Educational Psychology* 80(4). 424–436. DOI: 10.1037/0022-0663.80.4.424.

Teixeira, Carlos S. C. & Sharon O'Brien. 2019. Investigating the cognitive ergonomic aspects of translation tools in a workplace setting. In Hanna Risku, Regina Rogl & Jelena Milosevic (eds.), *Translation practice in the field: Current research on socio-cognitive processes*, 79–103. Amsterdam: John Benjamins. DOI: 10.1075/bct.105.05tei.

Thayer, Julian F., Fredrik Åhs, Mats Fredrikson, John J. Sollers & Tor D. Wager. 2012. A meta-analysis of heart rate variability and neuroimaging studies: Implications for heart rate variability as a marker of stress and health. *Neuroscience & Biobehavioral Reviews* 36(2). 747–756. DOI: 10.1016/j.neubiorev.2011.11.009.

Timarová, Šárka. 2015. Time lag. In Franz Pöchhacker (ed.), *Routledge encyclopedia of interpreting studies*, 418–420. Oxford: Routledge.

Timarová, Šárka, Ivana Čeňková, Reine Meylaerts, Erik Hertog, Arnaud Szmalec & Wouter Duyck. 2014. Simultaneous interpreting and working memory executive control. *Interpreting: International Journal of Research and Practice in Interpreting* 16(2). 139–168. DOI: 10.1075/intp.16.2.01tim.

Timarová, Šárka, Ivana Čeňková, Reine Meylaerts, Erik Hertog, Arnaud Szmalec & Wouter Duyck. 2015. Simultaneous interpreting and working memory capacity. In Aline Ferreira & John W. Schwieter (eds.), *Psycholinguistic and cognitive inquiries into translation and interpreting*, 101–126. Amsterdam: John Benjamins.

Timarová, Šárka, Barbara Dragsted & Inge Gorm Hansen. 2011. Time lag in translation and interpreting: A methodological exploration. In Cecilia Alvstad, Adelina Hild & Elisabet Tiselius (eds.), *Methods and strategies of process research: Integrative approaches in translation studies*, 121–146. Amsterdam: John Benjamins. DOI: 10.1075/btl.94.10tim.

Tiselius, Elisabet. 2015. Accuracy. In Franz Pöchhacker (ed.), *Routledge encyclopedia of interpreting studies*, 3–4. London: Routledge.

Tiselius, Elisabet & Kayle Sneed. 2020. Gaze and eye movement in dialogue interpreting: An eye-tracking study. *Bilingualism: Language and Cognition* 23(4). 780–787. DOI: 10.1017/S1366728920000309.

Tissi, Benedetta. 2001. Silent pauses and disfluencies in simultaneous interpretation. *The Interpreter's Newsletter* 10. 103–127. http://hdl.handle.net/10077/2455 (11 May, 2022).

Tommola, Jorma & Jukka Hyönä. 1990. *Mental load in listening, speech shadowing and simultaneous interpreting: A pupillometric study.* Paper presented at the 9th Meeting of the World Congress of Applied Linguistics, 2–11. Thessaloniki: ERIC.

Tommola, Jorma, Matti Laine, Marianna Sunnari & Juha O. Rinne. 2000. Images of shadowing and interpreting. *Interpreting: International Journal of Research and Practice in Interpreting* 5(2). 147–167. DOI: 10.1075/intp.5.2.06tom.

Tommola, Jorma & Pekka Niemi. 1986. Mental load in simultaneous interpreting: An on-line pilot study. In Lars S. Evensen (ed.), *Nordic research in text linguistics and discourse analysis*, 171–184. Norway: Trondheim.

Towse, John N. & Graham Hitch. 1995. Is there a relationship between task demand and storage space in tests of working memory capacity? *The Quarterly Journal of Experimental Psychology Section A* 48(1). 108–124. DOI: 10.1080/14640749508401379.

Treisman, Anne M. 1964. Selective attention in man. *British Medical Bulletin* 20(1). 12–16. DOI: 10.1093/oxfordjournals.bmb.a070274.

Treisman, Anne M. 1965. The effects of redundancy and familiarity on translating and repeating back a foreign and a native language. *British Journal of Psychology* 56(4). 369–379. DOI: 10.1111/j.2044-8295.1965.tb00979.x.

Treisman, Anne M. & Alison Davies. 2012. Divided attention to ear and eye. In Jeremy Wolfe & Lynn Robertson (eds.), *From perception to consciousness*, 24–31. Oxford: Oxford University Press. DOI: 10.1093/acprof:osobl/9780199734337.003.0005.

Tripepi Winteringham, Sarah. 2010. The usefulness of ICTs in interpreting practice. *The Interpreters' Newsletter* 15. 87–99. http://hdl.handle.net/10077/4751 (11 April, 2022).

Valentini, Cristina. 2001. *Uso del computer in cabina di interpretazione*. Forlì: Università di Bologna. (MA thesis).

Valentini, Cristina. 2002. *Uso del computer in cabina di interpretazione: Inchiesta sui bisogni terminologici degli interpreti prima e durante la simultanea*. https://aiic.org/document/470/AIICWebzine_FebMar2002_9_VALENTINI_Uso_del_computer_in_cabina_de_interpretazione_FULL_IT.pdf (22 June, 2022).

Van Cauwenberghe, Goran. 2020. *La reconnaissance automatique de la parole en interprétation simultanée*. Gent: Universiteit Gent. (MA thesis).

Van Merrienboer, Jeroen J. G. & John Sweller. 2005. Cognitive load theory and complex learning: Recent developments and future directions. *Educational Psychology Review* 17(2). 147–177. DOI: 10.1007/s10648-005-3951-0.

Vardaro, Jennifer, Moritz Schaeffer & Silvia Hansen-Schirra. 2019. Translation quality and error recognition in professional neural machine translation post-editing. *Informatics* 6(41). 1–29. DOI: 10.3390/informatics6030041.

Veisbergs, Andrejs. 2007. Terminology issues in interpreter training. In *Proceedings of the Baltic Sea Region university network "quality and qualifications in translation and interpreting II*". http : / / www . tlu . ee / files / arts / 645 / Quali698bb7e395eob88d73d603e33f5b153f.pdf (22 May, 2020).

Velásquez, Gonzalo. 2002. La traducción y la terminología en la comunicación bilingüe mediada. *Meta: Journal des Traducteurs/Meta: Translators' Journal* 47(3). 444–459. DOI: 10.7202/008030ar.

Vintar, Špela. 2001. Using parallel corpora for translation-oriented term extraction. *Babel* 47(2). 121–132. DOI: 10.1075/babel.47.2.04vin.

Vogler, Nikolai, Craig Stewart & Graham Neubig. 2019. Lost in interpretation: Predicting untranslated terminology in simultaneous interpretation. In *Proceedings of the 2019 conference of the North American chapter of the Association for Computational Linguistics: Human language technologies*, 109–118. Minneapolis: Association for Computational Linguistics.

Vuorikoski, Anna-Riitta. 1993. Simultaneous interpretation: User experience and expectations. In Catriona Picken (ed.), *Translation: The vital link. Proceedings of the 13th world congress of FIT*, 317–327. London: Institute of Translation & Interpreting.

Vuorikoski, Anna-Riitta. 1998. User responses to simultaneous interpreting. In Lynne Bowker, Michael Cronin, Dorothy Kenny & Jennifer Pearson (eds.), *Unity in diversity? Current trends in translation studies*, 184–197. Manchester: St. Jerome.

Wadensjö, Cecilia. 1993. The double role of a dialogue interpreter. *Perspectives* 1(1). 105–121. DOI: 10.1080/0907676X.1993.9961204.

Wadensjö, Cecilia. 1998. *Interpreting as interaction*. London: Routledge.

Wadensjö, Cecilia. 2005. *Interpreting as interaction*. 2nd edn. London: Longman.

Wagener, Leonie. 2012. *Vorbereitende Terminologiearbeit im Konferenzdolmetschen unter besonderer Berücksichtigung der Zusammenarbeit im Dolmetschteam*. Köln: Fachhochschule Köln. (MA thesis).

Wahlster, Wolfgang. 2000. *Verbmobil: Foundations of speech-to-speech translation*. Heidelberg: Springer.

Wang, Xinyu & Caiwen Wang. 2019. Can computer-assisted interpreting tools assist interpreting? *Transletters: International Journal of Translation and Interpreting* 2. 109–139.

Warren, Tessa, Sarah J. White & Erik D. Reichle. 2009. Investigating the causes of wrap-up effects: Evidence from eye movements and E–Z reader. *Cognition* 111(1). 132–137. DOI: 10.1016/j.cognition.2008.12.011.

Webex Help Center. 2022. *Real time translation in Webex meetings and events*. https://help.webex.com/en-US/article/7dzhht/Real-Time-Translation-in-Webex-Meetings-and-Events (13 August, 2022).

Weller, G. & P. Yanez. 1998. The audience's views on simultaneous conference interpreters performance in Mexico. In Muriel M. Jerome-O'Keefe (ed.), *Proceedings of the 38th annual conference of the American Translators Association*, 69–85. San Francisco: American Translators Association.

Wickens, Christopher D. 1976. The effects of divided attention on information processing in manual tracking. *Journal of Experimental Psychology: Human Perception and Performance* 2(1). 1–13. DOI: 10.1037/0096-1523.2.1.1.

Wickens, Christopher D. 1984. Processing resources in attention. In Raja Parasumaran & David R. Davies (eds.), *Varieties of attention*, 63–101. New York: Academic Press.

Wickens, Christopher D. 2002. Multiple resources and performance prediction. *Theoretical Issues in Ergonomics Science* 3(2). 159–177. DOI: 10.1080/14639220210123806.

Will, Martin. 2000. Bemerkungen zum Computereinsatz beim Simultandolmetschen. In Sylvia Kalina, Silke Buhl & Heidrun Gerzymisch Arbogast (eds.), *Dolmetschen: Theorie, Praxis, Didaktik – mit ausgewählten Beiträgen der Saarbrücker Symposien*, 125–135. Sankt Ingbert: Röhrig Universitätsverlag.

Will, Martin. 2007. Terminology work for simultaneous interpreters in LSP conferences: Model and method. In Heidrun Gerzymisch-Arbogast & Gerhard Budin (eds.), *Proceedings of the Marie Curie Euroconferences MuTra: LSP Translation Scenarios*, 65–99. Vienna: MuTra.

Will, Martin. 2015. Zur Eignung simultanfähiger Terminologiesysteme für das Konferenzdolmetschen. *trans-kom* 8(1). 179–201.

Will, Martin. 2020. Computer Aided Interpreting (CAI) for conference interpreters. Concepts, content and prospects. *ESSACHESS-Journal for Communication Studies* 13(25). 37–71.

Wintringham, Nils. 2009. *Terminus*. http://www.wintringham.ch/cgi/ayawp.pl?T=terminus (13 August, 2022).

Wright, Sue Ellen & Leland D. Wright. 1997. Terminology management for technical translation. In Sue Ellen Wright & Gerhard Budin (eds.), *Handbook of terminology management: Volume 1: Basic aspects of terminology management*, 147–159. Amsterdam: John Benjamins.

Wüster, Eugen. 1931. *Internationale Sprachnormung in der Technik, besonders in der Elektrotechnik: Die nationale Sprachnormung und ihre Verallgemeinerung* (Sprachforum: Zeitschrift fur angewandte Sprachwissenschaft Beiheft Nr. 2). Bonn: Bouvier.

Wüster, Eugen. 1979. *Einführung in die Allgemeine Terminologielehre und Terminologische Lexikographie*. Wien: Romanistischer Verlag.

Xu, Ran. 2015. *Terminology preparation for simultaneous interpreters.* Leeds: University of Leeds. (Doctoral dissertation).

Young, Laurence R. & David Sheena. 1975. Survey of eye movement recording methods. *Behavior Research Methods & Instrumentation* 7(5). 397–429. DOI: 10.3758/BF03201553.

Žganec-Gros, Jerneja, France Mihelič, Tomaž Erjavec & Špela Vintar. 2005. The VoiceTran speech-to-speech communicator. In Václav Matoušek, Pavel Mautner & Tomáš Pavelka (eds.), *Text, speech and dialogue*, 379–384. Berlin: Springer.

Ziegler, Klaus & Sebastiano Gigliobianco. 2018. Present? Remote? Remotely present! New technological approaches to remote simultaneous conference interpreting. In Claudio Fantinuoli (ed.), *Interpreting and technology*, 119–139. Berlin: Language Science Press. DOI: 10.5281/zenodo.1493299.

Zielinski, Daniel & Yamile Ramírez-Safar. 2005. Research meets practice: t-survey 2005: An online survey on terminology extraction and terminology management. In *Translating and the computer 27*, 1–27. London: Aslib.

Zwischenberger, Cornelia & Franz Pöchhacker. 2010. *Survey on quality and role: Conference interpreters' expectations and self-perceptions.* https://aiic.org/document/9646/ (24 July, 2021).

Name index

Ingram Content Group UK Ltd.
Milton Keynes UK
UKHW051856270323
419267UK00010B/359

9 783985 540556